CLARENDON LAW SERIES

Edited by
PETER BIRKS

CLARENDON LAW SERIES

CRIMINAL JUSTICE

LUCIA ZEDNER

OXFORD
UNIVERSITY PRESS

OXFORD

UNIVERSITY PRESS

Great Clarendon Street, Oxford OX2 6DP

Oxford University Press is a department of the University of Oxford.
It furthers the University's objective of excellence in research, scholarship,
and education by publishing worldwide in

Oxford New York

Auckland Bangkok Buenos Aires Cape Town Chennai
Dar es Salaam Delhi Hong Kong Istanbul Karachi Kolkata
Kuala Lumpur Madrid Melbourne Mexico City Mumbai Nairobi
São Paulo Shanghai Taipei Tokyo Toronto

Oxford is a registered trade mark of Oxford University Press
in the UK and in certain other countries

Published in the United States
by Oxford University Press Inc., New York

© Lucia Zedner 2004

The moral rights of the author have been asserted
Database right Oxford University Press (maker)

First published 2004

British Library Cataloguing in Publication Data

Data available

Library of Congress Cataloging in Publication Data

Data available

ISBN 0–19–876366–2

1 3 5 7 9 10 8 6 4 2

Typeset in Ehrhardt
by RefineCatch Limited, Bungay, Suffolk
Printed in Great Britain by
Ashford Colour Press, Gosport, Hampshire.

for Joshua

Preface

Keeping abreast of the relentless changes in criminal justice is a hindrance to quiet reflection. Standing back from the clamour of the latest Home Office Press Release, I hope in this book to offer the reader a sense of perspective and fresh discovery. It poses some very simple questions to which arise some surprisingly complex answers. What do we mean by criminal justice? And what is meant by crime? What is the role of punishment in our society and how do we justify it? What are the roles of the police and prosecutor, trial and sentence? What purposes do our institutions of punishment fulfil and why do they persist? And finally, can we predict the changes that criminal justice will next undergo?

I have incurred many debts in the long gestation of this book. First, warm thanks to Peter Cane, Tony Honoré, Jane Stapleton, and Richard Hart for first soliciting this work and to Peter Birks for encouraging its progress to completion. Secondly, I am especially grateful to Andrew Ashworth, Joshua Getzler, Roger Hood, and Declan Roche for reading and commenting on the entire book. Roger Hood deserves special mention for undertaking this thankless task whilst travelling in Cambodia and sending comments daily by e-mail on his return to Hong Kong. Thirdly, I am most grateful to Richard Ericson, Elizabeth Fisher, Carolyn Hoyle, and Liora Lazarus for reading and commenting on parts of the book. Fourthly, sincere thanks are due to Sam Freedman and Patricia Londono for their outstanding research assistance. Fifthly, I record my enormous gratitude to the British Academy for the award of a two-year Research Readership for another project entitled 'Security and Justice'. Their support both prompted me to add a final chapter on the rise of what I call 'the security society' and its implications for the practice of criminal justice as we know it, and made possible the completion of this book. Last and by no means least, my students first at the London School of Economics and over the past decade at the University of Oxford have taught me quite as much as I have taught them. In the writing of this book, both past and future students sat before me as my ideal audience and most feared critics.

This book is dedicated to my husband Joshua Getzler. He has been a source of inspiration and sustenance throughout. Special thanks also to our young daughters Naomi and Esther whose antics daily allow me to try my hand as police, prosecutor, judge, and jury and, in so doing, to gain direct insights into the problems of dispute resolution and order maintenance.

Lucia Zedner
February 2004

Contents

I

Criminal Justice

WHAT IS CRIMINAL JUSTICE?

Our familiarity with criminal justice is both a benefit and a blight. It is not necessary to have stepped inside a police station, courtroom, or prison to have the sense that you already know the central institutions of criminal justice. The news media are generous in their coverage of the workings of the criminal justice system. They report individual cases, political debates, and policy developments at length. And to this factual reporting, novels, dramas, and films add a fictional dimension replete with colour, if no little poetic licence. The familiarity fed by this daily diet of criminal justice stories (fact and fictional) has certain advantages. We share a basic perception of what the police do, what a courtroom looks like, and what happens inside the prison walls. But familiarity has its dangers also. We may be less inclined to question the very existence of the criminal justice system and the power it wields over us. The authority of the police and prosecutors is generally taken for granted. The trial appears as a natural forum for the resolution of criminal disputes. And the institutions of punishment appear as organic elements of our society, justified as much by their history as by any independent rationale.

If by a benign and temporary act of amnesia we were to forget all we know, the criminal justice system would appear a wonderful thing. Wonderful, that is, in the sense of exciting wonder or astonishment. The bewigged judge solemnly passing sentence would appear as curious as the sight of the Ming-Wahgi peoples who equally solemnly line up on opposing sides, arms clasped behind their backs, and kick at each other's shins until one side withdraws. This practice, known as the *tagba boz*, is an accepted response to the theft of a pig or the stealing of crops in the Western Highlands of Papua New Guinea. Likewise, the dome-helmeted police officer scathingly reprimanding the young delinquent would seem as peculiar as the Inuit song contest or *nith*-songs used as a form of public reprimand in which the aggrieved loudly chants the wrongdoing in a public place for all to hear.[1] You do not need to journey to Papua New Guinea or the frozen North but you do need to take a sizeable step back to enjoy the sense of distance and perspective so valued by anthropologists in studying the dispute resolution systems of other cultures. Nor, happily, do you need to engage in amnesia-inducing head bashing to look at the world anew. A little gentle eye opening is all that is required to observe the criminal justice system as if for the first time.

In this chapter, we begin this exercise by examining the general concept of criminal justice. Recourse to dictionaries will not help us since they, by their nature, reduce complex meanings to concise definitions that tend to obscure more than they reveal. Criminal justice must be a particular hazard for the dictionary writer because its meanings and usages are multiple. Our purpose, therefore, is not a reductive attempt to provide a general working definition (convenient as that would be) but to reveal the irreducible complexity of criminal justice and to tease out its many meanings.

Let us begin by identifying some of them. First, criminal justice is a form of governance.[2] It is the means by which the state, in collaboration with many other social institutions, seeks to make civil society sustainable. Though there are many ways of thinking about criminal justice as governance, three stand out. It is a means of imposing social order; a mechanism for resolving disputes; and a technique for managing risk. Secondly, criminal justice is a set of formal responses to suspected infractions of the criminal law. It is what law requires when wrongdoing occurs. Thirdly, it denotes a loose amalgam of institutions, agents, and practices, or put another way, of buildings and people and the things they do. Fourthly, it is a system with all the qualities and complexities a system entails. Fifthly, criminal *justice* implies a particular normative framework: a general theory of justice or, more modestly, a set of values and principles. Finally, criminal justice is also an emerging field of academic study or, if that is too large a claim, at least a proliferating set of university degree courses, journals, conferences, and departments. When reading and thinking about criminal justice, we need to be alert to the many possible meanings that may be intended: let us examine them more closely.

---

[1] Both examples are taken from Roberts, S., *Order and Dispute: An Introduction to Legal Anthropology* (Harmondsworth: Penguin, 1979) 58–61.

[2] On the concept of governance see Rose, N., 'Governing Liberty' in Ericson and Stehr (eds), *Governing Modern Societies* (Toronto: University of Toronto Press, 2000).

A FORM OF GOVERNANCE

That criminal justice is part of the apparatus of the state is self-evident. But to say that criminal justice is one means by which the state governs society only raises further questions. Governance signifies a blurring of the distinction between the state and civil society. Accordingly, it raises the question: what is the relationship of criminal justice to other forms, sources, and institutions of governance? And how best can we understand or characterize the particular form of governance that is criminal justice?

The criminal justice system is the product of its historical development and although parts of it have long historical roots, much of the present system is less than two hundred years old. Prior to the eighteenth century, the primary mechanisms of crime control were local and personal, depending on hierarchical social relations and the authority of local landowners to maintain order and resolve disputes. Methods of controlling crime were also entrepreneurial in the sense that thief-takers, justices of the peace, and gaolers took fees from their clients or imposed charges upon those subject to their authority. The development of the centralized, bureaucratic, and largely impersonal institutions of today's criminal justice system began only in earnest in the eighteenth century. Its growth ran alongside other larger socio-economic developments, not least industrialization and the shift from a rural to a predominantly urban population over the course of the nineteenth century. Whether and in what manner these parallel developments were related is the subject of considerable historical controversy to which we will return throughout this book.

The formal bureaucratic institutions of criminal justice may now dominate crime control but they do so in close relationship to the informal sources of governance that preceded them. Understood this way, criminal justice sits at the most coercive end of a continuum of institutions of social order. Informal methods of socialization and social control continue to play a large part in dealing with petty delinquencies, disputes, and other forms of deviance. The role of the family, the school, religious institutions, and that more amorphous entity, the community, play an enduring and integral role in maintaining social order.[3] Understanding criminal justice as a form of governance requires, therefore, that we

---

[3] See, for example, Donajgrodzki, A. P., *Social Control in Nineteenth Century Britain* (London: Croom Helm, 1977); Cohen, S., and Scull, A. (eds), *Social Control and the State: Historical and Comparative Essays* (Oxford: Basil Blackwell, 1983).

recognize that at no time has the state had exclusive jurisdiction over crime control.

The historic relationship between the formal institutions of criminal justice and the informal sources of social order is a subject of much academic interest. It is commonly argued that historically the strength of these informal sources rendered the formal institutions of criminal justice peripheral. Only as informal sources of social control grew weaker did the institutions of criminal justice develop to become the dominant means of imposing order. Thus, by the middle years of the twentieth century, crime control was largely reserved to the authority of so-called experts, who deployed their knowledge to assert the authority of the criminal justice state. A subsequent decline of faith in the reformative power of penal-welfarism has since eroded the authority of the agents and institutions of criminal justice and brought in its train the proliferation of other forms of policing and security beyond the state (about which we will have much more to say in the final chapter). In the face of this decline, the sovereign state has sought to reassert its authority by ever more punitive and inter-ventionist policies that declaim its ability to control crime.[4] But it is arguable this 'flexing of the muscles of the displaced state'[5] relies upon a mythic claim to a sovereignty it never possessed.

The expansion and decline of state responsibility for criminal justice relative to informal controls has been presented as inversely correlated. Whilst it is true that the strength of informal controls often correlates inversely with the strength of the criminal justice system and vice versa, it is not invariably the case. This simple equation is complicated by other factors. The levels of lawlessness a society is prepared or able to tolerate; the priority it gives to combating crime over other social problems; and the level of funding it is willing to commit to policing and institutions of punishment all contribute to the place criminal justice has in the larger governance of society. These factors vary historically and by jurisdiction, and the prominence given to criminal justice varies with them. It is per-fectly possible, therefore, for strong, even coercive institutions of informal control to be matched by an equally strong and coercive criminal justice system (contemporary Thailand might be a case in point).

---

[4] Garland, D., 'The Limits of the Sovereign State: Strategies of Crime Control' (1996) 36 *British Journal of Criminology* 445–71.

[5] Bauman, Z., *In Search of Politics* (Cambridge: Polity Press, 1999) 50; Loader, I. and Sparks, R., 'Contemporary Landscapes of Crime, Order, and Control: Governance, Risk, and Globalization' in Maguire *et al.* (eds), *The Oxford Handbook of Criminology* (3rd edn, Oxford: Oxford University Press, 2002) 86.

Likewise, in a society characterized by greater tolerance of deviance, weaker informal social controls may be mirrored by relative permissiveness on the part of criminal justice (more controversially, the example of the Netherlands springs to mind).

These broad typologies mask substantial variations in the shape and form of controls imposed by criminal justice upon different sections of the population and in respect of different kinds of crime. A few examples will illustrate the point. Women are underrepresented as subjects of criminal justice, forming only a small proportion of those brought before the courts or sentenced by them. It has been argued that women have been policed as much by informal social controls like the family as by the formal apparatus of the state.[6] Women were disciplined both by the structural constraints of a life lived principally within the family home and by the expectations placed upon them as wife and mother. In turn they were expected to police their own family members: a responsibility that placed further strictures upon their conduct.[7] The relatively low visibility of women as subjects of criminal justice might be explained, therefore, at least in part by the fact that they were being policed elsewhere and in other ways.

Another illustrative example is to be found by comparing juvenile justice in different countries. Different jurisdictions impose criminal liability at diverse ages: whereas in one jurisdiction (Ireland) 7-year-olds may find themselves in the criminal court as a result of their delinquencies, in another (Sweden) children under the age of 15 are excluded from criminal liability. The policing of children in the latter case is the responsibility not of criminal justice but of educational and welfare agencies. The nature and scope of juvenile justice in these jurisdictions is self-evidently very different from those where criminalization starts young. Quite another example arises in respect of drug policies. Whereas possession and personal use of soft drugs is tolerated in some jurisdictions,[8] in the USA it invites severe penalties and is the subject of a 'war on drugs'. Policies may also change over time, witness the reclassification of cannabis in England and Wales from Class B to Class C. Changes in who is, in law or in practice, subject to formal policing and

---

[6] Donzelot, J., *The Policing of Families: Welfare Versus the State* (London: Hutchinson, 1979).

[7] Zedner, L., 'Regulating Sexual Offences Within the Home' in Loveland (ed), *Frontiers of Criminality* (London: Sweet & Maxwell, 1995) 175–7.

[8] On the Netherlands as an example of this sort of permissiveness, see Downes, D., *Contrasts in Tolerance* (Oxford: Clarendon Press, 1993).

what is and is not defined as crime make it exceedingly problematic to make generalizing claims about the size and shape of criminal justice in relation to other institutions of governance.

How best can we understand or characterize the particular form of governance that is criminal justice? One obvious answer is that it is a set of practices devoted to coercion and punishment of those who transgress the criminal law. But to focus on punishment alone is to miss the larger role of criminal justice. That punishment is only a small part of the remit of criminal justice is evidenced by the fact that in England and Wales only 3 per cent of offences known to the British Crime Survey result in a caution or conviction, 2.2 per cent in a conviction, and 0.3 per cent in a custodial sentence.[9]

Putting punishment to one side for the moment, does it make sense to characterize criminal justice as a form of state coercion? Certainly when compared to other institutions of social order, criminal justice is coercive. The powers of the police to stop and search, to arrest, detain, interrogate, and caution suspects; of the courts to summon and arraign defendants, to summon witnesses and jurors, and to convict and sentence offenders all lie at the coercive end of state activity. But other state agents also act coercively. Social workers, doctors, psychiatrists, and teachers all have the power to coerce compliance whether in the 'best interests' of their clients or in accordance with wider social norms or statute. The requirement of attendance at school is a subtle but enduring act of coercion. The provision to hospitalize and forcibly treat those deemed to be at risk to themselves or society under mental health legislation is a more overt, if medically sanctioned form of coercion. Whilst coercion is an important facet of criminal justice it is by no means its exclusive preserve.

If punishment and coercion do not tell the whole story of criminal justice as governance, how else might it be characterized? A number of possibilities suggest themselves: no doubt there are more. One is as a form of order maintenance. The notion of order maintenance has the considerable virtue of capturing the minute and mundane activities of criminal justice agents in their everyday work. Much of this has little to do with crime control as conventionally understood but rather with the management of disorder. The ordering practices entailed in managing petty infractions, squabbles, and minor acts of anti-social behaviour

---

[9] Home Office, *Information on the Criminal Justice System in England and Wales: Digest 4* (London: Home Office, 1999) 29.

might better be characterized as asymmetrical negotiation than as outright coercion.

Beyond this instrumental role, criminal justice is also concerned with the symbolic construction of social order. As Durkheim observes, 'its real function is to maintain inviolate the cohesion of society by sustaining the common consciousness in all its vigour'.[10] Understood this way, criminal justice is engaged both in the instrumental activity of managing disorder and in practices positively informed by the desire to create the conditions of society's continued existence. Without it, continues Durkheim, 'there would result a relaxation in the bonds of social solidarity'. Although this characterization of criminal justice sounds benign, we should recognize the inherently conservative quality of the term 'continued existence'. By implication, the social order sought is that already in place, with all the socio-economic inequalities, injustices, and prejudices that this involves. Although criminal justice formally eschews social engineering, order maintenance implies (though it need not entail) the continuation of existing class, gender, racial, and ethnic divisions. Order is also delineated by reference to its more emotive antithesis—disorder. The 'well-ordered society', so beloved of politicians and police chiefs, is free not only from muggings and murder but also from the perceived threat posed by alternative lifestyles and political protests.[11] Those deemed to threaten order are less likely to be city brokers engaged in insider dealing or tax evasion, but street gangs, drug users, and discontented youths. Though both groups may evince equal disregard for law and though the cost of the activities of the former may be infinitely greater, it is the delinquent youth not the besuited broker who is seen primarily to threaten law and order. The idea of criminal justice as a mechanism for the maintenance of the social order relies, therefore, on a particular conception of the status quo and that which threatens it.

Notions of order and disorder are highly emotive and readily subject to political manipulation. The politics of law and order took a punitive turn in late twentieth-century Britain and America, becoming, according to von Hirsch, 'largely concerned with fostering and exploiting public

---

[10] Durkheim, E., *The Division of Labour in Society* (London: Macmillan, 1984) 76.

[11] For example, the Criminal Justice and Public Order 1994 conceives order to be threatened by travellers, gypsies, ravers, protest groups, and hunt saboteurs. The Act criminalizes forms of trespass to land, bans trespassory assemblies, criminalizes unauthorized camping, permits the removal and seizure of vehicles belonging to travellers, prohibits squatting, and criminalizes rave parties.

resentment of crime and criminals'.[12] That the experiences of many other European countries over the same period were altogether less punitive attests to the fact that the space occupied by crime in conceptions of social order and the prominence of criminal justice in order maintenance is a variable entity.[13] One way of unravelling the complex array of factors that underlie the significance of law and order as a matter of domestic politics is to juxtapose one jurisdiction against another. Comparative study thus provides a means of making transparent how different societies conceive disorder and how they perceive the role of criminal justice in responding to it.[14]

A second possible way of conceiving the form of governance that is criminal justice is as a mechanism for dispute resolution. The disputes with which criminal justice is concerned are of a particular kind. In theory, at least, they share a social dimension that differentiates them from the personal and private conflicts that are the subject of tort and contract law. This conception of criminal justice as dispute resolution can be traced to its historical origins. In Anglo-Saxon law little distinction was made between public and private wrongs. Both were dealt with by a system for the resolution of disputes through the making of compensatory redress or monetary payments known as the 'bot'.[15] Only with the growth of royal jurisdiction in the twelfth century was private dispute resolution sacrificed to the wider purposes of securing the 'King's Peace'. Crimes were differentiated from other social wrongs on the grounds that they were so serious as to offend not only against the interests of the direct party to the dispute, the victim, but against King and community as well. Over time, the notion of the crime as an interpersonal dispute was overlaid by the notion of crime as a threat to social order.

Only in the late twentieth century has the notion of crime as dispute been revived. A critical moment in its revival was the lecture delivered by Nils Christie in 1976 entitled 'Conflicts as Property'.[16] In this he argued that the conflicts that are crimes have been 'stolen' by the state, through

---

[12] von Hirsch, A., 'Law and Order' in von Hirsch and Ashworth (eds), *Principled Sentencing: Readings on Theory and Policy* (Oxford: Hart Publishing, 1998) 410–23 at 412.

[13] See, for example, Downes, D., *Contrasts in Tolerance* (Oxford: Clarendon Press, 1993); Zedner, L., 'In Pursuit of the Vernacular: Comparing Law and Order Discourse in Britain and Germany' (1995) 4 *Social and Legal Studies* 517–534.

[14] Nelken, D. (ed), *Contrasting Criminal Justice* (Aldershot: Ashgate Dartmouth, 2000).

[15] Pollock, F., and Maitland, F. W., *The History of English Law before the time of Edward I* (Cambridge: Cambridge University Press, 1895) 449.

[16] Later published as Christie, N., 'Conflicts as Property' (1977) 17 *British Journal of Criminology* 1–15.

the apparatus of criminal justice, from their rightful owners the offender and victim. The theft of the participants' property rights in their conflicts, he argued, denies them the chance to communicate directly and to resolve their disputes unaided by the dubious interventions of lawyers. The adversarial system further distances and embattles the two parties whilst the high standard of proof requires absolute attribution of culpability. The intimate relations between many victims and offenders; the blurred distribution of victim and offender status; and complexities of causation inimical to securing a conviction are diminished and denied.

Christie's writings, together with those of John Braithwaite, Howard Zehr, and others, have been influential in encouraging demands for the criminal justice system to return the dispute to its rightful owners, not least through the framework of restorative justice. Of course, this thesis, if accepted uncritically, would seem to suggest that criminal justice is devoted less to the resolution of disputes than to their amplification. In fact there are many, and an increasing number, of aspects of criminal justice which owe much to models of dyadic or, more usually, triadic dispute resolution. Provisions for mediation are longstanding features of criminal justice available prior to prosecution, pre-trial, pre-sentence, as an order of the court, and even post-sentence. Restorative justice conferences and restorative cautioning panels are more recent innovations which, in theory, seek to resolve disputes constructively and in a manner which recognizes the interests of many parties, not only the victim and offender but also family, friends, and other members of society.[17]

A third, increasingly prominent, way of thinking about criminal justice is as a mechanism for risk management. Understood this way, criminal justice is less about identifying known offenders, attributing blame or responsibility, and imposing punishment than about managing prospective dangers. It is less about responding to past offences than about preventing future ones. It is a device for identifying and classifying groups sorted by level of dangerousness and managing them through surveillance, prevention, and incapacitation. This conception of criminal justice, labelled in variant forms as the 'new penology' or 'actuarial justice',[18] captures perceived changes in the orientation of criminal justice and the

[17] For a study of restorative justice in practice, see Hoyle, C., Young, R., and Hill, R., *Proceed with Caution: An Evaluation of the Thames Valley Police Initiative in Restorative Cautioning* (York: York Publishing Services, 2002).

[18] Feeley, M., and Simon, J., 'The New Penology: Notes on the Emerging Strategy of Corrections and its Implications' (1992) 30 *Criminology* 449–74; Feeley, M., and Simon, J., 'Actuarial Justice: The Emerging New Criminal Law' in Nelken (ed), *The Futures of Criminology* (London: Sage, 1994).

development of new practices serving the ends of risk management and prevention. But it also identifies hitherto undisclosed or unobserved aspects of existing criminal justice practice, not least that policing is not only or primarily about crime control but about responding to institutional demands for knowledge of risk.[19]

Understood this way, criminal justice is less a mechanism for controlling or reducing crime than one for managing risk, where crime itself is a normal, and by implication therefore, inevitable and irreducible social fact.[20] Clearly some aspects of criminal justice practice fit this model better than others. Policing, situational crime prevention, surveillance, offender profiling, and certain aspects of probation (for example, Intensive Supervision and Surveillance Programmes for young offenders) and decision making on parole are centrally concerned with identifying and managing risk.[21] Other important aspects of criminal justice, not least trial, adjudication, and sentencing fit less well. To the extent that they remain central attributes of criminal justice practice, they suggest a greater concern with the culpability of the known offender than actuarial accounts allow. How far the future development of the trend toward actuarial justice is transforming the traditional role of criminal justice is a subject to which we return in the final chapter.

A LEGAL RESPONSE TO WRONGDOING

Every time parents intervene to adjudicate between squabbling infants, they engage in activities analogous to those that lie at the core of the criminal justice process. They identify wrongdoing, attribute responsibility, assess harm, and impose penalties in an attempt to do justice, restore order, or prevent recurrence. School teachers, the clergy, health and safety officials (to list a very few examples) also play a part in ensuring that law is observed and social order maintained. What differentiates criminal justice from other practices of social order is that law determines its defining ideology, scope, and structure. It is police, lawyers, and judges who, in our popular imagination, represent the law. And it is not by chance that the police are often referred to colloquially as 'the law'.

Criminal law sets out the categories of offending behaviour; rules of

---

[19] Ericson, R., and Haggerty, K., *Policing the Risk Society* (Oxford: Oxford University Press, 1997) 17–38.

[20] Felson, M., *Crime and Everyday Life* (3rd edn., London: Sage, 2002).

[21] Hood, R., and Shute, S., *The Parole System at Work: Home Office Research Study No. 202* (London: HMSO, 2000).

evidence dictate whether information is legally admissible; laws of procedure prescribe practice and limit the discretion allowed to criminal justice agencies. Formal laws are joined by subsidiary rules and regulations relating to police powers, prosecution decisions, conduct of the trial, sentencing, the administration of penalties, prison discipline, and provisions for release. Together, primary legislation, delegated legislation, common law, Home Office circulars, and codes of practice provide the legal authority for state action against suspected and known offenders. In practice these laws are mediated through the considerable discretion exercised by all agents of criminal justice in their application. Understanding discretion is fundamental to understanding criminal justice.

The criminal law plays a crucial role in defining behaviour and reconstructing it to fit the predetermined categories of existing offences. It is the essential first step in determining which behaviour is subject to criminal justice and which not. In defining what is and what is not crime, the law is far from merely responsive to offences committed. It actively maps out the contours of the criminal law. The power of the criminal law to shoehorn the untidy possibilities of human action into discrete legal categories is impressive. Human actions, motivations, and mental states often fit ill with the artificial categories of the criminal law. Offences against the person are a good example here: many a law student has puzzled over the difference between assault and battery or between causing grievous bodily harm with intent and malicious wounding.[22]

Legalism assumes the superiority of law as a means of knowing and regulating the social world. Shklar defines it as follows: 'It is the ethical attitude that holds moral conduct to be a matter of rule following, and moral relationships to consist of duties and rights determined by rules.'[23] It holds that justice is secured by adherence to the values of fairness, consistency, and certainty in the application of those rules. Legalism tends to doubt the validity of other forms of knowledge. The insights of other knowledges, be they sociological, psychological, or medical, are admitted only to the extent that they are, or can be rendered, consistent with legal rules, concepts, and categories. Where that knowledge is at variance with legal concepts or categories it is often denied or excluded. A good example here was the historic reluctance of the criminal courts to admit medical, as opposed to legal, definitions of insanity or lesser mental

---

[22] The first are offences at common law, the latter two are to be found in the Offences Against the Person Act 1861 s.18 and s.20.

[23] Shklar, J., *Legalism* (Cambridge, Mass.: Harvard University Press, 1964) 1.

abnormalities (such as diminished responsibility).[24] Of course scientific knowledge, shifting public values, or new research evidence can bring about changes in the law but there is no guarantee of legal reform. The medical definition of insanity and new understandings of the workings of the mind have had little sway within the criminal courts precisely because they do not fit with legal notions of responsibility. The result is that it is entirely possible for the most eminent of psychiatrists to declare a defendant insane but the court to decide otherwise.

The nature of legal rules is properly the subject of jurisprudence and, as such, beyond the remit of this book.[25] That said, thinking about the nature of rules, the values they enshrine, and the way they structure criminal justice is an important first step to recognizing the artificiality of categories, processes, and institutions we might otherwise regard as inevitable or organic. Let us examine just a few examples. Central to the criminal law is the idea of the responsible subject or, to put it another way, the individual who can be held to account for their actions.[26] The responsible subject is an artifice constructed in order to legitimate holding individuals to account. For all its artificiality, its centrality makes it difficult for the criminal law, and therefore the criminal justice system, to deal with wrongs committed by conglomerates of individuals such as commercial organizations or nation states.[27] The harms they cause are almost always on a far larger scale than those done by individual actors and may entail no less culpability but the difficulties of satisfying the requirements of an identifiable responsible subject hinder prosecution and conviction.

Another central tenet is the distinction between guilt and innocence. Anyone who has observed a brawl outside the pub at closing time will acknowledge that distinguishing between guilt and innocence can be a contrived exercise that does damage to the messy reality of social interaction. When tonight's aggressor loses the fight he may find himself defined as the victim. When those he set upon rise up and retaliate the following week, he may gain the upper hand and earn the label of

---

[24] Smith, R., *Trial by Medicine: Insanity and Responsibility in Victorian Trials* (Edinburgh: Edinburgh University Press, 1981).

[25] The first port of call for the student of this set of problems is Hart, H. L. A., *The Concept of Law* (Oxford: Clarendon Press, 1961; 2nd edn, 1994).

[26] Cane, P., *Responsibility in law and morality* (Oxford: Hart, 2002); Lacey, N., 'In Search of the Responsible Subject: History, Philosophy and Social Sciences in Criminal Law Theory' (2001) 64 *Modern Law Review* 350–71.

[27] Wells, C., *Corporations and Criminal Responsibility* (2nd edn, Oxford: Oxford University Press, 2001); Cohen, S., *States of Denial: Knowing about Atrocities and Suffering* (Cambridge: Polity Press, 2001).

offender. The dynamic process of interaction that characterizes much interpersonal crime is denied by the criminal justice process as inimical to the basic presumptions of legal guilt and the attribution of blame. If, instead of accepting the legal categories that frame criminal justice uncritically, we try to look at them as if for the first time we can begin to see their synthetic character and, frequently, their arbitrariness. Legal ideology is an important adjunct to legal rules. This ideology, or at least the rhetoric through which it is expressed, frames criminal justice. Of course neither legal ideology nor legal rules are omnipotent and much of this book will be concerned with the ways in which they are daily sidelined and subverted as criminal justice actors exercise discretion in deciding which laws to invoke, when, and in what ways. For example, contrary to popular expectation, much of the working day of the average police officer is taken up with mundane matters (for example, offering directions) far removed from the formal categories of the criminal law, procedure, or evidence. Seen this way, the police are only marginally involved in fighting crime or enforcing the law. This observation is often taken as evidence of the yawning gap between law in the books and law in practice. Arguably it is better understood as resulting from an overly formal conception of law, namely that law is to be found in the books in the first place.[28] The relationship between rules and the exercise of discretion in their application is one to which we will return throughout this book. Rather than doubt the importance of law, perhaps we need a more expansive conception of law that admits discretion as integral to its practice. This is not to deny the centrality of law, for that would be to miss the defining characteristic of criminal justice as a particular set of legally determined responses to disputes, deviance, and harmful behaviours.

AGENCY AND INSTITUTIONAL PRACTICE

The term 'criminal justice' is also commonly used descriptively to refer to all those agents, institutions, and practices entrusted with responding to crime. The practice of criminal justice ranges from identifying and investigating offences, gathering legally relevant information, assessing its seriousness, constructing a case, and proving its commission, through to conviction, judgment, sentencing, and punishment. Even to characterize these as responses to crime is problematic because it suggests that

---

[28] Twining, W. L., *Law in Context: Enlarging a Discipline* (Oxford: Clarendon Press, 1996).

crime is a fact of nature to which designated human agents merely react. Criminal justice agents are not merely responsive: they may actively determine what is to be the subject of their attention and they may target particular types of behaviour and particular social and ethnic groups as perpetrators. In this sense, criminal justice agents could be said to be interpretative or even constructive of crime. Only through the processes of investigation, classification, and verification does deviant or harmful behaviour come to be labelled criminal and become the subject of criminal justice at all.

It is relatively easy to identify the key agents of criminal justice, less so to recognize all those tangentially engaged in fulfilling criminal justice functions. Of the key agents and institutions, most prominent are the police, prosecutors, the criminal courts, and the prison. The prison stands out also as an institution of iconic status, whose dramatic appearance and associations have assured its place in our cultural and imaginative life. Other key criminal justice institutions are only a little less prominent. It is not by chance that it is the policeman's helmet, the scales of justice, the judge's wig, or the barred prison window that grace the covers of many criminal justice textbooks. Less visible but no less important, the work of defence lawyers, court clerks, the probation service, and the parole board also lies at the core of criminal justice. Less visible still are the government departments (in England and Wales the Home Office, the Department of Constitutional Affairs, the office of the Attorney-General, and the Director of Public Prosecutions) that play a central role in policy formation and the administration of criminal justice. The government of criminal justice extends downward to include local authorities whose responsibility for local by laws, local policy development, and enforcement practices is increasingly important.[29] It also extends outward to include international bodies, such as the United Nations, and the institutions of the European Union. International, trans-national, and European policing organizations and intelligence agencies like the United Nations Security Police, Europol, and Interpol, as well as the cooperation of domestic police forces under agreements like TREVI and the Schengen Convention, are also important both internationally and on the domestic scene. Many other authorities are less

[29] The development of local 'partnerships' and 'community-based' projects was formalized in the responsibility placed upon local authorities for 'community safety' under the ss. 5, 6, and 17 Crime and Disorder Act 1998 which in turn led to the setting up of Crime and Disorder Reduction Partnerships made up of police, social workers, teachers, housing officials, and health workers.

obviously associated with criminal justice but nonetheless play a significant role in the prosecution of crime: for example, in England and Wales, the Inland Revenue, Customs and Excise, and the Health and Safety Executive. These institutions are not principally agents of criminal justice, but as prosecuting bodies they fulfil a core criminal justice function. In later chapters we will have much more to say about what it is the agents of criminal justice do and the roles they fulfil.

To include the general public as agents of criminal justice might seem too expansive a definition. But without public involvement the criminal justice system could not function. As victims and witnesses to crime, the public plays a crucial role in reporting offences, providing information to the police, and, more rarely, giving evidence in court. The great majority of crimes are not detected by the police but come to their attention only as a result of reporting by the public. To this extent one could argue that it is not the police but the public who are the true gatekeepers of the criminal justice process. If people regard an offence as insufficiently important; do not have faith in the criminal justice process; or have other reasons for avoiding contact with state officials then that offence may never come to official notice.

Within the process itself, victims are increasingly consulted about procedural decisions; asked to report upon the impact of the crime on them prior to sentencing; and even to participate in mediation with the offender. Involving victims in decision making devolves to them functions that, it might be thought, should properly be reserved to the state. It is hardly surprising that moves to empower victims have attracted academic and political controversy, not least because they require the state to relinquish what has come to be seen as its prerogative and to invite partisan actors to influence key decisions.[30] Seen another way, the expansion of lay participation is merely a sop to the fact that criminal justice is heavily reliant upon the public to report offences and provide information about them. It could also be read as indicative of a larger reversion to the historic responsibility of lay actors for preventing and prosecuting crimes. Whether or not this trend signals a significant reconfiguring or diminution of state responsibility for crime control is a theme to which we return in our final chapter.

[30] For example, on victims and sentencing see Ashworth, A., 'Victim Impact Statements and Sentencing' (1993) *Criminal Law Review* 498–509; Erez, E., 'Who is afraid of the Big Bad Victim? Victim Impact Statements as Victim Empowerment and Enhancement of Justice' (1999) *Criminal Law Review* 545–56; Sanders, A., *et al.*, 'Victim Statements—Don't Work, Can't Work' (2001) *Criminal Law Review* 447–58.

Offenders are more usually thought of as passive subjects than as agents of criminal justice. And whilst it is true that most offenders have little say over whether proceedings are brought against them, in minor cases at least, a suspect's initial response to police enquiries may determine whether or not those enquiries take a formal turn. The powerful have greater opportunities to escape notice through strategies of avoidance and 'creative compliance'.[31] They can pre-empt prosecution by buying legal expertise to stay just within the law or to manipulate the law to their own financial advantage. They can negotiate their way out of prosecution, for example, by doing deals with the Inland Revenue for non-payment of tax or with Health and Safety officials for failures to abide by workplace legislation.

Even within the pre-trial process, offenders at all levels can influence the outcome positively by negotiating plea bargains or by providing information, or negatively by non-compliance. The offender's choice of plea, willingness or ability to make reparation, and compliance with or breach of penal orders imposed all affect the way criminal justice is administered. As will become clear in later chapters, offenders can and do have some control over their treatment within the criminal process, their reception in court, the penalties they receive, and even the manner in which they are applied. A striking example is the fact that offenders who continue to maintain their innocence in prison, or refuse to express any remorse, are likely to extend the period of their incarceration because denial of guilt is considered a failure to accept responsibility and a bar, therefore, on early release. This is an extreme example. Lesser everyday negotiations, it can be argued, render offenders not merely the subjects of criminal justice but also its agents.

Another notable and only marginally less controversial, lay element in the criminal justice system is the juries who serve as the finders of fact and arbiters of guilt in the Crown Court. Depending on one's view, the jury sits in court as popular legitimation of coercive state power; a bulwark against its abuse by bringing fair-mindedness and common sense to bear; an indefensible historical legacy; or a beacon of participatory justice. The fact that the jury is, more or less, randomly selected creates the theoretical possibility of exposing or countering class, race, and gender biases within the system that might otherwise go unchallenged. Historically, many black

---

[31] McBarnet, D., 'It's Not What You Do But The Way That You Do It' in Downes (ed), *Unravelling Criminal Justice* (London: Macmillan, 1992); Hawkins, K., *Law as Last Resort: Prosecution Decision-Making in a Regulatory Agency* (Oxford: Oxford University Press, 2002).

defendants have elected jury trial, and in so doing risked a more severe sentence in the Crown Court, probably because they hoped to receive justice from a more socially representative jury. In practice it is questionable whether the jury reduces discrimination and improves the quality of justice. Given the prohibition on research into the operation of the jury, it is a question that is impossible to answer. Whatever it is the jury does behind the closed doors of the jury room, there is no doubt that it remains strongly defended as an institution of public participation in criminal justice.

The public also participates as the 29,000 or so magistrates who are appointed to sit in the lower courts to try less serious or summary offences. Magistrates also have the power to commit crimes to the higher Crown Court if they deem them so serious as to lie beyond their competence or the extent of their sentencing powers. Magistrates are often referred to as lay magistrates in order to emphasize their voluntary non-professional character. Many a foreign law student has difficulty grasping the fact that magistrates need have no legal education, undergo limited training before sitting in court, are unpaid, and sit only part-time.[32] To the extent that the criminal process is about subjecting social action to legal jurisdiction, their presence would seem anomalous. In dealing with about 96 per cent of all criminal cases, it is an anomaly that nonetheless forms the mainstay of the system. The presence of the lay magistracy is probably best explained as a historical legacy that would be an unlikely feature of a modern, rationally conceived system. Whether the lay magistracy constitute a historic anachronism or whether, by virtue of their office and the powers vested in them, they have been incorporated into the state function (in the same way that police officers are said to be citizens in uniform) is open to debate. It is also debatable whether, like the jury, they can be said to legitimize coercive state power, introduce a tier of democratic accountability into the state system, or represent an element of community justice.

It is already clear that the formal agents and institutions of criminal justice interact with and sometimes co-opt citizens as witnesses, jurors, and lay magistrates. Less commonly observed is the considerable involvement of volunteers in supplementing the police as special constables, supporting crime prevention initiatives, and even administering community penalties.[33] Charitable organizations like Victim Support are

---

[32] In addition to the lay magistrates, legally qualified, salaried district judges (formerly named stipendiary magistrates) sit full-time alone in court.

[33] Mawby, R. I., 'The Voluntary Sector's Role in a Mixed Economy of Criminal Justice' in Matthews (ed), *Privatising Criminal Justice* (London: Sage, 1989) 135.

also important in mobilizing thousands of volunteers to offer support and advice to victims and to staff the Witness Service operating in every Crown Court centre and magistrates' court.[34] Volunteers also help the police in myriad community safety initiatives, as helpers in prison, and in staffing pre- and post-release programmes. Lobby organizations invoke popular support to bring pressure to bear on government decision making about criminal justice. The degree to which volunteers are incorporated into the criminal justice system or derogate from it is both variable in practice and open to debate. It is also debatable whether the growth of informal involvement by private citizens, community organizations, and private corporations in the administration of criminal justice represents a shift in power from state to citizenry or rather a change in the shape of state governance of crime—a debate to which we return in the final chapter.

The role of the state in criminal justice is today taken to be self-evident. But we should recall that the development of state responsibility for crime control is a relatively modern phenomenon. Only when the establishment of formal police forces became compulsory in the mid-nineteenth century did the state become the primary, though not sole provider of policing. The assumption that the state should have primary responsibility for crime control is therefore less than two centuries old. Today the modern state controls the legislative process that produces criminal, procedural, sentencing, and penal administration statutes. It is responsible for determining criminal justice policy and administration and for allocating funds to that end. Nonetheless, crime control has never been the exclusive prerogative of the state.

The involvement of politicians in criminal justice is a variable commodity. Decades of lack of political interest may leave as strong a mark on criminal justice as decades of intense 'politicization' of crime.[35] The importance a government gives to crime and crime control strategies powerfully determines the political and cultural environment within which the various agents of criminal justice operate and the expectations placed upon them. Ironically, the greater the political and financial investment in crime, the greater the risk that the problem appears to grow. Politicization of crime increases public awareness, fear, and reporting of crime. The growth in public concern about crime increases

---

[34] Victim Support alone has over 13,000 volunteers on its books.

[35] Downes, D., and Morgan, R., 'The Skeletons in the Cupboard: the Politics of Law and Order at the Turn of the Millenium' in Maguire *et al.* (eds), *The Oxford Handbook of Criminology* (3rd edn, Oxford: Oxford University Press, 2002) 286–321 at 287–91.

pressure for greater resources to be allocated to criminal justice agencies, which in turn risks increasing the number of crimes recorded. In making criminal justice a political priority, therefore, politicians face the danger of generating an ever-enlarging black hole. The growth of the prison population in Britain from around 15,000 in 1946 to over 75,000 in 2004 is testimony to the impact of public concern on penal policy. Politicians target law and order, therefore, at their peril.

It should by now be clear that a very expansive definition of the agencies and practices of criminal justice is possible and, arguably, desirable. One could go further to argue that economic, education, or employment policies also have implications for the problem of crime and how it is managed. Whilst this is true, to extend our analysis to include these institutions would dilute the concept of criminal justice too far. It is also arguable that criminal justice as a primarily state enterprise is being diminished by the growing privatization of its functions. Already the incursion of private industry into policing, prisoner transport, the building and management of prisons, and the administration of other penalties requires us to rethink classical accounts of criminal justice as a state responsibility. Private security guards, surveillance equipment like CCTV, and home security devices such as burglar alarms proliferate to create a shadow system of crime control that may eventually dwarf the formal criminal justice system in size, resources, and importance.[36] But sociologically important as private security is, for now it might better be seen as lying beyond the purview of the formal criminal justice system. What the expansion of private security implies for our conception of criminal justice is an issue to which we will return.

Within the core institutions of criminal justice, the roles of the various agents are diverse. There is little in common between the daily activities of the local beat officer and those of the circuit judge. The two may never speak other than in the artificial intercourse of the courtroom. Differences in background, education, and professional role are so great that criminal justice agents may not share the same values or any common conception of the scope or role of criminal justice. Even within a single agency such as the police, officers fulfil diverse roles and may have different values or understanding of their purpose. The administrative duties of the custody officer differ substantially from the undercover work of the

---

[36] Jones, T., and Newburn, T., *Private Security and Public Policing* (Oxford: Oxford University Press, 1998); Loader, I., 'Private Security and the Demand for Protection in Contemporary Britain' (1997) 7 *Policing and Society* 377–94.

Drug Squad or the social welfare role of the community policeman. And it should not surprise us if they do not share a common conception of the job of policing. The role of the rural magistrate is distant from that of the Old Bailey judge, the types of crime with which they deal, the sentences available to them, indeed, their entire world-view may be substantially different. The question then arises whether this disparate array of agents and institutions have sufficient commonality to fall under the umbrella term criminal justice. One possible answer is that whilst their values and roles are widely divergent, what holds them together is their mutual interdependence. Without the collection of evidence no charge can be laid, without a charge there is no basis for prosecution, without evidence there can be no trial, without conviction no grounds for punishment. The beat officer and the circuit judge may inhabit different worlds and have little in common, but each has limited *raison d'être* without the other.

A SYSTEM

Though the term criminal justice system is commonly used, it is less than clear what is meant by the word system in the context of criminal justice. Classic scientific usage of the term system suggests a set of relations so connected that deductions can be made from some relations to others or from relations among the various entities to the behaviour of the system as a whole. The term system has also been used by scientists to denote an entity that is explicitly distinguished from its environment, whose internal elements are clearly defined, and whose internal and external relationships can be unambiguously stated.[37] The problem with definitions derived from the biological sciences is that they set up criteria so demanding, it seems scarcely possible that they could be fulfilled by the muddled interactions of human agency. Sociologists think of systems as structured by particular value patterns, fulfilling certain functions if they are to survive,[38] and capable of evolutionary change. Adopting for the moment these less demanding criteria of coherence, is it plausible to describe criminal justice as a system?

Seen one way, criminal justice lacks unity and coherence. It encompasses diverse legal and non-legal, state and voluntary, coercive

---

[37] Feeney, F., 'Interdependence as a Working Concept' in Moxon (ed), *Managing Criminal Justice* (London: HMSO, 1985) 8.

[38] For Talcott Parsons these functions were 'adaptation', 'goal-attainment', 'integration', and 'pattern maintenance', see Parsons, T., *The Social System* (London: Routledge & Kegan Paul, 1951).

and compliance-based institutions and practices. For the most part, they are the product of historical accident and accretion rather than systematic planning and organization. The key institutions, procedures, and rituals have developed over centuries, often born out of some passing imperative, and maintained as often by inertia as by positive will. A good example is the prison, an institution whose use as a place of long-term confinement arose chiefly in response to the demise of transportation to the colonies. Set up as a means of replicating the exclusionary force of transportation, the prison has long outlived its founding *raison d'être* (though it does impose conditions of internal exile on offenders considered to be dangerous). Its persistence and assumption of a position of centrality within the penal repertoire can be seen as the product of its particular history.

The other penalties—significantly once named alternatives to custody or non-custodial penalties to distinguish them from the prison, now more commonly known as community penalties—are similarly haphazard products of historical development. Probation, for example, developed out of the work of nineteenth-century police court missionaries and, as a consequence, for much of its history was technically not a penalty but an order of the court in place of sentencing.[39] Criminal justice agencies are similarly products of historical evolution. The magistracy derives from its forebear the justices of the peace, a fourteenth-century reincarnation of an early policing body. By contrast, the Crown Court is the much more recent invention of the early 1970s, but it too replaced the ancient quarter sessions and assize courts.

As a consequence of their very different histories, criminal justice agencies appear atomized, operating independently of one another, pursuing differing aims with differing philosophies and little by way of shared priorities or common purpose. Inward looking, and sometimes defensive attitudes by practitioners in different parts of the system increase this atomization, particularly when decisions made by one body are inadequately explained to another. For example, a common source of complaint by the police is that prosecutors decide to discontinue cases prepared by them without explanation. Poor communication and co-ordination among agencies may result in professional isolation, mutual antipathy, and demoralization. The fragmentary jumble of activities that results may scarcely merit the label of system commonly applied to it.

Seen another way, even if criminal justice is far from coherent, there is

[39] Until it was made a sentence of the court in its own right under the Criminal Justice Act 1991 s. 8.

an identifiable cluster of agencies and institutions, of processes and practices, of values and goals that can plausibly be said to form a system. Criminal justice has systemic qualities, not least that changes in one part have effects elsewhere—an effect that has been described as 'practical interdependence'[40] or, more graphically, as the effect of squeezing 'the toothpaste of discretion'.[41] Thus although the various elements are diverse they are, to varying degrees, inter-reliant. Policy and operational decisions are not fully coordinated, but those made by one agency affect the workload, resource requirements, and output of others. Agents operate according to different priorities but they remain, nevertheless, interconnected or, to borrow a sociological term, loosely coupled. A few examples will illustrate these systemic qualities. The Crown Prosecution Service depends upon the police to present it with evidence upon which it then makes the decision whether or not to prosecute. In turn, decisions made by prosecutors determine the caseload of the courts and may determine the venue for the trial. Sentences handed down by the courts determine much of the workload of the probation and prison services. And the reports of prison officers may have a determinative influence on decisions made by the Parole Board. Policy shifts or strictures upon discretion at any one of the above points are likely to result in changes in practice elsewhere. In this more modest sense it is possible to see the criminal justice system as, indeed, a system.

Considerable effort is put into improving the systemic qualities of interdependence, coordination, and communication. Institutional attempts at coordination include the setting up of the national Criminal Justice Consultative Council and Local Criminal Justice Boards[42] that bring together representatives of the different criminal justice professions to consult with one another and increase mutual understanding. Likewise high-level conferences for senior members of the civil service, judiciary, criminal justice professions, and the voluntary sector are intended to increase mutual understanding, collective purpose, and shared objectives. The Sentencing Advisory Panel, set up under the Crime and Disorder

---

[40] Ashworth, A., *The Criminal Process: An Evaluative Study* (2nd edn, Oxford: Oxford University Press, 1998) 23.

[41] Braithwaite, J., and Pettit, P., *Not Just Deserts: A Republican Theory of Justice* (Oxford: Oxford University Press, 1990) 20.

[42] Introduced in 2003, these replace the Area Criminal Justice Strategy Committees that in turn replaced the Area Criminal Justice Liaison Committees established in the early 1990s, the Trial Issues Groups, Chief Officers Groups, and any existing Criminal Justice Boards.

Act 1998, is another example of an attempt to enhance the systemic qualities of criminal justice. It brings together sentencers, academics, members of other criminal justice agencies, and lay people to advise upon appropriate sentences for particular categories of offence. That the Sentencing Advisory Panel was explicitly intended to 'broaden the authorship' of Court of Appeal guideline judgments attests to the importance attached to broadening deliberation and consultation. The establishment of Youth Offending Teams (YOTs) as a means of securing coordination in the field of youth justice and the merger of the prison and probation services (into the new National Offender Management Service, NOMS) are other good examples. Similarly, the coordination of computing systems is designed to improve the free flow of information among the different computer systems operated by the various criminal justice agencies.[43] The setting of uniform data standards and the development of policies on information handling, data protection, and forward planning also suggest the aspiration, at least, to coordinate.

All these developments presume that coordination is a virtue. From the perspective of good management, it might appear self-evident that open channels of communication, as well as harmonization of purpose and practice, are desirable. They create the conditions for efficiency and economy in the processing of cases and are intended to increase the effectiveness of criminal justice agencies. However, it is open to question whether coherence within the criminal justice system is an unproblematic good. Another view is that the rivalries and tensions that beset the criminal justice system, though administratively inconvenient, serve to protect individual liberties. A powerful, centralized, all-embracing criminal justice system might pose a greater threat to the values of a liberal democratic state than one characterized by frictions, and even inefficiencies. Practical interdependence and fluid interaction might seem safer, if more modest, aspirations than the machine-like qualities of a wholly coordinated system.

It is possible to think of the criminal justice system in different ways than the one we have so far pursued. According to one branch of social theory, autopoiesis, a system is a mechanism designed to reduce the

[43] Criminal Justice Information Technology (CJIT, formed in 2001, works for all three of the principal criminal justice departments (Home Office, Department of Constitutional Affairs, and the Attorney-General's Department). Working in partnership with the other criminal justice organizations, its remit is 'to deliver the vision of a modernized, joined up Criminal Justice System'. See <http://www.cjit.gov.uk/home.html>.

complexity of the environment in which it is embedded.[44] The system achieves this by limiting interaction with its environment and by selecting relevant events from that environment which it then subjects to internal mechanisms of management and filtering. Faced with an environment that potentially threatens its autonomy, the system records and interprets that environment in such a way that, instead, enhances its autonomy. According to this account, the system is characterized by three dimensions: the code by which information is processed (as being, for example, significant or insignificant), the structure (of values, norms, and expectations), and the process itself. This account has particular promise for our understanding of criminal justice as a system.

Understood this way, the criminal justice system absorbs information about social action, filters it through internal criteria of truth and significance, subjects it to internal canons of validity, and processes it according to internal norms and values. The process is a means of reducing the complexity of social life to manageable proportions through organization, classification, and judgment. Put another way, the messy variety of human misery, aggression, hostility, and need is filtered, processed, and thereby rendered capable of regulation by the criminal justice system. There is, however, a danger that the criminal justice (or indeed any) system understood this way appears as an autonomous entity capable of processing and interpreting information and pursuing goals quite independently of the thoughts or actions of its individual actors.[45] The question is whether it is possible to resist the temptation to reify the criminal justice system, so as to see it as a closed communication system of the sort outlined here, without portraying it as one over which individuals have lost control.[46]

---

[44] Luhman, N., *The Differentiation of Society* (New York: Columbia University Press, 1982); Luhman, N., 'The Unity of the Legal System' in Teubner (ed), *Autopoietic Law: A New Approach to Law and Society* (Berlin: de Gruyter, 1988); Luhman, N., *Social Systems* (Palo Alto, Calif.: Stanford University Press, 1992).

[45] Teubner, G., 'How the Law Thinks: Toward a Constructivist Epistemology of Law' (1989) 23 *Law and Society Review* 727–57.

[46] Cotterrell, R., 'Sociological Perspectives on Legal Closure' in Norrie (ed), *Closure or Critique: New Directions in Legal Theory* (Edinburgh: Edinburgh University Press, 1993) 175–93.

A NORMATIVE THEORY

There is a sad irony in the fact that the well-documented injustices of the criminal process and much-publicized cases of miscarriage of justice[47] form a more immediate association with the term criminal justice than any positive conception. No wonder then that the presence of the word *justice* appears as a false promise and that its apparent claim to legitimize criminal justice is difficult to sustain. Even leaving aside miscarriages of justice, much that is done in the name of criminal justice seems morally wrong and as such requires special justification.[48] On the face of it, it is wrong to coerce, to interrogate, to incarcerate, and to exact monetary payment or physical labour for no return, yet the state does all these things in the name of criminal justice. The attempt to justify them is the subject matter of criminal *justice*.[49] In this sense, criminal justice is a negative account of why apparently bad things are warranted. Or, more negatively still, of why a system of criminal justice is a practical necessity. Although it may not deliver justice, it is defensible on the grounds that the consequences of its abolition would be even worse.[50]

Happily, a positive account of criminal justice as a normative theory is also possible. It can be argued that law enforcement agents aspire to a particular form of legitimacy that resides in the notion of criminal justice. This legitimacy requires that criminal justice is properly the duty of the state and that state agents discharge that duty in the best manner possible. No one claims that any actual system of criminal justice will live up to that ideal in all respects. But the fact that criminal justice is a theoretical aspiration does not undermine its importance in structuring and legitimating the actions of its agents. The question then arises, where does this legitimacy reside? Is it in the articulation of particular aims, values, and principles specific to criminal justice? Is it in an overarching general

---

[47] The miscarriages of justice concerning those convicted of IRA bombings in the 1980s are one such example. The scandal surrounding the bungled police investigation into the murder of a black British teenager Stephen Lawrence in 1993 is another. Rose, D., *In the Name of the Law: The Collapse of Criminal Justice* (London: Jonathan Cape, 1996).

[48] As Duff and Garland have observed of punishment: Duff, R. A., and Garland, D. (eds), *A Reader on Punishment* (Oxford: Oxford University Press, 1994) 2.

[49] Lacey, N., 'Introduction: Making Sense of Criminal Justice' in Lacey, (ed), *A Reader on Criminal Justice* (Oxford: Oxford University Press, 1994) 4–6. In Chapter 3 we shall have more to say about the particular need to justify punishment.

[50] A point conceded even by those who would see its role radically reduced: Mathiesen, T., *The Politics of Abolition: Essays in Political Action* (Oxford: Martin Robertson, 1974).

theory of criminal justice? Or is criminal justice better conceived as one part of a larger framework of social justice?

Let us examine the last proposition first. It is arguable that criminal justice can only be achieved (or even conceived) within **a general theory of social justice**.[51] If this is true, then we are obliged to abandon any idea of a discrete conception of *criminal* justice. We can aspire to justice in respect of wrongdoers only if we can first imagine the just society. And perhaps this is a task better left to social and political theorists and philosophers. Whether a theory of criminal justice might contribute to a larger theory of social justice remains open to question. Arguably, where economic and social inequality are endogenous, where racism is endemic, and gender discrimination widespread, it is unrealistic to think of criminal justice as a mechanism for transforming an unjust society into a just one.[52] But does this mean that in an unjust society we must relinquish any hope of aspiring to justice within the criminal process?[53] Is it arguable that in an unjust society criminal justice can have no legitimacy and should be abolished until the just society is realized? Abolitionists, for example, question the continued existence of the central institutions of criminal justice and claim that reform only strengthens the very institutions whose legitimacy they doubt.[54]

A less radical view is that, even in a society that is less than just, **a general theory of criminal justice** might aspire to minimize the perpetuation of injustice within its own purview.[55] The pursuit of criminal justice would not constitute a claim to wider social justice, but the specific achievement of a normative framework for regulating the criminal process, the trial, and punishment. A general theory of criminal justice would have to arch over the entirety of the process (from criminalization through the pre-trial process, trial, sentencing, and disposal) and it would not suffice for it to apply to one part alone. One reason for developing

[51] As Marxists, for example, are inclined to argue. A classic statement is to be found in Rusche, G., and Kirchheimer, O., *Punishment and Social Structure* (New York: Columbia University Press, 1939).

[52] von Hirsch, A., *Censure and Sanctions* (Oxford: Oxford University Press, 1993) 97–9; Smart, C., *Feminism and the Power of Law* (London: Routledge, 1989).

[53] Hudson, B., *Penal Policy and Social Justice* (London: Macmillan, 1993) 12–13.

[54] One leading abolitionist, Thomas Mathiesen, resolves this dilemma by condoning only those reforms that could be expected to weaken the existing institutions of punishment: Mathiesen, T., *The Politics of Abolition: Essays in Political Action* (Oxford: Martin Robertson, 1974).

[55] As I have argued in respect of young offenders: Zedner, L., 'Sentencing Young Offenders' in Ashworth and Wasik (eds), *Fundamentals of Sentencing Theory* (Oxford: Clarendon Press, 1998) 175.

such a theory is that given the interconnectedness of different parts of criminal justice, a theory applicable to only one part of the criminal process will likely find itself in conflict with, or defeated by, contrary impulses in another part of the process. Whether it is in practice possible for theories developed with regard to one stage to be expanded to another is open to debate and has been the subject of intense discussion among leading penal theorists.[56]

We can examine the difficulties involved by taking the example of desert theory. Desert theory (known also as the justice model) is an important and sophisticated theory, developed in respect of the sentencing stage.[57] We shall give a fuller account of desert theory in Chapter 3. Suffice it to say here that it promotes proportionality of punishment and is committed to legal formalism, to due process, and to parsimony in the use of punishment. In these respects, it could be argued that desert theory has wider applicability to pre-trial procedure and the trial stage. Proportionality requires that there should be correspondence between the gravity of the offence and the burdens imposed upon an offender.[58] At the pre-trial stage, when the offence has not yet been proven, requirements imposed upon offenders should be less onerous than those imposed by the courts as penalties. The concentration by desert theory upon the gravity of the present offence also requires that multiple cautions be available for repeat offenders and that there be no undue increase in severity of response based on past record. Beyond these issues, however, desert theory is less obviously applicable to the very different normative questions that arise in respect of the criminal process prior to sentencing. To be clear, proponents of desert theory make no claim that theirs is a general theory of criminal justice. They propound it as a theory of sentencing alone.[59]

Other theories make more ambitious claims of general applicability to

---

[56] For example, see Braithwaite, J., and Pettit, P., *Not Just Deserts: A Republican Theory of Justice* (Oxford: Oxford University Press, 1990); Ashworth, A., and von Hirsch, A., 'Not Not Just Deserts: a Response to Braithwaite and Pettit' (1992) 12 *Oxford Journal of Legal Studies* 83–98; or von Hirsch, A., *Censure and Sanctions* (Oxford: Oxford University Press, 1993) ch. 2.

[57] von Hirsch, A., *Doing Justice: The Choice of Punishments* (New York: Hill & Wang, 1976); von Hirsch, A., *Censure and Sanctions* (Oxford: Oxford University Press, 1993); Ashworth, A., 'Criminal Justice and Deserved Sentences' (1989) *Criminal Law Review* 340–55.

[58] Ashworth, A., *The Criminal Process: An Evaluative Study* (2nd edn, Oxford: Oxford University Press, 1998) 62.

[59] Ashworth, A., and von Hirsch, A., 'Not Not Just Deserts: a Response to Braithwaite and Pettit' (1992) 12 *Oxford Journal of Legal Studies* 83–98 at 98.

criminal justice. The 'republican theory of dominion' advanced by Braithwaite and Pettit, for example, harks back to the classical notion of liberty espoused by the ancient republics. Put briefly, it sets as its target 'the maximisation of the dominion of individual people',[60] where dominion is the promotion of a negative concept of individual liberty, namely protection from interference by others. This attempt to frame a general theory of criminal justice has the advantage that, unlike desert theory, it does not rely on a theory of punishment to generate a larger normative framework. To focus on sentencing (as desert theory does) presumes punishment as the end goal of criminal justice. In this sense, desert theory presumptively legitimates the system of punishment rather than subjecting it to the kind of critical scrutiny that might question its very existence. By contrast, republican theory could conceivably conclude that its ends were best served by another mechanism for protecting dominion entirely. Republican theory claims to be a 'comprehensive theory of criminal justice . . . capable of generating a set of answers to policy questions which is complete, coherent, and systematic'.[61] It is arguable that such ambition is also a weakness of republican theory. It purports to provide a normative framework for the entirety of a system whose inherent diversity defies any unifying rationale. The leading critics of republican theory, von Hirsch and Ashworth, challenge its claim to comprehensiveness and doubt that a single theory can hold good for every stage of the criminal process: 'Philosophers have become increasingly sceptical of sweeping, foundationalist moral and social theories. The conception that purports to answer every question is apt to yield answers that are meagre at best and, at worst, plain wrong.'[62] Whether republican or any other general theory of criminal justice is ultimately convincing or desirable is a question to which we shall return.

Given the complexity of criminal justice, von Hirsch and Ashworth may well be right to argue that the search for an overarching theory capable of framing the entire process is overly ambitious. The need to identify a single purpose for criminal justice or a comprehensive normative structure that makes sense of all parts of the process is a daunting intellectual challenge. Moreover, it requires that parts of the process that can legitimately claim to pursue different goals be forced into a single

---

[60] Braithwaite, J., and Pettit, P., *Not Just Deserts: A Republican Theory of Justice* (Oxford: Oxford University Press, 1990) ch.2 'For a Comprehensive Theory' at 54.

[61] Ibid. 15.

[62] Ashworth, A., and von Hirsch, A., 'Not Not Just Deserts: a Response to Braithwaite and Pettit' (1992) 12 *Oxford Journal of Legal Studies* 83–98 at 98.

mould. Indeed it is arguable that the very term 'criminal justice' conflates two quite distinct processes. The process of detection, investigation, prosecution, and trial rests upon presumptions and enshrines values that are subtly different from those that apply once the offender has been found guilty. After conviction other values come into play.[63] Accordingly, it might make more sense to develop distinct models for the pre- and post-trial phases. This need not entail the complete abandonment of coherence. Given the evident interdependence of the two parts of the process, one would still need to find ways of linking, for example, the values of due process in the pre-trial stage with those of desert theory at the point of sentencing.

Our third conception of criminal justice is less ambitious but potentially more powerful. It conceives of criminal justice not as a general theory but as **a set of values** applicable both to procedure and to disposal by which the otherwise unfettered discretion of criminal justice agents can be subject to principled control. This approach concedes that different considerations apply at the pre- and post-trial stages and that these may not be reconcilable. It also recognizes that, without adherence to specified values, the operation of the powerful machinery of the state criminal justice system against lone, often vulnerable, or inadequate individuals has the potential to be harsh.[64] Identifying the values that criminal justice should embrace and the ethical standards with which its agents should comply thus takes precedence over the pursuit of meta-enquiries into criminal justice's larger role or purpose.[65] The advantage of this approach is that identifying particular values such as fairness, balance, transparency, accountability, and respect for individual rights potentially provides a working guide for decision making. Respect for rights has become central to thinking about criminal justice, not least as a consequence of the Human Rights Act 1998. By incorporating the European Convention on Human Rights into English law, the 1998 Act provides a normative framework that pertains to many aspects of criminal justice. Accepting that the criminal justice process is strongly characterized by

---

[63] Lacey, N., 'Discretion and Due Process at the Post Conviction Stage' in Dennis (ed), *Criminal Law and Criminal Justice* (London: Sweet & Maxwell, 1987).

[64] On 'the return to respectability of cruelty as a penal value' see Simon, J., ' "Entitlement to Cruelty": The End of Welfare and the Punitive Mentality in the United States' in Stenson and Sullivan (eds), *Crime, Risk, and Justice* (Cullompton, Devon: Willan Publishing, 2001).

[65] On the application of this approach to the pre-trial process see Ashworth, A., *The Criminal Process: An Evaluative Study* (2nd edn, Oxford: Oxford University Press, 1998) particularly chs 2 and 3.

the exercise of discretion, a principled approach, whether based on rights or some other model, has the potential to steer and constrain decision making. If backed up by appropriate measures of enforcement, it has the power to discipline gross derogation from the principles enunciated in legislation and case law.

One possible criticism of this approach is that it is less a conception of criminal justice than a subset of values. Without a larger conception of the proper role of criminal justice, it provides little steer where these values conflict. The promotion of the rights of the defendant under the Human Rights Act 1998, for example, is constrained by the requirement implied into Article 6 of the European Convention that such rights can, in theory, be restricted by balancing them against the public interest.[66] If offenders' rights are not to be 'balanced away', then we need a clear conception of the extent of legitimate public interest. The evident difficulty of deciding how to weigh different values tempers the normative power of the principled approach to criminal justice. Although it has the power to ameliorate, it is arguable that it cannot effectively challenge the status quo.

We have sketched three possible normative conceptions of criminal justice: as an element in a larger conception of social justice; as a general theory of criminal justice; or as a principled approach encompassing subsets of procedural and dispositive values. We have said little about the subject to whom justice is to be done. It hardly needs to be said that most normative conceptions of criminal justice have in mind the defendant and, post-conviction, the offender as their primary subject. Arguably, this conception of criminal justice is too narrow. Through the criminal process, justice is also sought on behalf of society in repairing the damage done to its normative order; in making good tangible harms to persons and property; and in reaffirming moral values. The victim also has a claim to be recognized as a legitimate subject of criminal justice whose losses and suffering furnish the basis of claims to information; to participation in decision making; and, to a more limited degree, in the outcome of the process. Despite political pronouncements that a 'victim justice system' should replace the existing criminal justice system,[67] it remains unclear what this might look like, how it would operate, and at what cost.

The stakes legitimately held by each of these parties—offender, victim, and society—are not readily reconcilable and their pursuit creates the

---

[66] Ashworth, A., 'Criminal Proceedings after the Human Rights Act: The First Year' (2001) *Criminal Law Review* 855–72 at 865.

[67] Rt. Hon. Tony Blair, Prime Minister, the Queen's Speech, November 2002.

potential for conflict. Managing their respective interests involves making difficult judgments about how to balance one against the other. An illuminating example arises in the need to protect vulnerable witnesses called to give evidence in court. Screening witnesses from their alleged abusers may reduce the trauma of giving evidence in open court and increase the likelihood of securing a conviction. But it may also damage the interests of the defendant whose right to be presumed innocent is threatened by the visual presumption of guilt that the screen signals to the jury. A normative conception of criminal justice, at whatever level of abstraction, cannot avoid addressing and seeking to reconcile these competing interests.

A final but all-pervading normative issue is whether criminal justice can 'do justice to difference'.[68] Legality assumes the juridical subject: it assumes that those subject to law are identifiable individuals with the capacity to make choices for which they may justly be held accountable. The central tenets of criminal justice rely on this assumption of equal legal capacity. At most stages of the criminal justice process it is assumed that fairness is achieved by treating all equally. Limited recognition is given to the fact that offenders have different capacities, means, and resources. The criminal law excludes from liability those deemed to be below the age of criminal responsibility, the insane, and others lacking mental capacity but it places strict limits on other qualifications to the presumed capacity of the offender. Similarly, although police and pro-secutors have discretion to exclude on grounds of capacity, the starting assumption is that individuals enjoy free will and are so situated as to be able to exercise it. In sentencing, judges are exhorted to focus on the seriousness of the offence, and have little regard for the constrained eco-nomic circumstances; the vulnerable social situation; or the limited abil-ities or life chances of the offender. An alternative view is that justice is not served by the presumption of equity among juridical subjects. According to this view, it is not enough to treat women, for example, equally to men.[69] To do so ignores differences in their psychological make up, socialization, opportunities, social situation, and responsibilities for childcare. It also fails to recognize that women's experience of interroga-tion, trial, sentencing, and punishment is different from that of men and

---

[68] Hudson, B., 'Doing Justice to Difference' in Ashworth and Wasik (eds), *Fundamentals of Sentencing Theory* (Oxford: Clarendon Press, 1998).

[69] Heidensohn, F., 'Models of Justice; Portia or Persephone? Some Thoughts on Equality, Fairness and Gender in the Field of Criminal Justice' (1986) 14 *International Journal of the Sociology of Law* 287–98.

that injustice is likely to be done if these differences are not recognized. More generally, recognition that formal equality in sentencing may not result in equality of impact in practice has been central to the case for varying financial penalties according to the means of the offender. Perhaps the most established case for differentiation is the distinct concept of juvenile justice. This acknowledges young offenders' limitations and the potential unfairness of treating them like adults. As a particularly well-developed instance of differentiation, juvenile justice provides a model for other possible derogations from the prevailing model of formal equality—on grounds of gender, race, disability, and old age for example. To the extent that the formal neutrality of criminal justice results in discriminatory treatment of those whose characteristics, needs, or interests differ from the norm, it would seem that an undifferentiated conception of criminal justice will not suffice. Evidence that the application of supposedly 'neutral criteria' at each stage of the criminal justice process has resulted in 'cumulative disadvantage' to Afro-Caribbean defendants,[70] for example, would seem to suggest that justice can only be done where the grounds for differential treatment are fully articulated and integral to the larger conception of criminal justice.[71]

A FIELD OF STUDY

Finally, we consider criminal justice as a field of study. There has been an extraordinary growth of masters and even undergraduate degree courses, of full-time academic posts, of research centres, of conferences, colloquia, and seminar series, of monographs and journals bearing the name criminal justice. Despite this flowering of academic interest and endeavour, it is open to question whether criminal justice can plausibly be considered a distinct branch of knowledge. Historically, it is best seen as a sub-field of criminology, a discipline that is little more than a century old.

Although criminologists have long been interested in crime control, its institutions, and its effectiveness, we tend to think of criminology principally as the study of the causes, patterns, and nature of crime itself. The difficulties encountered in trying to isolate these causes or explain crime

---

[70] Phillips, C., and Bowling, B., 'Racism, Ethnicity, Crime and Criminal Justice' in Maguire, *et al.* (eds), *The Oxford Handbook of Criminology* (3rd edn, Oxford: Oxford University Press, 2002) 612.

[71] Hudson, B., 'Doing Justice to Difference' in Ashworth and Wasik (eds), *Fundamentals of Sentencing Theory* (Oxford: Clarendon Press, 1998).

have led many scholars to abandon the unequal struggle.[72] The acceptance of crime as an inevitable fact of modern social life has further tended to remove crime from the centre of scholarly attention and promote instead study of the state's response to it. Viewed this way, the expansion of studies in the field of criminal justice is a retreat from the big, important questions about the sources, causes, and meanings of deviance. But a more positive account is also possible. The study of criminal justice recognizes the importance of a key area of state power and can thus be seen as fundamental to understanding the working of the modern state. Seen this way, criminal justice is less the orphan of criminology than the vibrant child of socio-legal studies, law in context, political science, and emerging studies in governance and regulation.

An alternative structural explanation for the growth in interest in criminal justice is to be found in the educational background of the criminological community. Whereas the majority of those graduating in the post-war period had studied social sciences, particularly sociology, latter generations increasingly trained first in law.[73] A parallel movement of criminologists into law faculties where the majority now teach, research, and write mirrored this educational shift. Whereas in other European countries criminal lawyers and criminologists retain a strong sense of their separate intellectual identities, in England a growing convergence of approach, method, and substance began to blur these distinctions. Increasing pressure on academics to obtain outside funding also had the effect of obliging criminologists to adopt the interests of policymakers and government officials in order to secure research grants. These factors have contributed to the reorientation of criminology, away from its sociological origins and its primary interest in the phenomenon of crime, towards the legal classification of activities as criminal, and the institutions, procedures, and practices that together make up the criminal justice system. Given these circumstances it is not surprising that there is convergence between criminal lawyers and criminologists interested in criminal justice. In many cases they are one and the same person.

These developments tell us something about why criminal justice is the subject of scholarship and study. They do not tell us whether or not it has yet attained the status of an academic discipline. Although we can readily identify the substantive subject matter of criminal justice, it is less clear

---

[72] Sumner, C., *The Sociology of Deviance: An Obituary* (Buckingham: Open University Press, 1994).

[73] Rock, P., 'The Social Organisation of British Criminology' in Maguire *et al.* (eds), *The Oxford Handbook of Criminology* (Oxford: Oxford University Press, 1994) 129.

that it connotes a distinct intellectual approach or set of methodological tools. Sitting uncomfortably on the margins between criminal law and criminology, criminal justice, it could be argued, is best seen not as a discrete discipline but as drawing parasitically upon those adjacent to it. It draws heavily also upon other established disciplines including sociology, jurisprudence and political philosophy, psychology, political science, social and economic history, and social administration. Like criminology, it might well be described as a *rendezvous* subject, enjoying little coherence of approach and method but providing a meeting place where scholars of different disciplinary backgrounds, but common substantive interests, converge and converse.

A more aggressive account of the emergence of criminal justice is also possible. This account recognizes that academics are motivated not just by intellectual curiosity but also by the competition for financial capital (research grants), symbolic capital (the authority to define), and social capital (networks of influence).[74] Establishing the independence and prestige of criminal justice as a discipline is essential to the promotion of academic careers built upon its pursuit. In the attempt to establish its independent existence, protagonists of criminal justice have raided neighbouring disciplines for methods and conceptual tools. In so doing they sought to carve out a distinct and defensible space or disciplinary turf. This intellectual looting and pillaging was followed by a period of consolidation in which the structures necessary to the continuation of the discipline were put in place. Hence the establishment of permanent university posts, of research centres, of courses, and (more rarely) of departments to which we alluded above. The availability of funding from external sources, most notably in the policy arena, has been an important factor in permitting criminal justice to lure staff and students from neighbouring disciplines like sociology with the promise of present or prospective employment. As both academics and their student progeny come to identify themselves as practitioners of criminal justice (no convenient 'ology' yet springs to mind), they look to the nascent discipline to set out the parameters of what they need to know (and, importantly, what they need not know), what research practices, what explanatory tools, and what normative frameworks to employ.

Of course the items on this disciplinary shopping list are not as distinct as the format of the list suggests. Description inevitably involves selection

---

[74] Ericson, R., 'The Culture and Power of Criminological Research' in Zedner and Ashworth (eds), *The Criminological Foundations of Penal Policy* (Oxford: Oxford University Press, 2003) 45.

and that selection is guided by ideas about what is valuable (or not). The normative frame within which research is carried out may not be made explicit but it is there nonetheless. Likewise explanation and analysis are heavily reliant upon empirical research that seeks to uncover how the institutions of criminal justice really operate, what motivates criminal justice actors in their decision making, how offenders experience and influence the processes and the punishments imposed on them, and so on. Similarly, normative accounts of criminal justice are grounded in a strong appreciation of criminal justice history and present practice. Without this descriptive content, criminal justice would scarcely be differentiable from an exercise in moral philosophy. And to the extent that law frames criminal justice practice, its study also has to have regard for rules and their application. The study of criminal justice depends upon constant movement between these descriptive, explanatory, normative, and legal frames. Some, namely the descriptive and explanatory, are more developed than others, and the normative project remains least developed. It is for this reason, above all, that it seems premature to talk of criminal justice as a discipline.

Given the difficulty of identifying whether or in what degree criminal justice has attained the prerequisites of discipline-hood, it is tempting to seek some more tangible test. Abbott suggests one simple but compelling condition for determining whether a new discipline has arrived. He says 'we can think of them as having become true disciplines in the social structural sense once they hire mainly Ph.D.s in their own field'.[75] According to this test at least, criminal justice remains firmly in the category of raider tribe rather than settled disciplinary state.

CONCLUSION

In this chapter we have explored just some of the many ways in which the term criminal justice is commonly employed. We have considered whether criminal justice can usefully be understood as a form of governance, whether as a social ordering practice, as a means of dispute resolution, or as risk management. We have suggested that criminal justice is a particular type of legal response to wrongdoing; that it refers to a particular set of institutions and practices engaged in that response; and that reference to the criminal justice system implies a particular set of relations among those institutions and practices. We have considered

---

[75] Abbott, A., *Chaos of Disciplines* (Chicago: Chicago University Press, 2000) 139.

criminal justice as embracing normative theory and explored at what level of specificity or generality it plausibly operates. Finally, and more controversially, we have raised the question of whether criminal justice can claim the status of emerging discipline. In these various capacities, the term criminal justice is used descriptively, analytically, and normatively (presuming that these are distinct and separable). It refers both to a process and the desired outcome of that process. It identifies a substantive subject and, simultaneously, the study of that subject. Of course, it would be both convenient and intellectually satisfying if it were possible to formulate an elegant inclusive account of criminal justice capable of embracing all the ideas we have set out in this introductory chapter. But such elegance could be achieved only at the cost of obscuring the disparate and tangled meanings presently embraced by criminal justice.

2

Crime

WHAT IS CRIME?

Criminal justice, it might be said, presupposes crime. The existence of police, prosecutors, judges, courtrooms, and prisons might seem evidence enough of crime. It might even be said that crime calls the rules and practices, the agencies and institutions of criminal justice into existence. As Marx wryly observed: 'The influence of the criminal upon the development of the productive forces can be shown in detail. Would the locksmith's trade have attained its present perfection if there had been no thieves? Would the manufacture of bank notes have arrived at its present excellence if there had been no counterfeiters?'[1] Texts on criminal justice might also be said to owe their existence (if not their perfection) to crime. Yet even if, on the evidence of their existence, we could take crime as a given, we would still be left uncertain as to its meaning. What is this phenomenon that provokes such public concern, political interest, institutional endeavour, and expense? How is it defined? By whom? And to what ends?

Historically, these questions have been the focus of two adjacent but distinct academic disciplines: criminal law and criminology. In defining crime, the criminal law identifies those forms of behaviour, action, or, in certain circumstances, inaction that the state prohibits as offences against society (differentiable from civil wrongs deemed to offend only against the individual). The criminal lawyer's main concerns are with the way law structures crime, the principles underlying that structure, and the values that the law professes to uphold. In criminal law, the central components of crime are the mental and conduct elements according to which liability for wrongdoing without justification or excuse arises. It follows that in defining crime, the criminal law also lays down the parameters of liability and determines how offences should be ranked. Criminology, on the

---

[1] Quoted in Greenburg, D. F., *Crime and Capitalism: Readings in Marxist Criminology* (Philadelphia: Temple University Press, 1993) at 53 taken from Marx, K., *Theories Of Surplus Value* (London: Lawrence and Wishart, 1969).

other hand, is less concerned (and arguably less concerned than it should be) with the legal definition of crime than with its complex social role. The criminologist is inclined to characterize crime as a problematic social phenomenon, as a social construct or label, as the exercise of power, or as a means of governance, as much as individual wrongdoing. The fundamentally different world-views that structure the twin disciplines of criminal law and criminology served for a long time to keep them asunder despite their common subject matter.

More recently, strenuous efforts have been made to reconcile legal and social scientific approaches to the study of crime. Socio-legal studies, critical legal studies, and 'law in context' scholarship have done much to integrate social scientific knowledge and insight into legal scholarship. This scholarship asks how and why legal categories are framed and, in seeking to answer these questions, recognizes that definitions of crime are historically and politically contingent. The drive to set law in context has touched most areas of legal scholarship and in the field of criminal law has proved particularly strong.[2] Enquiries about the social, political, and economic circumstances in which laws arise, who promotes particular laws, in whose interests, and to what ends are increasingly the staples of criminal law scholarship. These enquiries seek to reveal the power relationships and political imperatives that underlie criminalization. Criminology reveals that acts are criminalized along lines of class, race, and gender and that criminalization protects certain interests over others. Studies of core criminal categories, like theft and offences against the person, reveal that they are not unproblematically engaged in protecting property, sexual integrity, or bodily autonomy. Rather they safeguard particular types of property and provide differential levels of protection for different categories of person. Studies of 'new' offences like city fraud, insider dealing, workplace negligence, and environmental pollution go further still to reveal how the categories of the criminal law are politically contingent.[3] They make it abundantly clear that the criminal law is far from a simple, still less an apolitical, response to wrongdoing or harmful behaviour.

This scholarship allows us to overcome traditional disciplinary boundaries and to pose anew the question, what do we mean when we talk of

---

[2] For example, Lacey, N., and Wells, C., *Reconstructing Criminal Law: Text and Materials* (3rd edn, London: Butterworths, 2003).

[3] For example, Wells, C., *Corporations and Criminal Responsibility* (2nd edn, Oxford: Oxford University Press, 2001).

crime?[4] We will consider crime as a contestable concept with many possible meanings, not least: a form of labelling, a social construct, and the product of power relations, whether between classes, races, states, or individuals and the state. It is also used to designate a form of wrongdoing that violates a social code or does violent offence to moral feelings. It is used to describe harm doing or the violation of duties to the community. Together these form the basis for the legal categorization of crime. Understanding the classificatory role of the criminal law is essential for the student of criminal justice, but, as we shall see, the legal definition of crime is problematic, especially for those principally interested in criminological questions. Finally, in order to examine the relationship between the normative and the consequential aspects of crime, we consider the proposition that it is a condition precedent to punishment. The more recent characterization of crime as a normal fact of everyday life or routine activity is a topic to which we will return in the final chapter.

Given the range and variety of these ways of thinking about crime, the possibility of an elegant overarching theory or definition of crime looks remote. As Braithwaite observes: 'Crime is not a unidimensional construct. For this reason one should not be overly optimistic about a general theory which sets out to explain all types of crime.'[5] The various definitions of crime explored below lack coherence, they jostle uncomfortably together, overlap, correspond, and contradict. They slide between positive and normative statements about what is and what ought to be criminal, between depictions of action and descriptions of responses to that action.

A SOCIAL CONSTRUCT

Thinking about crime as a social construct departs from naturalistic conceptions that employ unproblematic categories of normal and deviant behaviour. Instead, it illuminates the artificial way in which normality and abnormality is defined and defended. It moves beyond legal categories to examine their genesis, application, and effect. It asks why certain

---

[4] For other answers to this question, see Muncie, J., 'The Construction and Deconstruction of Crime' in Muncie and McLaughlin (eds), *The Problem of Crime* (2nd edn, London: Sage, 2001); Lacey, N., and Wells, C., *Reconstructing Criminal Law: Text and Materials* (3rd edn, London: Butterworths, 2003) ch. 1; Loveland, I. (ed.), *Frontiers of Criminality* (London: Sweet & Maxwell, 1995).

[5] Braithwaite, J., *Crime, Shame and Reintegration* (Cambridge: Cambridge University Press, 1989) 1.

activities are deemed criminal and not others and why at some times and not others; who creates the rules and in whose interests; and who enforces them and with what consequences. It focuses on the processes by which certain types of behaviour, and certain categories of person, are identified as criminal. Particularly important is the recognition that action is context specific. For example, rowdy behaviour by local youths is thought about quite differently from the 'high spirits' of undergraduate celebrations even where, objectively, the behaviour in each case is all but identical. The fact that the first attracts the less than friendly attention of the police, whereas the latter merits only the quiet intervention of the university authorities is a paradigm example of social construction.

Criminal justice courses often begin with the proposition that crime is a social construct, not least to encourage students to consider how meaning is attached to social action. Hulsman puts it more strongly, 'Crime is not the *object* but the *product* of criminal policy. Criminalization is one of the many ways to construct social reality.'[6] To say crime is a social construct contests the presentation of crime as a positive or natural phenomenon that can be observed and recorded, and its causes identified. Seeing crime instead as culturally relative, social constructionist approaches observe the ways in which definitions of crime vary by time and place, according to circumstance, and to the personal characteristics of the perpetrator, as well as the victim. What is theft in one society is legitimate appropriation in another; what is assisted suicide in one is euthanasia in another; what is child murder in one is lawful abortion in another, and so on.

Historically, the scope of crime has altered enormously. Sexual offending is a good example of a sphere in which changing mores have radically altered the scope of what is deemed criminal and what legitimate personal expression.[7] The persistence in Britain of the marital rape exemption permitted non-consensual sexual intercourse between spouses to go unpunished until its belated abolition in 1991.[8] Child sexual abuse was scarcely recognized until after the Second World War and then rapidly came to be regarded as one of the most heinous forms of wrongdoing.

---

[6] Hulsman, L., 'Critical Criminology and the Concept of Crime' (1986) 10 *Contemporary Crises* 63–80 at 71 quoted Muncie, J. (ed), *Criminological Perspectives: A Reader* (London: Sage, 1996) 300–1.

[7] Zedner, L., 'Regulating Sexual Offences Within the Home' in Loveland (ed), *Frontiers of Criminality* (London: Sweet & Maxwell, 1995). Likewise, domestic violence: see, for example, Hoyle, C., *Negotiating Domestic Violence* (Oxford: Clarendon Press, 1998).

[8] R v R [1991] 4 All ER 481, HL.

Homosexuality was outlawed until 1967 and only then permitted between consenting adults in private.[9] As in these examples, an activity that was yesterday barely a matter of notice may, overnight, become the subject of media attention and therefore public concern.[10]

Mugging, joy-riding, and mobile phone theft are all examples of crimes thrown into the public spotlight by media attention. Public opinion, often fanned by the headlines of the news media, can exert significant leverage on what, at any given time, is taken to be a serious crime problem. The term 'moral panic', a sociological term of art, has entered popular vocabulary to capture the impact which news-inspired hysteria may have on popular reactions to offending behaviour and on the consequences of this reaction for criminal justice policy and enforcement practice.[11] Of course, not all examples of criminalization brought about by social pressure are irrational or undesirable. The ending of the immunity for rape within marriage was brought about partly by lobby organizations pressing the Crown Prosecution Service to bring the criminal law in line with modern morality. More controversially, activities once outside the criminal law like organizing raves, possessing combat knives, and stalking have been added to the statute book under the pressure of public opinion and media campaign.[12]

Politicians, too, may be subject to media and other forms of popular pressure to criminalize behaviour or increase the gravity of responses to it.[13] Populist punitivism, a term coined by Bottoms, captures the willingness of politicians to be led by popular sentiment; whether in the hope of strengthening the moral consensus or of satisfying a particular electoral constituency.[14] But despite political claims to be acting in response to popular demand, it is debatable whether politicians are led by or lead

---

[9] Sexual Offences Act 1967 s.1.

[10] Sparks, R., *Television and the Drama of Crime: Moral Tales and the Place of Crime in Public Life* (Buckingham: Open University Press, 1992).

[11] Cohen, S., *Folk Devils and Moral Panics* (2nd edn, Oxford: Martin Robertson, 1980); Hall, S. *et al.*, *Policing the Crisis: Mugging, the State, and Law and Order* (London: Macmillan, 1978).

[12] Under the Criminal Justice and Public Order Act 1994, the Knives Act 1997, and the Protection from Harassment Act 1997 respectively.

[13] A classic example of a hasty and ill-thought-out political response to a minor panic is the Dangerous Dogs Act 1991, whose provisions for the mandatory destruction of dangerous dogs were so harsh they had later to be moderated by the Dangerous Dogs (Amendment) Act 1997.

[14] Bottoms, A. E., 'The Philosophy and Politics of Punishment and Sentencing' in Clarkson and Morgan (eds), *The Politics of Sentencing Reform* (Oxford: Clarendon Press, 1995) 39–40.

public opinion. Having direct control of the legislative process, politicians can determine current live issues and government's responses to them. In defining the parameters of crime and determining the prevailing crime problem, they in turn influence journalists, the public, and criminal justice officials so that the resultant crime figures become as much a function of political will as any actual change in crime trends. An apparent crime wave may, on later reflection, appear more a product of political construction than of any palpable change in offending behaviour. For example, espousal of policies of 'zero tolerance' and growing political resentment of so-called anti-social behaviour has resulted in broad-reaching changes to the law.[15] It is also the case that criminal statutes introduced to deal with one problem may be invoked against other unanticipated forms of action.[16] In other cases, legislation defining a new area of criminality may not in practice appreciably extend the existing scope of the criminal law.[17] Where the problem could have been dealt with within the scope of the existing law, legislation may be little more than an acknowledgement of public concern or an opportunistic reaction by politicians.

Existing crimes can also be subject to the process of social construction. Criminal justice agencies coming under pressure to do something about an activity, be it squeegee merchants, mobile phone theft, or underage sex, indirectly contribute to the criminalization process by bringing ever more cases before the courts. The police may also initiate changes by targeting particular activities because they regard them as a local menace (for example, drug abuse and dealing) or for internal reasons of audit (policing traffic offences, for example, is a sure way of meeting performance targets). Here the boundaries of what is constituted as crime may shift without any change in the law.

It would be simplistic to suggest that the criminal law is directly determined by public opinion or vice versa. If law neither directly follows nor straightforwardly determines public opinion but rather shapes and is

---

[15] Under the Crime and Disorder Act 1998 and the Anti-Social Behaviour Act 2003 which together considerably extend police powers to tackle instances of minor nuisance and anti-social behaviour.

[16] The widespread powers introduced by the Terrorism Act 2000 and, more particularly, the Anti-Terrorism, Crime and Security Act 2001 are good examples. Extensive provisions, particularly in the latter act, targeted against terrorists in fact have far wider applicability and permit disproportionate response and license unwarranted intrusions upon human rights: Fenwick, H., 'The Anti-Terrorism, Crime and Security Act 2001: A Proportionate Response to 11 September?' (2002) 65 *Modern Law Review* 724–62.

[17] As would appear to be the case in respect of legislation on stalking. See Wells, C., 'Stalking: The Criminal Response' (1997) *Criminal Law Review* 463–70 at 470.

shaped by it, then the law in the books can tell no more than part of the story. An activity that is designated criminal by statute may effectively be rendered void if it is out of line with popular sentiment. An example here might be the widespread use and acceptance of drugs like cannabis in some inner city areas. The resulting policy of virtual non-enforcement by the police left the law unmodified but its practical bite negligible. Given time, the pressure of public opinion, and the need to preserve the dignity of the law by excising laws that are unworkable, may lead to reform.[18] In turn the passing of laws may have an educative effect on public opinion. The formal designation of an activity as criminal does not, overnight, prompt people to accept as criminal that which was formerly permitted, nor will it necessarily persuade them to see as harmless or acceptable that which was once outlawed. In time, however, the declaratory impact of court cases may prompt a realignment in public attitudes. Public perceptions, media pressures, the attitudes and practices of criminal justice professionals intermingle in complex, sometimes conflicting ways to determine what, at any given time, has operative effect, as opposed to the mere legal label of crime.

Yet conceiving of crime as socially constructed also suffers from certain limitations. To suggest that crime is a social construct may sound less than persuasive to the victim sporting a black eye or the householder returning to find their house trashed and their possessions gone. Criminological theories that characterized crime as a form of labelling[19] were rightly criticized for failing to take crime and the pain it inflicts seriously. Beyond the immediate issue of failing to acknowledge suffering, Left and Right Realists regard social construction as problematic for strikingly different reasons. For the Right it is problematic because it tends to downplay the sources of social and moral breakdown that foster crime and to deny the culpable wrongdoing of its perpetrators.[20] It also denies the possibility of responding to crime by altering the environment, conditioning behaviour, and inculcating conscience in such a way as to elicit 'correct' moral choices and conformity to rules.[21] For the Left it is problematic because it sidelines the social and economic inequalities that

---

[18] Cannabis has now been reclassified from Class B to Class C, through this downgrading has sparked a moral panic about the drug's capacity to induce psychosis.

[19] Becker, H., *Outsiders: Studies in the Sociology of Deviance* (New York: The Free Press, 1963); Erikson, K., *Wayward Puritans: A Study in the Sociology of Deviance* (New York: Wiley, 1966).

[20] For example, Wilson, J. Q., *Thinking about Crime* (New York: Vintage, 1985).

[21] Wilson, J. Q., and Herrnstein, R., *Crime and Human Nature: The Definitive Study of the Causes of Crime* (New York: Simon & Schuster, 1985).

underlie offending; ignores the costs of crime for offenders as well as victims; and overplays the role of the police in its combat.[22]

A further trenchant criticism of social construction or labelling theories is that, in focusing on the opinions and activities of those who label, they fail to explore the larger political issues at stake. Behind the construct lie political interests and power relations underlying the authority to criminalize. Recognizing the ideological nature of crime emphasizes the selective nature of criminal law creation and enforcement by revealing that purportedly objective categories are often politically loaded. Put more pointedly, criminalization is the power to translate private interests into public policy.[23]

Marxist criminology characterizes criminalization as an instrument of class oppression in capitalist societies.[24] According to Marx, criminalization is a means by which the ruling classes retain power by suppressing indiscipline and challenges to order by the proletariat. It permits the repression, incapacitation, or exclusion of the surplus, or marginal population who most threaten the capitalist order. It is not necessary to be a Marxist in order to accept that crime is a vehicle of power. Power is wielded by those who have it in order to designate certain activities by those who do not as criminal. The result is that it is by no means the most serious of offences that dominate popular culture, political life, and the criminal justice process. As Box observed, the key to 'understanding the most serious crimes can be located in power, not weakness, in privilege, not disadvantage, in wealth, not poverty'.[25] A paradigm example is theft. Ostensibly a means of protecting universal property interests against illegitimate incursion, the law of theft has, historically, been deployed to protect particular types of property against particular types of depredation, typically by the urban poor. Until recently, this protection was not extended to the loss of property caused by corporate crime, city fraud, or tax evasion.[26] It is not by chance that when we hear the word thief we

---

[22] Young, J., 'Ten Points of Realism' in Young and Matthews (eds), *Rethinking Criminology: The Realist Debate* (London: Sage, 1992).

[23] Muncie, J., 'The Construction and Deconstruction of Crime' in Muncie and McLaughlin (eds), *The Problem of Crime* (2nd edn, London: Sage, 2001) 19.

[24] Spitzer, S., 'The Rationalizations of Crime Control in Capitalist Societies' in Cohen and Scull (eds), *Social Control and the State: Historical and Comparative Essays* (Oxford: Basil Blackwell, 1983).

[25] Box, S., *Power, Crime and Mystification* (London: Tavistock, 1983).

[26] Though it is beginning to attract academic attention: Wells, C., *Corporations and Criminal Responsibility* (2nd edn, Oxford: Oxford University Press, 2001); Gobert, J., 'Corporate Criminality: New Crime for the Times' (1994) *Criminal Law Review* 722–34.

think of the mobile phone snatcher or pickpocket and not the boardroom executive.

Power relations also determine the very bases of criminal liability. The construction of crime around concepts of individual responsibility, culpability, capacity, and individual action obscure the fact that corporate bodies, commercial organizations, and the state have the capacity for wrongdoing. It might even be said that this individualist construction of crime deliberately resists the labelling of state activities as criminal. Hence wrongs of a scale far beyond the capabilities of even the most heinous individual, such as state corruption, torture, illegal expulsion, mass killing, and genocide, have been denied and, effectively, decriminalized.[27] The establishment of the Truth and Reconciliation Commission in South Africa, of international tribunals for the prosecution of genocide, and of the International Criminal Court may be possible indicators of change, though it is too early to say how the last of these will fare. Below the level of the state, corporate crimes such as financial misconduct, environmental damage, and manslaughter also tend to resist criminalization. Lest it be thought that the historic construction of criminal responsibility around the individual subject always inhibits the criminalization of corporate action, note that this has not similarly protected other less powerful corporate bodies. The members of protest groups and trade unions find little parallel protection in their corporate membership. To the extent that their activities are deemed to endanger the state or other powerful interests, their activities are criminalized as inimical to public order or the social good.

The advantage of interpreting criminalization as the exercise of power is that it focuses on its ideological and instrumental underpinnings; invites historical analysis of its development and application; and provides the basis for critique. Its most striking weakness is that, with the exception perhaps of feminist criminology, it tends to focus on the exercise of power by those who determine what is labelled crime. It ignores the capacity of those so labelled to resist and to develop 'techniques of neutralization' which downplay or deny wrongdoing using 'vocabularies of motive'.[28] Although those labelled as criminal tend to be the least powerful in society, their offending behaviour nonetheless constitutes an exercise of power itself, often over those less powerful still. It is for this

---

[27] Cohen, S., *States of Denial: Knowing about Atrocities and Suffering* (Cambridge: Polity Press, 2001).

[28] Downes, D., and Rock, P., *Understanding Deviance* (3rd edn, Oxford: Oxford University Press, 1998) 189.

reason that Henry and Milovanovic state that 'crimes are nothing less than moments in the expression of power' and that crime 'is the power to deny others'.[29] In the case of domestic violence or child abuse, for example, the most significant power relation is arguably not between state and offender but between assailant and assailed. Similarly, in respect of property crimes, the great mass of victims are not the power elites but fellow members of the very populations from whom offenders are themselves drawn. To describe the categories of theft or burglary as tools of class oppression misses the important fact that it is the offender's equally impoverished neighbours who typically suffer most as his prey. The interest being protected here is that not of the propertied powerful but of precisely those who can least afford to lose what little they have. Without careful regard to the practice of crime and the facts of victimization, characterizing crime as an exercise in power relations risks becoming an ideological exercise that obscures more than it reveals.

Arguably a more persuasive social construction of crime is to see it as an instrument of governance. Simon has developed the idea of 'governing through crime' to capture the way in which crime is used to shape conduct: 'We govern through crime to the extent to which crime and punishment become the occasions and the institutional contexts in which we undertake to guide the conduct of others (and ourselves).'[30] According to Simon, crime is also used to frame larger social problems and to supply the narratives and metaphors for people to seek to make claims upon those who govern. Disparate economic and social problems of unemployment, poverty, failing education, poor housing, and even environmental harm are recast as crime problems. The redirection of central state resources to crime prevention initiatives leads local authorities to redefine a host of local social and economic problems as crime problems simply in order to obtain funds.[31] And crime, or fear of crime, is the driving force behind a host of present-day social developments: the gated housing community, the sports utility vehicle (SUV), and the mobile phone, all of which are sold, at least in part, as a means to personal security and which, as such, exemplify 'how governing through crime is

---

[29] Henry, S., and Milovanovic, D., *Constitutive Criminology: Beyond Postmodernism* (London: Sage, 1996) 104.

[30] Simon, J., 'Governing Through Crime' in Friedman and Fisher (eds), *The Crime Conundrum: Essays on Criminal Justice* (Boulder, Colo.: Westview Press, 1997) 174.

[31] Crawford, A., *The Local Governance of Crime: Appeals to Community and Partnership* (Oxford: Clarendon Press, 1997).

embedded in our self governing'.[32] Understood this way, crime is no mere narrow subject of the formal institutions of criminal justice but holds a 'pivotal place in the production of order and security'.[33]

WRONGDOING

In the light of all we have said so far, it should be evident that the classic definition of crime as wrongdoing is, to say the least, problematic. In what follows we will examine the several bases for describing crime as wrongdoing before going on to explore some of the more serious difficulties inherent in the claim that crime is wrongful behaviour.

To say that crime is wrongdoing has a strong intuitive appeal. It is precisely this understanding of crime that is captured in the colloquial contention that 'his behaviour was downright criminal'. The statement is not primarily or even necessarily a reference to the legal status of the behaviour in question, but rather a moral claim about its wrongfulness. The behaviour, action, or inaction so described is said to offend our moral feelings. The claim to offence runs as follows: crime offends us because it transgresses our common expectation as to how those around us should conduct themselves. The offence to our moral feelings is not trivial: we cannot dismiss it as a mere aberration or fault worthy of note but not response. It offends us so gravely as to demand, at the very least, public notice, apportionment of blame, or rebuke, at worst, temporary banishment from civil society. Nor is the offence to individual moral feelings. There is an implied collective moral reaction that extends to a sufficient proportion of society for the wrong to be deemed a public one. It is this aspect that allows crime to be declared an offence against the public interest even where the action in question occurs behind closed doors, as is the case in domestic violence or much child abuse.

Conceiving of crime as wrongdoing underpins the criminalization of behaviour that entails no harm to others, for example the offences that surround prostitution. Purely moral wrongs are criminalized not because they entail physical harm or risk to safety but because they are said to contravene common standards of morality. Where there is no harm element, limitations upon personal freedom entailed by criminalization

---

[32] Simon, J., *Governing Through Crime: Criminal Law and the Reshaping of American Government, 1965–2000* (New York: Oxford University Press, forthcoming) ms.17.

[33] Loader, I., and Sparks, R., 'Contemporary Landscapes of Crime, Order, and Control: Governance, Risk, and Globalization' in Maguire *et al.* (eds), *The Oxford Handbook of Criminology* (3rd edn, Oxford: Oxford University Press, 2002) 84.

and the pains of punishment are social costs that have to be balanced against the supposed offence to morals.

If it were possible to identify a standard or common moral code, then the definition of crime might be expanded to encompass all violations of that code rather than those that happened to have attracted the attention of the legislators. An obvious advantage of this definition is that it would furnish a basis both for recognizing wrongs irrespective of their legal status and for external critique of the scope of existing laws. It might furnish the basis of an independent standard for identifying what it 'truly' criminal. It would also draw attention to the fact that the criminal law is a product of historical accident, changing social mores, and political exigencies. It would highlight the fact that many wrongs are committed against marginalized or disadvantaged groups whose interests are not adequately protected by law, for example children, members of racial or religious minorities, or other minority interest groups. Finally, it would recognize wrongs by the powerful that have hitherto tended to escape criminal sanction precisely because the perpetrators were well placed to evade criminalization. Examples here include dangerous working practices, environmental pollution, and fiscal impropriety.

The crucial question is whether it is in fact possible to agree upon an absolute standard that exists independently of law and against which aberrations can be measured. Such agreement presumes a common moral code. Around a core of activities there is a high level of concord. Murder, rape, and robbery attract common repugnance and few would have difficulty in accepting their designation as criminal. This core is replicated in the criminal law. Beyond it, however, concord is far less clear. Public opinion surveys reveal wide disagreement about what ought and what ought not to be recognized as criminal.[34] Even where there is rough accord about the appropriateness of attaching the label crime to a given activity, there is often disagreement about the seriousness of the offence. Insider dealing and driving with excess alcohol are useful examples of disparate activities that each attract widely different moral responses and levels of condemnation. The degree of seriousness with which each is regarded varies by age, social class, and sex. Nor does the degree of public opprobrium that attaches to different behaviour necessarily reflect the gravity of the harm done. Corporate wrongdoing, for example, may entail

---

[34] Useful data can be found in the national *British Crime Survey*, which has been carried out at regular intervals by the Home Office since 1982 and annually since 2001.

serious damage to financial and other interests but more rarely attracts such opprobrium or the attention of the criminal justice system.[35]

The question of whether it is possible to identify a common moral code and whether such a code would provide a safe or desirable basis for labelling activity criminal was famously the subject of debate between Patrick Devlin and H. L. A. Hart in the 1960s. Lord Devlin contended that there is a common morality that must be protected in order to ensure the cohesion of society.[36] Hart doubted the degree of 'moral solidarity' assumed by Devlin and posited instead a 'number of mutually tolerant moralities'.[37] To use 'legal punishment to freeze into immobility the morality dominant at a particular time' seemed to Hart both morally conservative and potentially harmful.[38] His warning rings even more loudly today: in a multi-cultural, multi-ethnic, multi-faith society, the imposition of any single moral code risks overriding the interests of the minority. And it licenses an unhappy measure of intolerance towards non-conformist or unorthodox behaviours and lifestyles that do not satisfy the expectations of the moral majority.

A second idea captured by crime as wrongdoing is that behaviour so described is the product of a wrongful moral choice by the offender. The making of wrongful moral choices presumes the capacity to distinguish between right and wrong. It is for this reason that we tend to exculpate those whose capacity is diminished and that we are loathe to describe the wrongful behaviour of infants or the insane as criminal. Similarly, where situational constraints seriously limit a person's capacity for choice, we may be reluctant to impose liability. Which situational constraints so limit capacity is a matter for fierce debate however. Should poverty count? Or hunger?

Where an individual can be held responsible for their behaviour, it is often argued that as a matter of respect for their capacity as a free-willed moral agent they should be held to account for their actions.[39] The precise stipulation of capacity and of the particular mental elements required before criminal responsibility can be ascribed by the criminal law is something to which we will return below. The notion of wrongfulness to which we refer here is less precisely drawn than its legal analogue, *mens*

---

[35] Wells, C., *Corporations and Criminal Responsibility* (2nd edn, Oxford: Oxford University Press, 2001).

[36] Devlin, P., *The Enforcement of Morals* (Oxford: Oxford University Press, 1965).

[37] Hart, H. L. A., *Law, Liberty and Morality* (Oxford: Oxford University Press, 1963) 62–3.

[38] Ibid. 72.

[39] Cane, P., *Responsibility in law and morality* (Oxford: Hart Publishing, 2002).

rea, but requires no less a factual statement about the capacity of the offender and a moral statement about the choice made. As we suggested above, that moral statement must imply a degree of culpability so grave that no designation less than crime will suffice to capture the degree of trespass entailed. The moral wrong done carries with it an implied blameworthiness that requires some form of holding to account.

Inherent in the designation of crime as wrongdoing is the claim that the perpetrator, formally proven, bears the entire burden of culpability. The advantage of this claim is that it tallies with the requirement in criminal law that the offender be held guilty of his or her offence. With the exception of certain designated partial excuses such as diminished responsibility or provocation, there is little possibility of saying that the offender was merely 'partly wrong', still less 'a little bit wrong'.[40] Where the interests at stake are clear, and the violation all in one direction, this is not problematic. The thief who seizes your mobile phone is under no illusion as to its rightful ownership and it is clear that he is infringing your property rights when he takes it without authority. The problem arises where, as is the case in respect of very many crimes, the distribution of wrongs is less clear-cut. Many instances of interpersonal violence, for example, arise in situations where the attribution of blame is hazy.

Where crimes take the form of disputes over ownership of property; a disagreement about an alleged affront to personal space or honour; or contests between competing world-views then the designation of wrongdoing is less appropriate still. Conceiving of crimes as disputes rather than wrongdoing is controversial and cannot apply in every case but it does recognize that moral wrongs cannot necessarily be neatly apportioned to one party alone. It recognizes also that the parties have a property interest in the dispute between them that is, in a sense, stolen when the blame-apportioning apparatus of the criminal justice system intervenes.[41] And it provides the occasion for discussion about the moral status of the wrong supposedly done: a discussion that tends ordinarily to be suppressed in a system devoted to apportioning, but not scrutinizing, blameworthiness.

A further problem is that many offences under criminal law are not moral wrongs but mere prohibitions, the product of legislative proscription for social or policy reasons.[42] Many road traffic offences; violations of

---

[40] Though this may be taken into account in mitigation at the sentencing stage.
[41] Christie, N., 'Conflicts as Property' (1977) 17 *British Journal of Criminology* 1–15.
[42] Lacey, N., 'Contingency and Criminalisation' in Loveland (ed.), *Frontiers of Criminality* (London: Sweet & Maxwell, 1995) 4.

general public interests such as offences against state security or the administration of justice; and violations of the environment, health and safety, and public order do not offend us morally. In some cases it is a moot point why they do not: for example, road traffic or health and safety offences may entail grave harms but rarely attract the same opprobrium as 'real' crimes. They are proscribed in order to avert danger and to ensure effective administration and the smooth and fair running of modern society. Many are offences of strict liability requiring no mental element to be proven. They do not fit the conception of crime as the deliberate taking of wrong moral choices. Nor are the perpetrators of such offences invariably thought of as wrongdoers in the sense described above. To the extent, therefore, that it seems inappropriate to describe inadvertent parking on a double yellow line, for example, as wrongdoing there is a lack of fit between this designation and the current scope of the criminal law. It is debatable whether this should give rise to criticism of the conception of crime as wrongdoing or of the criminal law itself. If wrongdoing does not suffice to capture all that is encompassed by the criminal law, it raises the question whether activities that are not morally wrong should be designated criminal in law. If they are not wrongdoing, should their perpetrators be blamed and receive punishment as the criminal law requires? Or might they better be reconceived as regulatory offences, worthy of civil penalty but not punishment?[43]

A third idea captured by the designation of crime as wrongdoing relates not to the action, or inaction, but to the perpetrator. It might appear self-evident to observe that for every wrongdoing there must be a wrongdoer. It is less self-evident that their wrongdoing should become that person's 'master status'; still less that concern about criminals should outstrip concern about crime. And yet it is not uncommon for the news media, and even Home Office mandarins, to talk about sex offenders rather than sexual offences, about joy-riders rather than car theft, or about bogus asylum seekers rather than offences against immigration laws. Seen one way, talk about criminals is an unobjectionable reference to those who commit crime. Seen another way, it is worrisome and potentially dangerous. It carries with it the implied presumption that those who offend once can safely be labelled as offenders. And it tends to reconfigure crime as wrongdoing from single acts by individual offenders

---

[43] It was reasoning along these lines that led Germany to redesignate many lesser crimes as regulatory offences, or *Ordnungswidrigkeiten*, subject only to administrative fines.

to the activities of entire suspect populations.[44] The identification of suspect populations through the use of statistical profiles allows state officials to target, monitor, and in some cases stop, search, and even arrest potential wrongdoers on the basis of dubious predictions of their potential danger.[45]

HARM DOING

Harm doing has a central place in our conception of crime and, like wrongdoing, has an intuitive appeal as a basis for defining crime. Yet harm is more slippery and less readily defined than may at first appear.[46] To describe it as an incursion upon another's interests takes us some way toward a definition but leaves open key questions such as which interests and in what degree? Unwarranted infringement of bodily autonomy is clearly a form of harm doing but even here there is plenty of scope for controversy. What if the infringement, though harmful, is invited? If we are willing to permit tattooing, and even branding where the victim consents, what grounds do we have to label sadomasochist acts as crimes? What if the harm is such as to be expected in the context of sporting activity or rough play? Is it plausible to say that such harms are consistent with the public good or simply part of the rough and tumble of everyday life? And what should happen if the harm is compounded by the action or inaction of the victim?

In the case of other types of harms, the issues are more complex still. Infringement of property interests is the basis of much crime but constitutes harm only where the initial interests are legitimate. Profound disagreement exists as to the legitimacy of property interests in different circumstances and according to different political ideologies. The clear-cut case of theft of one person's property by another appears altogether less clear-cut where the object is a loaf of bread, the owner a supermarket

---

[44] Labelling theory reveals all too starkly the damage done by designating people as offenders: Becker, H., *Outsiders: Studies in the Sociology of Deviance* (New York: The Free Press, 1963); Cicourel, S., *The Social Organisation of Juvenile Justice* (New York: Wiley, 1968).

[45] Feeley, M., and Simon, J., 'Actuarial Justice: The Emerging New Criminal Law' in Nelken (ed), *The Futures of Criminology* (London: Sage, 1994) 177; Pratt, J., 'Dangerousness and Modern Society' in Brown and Pratt (eds), *Dangerous Offenders: Punishment and Social Order* (London: Routledge, 2000).

[46] There is a sizeable literature on theories of harm, most importantly Joel Feinberg's extensive writing on the subject including: Feinberg, J., *Harm to Others* (New York: Oxford University Press, 1984); Feinberg, J., *Harm to Self* (New York: Oxford University Press, 1986).

chain, and the thief a starving tramp. Conflict of interests are also common in the case of social order, where preventing harm to one class's enjoyment of order may entail substantial curtailment of another's freedom of expression or social life. My right to peace and quiet has to be balanced against your right to party, and your right to foxhunt against my peaceful enjoyment of the countryside. Whether infringements of other interests, such as reputation or sensibility, constitute harms of sufficient gravity to deserve the protection of the criminal law is more controversial still.

Problematic as it clearly is to talk of crime as harm doing, harm is nonetheless central to our thinking about crime. When we think of crime it is serious cases like murder, rape, assaults, robbery, theft, and riot that spring to mind. In these the harm—be it violation of individual autonomy, bodily integrity, sexual freedom, property, or social order—is clear-cut. So dominant is the presumption that crime entails serious harm that we tend not to concern ourselves as much as we might about the very many cases where the harm is less clear-cut.

Whereas wrongdoing requires culpability on the part of the offender, conceiving crime as harm doing does not. It has no difficulty in recognizing as crime offences of strict liability or those involving serious harms but partial intention such as causing death by dangerous driving, or gross negligence manslaughter. It has also been argued that emphasizing harm stands as an important corrective to theories of crime as social construction, crime as governance, or the exercise of power that tend to downplay the impact of crime or assert that it is an externally manufactured category or label. Focus on harm provides the stimulus to victim surveys enquiring into the immediate and longer-term impact of victimization. These surveys reveal that crime often imposes grave costs upon its victims, that the working classes are prime victims of crime, and that they generally want it to be dealt with. Findings such as these led Left Realist criminologists like Jock Young and John Lea to insist that we 'take crime seriously'.[47]

One important aspect of the pressure to take crime seriously is that it draws attention to the aggregate effects of crime. Rather than focusing on individual offenders or individual incidents, focusing on harm allows for a clearer assessment of the larger impact of crime upon its victims' lives. It highlights fear of crime and its attendant costs; the impact of crime

---

[47] Lea, J., and Young, J., *What is to be Done About Law and Order?* (Harmondsworth: Penguin, 1984).

upon lifestyle and freedom of movement; and the possibility of long-term psychological and other harms. Nowhere is this truer than in the case of repeat or multiple victimization where the impact is likely to be compounded with each occurrence. At worst it may become impossible to distinguish the harm done by each crime from the generally impoverished quality of life suffered by the victim as a result.[48] Examples here are domestic violence and racial harassment whose victims suffer the aggregate effects of multiple offences against them.[49] The enduring social costs of living on estates with high crime rates in deprived inner city areas also invite reassessment of the notion of a crime as a discrete incident.

Thinking about crime as harm doing also draws attention to the wider impact of crime beyond its immediate and readily identifiable victims. Secondary victims of crime may be members of the same household, relatives, or friends emotionally burdened by the harm suffered by a friend or family member or who bear financial loss as a result. In the case of financial crimes, the extended burden of large-scale fraud and other corporate crimes may fall upon employees, pensioners, tenants, consumers, and, ultimately, taxpayers.[50] Corporations may themselves be the victims.[51] Much crime is committed against government, local authorities, non-governmental agencies, commercial companies, charitable and other foundations. The harms inflicted by crime give rise to larger social and economic costs: policing, crime prevention, private security, and insurance are all industries spawned by crime. Economists conceive the financial burden of these industries as 'externalities' or costs spilling over from the direct incidence of criminal harms (though this calculative approach attenuates the concept of crime as especially disruptive breaches of moral order).

Although thinking about crime as harm doing has a number of conceptual advantages, we have said enough to show that harm is a problematic and contested category. Just who gets to determine what constitutes

[48] Genn, H., 'Multiple Victimization' in Maguire and Pointing (eds), *Victims of Crime: A New Deal?* (Milton Keynes: Open University Press, 1988); Pease, K., 'Repeat Victimization' in McLaughlin and Muncie (eds), *The Sage Dictionary of Criminology* (London: Sage, 2001).

[49] Bowling, B., *Violent Racism: Victimization, Policing, and Social Control* (Oxford: Clarendon Press, 1998) ch. 5; Saraga, E., 'Dangerous Places: the family as a site of crime' in Muncie and McLaughlin (eds), *The Problem of Crime* (London: Sage, 2001).

[50] Young, R., 'Integrating a Multi-Victim Perspective into Criminal Justice Through Restorative Justice Conferences' in Crawford and Goodey (eds), *Integrating a Victim Perspective within Criminal Justice* (Aldershot: Ashgate Dartmouth, 2000) 230.

[51] Young, R., 'Testing the Limits of Restorative Justice: The Case of Corporate Victims' in Young (ed), *New Visions of Crime Victims* (Oxford: Hart Publishing, 2002).

harm, to whom, and in what circumstances is a political and practical minefield. This has not prevented harm from standing at the core of a normative framework upon which both the criteria for criminalization and a critique of existing laws have been based. The 'harm principle' enunciated by John Stuart Mill states, 'the only purpose for which power can rightfully be exercised over any member of a civilized community against his will, is to prevent harm to others'.[52] To provide the further and necessary justification for state punishment, two additional criteria are added: namely, that the harm be of sufficient gravity and that it be done to wider society. Read sympathetically, this principle provides an important framework for determining when state authority over the individual may be exercised. Read critically, its failure to elaborate an adequately specified concept of harm permits an untrammelled expansion of the scope of crime that is both conceptually vague and politically dangerous.

The dangers inherent in the harm principle have not prevented it from becoming one of the dominant bases for criminalization: for this reason alone we need to explore it further. Let us begin by examining the requirement that the harm be done to others. Obviously this requires both that there be harm and that it be done to someone other than the perpetrator. Where the activity or behaviour does not entail harm or where the harm inflicted falls upon the perpetrator alone, criminalization, according to this principle, should not occur. Unless it is possible to justify describing inchoate offences, conspiracy, and incitement as furnishing prospective or remote harms, they would also appear to require separate justification. Similarly, victimless offences like possession of prohibited drugs could be said to entail no harm other, again, than the remote prospect of harm ensuing. Likewise self-harm, even to the extent of suicide, would appear to fall outside the harm principle, except where paternalism permits protection of the vulnerable.[53] Paternalism is a heading under which substantial inroads into the harm principle are sometimes justified or, at least, defended. It is relatively uncontroversial to say that sexual intercourse with minors or the mentally ill should be criminalized on the grounds that they are not capable of consenting to violation of their sexual or bodily integrity. It is more controversial to argue that the state should intervene to criminalize drug abuse by adults. Since the

---

[52] Mill, J. S., *On Liberty* (Harmondsworth, Middlesex: Penguin, 1979) 68.
[53] Hart, H. L. A., *Law, Liberty and Morality* (Oxford: Oxford University Press, 1963) 30–4.

harm in this latter case is done to the perpetrator, it is only by the attenuated claim that harm arises in the burden consequently thrown upon the medical and social services, upon those who care for drug addicts, or upon the addict's dependants, that it can be brought within the harm principle.

Secondly, we suggested that in order for harm to attract the designation crime and the consequence of punishment, rather than other state action, it must be of sufficient gravity. In theory the law does not concern itself with trifles.[54] In practice, in many cases of statutory crimes, the harm is so trifling as to risk contravening this principle. In the case of illegal parking, dropping of litter, or non-payment for a television licence we might more naturally describe the wrong as anti-social behaviour than harm doing. The question then arises, can conduct legitimately be criminalized where harm does not result? The affirmative answer supplied by Joel Feinberg resorts to the offence principle: namely that where conduct results in serious offence and criminal prohibition is a necessary and effective means of preventing that offence, then criminalization is justified.[55] This principle has been criticized on the grounds that it is too expansive and, particularly in a climate of diminishing tolerance, liable to result in the criminalization of minor incivilities.[56] Stringent legal measures in the form of Anti-Social Behaviour Orders and Curfew Orders employed against noisy neighbours and rowdy youths under the Criminal Justice and Disorder Act 1998 are prime examples of the potentially expansive application of the offence principle. The Anti-Social Behaviour Act 2003 pushes this trend further still by making it possible to impose on-the-spot fines on teenage 'yobs' and stop the payment of housing benefit to anti-social tenants. It reflects a growing willingness to deploy criminal sanctions in furtherance of official determination to be 'much tougher about forcing people not to behave anti-socially'.[57]

If the requirement that the harm be of sufficient gravity does not always apply, it is equally the case that not all grave harms attract the label crime. Many forms of harmful behaviour by individuals—such as standing by as a child drowns—are not designated as criminal (though would be in many continental European countries). Some of the most harmful

[54] A principle captured in the maxim *de minimis non curat lex*.

[55] Feinberg, J., *Offense to Others* (New York: Oxford University Press, 1985).

[56] Simester, A. P., and von Hirsch, A., 'Rethinking the Offense Principle' (2002) 8 *Legal Theory* 269–95.

[57] Foreword by the Home Secretary, Home Office, *Respect and Responsibility—Taking a Stand Against Anti-Social Behaviour* (London: HMSO, 2003) 4.

activities by industry, commercial companies, and the state, like failing to ensure safety at work, dumping of toxic waste, and the export of arms to undesirable regimes, have not historically been recognized as crime at all. For reasons we will explore further below, infliction of harm or injury or the creation of danger does not always eventuate in criminalization. In sum, much of the activity that daily engrosses the criminal justice system entails only minor or remote harms whilst large-scale injury and destruction escape its attention altogether. Part, but only part, of the problem is that the harm principle is permissive not prescriptive, and the gravest harms continue to go unpunished.

A third aspect of the harm principle is that the harm must be done to wider society. This requires that the perpetrator has violated a duty to the community irrespective of the fact that their offence was perpetrated against a single individual or took place entirely in private.[58] Crime can be said to offend against society on several grounds. It violates a duty owed by the offender to his or her fellow citizens not to trespass upon their interests unwarrantedly. It threatens their wider sense of security, by inviting the question 'will it be me next?' It punctures the sense that society offers a minimum level of moral order. And, as we have already observed, it often imposes burdens beyond the individual victim (upon family and friends, welfare and medical services, employers, insurers, and so on). It is for these reasons that crime is said to legitimate the response of the criminal justice state rather than private action. Economists, in their inimitably amoral style, call these harms 'demoralization costs', but this only invites enquiry whether society ought to recognize an inchoate state of insecurity or offence as a harm requiring coercive social control.

All these stipulations leave open the question why harm should be central to our conception of crime. One obvious answer is that we value the security of our persons and our property, and we wish to protect our interests against unwarranted detriment. Yet this simple statement presumes a common interest that rarely pertains. First, the fact of unwarrantedness is important since we are willing to suffer harms where we are persuaded that good reasons outweigh the suffering entailed. The surgeon who wounds our flesh and the taxman who deprives us of our income commit warranted harms upon us and we have little difficulty in distinguishing their actions from those of the knifeman or the thief. To the extent that harms are without warrant we share a strong interest in

---

[58] For a cogent argument why domestic violence, despite its 'private' qualities, must be the subject of criminal law see Duff, R. A., *Punishment, Communication and Community* (Oxford: Oxford University Press, 2001) 62.

deterring or preventing their occurrence. The difficulty here lies in agree-ing which harms are unwarranted and which are not. As in so many aspects of crime, it is those with the power to further their interests who determine what constitutes an unwarranted harm.

Secondly, it is said that the harms entailed by crime commonly amount to the taking of an unfair advantage. The harm-doer gives vent to feelings of violence or avarice that we suppress in ourselves. They enjoy this unfair advantage not only over their victim but over all who have success-fully suppressed their baser urges. The problem is that the notion of crime as unfair advantage does not fit in very many cases. For most of us, most of the time, it does not make sense to say that the murderer has taken an unfair advantage. We fail to kill not because we repress our desires but because we consider it morally wrong to do so irrespective of the designation of murder as a crime.

Finally, identifying unwarranted and serious harms as crimes is said to serve the function of fair labelling: namely that conduct should be labelled appropriately and according to its gravity. Fair labelling is important: it ensures that the label attached is appropriate to the offence and that the consequences that follow are likewise fitting. It could be argued, however, that the very label crime itself strains the principle of fair labelling since this single word encompasses a vast range of harms from illegal parking to murder. Again we might wonder whether, as in Germany, lesser harms would be better excluded from the category of crime in order that the resonance associated with that label be applied to grave harms alone.

LEGAL CLASSIFICATION

Thinking about crime as a legal category poses problems for students of criminal justice. It tends to downplay the contingency of crime and, by imposing fixed definitions, to deny its open and contested nature. Under-standing the central components of the legal classification of crime is indispensable but it is also fraught with difficulties.

First, central to the legal classification of crime is its public quality. A wrong that arises primarily in respect of the rights and duties owed only to individuals is the subject of civil law, whether as a tort, a breach of contract or trust and property rights. A crime is differentiable by the fact that the wrong is deemed to offend against duties owed to society. Just to complicate matters, the same conduct (or inaction) may be both a civil and a criminal wrong; in which case proceedings may generally be taken in both civil and criminal court simultaneously. For example, an assault is potentially both a tort and a crime, and a deception may entail a tort, a breach of contract or trust or be treated as a crime. Given this overlap it is important to identify the differences that determine whether civil or criminal liability, or both, arise. The liability of the civil wrongdoer is based principally upon the loss he or she has occasioned, whereas the criminal wrong resides, in principle at least, in the voluntary action of the perpetrator, their culpability, and the harm caused. And whereas in civil law proceedings are generally brought by the injured party in order to secure compensation or restitution, it is generally the state that prosecutes and punishes crime. A serious problem with the legal classification of crime as public wrong is that it is uninformative: a crime is that which is legally designated as criminal. But the classification does not tell us how, why, or to what end that legal designation has arisen. It cannot explain why some forms of deviance attract the response of the law and not others. It does not explain what determines whether that response is criminal, or civil, or both.

A second facet of the legal classification of crime is that every crime must be so designated by statute or case law and its component parts clearly specified. Every crime consists of a conduct element and, unless it is a crime of strict liability, an accompanying mental element.[59] The conduct element specifies the act or conduct, omission, consequence, or state of affairs that is the substance of the offence. The mental element specifies the state of mind that the prosecution must prove the defendant had at the time of committing the offence. Both must be set down in law to define an offence and both must be proven in order to secure a conviction. For lawyers, this definition has some important attractions. It honours the principle that there be no crime without law and that liability arises only in respect of actions or omissions already proscribed by law as criminal. This principle allows people to go about their daily business free from fear of arbitrary punishment. It gives fair warning to those who choose to offend against the law that they may expect punishment to ensue. It respects the presumption of innocence by making it improper to speak of someone as a criminal until all aspects of liability for a crime have been proven in a court of law. If it is right to refer to suspects, not offenders, in the pre-trial process, then it must be right also to talk only of alleged crimes and alleged victims until the case has been proven in court.

As a substantive definition of crime, however, legal classification is

[59] The two elements are known in criminal law by the Latin tags *actus reus* and *mens rea*.

problematic. Although it specifies the structural conditions (principally the mental and conduct elements) that must be met before a court of law will convict, it provides little purchase on the social phenomenon that is crime. To say both that criminal law responds to crime and that crime is defined by the criminal law creates an unfortunate circularity. Taken at face value, it suggests that without criminal law there can be no crime or even that the criminal law is, in some bizarre sense, the formal cause of crime.

A third aspect is that legal ideology makes certain claims as to the objectivity and political neutrality of legal doctrine and the autonomy of legal reasoning by which judgment is reached. Critical scrutiny of the criminal law allows the student of criminal justice to understand that doctrinal framework and the larger values and political factors that underlie it. For example, attention to the centrality of the mental element in the general part of the criminal law attests to its importance as a mechanism for assigning responsibility.[60] But legal ideology can be problematic too. The proclaimed authority of the judgment and bringing in of the guilty verdict are brutal techniques for imposing order on social strife or messy disputes in which attribution of blame is often far less clear-cut than the law pretends.

A fourth aspect of legal classification is the requirement that crime be subject to a distinctive set of procedures. The rules of evidence, the standard of proof, the requirement that crime be adjudicated in a designated forum, subject to its own procedural rules, and staffed by its own personnel, are all intrinsic to the legal definition of crime. The requirement of proof beyond all reasonable doubt, the principle of orality, and the rules and conventions of the adversarial system combine with the legal institutions of the magistracy, judiciary, and lay jury as distinctive features of the criminal process. Understood this way, crime can be defined as that which is the subject of the criminal process: without prosecution and conviction, no liability for crime can be said to have occurred. The chief problem with this approach is that it is doubtful whether defining crime by reference to laws of evidence and procedure takes one much further.

For the student of criminal justice, the larger problem lies less in the elements so far discussed than the fact that most criminal law scholarship does not address the ways in which law is in practice applied by police,

---

[60] Lacey, N., 'Legal Constructions of Crime' in Maguire *et al.* (eds), *The Oxford Handbook of Criminology* (3rd edn, Oxford: Oxford University Press, 2002) 270.

prosecutors, defence lawyers, magistrates, and judges. A simple application of legal definitions misses important variations in social attitudes and moral judgments that determine how those definitions are in practice imposed. And it cannot account for disparities in the application of the law according to the age, sex, class, and race of the supposed perpetrator.[61]

To think about crime, as some criminal law textbooks still do, as comprising discrete, autonomous legal categories remote from the social world, is to engage in an absorbing but esoteric intellectual activity. The exercise of the law is not an arcane clerical task of filing different behaviours in discrete and precisely labelled boxes to achieve nothing more than a semblance of order. Of course, conceptual clarification and normative critique are essential elements of criminal law. Criminal law must define crimes clearly and crimes so defined should be worthy of their label. But the emphasis given by some textbooks to the legal requirements of mental and conduct elements is at odds with the practice of the criminal law, where these concepts play a more marginal role. To illustrate, students of criminal law typically begin their studies by minute examination of the intricacies of the mental elements of crime. They are less often asked to begin by reflecting upon the fact that the great bulk of the 8,000 offences in English criminal law are crimes of strict liability and, as such, require no intention.[62] The sheer number of offences of strict liability raises doubts about the centrality of intention to criminal liability and about the centrality of individual responsibility. It might even be said to place in question what the criminal law is for. With respect to offences of strict liability at least, it is difficult to sustain the notion that crime is principally defined by culpable wrongdoing.

The misapprehension that practising lawyers devote their energies to tortured discussion about the degree of certainty needed to infer or find intention from evidence of foresight would similarly be dispelled by observation of the caseload and working patterns of magistrates' courts where intention is rarely at issue. Likewise, although university courses generally focus on serious offences such as murder, manslaughter, assault, and rape, in practice petty property, public order, and driving offences are

---

[61] Naffine, N., *Feminism and Criminology* (Cambridge: Polity Press, 1997) 6–7; Phillips, C., and Bowling, B., 'Racism, Ethnicity and Criminology: Developing Minority Perspectives' (2003) 43 *British Journal of Criminology* 269–90; Hudson, B., 'Doing Justice to Difference' in Ashworth and Wasik (eds), *Fundamentals of Sentencing Theory* (Oxford: Clarendon Press, 1998).

[62] See, for example, Aldridge, P., 'What is Wrong with the Traditional Criminal Law Course?' (1990) 10 *Legal Studies* 38–62.

the staple work of the lower courts.[63] It is not surprising that generations of students of criminal law are misled into thinking that serious offences and jury trials are the norm, and that sentences of imprisonment are common punishment. Attention to the statistics of recorded crime; to the proportion of cases going to magistrates' and Crown courts; and to patterns of punishment quickly reveals another truth.

Most importantly, for a criminologist to accept that crime is that which is defined by law would lead to some perverse results. To proceed from the idea that crime exists only in law and only insofar as it has been proven in a court of law would excise from criminology a good part of its present subject matter, scope, and interest. By this definition there could be no dark figure of unrecorded crime since, legally, it is not crime at all. It would also require that the *British Crime Survey* be renamed the British Survey of Alleged Crime and its respondents called not victims but claimants. Official criminal statistics, on the other hand, would enjoy a perfect fit with crime. For by definition only those acts and omissions proven to satisfy the legal requirements of crime before a court of law and recorded as such would count as crime. Studies of attrition rates would also need to be re-conceptualized. There could be no gap between the commission and reporting of crime, nor between reporting of crime and recording by police, and no failure of clear-up rates either. Likewise there could be no offenders other than those convicted, nor any victim whose offender has not been so convicted. In sum, the possibility of hidden crime,[64] of unreported crime, of unsolved crime, or of unknown or undisclosed victims would evaporate and much criminological endeavour with it.

This emphatically doctrinal account of criminal law is diminishing as legal and criminological scholarship converge. Criminal lawyers have fruitfully extended their scrutiny to the social world in which the laws they study are constructed, applied, and enforced. And criminologists reflect more and more upon the legal categorization of activities as criminal: to ask not only why people offend, but also why this behaviour, but not that, is legally designated criminal. If, as is currently the case in England, the study of criminal justice increasingly takes place within law schools, then a conception of crime that speaks little to its legally trained

---

[63] As the classic studies by Hood revealed: Hood, R., *Sentencing in the Magistrates' Courts* (London: Tavistock, 1962); Hood, R., *Sentencing the Motoring Offender* (London: Heinemann, 1972).

[64] Stanko, E., 'Hidden Violence Against Women' in Maguire and Pointing (eds), *Victims of Crime: A New Deal?* (Milton Keynes: Open University Press, 1988) 40–6.

students must be undesirable. But convergence is not union and criminal justice scholars sitting at the margins of the two disciplines have to hold two different definitions of crime, the criminological and the legal, simultaneously in play. Those reading their work had better be quite clear which meaning they employ on each occasion. The crime that is the verdict of a jury persuaded beyond all reasonable doubt of the guilt of the offender is, of necessity, a different phenomenon from the crime concealed in the dark field that has yet to face the bright light of the legal process.

A CONDITION PRECEDENT TO PUNISHMENT

In the previous section we focused upon the notion of crime as a legal category and the criminal law as a particular kind of declaratory or duty-imposing law. The criminal law seen this way sets out the scope and conditions of criminal liability but does not concern itself beyond classification. Although the criminal law is a sophisticated and authoritative method of classifying deviant behaviour, the danger is that classification appears as the end rather than the means to something else. Classification is an important way of making sense of the world and imposing upon it a certain order but it might be said to have little purpose beyond taxonomy. Criminal law has an ulterior purpose: it defines action (and more rarely inaction) that is punishable by the state. The perpetrator, if prosecuted and found guilty without excuse or justification, is liable to sanction. The relationship between criminal law and criminal justice is vital because only through punishment does criminal law move from being merely declaratory to sanction conferring. This relationship is much more transparent in other jurisdictions where the very word for criminal law refers directly to its consequence, for example in French 'droit pénal' or in German 'Strafrecht'. In English it is too easy for criminal law and criminal justice to appear to be categorically distinct and the historic English irrelation between the two has obscured their mutual dependence.[65] We tend to think of criminal law as defining the categories of offending, criminal justice their legal consequences. But this categorical view of criminal law obscures the fact that crime is the trigger, the condition precedent to punishment.

---

[65] Nelken, D., 'Criminal Law and Criminal Justice: Some Notes on their Irrelation' in Dennis (ed.), *Criminal Law and Criminal Justice* (London: Sweet & Maxwell, 1987); Jung, H., *Was ist Strafe?* (Baden-Baden: Nomos, 2002).

Despite the continued pedagogic presentation of criminal law as an end in itself, it is inherently consequentialist. Far from simply attaching fair labels to action, the criminal law invokes condemnation of the offender and furnishes an occasion for making authoritative statements about moral and social values. It is this expressive, communicative function that is overlooked in doctrinal accounts that divorce the criminal law from its social world and that is so effectively recaptured by studies that reconnect criminal law with discussion of its penal purpose.[66] Lacey argues that the criminal law can properly be recast as two questions: 'should a defendant be punished for this conduct in these circumstances, and, if so, how severely?'[67] If there were a perfect fit between the normative answers to these questions and the punishment that actually ensued, then much could be learned about the social and moral meaning of crime from studying punishment. Punishment might be conceived not only as a communicative device for conveying society's opprobrium of the offender but also as a precise measure of the cultural value of the offence. In reality there is no perfect congruence between penal value and sentencing practice. The wide discretion enjoyed by sentencers, the diverging cultures of different courthouses, and the variable availability of penal measures introduce a degree of uncertainty and inconsistency in practices of punishment that require a third and fourth question to be added to Lacey's initial two: 'but what punishment does the defendant in practice receive, and why?'

Practices of enforcement are essential to understanding the reality of the criminal law and, by implication, crime. The exercise of discretion at every stage of the criminal process, whether by police, prosecutors, or the judiciary has been the subject of important criminological scholarship.[68] Research studies show that law enforcement is contingent upon its institutional and social context, and that the exercise of discretion is often a more powerful determinant of criminalization than the mechanical application of rules. Far from being applied universally, equally, and fairly,

---

[66] See, for example, Duff, R. A., *Punishment, Communication and Community* (Oxford: Oxford University Press, 2001) 79–82.

[67] Lacey, N., 'The Territory of Criminal Law' (1985) 5 *Oxford Journal of Legal Studies* 453–62 at 460.

[68] For example, McBarnet, D., *Conviction: Law, the State, and the Construction of Justice* (London: Macmillan, 1983); McConville, M. *et al.*, *The Case for the Prosecution: Police Suspects and the Construction of Criminality* (London: Routledge, 1991); Hood, R., *Race and Sentencing* (Oxford: Oxford University Press, 1992); Hawkins, K., *Law as Last Resort: Prosecution Decision-Making in a Regulatory Agency* (Oxford: Oxford University Press, 2002).

criminal laws are mediated through the culture and professional interests of the police, prosecutors, and judiciary.[69] The dominant cultural definitions and legal rules are subverted by the codes, values, or 'working rules' of the professions officially employed to apply them. Between the law laid down in legislation and judicial precedent and the law as actually applied lies a varying, and often sizeable, interval. This interval arises in part from considered judgments about which crimes are worthy of pursuit and which are not, and these judgments do much to temper what might otherwise be an unduly punitive legal code.[70] It may also derive, however, from racial prejudice, gender, and class bias in the enforcement of the criminal law.[71] Recognition of these partialities, however unpalatable, is an important counter to claims of law's supposed neutrality.

Practical factors also play an important role in determining the impact that the criminal process has upon the effective content of the law. The structure, rhythms, and efficacy of the criminal process profoundly affect the substance of the criminal law.[72] If the process is cumbersome, slow, or poorly resourced it will achieve fewer convictions and formal punishment may become a less salient response than it is in a system where the conveyor belt runs smoothly. If the police consider that pursuing a case to court is too time-consuming, tedious, or unlikely to result in conviction, then resort to diversionary tactics such as cautioning or other informal measures of social discipline increases.[73] Where in the pursuit of greater 'efficiency, economy and effectiveness', due process constraints are minimized and the path to conviction smoothed, rates of convictions are likely to go up. Much depends also on the prevailing priorities of criminal justice policy. However draconian the substantive laws on public order offences, for example, if the police have been withdrawn from foot

---

[69] On the importance of the 'cop culture' of the police see Reiner, R., *The Politics of the Police* (3rd edn, Oxford: Oxford University Press, 2000).

[70] The exercise of discretion and, through discretion, mercy has long been essential to the operation of the criminal law. See Hay, D., 'Property, Authority and the Criminal Law' in Hay *et al.* (eds), *Albion's Fatal Tree: Crime and Society in Eighteenth Century England* (London: Allen Lane, 1975) 40–9. On the centrality of mercy to the exercise of eighteenth-century criminal law, see King, P., *Crime, Justice and Discretion in England, 1740–1820* (Oxford: Oxford University Press, 2000).

[71] Hood, R., *Race and Sentencing* (Oxford: Oxford University Press, 1992); Heidensohn, F., 'Gender and Crime' in Maguire *et al.* (eds), *The Oxford Handbook of Criminology* (3rd edn, Oxford: Oxford University Press, 2002).

[72] Packer, H. L., *The Limits of the Criminal Sanction* (Stanford, Calif.: Stanford University Press, 1968) 150.

[73] Choongh, S., *Policing as Social Discipline* (Oxford: Clarendon Press, 1997).

patrols, then fewer instances of disorderly behaviour, vandalism, or criminal damage will be detected. By contrast zero-tolerance strategies can substantially increase the policing and subsequent punishment of minor acts of disorder. Between the determination that the wrongdoer ought to be punished and the punishment actually imposed, a host of political, economic, institutional, and cultural factors intercede. If crime is a condition precedent to punishment it is only one among many.

To say that punishment follows from crime is not merely a factual or predictive statement about the causal relationship between the two but also a normative statement about what ought to follow. The prescription that punishment follows conviction contains within it also an imputed obligation upon the state to impose sanctions if a norm is violated.[74] Understood this way, crime not only licenses but also obliges state officials to punish its perpetrators. Thomas sums up this dual function of the criminal law as follows:

A law which marks the boundaries of acceptable conduct to the citizen also defines the power of the agencies of social control. The prohibition inherent in a criminal statute is dual: it addresses the citizen in identifying the proscribed behaviour, and it addresses the organs of the state in establishing conditions precedent to punitive reaction.[75]

Of course this licence is not unconstrained and the criminal law simultaneously prescribes what state officials may and may not do. Nor is the obligation to punish universal and invariable: for example, diversion schemes license state officials to deflect offenders from the criminal process in order to reduce the labelling effects and stigma of conviction. All the problems we have so far observed concerning the designation of crime and the apportionment of liability likewise render problematic the assumption that crime entails an obligation to punish.

Criminal law is just part of the complex network of laws relating to criminal procedure, evidence, and sentencing, together with subsidiary rules and regulations relating to police powers, prosecution, the administration of penalties, prison discipline, and provisions for release. Together they combine to shape and limit the criminal justice system. The legal powers according to which state agents are licensed to investigate, arrest, prosecute, sentence, and punish are characterized by a high degree of discretion. Given this, there is much profit to be had in close scrutiny of

---

[74] Kelsen, H., 'On the Pure Theory of Law' (1966) 1 *Israeli Law Review* 1–7 at 3.
[75] Thomas, D., 'Form and Function in Criminal Law' in Glazebrook (ed.), *Reshaping the Criminal Law: Essays in Honour of Glanville Williams* (London: Stevens & Sons, 1978) 21.

the design of statutes and, in particular, the internal structure of individual offences. Declaring an activity illegal clearly does not convey a blanket permission to criminal justice agents to act against wrongdoers. The precise wording of the prohibition determines whether it is this offence or another which is to be prosecuted, in which court charges may be laid, the limits of the defendant's liability, the powers of the jury in determining guilt, and of the magistrate or judge in sentencing. If the definition of the criminal behaviour is not precisely drafted or fails to specify the conduct exactly, considerable discretion is vested in prosecuting agents, acting in quasi-legislative manner, to determine the appropriate charge.[76]

Likewise, where there is flexibility as to forum or mode of trial, discretion is again handed over to criminal justice officials and, to a more limited extent, to the accused as well. The flexibility introduced by allowing a degree of licence as to mode of trial may be a convenient way of ensuring that crimes of differing seriousness are dealt with appropriately. It can have significant implications, however, for the severity of punishment that then ensues. Later in the process, the determination of guilt is also limited (or not) by the degree of precision with which legal categories are framed. If they are too widely defined or lack clarity, then the scope of the magistrate's or the jury's discretion will be large.[77] Sentencing is perhaps the least law-bound of any stage in the criminal process and it has moved more than one commentator to observe how procedural controls slip away at the sentencing stage to be replaced with a degree of licence not conceivable earlier in the criminal process.[78] Detailed distinctions within doctrinal law can curtail discretion but since sentencing involves making judgments as to the seriousness of the offence, and the personal circumstances, attitudes, problems, and prospects of the

---

[76] A good example here is the draconian powers laid down in s. 63 of the Criminal Justice and Public Order Act 1994 against so-called raves that could apply equally to outdoor festivals and other gatherings. Similarly, provisions directed against trespassory assembly under s. 70 aimed at prohibiting the mass summer solstice gatherings around Stonehenge could also be applied against large-scale demonstrations by trade unions or other political organizations in city parks.

[77] Thomas gives the example of 'to deprave and corrupt' under the Obscene Publications Act 1959 or 'dishonesty' under the Theft Act 1968. Terms that no longer attract consensus as to their meaning will fail to fetter the jury leaving the outcome dependent on their idiosyncratic and probably variable definitions: Thomas, D., 'Form and Function in Criminal Law' in Glazebrook (ed.), *Reshaping the Criminal Law: Essays in Honour of Glanville Williams* (London: Stevens & Sons, 1978) 32.

[78] Lacey, N., 'Discretion and Due Process at the Post Conviction Stage' in Dennis (ed), *Criminal Law and Criminal Justice* (London: Sweet & Maxwell, 1987).

offender this power to curtail is limited. To the extent that the exercise of judicial discretion is necessary to ensure the just application of doctrinal law, the imposition of mandatory sentences is likely to be productive of injustice.[79]

Thinking of the criminal law as licensing action by the officials of the criminal justice system has the advantage that it suggests a different conception of the relationship between crime and criminal justice than that which ordinarily comes to mind. To say that crime compels punishment or requires action by criminal justice officials is a stronger, normative statement that goes beyond our earlier observation that crime is a trigger of the criminal justice process. The disadvantage of thinking about criminal law as licence is that it forecloses critical discussion about the justification of punishment. Against the argument that punishment is justified by crime, there is a strong counterclaim that two wrongs do not make a right. To add state-inflicted pain to offender-inflicted pain is merely to double the sum of suffering. If it is not self-evident that crime requires that there be punishment, a line can be drawn between censure and hard treatment. Whilst crime legitimates censure, some further justification is needed for inflicting pain and it is to this we turn in the next chapter.

CONCLUSION

This chapter has explored just some of the ways of thinking about crime, namely: crime as a social construct, exercise in power, or form of governance; as wrongdoing; as harm doing; as a legal category; and as a condition precedent to punishment. These are by no means the only way of conceiving crime. Other possibilities include conceiving crime as a form of ideological censure,[80] social injury,[81] moral consensus,[82] political conflict,[83] means to political unity,[84] and of course, as a positive fact.[85] No doubt the list could be extended further still. Increasingly, criminologists

[79] Thomas, D., 'The Crime (Sentences) Act 1997' (1998) *Criminal Law Review* 83–92.

[80] Sumner, C. (ed.), *Censure, Politics and Criminal Justice* (Milton Keynes: Open University Press, 1990).

[81] Quinney, R., *Class, State and Crime* (New York: David McKay, 1977).

[82] Michael, J., and Adler, M., *Crime, Law and Social Science* (New York: Harcourt, Brace & Jovanovich, 1933).

[83] Taylor, I. *et al. The New Criminology* (London: Routledge & Kegan Paul, 1973).

[84] Hall, S. *et al.*, *Policing the Crisis: Mugging, the State, and Law and Order* (London: Macmillan, 1978).

[85] Lombroso, C., *Crime: Its Causes and Remedies* (Boston, Mass.: Little, Brown, 1913).

see crime as a 'normal social commonplace aspect of modern society',[86] a routine activity or 'fact of everyday life,'[87] or a form of economic loss.[88] We will return to these later possibilities in our final chapter and examine their implications for criminal justice. Suffice it to say here that crime is a problematic category used routinely to describe a set of behaviours that, beyond a central core, are highly contested. Legal definition alone cannot adequately recognize the historical development, social relationships, practices, ideologies, and interests that determine what, at any given moment, is designated criminal. And yet it is only that which is legally defined as crime that can legitimately be subject to the criminal justice process and to punishment.

[86] Garland, D., *The Culture of Control: Crime and Social Order in Contemporary Society* (Oxford: Oxford University Press, 2001) 128.

[87] Felson, M., *Crime and Everyday Life* (3rd edn, London: Sage, 2002) ch. 11.

[88] Shearing, C., 'Punishment and the Changing Face of Governance' (2001) 3 *Punishment and Society* 203–20.

3

Punishment

WHAT IS PUNISHMENT?

Punishment is so entrenched an institution of our society that we can scarcely envisage life without it. Yet, anthropological studies of societies other than our own reveal that punitive responses to wrongdoing, or indeed any response to wrongdoing, are not inevitable. Whereas in one society wrongdoing provokes aggression and immediate physical retaliation, often backed up by members of the aggrieved person's kinship group, in another society restraint and silence even under severe provocation are expected. In these latter societies any retaliation would earn the respondent as much opprobrium as the original wrongdoer. As Roberts observes, 'a response representing the minimum which "honour" demands in one society may thus seem an inconceivable over-reaction in another'.[1] Whereas the Tswana tribesman of Southern Africa would allow himself no more than a monosyllabic response or merely remain silent, his counterpart amongst the Tangu of the Papua New Guinea Highlands hearing that his piglet had been accidentally killed responded by 'whooping, yelling, leaping in the air and thwacking his buttocks'.[2] In part this variety of reaction is explicable by reference to different cultural expectations, in part to different structural arrangements. Where, as is the case in nomadic societies, ostracism or voluntary withdrawal by the wrongdoer removes them from social interaction with those they have wronged, no further response may be thought necessary. Where kinship relationships are so complex as to render retaliatory action too costly for those who have ties to both the wronged and wrongdoing factions, non-punitive responses tend to take their place. Nor is resort to third parties inevitable. But, where it does occur, it too varies from diversion, through discussion and dispute resolution, to shaming, retaliation, removal, and even destruction of the offender. Likewise the response itself takes a surprising

---

[1] Roberts, S., *Order and Dispute: An Introduction to Legal Anthropology* (Harmondsworth: Penguin Books, 1979) 54.
[2] Ibid. 53–4.

variety of forms catalogued by anthropologists: from silent gestures of reproach, through rituals of ridicule and jest, song-contests, competitive food-exchanges, sorcery, ordeals, and ostracism. A famous example is Malinowski's description of the Trobriand Islanders' *buritila' ulo*, the exchange of yams between two villages where a dispute had taken place, in which members of each village worked furiously to ensure that their gift of yams matched in size and quality.[3] Honour restored, the original dispute was forgotten and all thought of retaliation abandoned.

If punishment is not always and everywhere the common response to wrongdoing, it is a certainly a central feature of most Western criminal justice systems. As these few observations show, our system of punishment is neither inevitable nor fixed in form or purpose: it is rather an equally peculiar and contingent condition of our own societies. We would do well to keep in mind the Trobriand Islanders' yam exchange, and the very great variety of possible responses to wrongdoing, as we go on to consider the particularities of punishment as we know it.

As with crime, our over-familiarity with punishment carries the further danger that we are imprecise, overly expansive, or uncritical in our usage. Part of the problem is that we tend to use the term colloquially to refer to any unpleasant or painful experience—a punishing exercise regime or punishing work schedule, for example.[4] We use it also to refer to informal sanction by gangsters upon wayward or rival gang members or, more legitimately, by parents of children or by teachers of pupils.

Punishment in the context of criminal justice has a narrower meaning, which may be focused on six questions. What are the prerequisites of formal punishment? What are its component parts? By whom is it imposed? Upon whom? What social roles does it fulfil? And with what justification or to what end is it inflicted? In answering these questions we should be aware that both positive and normative answers are possible. Sometimes we are describing punishment as it currently is and sometimes as we should wish it to be. This distinction is reflected in scholarship about punishment. Whereas penology concerns itself with the study and evaluation of existing penal institutions, normative penal theory seeks to establish the aims and justifications of punishment. Before we examine these two avenues, let us begin by focusing on the conceptual question, what is punishment?

---

[3] Malinowski, B., *Coral Gardens and their Magic* (2nd edn, London: Allen & Unwin, 1966) 182–7.

[4] Hudson, B., *Understanding Justice: An Introduction to Ideas, Perspectives and Controversies in Modern Penal Theory* (Buckingham: Open University Press, 1996) 1.

Formally, punishment is the punitive response to the commission of an existing offence in criminal law. Two basic principles formally govern punishment: that there can be no crime without law and that there can be no punishment without law.[5] The principle that no conduct be considered criminal unless it has been declared so in law works well in respect of those offences clearly defined in common law or statute. It is more problematic in respect of crimes that are so broadly cast that they lack definition until refined in future cases—many public order offences seem unduly vague according to this criterion. It is also undermined by the judicial practice of extending or creating new offences in order to reflect changing moral values. The second principle requires that punishment follow only upon conviction, that it be in accordance with existing statutory provisions, and that it be declared in the sentence of the court. Whether the principle is attenuated by the considerable discretion given to sentencers to decide upon the appropriate level of punishment under designated maxima is a matter of some debate to which we return in Chapter 5.

Our second question is what are the characteristics or component parts of punishment? Two key components appear common to most, though not all, definitions of punishment, namely censure and sanction. Censure is the means by which punishers express disapproval of the offender and publicly declare the wrongfulness of the offence.[6] Censure is addressed to several different parties simultaneously. To offenders it conveys societal condemnation of their actions and may provide an occasion for reflection or penitence.[7] To victims it acknowledges not only that they have been hurt or suffered loss but also that this has occurred through another's fault. To society in general it reaffirms the limits of acceptable behaviour and provides reasons for desistence from wrongdoing. To load censure with these several functions is to impose a considerable burden and it is questionable whether censure alone is equal to the task. It is principally for this reason that many theorists consider it necessary to add the further element of sanction in order adequately to convey the multiple messages that censure alone cannot.[8] From this point of view, pain (broadly conceived as unpleasant consequences) is not simply a common characteristic

---

[5] Each enunciated in Latin: *nullum crimen sine lege* and *nulla poena sine lege*.

[6] von Hirsch, A., *Censure and Sanctions* (Oxford: Oxford University Press, 1993) 9.

[7] Duff, R. A., *Punishment, Communication and Community* (Oxford: Oxford University Press, 2001) ch. 6.

[8] Narayan, U., 'Appropriate Responses and Preventative Benefits: Justifying Censure and Hard Treatment in Legal Punishment' a (1993) 13 *Oxford Journal of Legal Studies* 166–82.

or coincidental side effect but an essential element of punishment. Before we concede this point uncritically, however, we should ask whether and in what circumstances censure alone might suffice. Where censure can convey the multiple messages listed above then it is arguable that we should place a definitional stop after censure and demand some justification before any further consequence can be inflicted. From this perspective, sanctioning is not an essential element of punishment but one whose infliction must be shown to be necessary to its purpose.

What this leaves open, of course, is what purpose the sanction fulfils. Does the importance of the sanction reside in the intention of the agent imposing punishment or the experience of the person receiving it? And if pain can be said to be integral to punishment, is it still punishment where the intention of the punisher is to do good or reform rather than to impose pain? Is it punishment where the person so subjected experiences it as a benefit rather than a burden? For example, in providing a warm, dry, relatively safe shelter and regular meals is the prison a burden or a benefit for a homeless and hungry person? In answering these questions we should be wary about claims to be 'doing good' or conferring benefits because so much that is done in the name of rehabilitation or reform might then escape the definition of punishment, even though it is done coercively and imposes burdens upon the offender.

Our third question is by whom is punishment inflicted? Is punishment solely the responsibility of the state and its agents? In order to distinguish it from other punitive action, punitive damages in tort for example, should we further require that punishment be that which is imposed by officials of the criminal court following trial and conviction? Asserting the requirement that punishment be imposed by criminal justice agents raises doubts about the power to delegate. Is the concept of punishment as a state prerogative undermined by delegation to private agents, for example, employed by contractors in privatized prisons? Apologists for privatization rely on the distinction between the allocation and the delivery of punishment. According to this line of argument, provided the allocation of punishment remains under state control, its administration can be delegated to private agents without derogating from the principle that punishment is the responsibility of the state.[9] Opponents, on the other hand, argue that to delegate the delivery of punishment to private agents is a clear derogation. Sparks, for example, argues that by

---

[9] Harding, R. W., *Private Prisons and Public Accountability* (Buckingham: Open University Press, 1997) 22.

attempting to distinguish between allocation and delivery, proponents of privatization seek to divorce the penalty from its essential characteristic, the delivery of pain or unpleasant consequences. In respect of prison privatization, Sparks argues:

the sharp distinction between allocation and delivery of punishment serves rhetorically to insulate the two areas of discussion from one another. It protects the original act of sentencing (a judicial specialism—one sphere of expertise) whilst at the same time it presents the delivery of imprisonment in a moderated and sanitized language (a correctional specialism—another sphere of expertise—nothing to do with the intended delivery of pain).[10]

It is precisely because he sees pain as integral to both allocation and delivery that Sparks argues punishment must remain a state function.

For the moment, our interest is less in the rival merits of these debates than in the doubts they cast upon the conceptual distinction between allocation and delivery of punishment. The practical decisions as to which security classification prisoners are given; to which type of prison they are allocated; and what further punishments may be awarded as a result of internal disciplinary proceedings each blur the distinction further still. If both allocation and delivery of punishment are properly state functions, would we do better to talk only of state punishment?[11] Or, given that private agencies encroach ever further upon the delivery of punishment, should we adopt a more expansive definition of punishment, if only to make clear that what private agents deliver is indeed pain and not some more benign product? How one answers these questions will be determined largely by one's attitude to privatization (an issue to which we will return in Chapter 7).

Having addressed the question of by whom, we turn to our fourth question. Upon whom is punishment imposed? Our earlier requirement that punishment be for a criminal offence would seem to presuppose an offender. To say this leaves open the question of the means by which we determine who is and who is not an offender. Does the term offender apply only to those whose culpability has been determined in a criminal court? If punishment is that which follows conviction and sentence, then the object of punishment must be someone so convicted. In practice, several apparent derogations from this principle occur. First, agents of

---

[10] Sparks, R., 'Can Prisons be Legitimate? Penal Politics, Privatization, and the Timelessness of an Old Idea' (1994) 34 *British Journal of Criminology* 14–28 at 23–4.

[11] As Nicola Lacey proposes: Lacey, N., *State Punishment: Political Principles and Community Values* (London: Routledge, 1988).

criminal justice do not always wait until the determination of guilt before they inflict pain upon putative offenders. As we shall see in Chapter 4, studies of policing suggest that informal punishment of offenders on the street, in the police car, in cells, or in an interview suite is common.[12] Whether one can legitimately describe police treatment of suspects, yet to be convicted of any crime, as punishment is open to question. Indeed one might argue that to do so is to endow illegitimate practices with a spurious legitimacy. Admonishment and deprivation of basic liberties in pursuit of confession or contrition may be common police practice but do not constitute lawful punishment. Suspects held on remand in prison likewise constitute a derogation from the principle outlined above in that, although presumed innocent, they are often held in significantly more arduous circumstances than are convicted prisoners.

A further derogation is the painful consequences imposed by the courts in response to civil wrongs. An illuminating example here was the introduction of Anti-Social Behaviour Orders (ASBOs). These define 'anti-social' behaviour as that which 'caused or was likely to cause harassment, alarm or distress to two or more persons not of the same household'.[13] ASBOs are civil orders that rely upon the lower, civil law standard of proof—'balance of probabilities' (rather than the criminal requirement of 'beyond all reasonable doubt'). As such, they attract none of the protections of the criminal process. They have the power, however, to impose burdensome and disproportionate penalties (up to five years' imprisonment if the order is proven to have been breached) for behaviour that is by definition not criminal but merely 'anti-social'. Do these orders constitute punishment or not? Those upon whom they are imposed are not criminal and their 'offences' are not crimes. But, as Ashworth and others have argued, where the effect is to criminalize and the outcome is the coerced imposition of pain, the technical designation of such an order as civil rather than criminal ought not to take it outside the realm of punishment.[14] In answering the question upon whom is punishment inflicted, we should be prepared, therefore, to consider including not only proven

---

[12] Feeley, M., *The Process is the Punishment: Handling Cases in a Lower Criminal Court* (New York: Russell Sage Foundation, 1979); Choongh, S., *Policing as Social Discipline* (Oxford: Clarendon Press, 1997).

[13] Crime and Disorder Act 1998 s.1(1) (as amended by the Anti-Social Behaviour Act 2003 s. 85).

[14] Ashworth, A. *et al.*, 'Neighbouring on the Oppressive: the Government's "Anti-Social Behaviour Order" Proposals' (1998) 16 *Criminal Justice* 7–14.

but also putative offenders and also those neither suspected nor convicted of any criminal offence.[15]

THE SOCIAL ROLES OF PUNISHMENT

The philosophical attempts to justify punishment to which we will turn in the latter part of this chapter tend to posit punishment as an abstract and unvarying institution. It is arguable, however, that we cannot begin to ask whether punishment is justified until we have in mind the roles it fulfils, the concrete forms it takes, and the effects it has in our society. The forms and functions of punishment vary over time in close parallel with larger changes in society. Explaining punishment can thus be seen as an exercise in social theory. In studying punishment we explore the means by which society, at any given point, governs itself and maintains order in the face of challenges to its authority. How punishment relates to other state institutions, contributes to social order, and the values it expresses have been the subject of extensive sociological and historical enquiry.[16] What follows is a broad taxonomy of the main lines of thought and an indication of their principal exponents.

CONSCIENCE COLLECTIVE

Perhaps the most important sociological interpretation of punishment is as a mechanism by which social order is maintained. By tackling and neutralizing problems of disorder that threaten society's peace and ability to function, punishment ensures society's continued existence. This way of thinking of punishment was first elaborated by the sociologist Émile Durkheim (1858–1917) who saw punishment as playing a crucial role in the development and maintenance of social bonds.[17] In traditional societies, crime offended against the 'conscience collective' or totality of shared social beliefs and evoked collective repression in the form of brutal punishment. Punishment served simultaneously to denounce offences to the conscience collective and to restore and fortify common social beliefs about the limits of acceptable behaviour. By buttressing social consensus

---

[15] Ashworth, A., 'Social Control and Anti-Social Behaviour Order: the Subversion of Human Rights?' (2004) 120 *Law Quarterly Review* 264–92.

[16] For an extensive and sophisticated analysis of the sociology of punishment see Garland, D., *Punishment and Modern Society: A Study in Social Theory* (Oxford: Oxford University Press, 1990).

[17] Durkheim, E., *The Division of Labour in Society* (London: Macmillan, 1984). Conveniently, Lukes, S., and Scull, A. (eds), *Durkheim and the Law* (Oxford: Martin Robertson, 1983) collects Durkheim's writings on punishment in chs 3 and 4.

or what Durkheim terms 'mechanical solidarity', punishment was thus an essential means of ensuring peace and social order.

In modern societies characterized by specialization of labour and differentiated beliefs and attitudes, it becomes necessary to create new means to sustain social solidarity. Where social solidarity is not strongly shared, institutions like the law are invoked to generate the rules whereby members of society with different sentiments can agree to reconcile their differences. In place of the conscience collective, the rule of law provides the authoritative means by which common values may be affirmed—what Durkheim terms 'organic solidarity'. The function of punishment is less to control crime than to provide a vehicle for the expression of outrage when crime is committed and thus to reaffirm the social value transgressed. The subject of punishment is, therefore, less the offender than society as a whole.

Many criticisms can be levelled at this interpretation of punishment not least that Durkheim's theory of penal evolution is flawed; that contemporary punishment is not directly determined by public sentiment; that it is better understood as a legal and administrative device than as an expressive one; and that it leads, as much as it reflects, public opinion. More importantly still, Durkheim's analysis suggests a degree of consensus that is at odds with the realities of power imbalance, economic inequality, and class hostility that characterize modern society. For his critics, law and the legal institution of punishment are less the means of ensuring social consensus than an arena of social conflict and power struggle. Although some have criticized Durkheim's insistence on the functionality of punishment, it is arguable that this is to misrepresent his thesis. Durkheim's claim is rather that punishment has an importance for society that outweighs its functionality as a means of controlling crime. Seen this way, his insights into the meaning of penal rituals and the relationship between penal institutions and public sentiment survive doubts about his larger characterization of society.[18]

BUREAUCRATIC GOVERNANCE

A second leading sociological interpretation of punishment is as a form of bureaucratic governance or as the means by which modern societies govern themselves. This interpretation is derived from the sociological writings of Max Weber (1864–1920). Weber differentiates modern *legal*

---

[18] Garland, D., *Punishment and Modern Society: A Study in Social Theory* (Oxford: Oxford University Press, 1990) ch. 2.

authority from the ideal types of *traditional authority* (the power to rule handed down by tradition, for example hereditary monarchy) and *charismatic authority* (the endowment of certain individuals or groups with special qualities or characteristics).[19] Modern legal authority is characterized rather by impersonal rule: those entrusted to rule are selected by legal processes such as elections and are obliged to obey the laws they pass. Weber proposes *bureaucratic rationality*, characterized by established rules and procedures, formal systems of law making, and prescribed legal rules, as the most appropriate form of legal authority for modern societies.[20] Although Weber does not directly address punishment, it can be extrapolated that it requires a formal legal criminal code, legal rules of procedure and adjudication, formal professional functionaries, and a rational, graduated penal code. Reliance on lay people acting as magistrates or juries is at odds with Weber's expectation of legal rationality, as is resort to inhumane or cruel punishment. The rationalization of punishment is not without costs however, as Weber acknowledges: bureaucratic rationality replaces moral judgments with technical imperatives which reduce life to a routine.

Conceiving modern punishment as a form of bureaucratic rationality can be criticized on the grounds that it is simplistic to suggest that traditional societies have irrational means of social control and modern societies' rational ones. The development of rational bureaucratic forms does not eclipse or excise non-rational motivations though it may conceal them or limit their sway. Indeed it is likely that although managerialism and the technical administration of punishment limits the influence of populist demands for vengeance, this urge is not wholly repressed. Bureaucratic rationality does not replace irrationality but becomes rather a means of managing it so that punitive desires are exercised in a concealed, neutral, and socially acceptable manner. This is not necessarily to contradict Weber's typology, which acknowledged that differing forms of authority coexist and intersect in historical time.

ECONOMIC DETERMINISM

The Durkheimian and Weberian sociologies of punishment discussed so far portray society as more cohesive than sociologists in the Marxist tradition find plausible. Karl Marx (1818–83) saw society as riven by conflicts based on class division or economic relationship to the mode of

---

[19] Weber, M., *Economy and Society: An Outline of Interpretive Sociology* (Berkeley: University of California Press, 1978) ch. 3 'The Types of Legitimate Domination'.

[20] Ibid. 217–26.

production. According to Marx, the economy not only provides the base upon which the superstructure of political and ideological relations are constructed but also determines their shape and form. Aside from brief discussions of the criminalization of gathering fallen wood and the punishment of vagrancy, Marx himself had little to say about punishment. This has not inhibited neo-Marxists from identifying punishment as a key institution in the superstructure, likewise reliant upon the underlying mode of production. Changes in the mode of production thus bring about changes in the form and function of punishment. When labour is in plentiful supply, life is cheap and punishment treats it as such so that capital and corporal punishments predominate. When demand for labour exceeds supply, the state is more careful to conserve human resources and to subject offenders to the discipline necessary to reintegrate them into the workforce, for example via captive penal labour in workhouses and prisons.[21] Conceiving punishment as economically determined focuses attention on its historical specificity. According to perhaps the most important exponents of Marxist penal theory, Rusche and Kirchheimer, 'punishment as such does not exist, only concrete forms of punishment and specific criminal practices exist'.[22] Understood this way, punishment takes on a very different guise from the abstract and unchanging entity envisaged by philosophers and becomes rather a concrete product of historical moment.

A second facet of Marxist analysis is the central place of class struggle between the subordinate, labouring classes and the dominant class dedicated to appropriating the fruits of their labour. According to Marx, the dominant class secure their position by using the institutions of the state to suppress opposition and further their class interests. Again Marxists have identified punishment as essential to the maintenance of class rule and as a particular site of order maintenance.[23] The many analyses of punishment following Marx vary in their emphasis and interpretation but share a common view of punishment as linked to a particular set of property relations and the struggle to maintain power by the ruling

---

[21] Melossi, D., and Pavarini, M., *The Prison and the Factory* (London: Macmillan, 1981).

[22] Rusche, G., and Kirchheimer, O., *Punishment and Social Structure* (New York: Columbia University Press, 1939) 3.

[23] Hay, D., 'Crime in eighteenth- and nineteenth-century England' in Tonry and Morris (eds), *Crime and Justice: An Annual Review of Research* (Chicago: University of Chicago Press, 1980); Hay, D., 'Property, Authority and the Criminal Law' in Hay *et al.* (eds), *Albion's Fatal Tree: Crime and Society in Eighteenth Century England* (London: Allen Lane, 1975). For a spirited rebuttal see Langbein, J. H., 'Albion's Fatal Flaws' (1983) 98 *Past and Present* 96–120.

classes over those below them in society. Subsequent Marxist analysis tended to shift away from its earlier focus on the mode of production toward greater concern with the institutions of class domination, identifying punishment as a site of ideological conflict and class struggle.[24]

Marxist analysis of punishment has been subject to extensive criticism, not least on the grounds that it tends to overstate the power of economic determinism and simultaneously to underestimate the countervailing or inhibiting influence of other factors such as professional interests and institutional dynamics. Further, to claim that punishment is economically determined fails to explain the means by which the economy brings about changes in penal institutions. Characterizing punishment as a mechanism for regulating labour supply is arguably both reductive and overly functionalist. Finally, the assertion that punishment is an instrument of class domination has prompted critics to observe that the lower orders have resort to the protections of the criminal law quite as much as those ruling classes whose interests punishment supposedly serves. To the extent that it is the lower orders who suffer chiefly as victims of crime, their interests are bound up in punishment quite as much as those who rule.[25] And yet, despite these criticisms, Marxist analysis has proved powerfully enduring. Its persistence is explicable, not least by the fact that it provides a framework for thinking about punishment as a governmental strategy, inherently linked with power relations, economic struggle, and social conflict: none of which necessarily assumes full-blown Marxist economic determinism.

DISCIPLINE

The role of punishment as a disciplinary device central to modern capitalism was further developed in the work of Michel Foucault (1926–84), though his analysis is far removed from the economic determinism of Marxism. Instead Foucault focuses on the exercise of power and the role of punishment in governing individuals in modern society. His particular concern is with what he terms 'the microphysics of power', namely the detailed ways in which individuals are governed through technologies that provide information about them and thus exercise power over

[24] Lea, J., and Young, J., *What is to be Done About Law and Order?* (Harmondsworth, Middlesex: Penguin Books, 1984).

[25] Left Realism, for example, drew attention to the fact that the costs of crime fall most commonly upon those least able to bear them: Young, J., 'Ten Points of Realism' in Young and Matthews (eds), *Rethinking Criminology: The Realist Debate* (London: Sage, 1992).

them.[26] Modern punishment is such a technology. It is designed not to avenge through brutal corporal punishment but rather to discipline through strategies of isolation or 'partitioning', diagnosis, assessment, and correction.

That the disciplinary power of punishment fails in practice to correct the majority of offenders might be thought an indictment of Foucault's analysis. Instead Foucault acknowledges this failure and he reinterprets it as a covert success. The creation of a permanent class of delinquents channels potential revolt into forms that are politically harmless, maintains criminals on the margins of society, and serves to keep in check the respectable working classes anxious to differentiate themselves from the delinquent underclass.[27] The manufacture of delinquents is thus a central and functional feature of punishment, a primary means of 'moralizing' the poor.

Foucault's account of punishment has attracted enormous interest and no little criticism. By focusing on the institution of the prison, Foucault gives a primacy to the disciplinary quality of imprisonment that is not self-evidently true of all penal measures.[28] Secondly, there is an uncomfortable disjuncture between his analysis of punishment as simultaneously disciplinary and yet as failing in its disciplinary project.[29] Thirdly, his designation of who wields the power to punish swings precariously from the middle classes, to the 'dominant class', to the state, and more frequently still fails to identify any recognizable agent. This negation of human agency extends also to the subjects of power who are portrayed as wholly passive; their ability to frustrate or subvert the regime beyond simple physical resistance is barely acknowledged. Finally, it is objected that Foucault's account of punishment is overly instrumental, focusing on the function of punishment (and indeed making questionable assumptions about its functionality) to the detriment of its expressive qualities.[30] These criticisms notwithstanding, Foucault's account of punishment as discipline has been enormously influential in

---

[26] On the relationship between knowledge and power see Foucault, M., *The Archaeology of Knowledge* (London: Routledge, 1972).

[27] Foucault, M., *Discipline And Punish: The Birth of the Prison* (reprint, Harmondsworth, Middlesex: Penguin Books, 1982) ch. 2.

[28] Bottoms, A. E., 'Neglected Features of Contemporary Penal Systems' in Garland and Young (eds), *The Power to Punish: Contemporary Penality and Social Analysis* (London: Heinemann Educational Books, 1983).

[29] Garland, D., 'Sociological Perspectives on Punishment' (1991) 14 *Crime and Justice: A Review of Research* 115–65 at 139–40.

[30] Garland, D., *Punishment and Modern Society: A Study in Social Theory* (Oxford: Oxford University Press, 1990) ch. 7.

framing subsequent thinking about punishment and in providing the very vocabulary and concepts of modern penology.

A CULTURAL FORM

In reaction to functionalist accounts of punishment, modern social theorists have focused instead on the expressive quality of punishment. They represent punishment as a cultural form and replace questions about its role with enquiries into its meaning and significance. Punishment is seen both as the product of cultural mentalities and prevailing sensibilities and as contributing to the larger formation of culture. This larger terrain is the subject of wide-ranging sociological enquiry and a central focus of social anthropology. For the anthropologist Clifford Geertz, the analysis of culture is 'not an experimental science in search of law but an interpretive one in search of meaning'.[31] One of the leading exponents of the cultural analysis of punishment is David Garland.[32] Drawing upon Geertz, Garland argues that a fully developed notion of culture must recognize both its intellectual aspects (conceptions, values, categories, frameworks of ideas, and systems of belief) and its emotional ones. He thus views punishment as a 'complex cultural artefact' informed and shaped by both the cognitive mentalities and the affective sensibilities of the day. This interpretation of punishment moves beyond the institutional focus of earlier sociological accounts to 'take seriously the rhetoric and motivational formulations of penal reformers'.[33] The language of penal reform, debate, legislation, and policy are seen as patterns of cultural expression encoding the wider culture, though, as Garland warns, 'any "cultural" or "discursive" approach to the phenomena should never lose sight of the fact that punishment is also, and simultaneously, a network of material social practices in which symbolic forms are sanctioned by brute force as well as by chains of reference and cultural agreement'.[34] This is not to say that Garland distinguishes between the cultural forms and the practices of punishment. Rather, as he makes clear, 'instrumental practices are always conceived within a context of cultural mentalities and sensibilities, so that instrumental and cultural forms are one and the same

---

[31] Geertz, C., 'Thick Description: Toward an Interpretive Theory of Culture' in Geertz (ed), *The Interpretation of Cultures* (London: Fontana Press, 1993) 5.
[32] Garland, D., *Punishment and Modern Society: A Study in Social Theory* (Oxford: Oxford University Press, 1990) ch. 9; Garland, D., *The Culture of Control: Crime and Social Order in Contemporary Society* (Oxford: Oxford University Press, 2001).
[33] Garland, D., *Punishment and Modern Society: A Study in Social Theory* (Oxford: Oxford University Press, 1990) 198.
[34] Ibid. 199.

thing'.[35] If the cultural analysis of punishment moves beyond sociology, therefore, it certainly does not abandon it but rather requires a marriage of the two.

The model of cultural analysis propounded by Geertz further requires that one abandon generic discussion of culture in favour of detailed ethnography or 'thick description' of the particular institution, act, or event.[36] Applied to punishment, this requires that one forsake generalization for specific analysis of the particularities of penality at any given time or place:

the diverse practices, routines, and procedures which make up the penal realm are always undertaken within an immediate framework of meaning which one might term 'penal culture'. This penal culture is the loose amalgam of penological theory, stored-up experience, institutional wisdom and professional common sense which frames the actions of penal agents and which lends meaning to what they do.[37]

By way of example, Garland takes the concept of justice. Rather than conceiving of justice as a timeless, unchanging category 'beyond culture and outside history', one should see it as specific to the prevailing mentality of the time. To illustrate: the intimate and personalized qualities of the eighteenth-century criminal process were by the nineteenth century regarded as scandalous and unjust. Yet the strict formality of nineteenth-century justice was challenged again in the early twentieth century by new concerns for individual welfare and rehabilitation. The emerging 'psy' professions promoted indefinite sentences whose length was determined not by the gravity of the offence but by the requirements of the reform process. Welfarism posited alternative purposes for the criminal justice system, orientated toward rehabilitation, reparation, and, to a lesser extent, social defence. These goals sat uncomfortably against a legal framework that was predicated upon notions of individual responsibility and invoked its power to chastise within carefully prescribed legal limits. The resulting tensions between the prevailing social purposes of criminal justice and the legal forms and processes through which these were to be achieved haunted the courtroom. Only when disillusionment with the efficacy of rehabilitation motivated a return to classical notions of justice did formalism again come to the fore in sentencing. It follows from this

---

[35] Ibid.

[36] An exemplar of which is Geertz, C., 'Deep Play: Notes on the Balinese Cockfight' in Geertz (ed), *The Interpretation of Cultures* (London: Fontana Press, 1993) 412–53.

[37] Garland, D., *Punishment and Modern Society: A Study in Social Theory* (Oxford: Oxford University Press, 1990) 209–10.

brief historical survey that the meaning of justice can only be understood within the specific culture to which punishment itself contributes.

There is much that is potentially profitable in the analysis of punishment as culture. It places the meaning of punishment at the centre of the enquiry; it reveals how culture determines punishment; and, perhaps more importantly, how punishment contributes to the generation of culture. But there are also dangers in conceiving punishment as a creation and agent of cultural production. Reading punishment as a cultural text invites a focus on penal discourse that has an unnerving tendency to mistake talk for action and in so doing to ignore the countervailing realities of penal practice. Focus on the meaning of punishment tends also to privilege deconstruction over critique: that is, it permits its practitioners to analyse and interpret without the additional burden of taking an evaluative, critical, or normative stance. Finally, by positing punishment as a primary agent in the creation of cultural order, cultural analyses risk overstating the centrality of punishment in modern society. We need to keep firmly in mind the constitutive elements, the varieties in nature and form, and the multiple social roles of punishment, as we turn to the philosophical question, is punishment justified? To do otherwise would create the risk that, though we claim to offer a justification for punishment in the abstract, we find ourselves obliged to acknowledge that, for this particular punishment, no viable justification is after all available.

IS PUNISHMENT JUSTIFIED?

The questions with what justification or to what end is punishment invoked have been the subject of an immense literature spanning penal theory, legal philosophy, and political theory. This literature arises as much from the sense that this particular instance of state action is in need of special justification as from interest in the concept or purpose of punishment per se. Punishment poses a particular moral conundrum, as Duff and Garland observe: 'Punishment requires justification because it is morally problematic. It is morally problematic because it involves doing things to people that (when not described as "punishment") seem morally wrong.'[38]

Literature on the justification of punishment typically asks two questions: 'upon what grounds may the State inflict pain and how much pain

---

[38] Duff, R. A., and Garland, D. (eds), *A Reader on Punishment* (Oxford: Oxford University Press, 1994) 2.

is the State justified in using in this case?' Punishment is one of the most coercive exercises of state power over the individual and, in most instances, causes unpleasant consequences for that individual. It is hardly surprising that it provokes us to question its legitimacy and to think about the limits that should be imposed upon its use. Our attempt to justify occurs at several levels. First, we seek to justify having a coercive system of state punishment at all. Given that it is not only painful to the offender and his or her relatives and dependants but costly also to the taxpayer, we need to offer reasons for persisting with the institution of punishment. The question 'why punish?' is thus an attempt to identify a general justifying aim.[39] Secondly, the question 'how much?' seeks to elicit justification for the level and distribution of punishment and for its particular forms and institutions. Philosophies that focus exclusively on the initial justification of punishment tend to overlook the further question of quantum.[40] If a positive answer to the question 'why punish?' is not to be tantamount to carte blanche for the punisher, then the question 'how much?' is an essential restraint on the infliction of pain.

Whether we can plausibly aspire to a single unitary theory capable of justifying punishment in all its guises seems open to doubt, given the variety and incoherence of penal practice. It is seems unlikely that the same justification could serve for a compensation order as for life imprisonment, or for a fine and for a community rehabilitation order. The sceptically minded might further doubt whether attempts at justification really supply the criteria by which state punishment is justified, its proper quantum calculated, and its just distribution determined. Or are they principally subjects of intellectual industry upon which academic reputations are made but which are of little practical relevance to those who punish; other perhaps than as post-hoc justificatory devices for decisions reached by other means? And what is the status of these justifications in respect of policy making and legislation? Politicians and Home Office mandarins often avert to the various justifications of punishment when announcing policy changes or legislative reform. On some occasions this reflects a genuine attempt to establish a coherent basis for reform.[41] On others, resort to philosophical principles appears as little more than

[39] Walker, N., *Why Punish?* (Oxford: Oxford University Press, 1991).

[40] von Hirsch, A., 'Proportionality in the Philosophy of Punishment: From "Why Punish?" to "How Much?"' (1990) 1 *Criminal Law Forum* 259–90.

[41] Despite the ludicrous misspelling of 'dessert' theory in the White Paper preceding it, the Criminal Justice Act 1991 can be seen as a concerted attempt to base sentencing upon desert theory.

political window-dressing of reforms instituted for other reasons entirely. It is in this somewhat sceptical frame of mind that we turn to the justifications themselves.

RETRIBUTION AND DESERT THEORY

Retribution is probably the oldest and most widely invoked justification of punishment. It is a backward-looking theory in the sense that punishment derives its justification by reference back to the crime rather than from any claim as to future good. The idea of retribution derives historically from the Roman concept of *lex talionis*; illustrated by the biblical phrase, 'Wherever hurt is done, you shall give life for life, eye for eye, tooth for tooth, hand for hand, foot for foot, burn for burn, bruise for bruise, wound for wound.'[42] Immanuel Kant elaborated the philosophical basis for retributivism by arguing that any forward-looking justification for punishment risked treating the subject of punishment solely as a means to an end rather, as retributivism does, as an end in him or herself. Viewing the offender as the end of punishment, Kant required that even 'the last murderer remaining in prison would . . . have to be executed, so that each has done to him what his deeds deserve'.[43]

The cruelty inherent in strict equivalence, and the inapplicability of this equation to much of today's more complex crime, has ensured its demise in modern Western countries.[44] Indeed, there is good evidence that the biblical practice of retributive punishment was never based on strict equivalence. The basic premise that there should be a direct relationship between offence and penalty has proved enduring and has been revived under the guise of desert theory. Modern-day desert theorists share with their retributivist forebears the belief that individuals are free willed and that offenders can therefore be held morally responsible for their actions.[45] Censure and sanction are said to be the appropriate or just response to offending behaviour:[46] not to punish would constitute a failure to acknowledge the offender as a moral being. For the same reasons, desert theory strongly prohibits punishment of the innocent and pays

---

[42] Exodus 21: 23–5.

[43] Cited in Bix, B., *Jurisprudence: Theory and Context* (London: Sweet & Maxwell, 1999) 110.

[44] For a forthright critique of *lex talionis* see Lacey, N., *State Punishment: Political Principles and Community Values* (London: Routledge, 1988) 17–18.

[45] von Hirsch, A., 'Proportionate Sentences: a Desert Perspective' in von Hirsch and Ashworth (eds), *Principled Sentencing: Readings on Theory and Policy* (Oxford: Hart Publishing, 1998) 168–79 at 169–71.

[46] von Hirsch, A., *Censure and Sanctions* (Oxford: Oxford University Press, 1993).

close attention to the capacity of the offender on the grounds that it is only just to punish those who may fairly be held responsible for their wrongdoing. By declaring the gravity of each offence, desert theory is said to permit the rational offender to know in advance how serious their misdeed will be judged to be and what sanction will follow. By recognizing and taming what desert theorists see as an instinctive desire for vengeance, they seek to prevent angry citizens from taking retaliatory action. By insisting that the penalty must be no more than that justified by the gravity of the offence, modern proponents of desert, like von Hirsch and Ashworth, argue that it is a powerful means of limiting judicial discretion and of ensuring parsimony.

By establishing the quantum of punishment proportional to the gravity of the offence, desert theory seeks to secure certainty, consistency, and, most importantly, fairness in punishment.[47] Desert theory relies upon establishing two scales of proportionality: ordinal proportionality ranks offences hierarchically according to their relative seriousness and cardinal proportionality furnishes the overall scale of punishments. In pursuit of ordinal proportionality von Hirsch and Jareborg attempt to scale harm according to the 'living standard analysis' developed by the economist Amatya Sen. This provides an elaborate basis for scaling quality of life and hence measuring intrusions against personal resources and interests such as physical integrity, material support and amenity, freedom from humiliation, privacy, and autonomy.[48] As such it provides one possible basis for scaling harms in order to inform the ordinal scaling of offences. What it cannot protect against, however, is political intervention in the cardinal scaling of overall levels of punishment. The parameters of that scale will always be determined by the most severe penalty; thus a system in which imprisonment is the most severe penalty will inevitably be less punitive than that in which capital punishment sits at its apex.

Several criticisms have been made of the idea of proportionality. The ordinal ranking of offences is problematic. Clearly rape is more serious than indecent assault but how one should rank other offences is less obvious. Is bank robbery more serious than burglary or less? Determining proportionality is more difficult still in the case of inchoate offences

---

[47] von Hirsch, A., *Doing Justice: The Choice of Punishments* (New York: Hill & Wang, 1976); von Hirsch, A., *Past or Future Crimes: Deservedness and Dangerousness in the Sentencing of Criminals* (Manchester: Manchester University Press, 1986); Ashworth, A., 'Criminal Justice and Deserved Sentences' (1989) *Criminal Law Review* 340–55.

[48] von Hirsch, A., and Jareborg, N., 'Gauging Criminal Harm: A Living-Standard Analysis' (1991) 11 *Oxford Journal of Legal Studies* 1–38 at 19.

where no harm has yet occurred. Problems arise also in respect of cardinal proportionality since the location of the scale is vulnerable to external factors such as the punitiveness of the public and politicians, and the willingness of government to commit public funds to punishment. Although proportionality purports to import objectivity into sentencing, it has been argued that its reliance upon an abstract scale of punishments places it at the mercy of the prevailing political climate.[49] Ashworth and von Hirsch seek to rebut this criticism by arguing that no penal theory can wholly withstand political pressure and that, despite claims to the contrary, desert theory 'does not support escalated severities of punishment'.[50] They go on to show that the application of desert theory in many jurisdictions (including Finland, Sweden, Minnesota, and Oregon) has had a significant limiting effect. In fairness, it should also be observed that the immediate effect of desert-based legislation in England was also to reduce the prison population.[51]

Classical desert theory was predicated upon the assumption that offenders are rational, autonomous individuals who, having made the decision to offend, 'deserved' punishment for their wrongdoing. This presumption was criticized by those who counter that desert theory risks ignoring social and economic inequalities among offenders.[52] Thus the starving tramp who steals in order to eat is deemed to deserve the same measure of punishment as the casual, well-fed shoplifter. The acknowledgement that many offenders operate in conditions of structural disadvantage has led desert theorists to abandon the claim to be removing an unfair advantage in order to restore a pre-existing equilibrium;[53] since, on one view at least, that equilibrium is in fact a dis-equilibrium. This leaves open the question of whether desert theory can adequately acknowledge gender, racial, and other significant differences among offenders.[54]

In the face of these criticisms, Duff promotes desert theory as a communicative device for censuring wrongful behaviour in such a way

[49] Garland, D., *The Culture of Control: Crime and Social Order in Contemporary Society* (Oxford: Oxford University Press, 2001) 9.

[50] von Hirsch, A., and Ashworth, A., *Punishment and Proportionality* (Oxford: Oxford University Press, 2005 forthcoming) ch. 8.

[51] The failure of the desert-based Criminal Justice Act 1991 to bring about long-term reduction can best be explained by the subversive attitudes and actions of the judiciary and the repeal of key sections under the Criminal Justice Act 1993.

[52] Hudson, B., *Justice through Punishment: A Critique of the 'Justice' Model of Corrections* (Basingstoke: Macmillan, 1987).

[53] von Hirsch, A., *Censure and Sanctions* (Oxford: Oxford University Press, 1993) 7–8.

[54] Hudson, B., 'Doing Justice to Difference' in Ashworth and Wasik (eds), *Fundamentals of Sentencing Theory* (Oxford: Clarendon Press, 1998).

that it permits the offender to rejoin the moral consensus.[55] Whether the notion of a moral consensus is less problematic in a modern pluralist, multi-cultural, multi-faith society than the notion of social equilibrium is another question. It is also open to doubt whether censure can be communicated without imposing stigma, which is itself counterproductive to readmission. One attempt to overcome these criticisms is to be found in von Hirsch's moral theory of human agency in which he suggests that the communicative power of punishment lies in providing offenders with the opportunity to reflect upon what they have done:

A response to criminal wrongdoing that conveys blame gives the individual the opportunity to respond in ways that are typically those of an agent capable of moral deliberation: to recognize the wrongfulness of the action; feel remorse; to make efforts to desist in future—or to try to give reasons why the conduct was not actually wrong.[56]

To do otherwise, he argues would be to treat individuals as 'beasts in a circus' who must be coerced into submission because they are incapable of understanding that their conduct is wrong. On this view, hard treatment is less a means of communicating censure than an additional prudential reason for obedience. This approach thus moves away from the much-criticized presumption of perfect moral agency to acknowledge that we are 'moral but fallible agents who need some prudential supplement to help us resist criminal temptation'.[57]

CONSEQUENTIALIST THEORIES

Consequentialist theories go beyond the crime to justify punishment by making claims about the desirability of its future consequences. These theories are sometimes also known as reductivist because they claim that 'the incidence of crime will be less than it would be if no penalty were imposed'.[58] In general, though not invariably, they are based upon Utilitarianism, a moral theory advanced by Jeremy Bentham that relies upon a 'felicific calculus' as the proper basis for morality and legislation. This calculus is often captured in Bentham's maxim 'the greatest happiness of

---

[55] Duff, R. A., *Punishment, Communication and Community* (Oxford: Oxford University Press, 2001) 27–30.

[56] von Hirsch, A., 'Proportionate Sentences: a Desert Perspective' in von Hirsch and Ashworth (eds), *Principled Sentencing: Readings on Theory and Policy* (Oxford: Hart Publishing, 1998) 170.

[57] Ibid. 171.

[58] Cavadino, M., and Jignan, J., *The Penal System: An Introduction* (3rd edn, London: Sage, 2002) 34.

the greatest number', though this phrase slightly obscures Bentham's original intention that felicity of the community be derived by summing up the pleasure and pain of each individual within it.[59] Punishment of the individual is justified, therefore, only where it can be shown that the good derived thereby outweighs the pain. To the Kantian objection that this is to use individuals as means to others' ends, it might be replied that to the extent that the individual also derives benefit—from being reformed, living in a society in which attempts are made to reduce crime, and being readmitted to civil society—the individual is not merely a means but also the end or beneficiary of punishment.

General deterrence

Deterrence is at least as old as retribution and historically was the predominant basis for punishment. Even today deterrence has a strong intuitive appeal. If we ask ourselves what punishment is for, we instinctively respond that it is about reducing crime by discouraging others. Deterrence has a simple rationale: it presumes that the knowledge that criminal acts will be punished works upon the minds of anyone contemplating committing a crime or tempted to do so to inhibit wrongdoing (general deterrence); whilst the infliction of punishment on actual offenders will encourage them, through the experience of painful consequences, to desist in the future (specific or individual deterrence). Deterrence can further be subdivided into initial and marginal effects. As von Hirsch and colleagues observe: 'initial deterrence concerns the effects of initiating a prohibition against previously permissible conduct . . . Marginal deterrence concerns the increased (or decreased) deterrence that results from altering enforcement policies or penalties concerning conduct which already is punishable.'[60] Whilst it is the former claim of initial deterrence that provides the overarching justification for punishment, it is the latter claim to marginal deterrence that provides the justification for any given mode or amount of punishment.

Another crucial distinction in deterrence theory lies between certainty and severity of punishment. Certainty refers to the likelihood of being caught and punished, and severity to the stringency of the punishment imposed. Where the perceived risk of detection is low, then deterrence theory would require the perceived severity of the penalty to be cor-

---

[59] Bentham, J., *Introduction to the Principles of Morals and Legislation* (London: Methuen, 1982) ch. 13.

[60] von Hirsch, A. *et al. Criminal Deterrence and Sentence Severity: An Analysis of Recent Research* (Oxford: Hart Publishing, 1999) 5.

respondingly high. For example, prior to the establishment of formal police forces in the early nineteenth century, the chances of detection were low. In the eighteenth century, it was deemed necessary to impose draconian penalties under the so-called 'Bloody Code' to persuade people of the risks of breaking the law. The risk of apprehension was slight but the consequences if caught were so severe as to play upon the mind of the prospective sheep stealer or purse-snatcher. The terrifying spectacle of public execution or the offender's corpse rotting on the gibbet was intended to have a powerful effect on the minds of its observers.[61] Only later in the eighteenth century did Enlightenment thinkers, such as Cesare Beccaria, baulk at the brutality of such punishments and suggest that certainty of punishment might serve the purpose of deterrence better than spectacular, barbaric punishment of the few.[62] Although we generally no longer resort to such barbaric penalties,[63] it is still the case that where crimes are difficult to police the threatened consequences of detection are set correspondingly high. Fare evasion, smoking, and vandalism on public transport are all examples of offences which, being hard to police, attract high fines. So too non-purchase of television licences, non-payment of taxes, and other such offences that are difficult to detect are attended by costly consequences for evasion.

Theories of general deterrence draw upon Bentham's philosophy of Utilitarianism. They claim that the pain of punishment and the costs of imposing that pain upon the offender are outweighed by the social benefits consequently enjoyed. If punishment deters prospective offenders and thus reduces the risk of crime, citizens enjoy a greater sense of security. Deterrence also relies upon rational choice theory in that it assumes that individuals make rational calculations in order to maximize their preferences.[64] Individual rationality may be bounded in the sense that in assessing the costs and benefits entailed, individuals will be influenced by their values, attitudes and beliefs, and the information (however inaccurate or incomplete) available to them. What individuals believe the certainty or severity of punishment to be is, therefore, crucial. Their

---

[61] Hay, D., 'Property, Authority and the Criminal Law' in Hay *et al.* (eds), *Albion's Fatal Tree: Crime and Society in Eighteenth Century England* (London: Allen Lane, 1975) 17–63.

[62] Sharpe, J. A., *Judicial Punishment in England* (London: Faber & Faber, 1990) 6–7.

[63] Though see Simon, J., ' "Entitlement to Cruelty": The End of Welfare and the Punitive Mentality in the United States' in Stenson and Sullivan (eds), *Crime, Risk, and Justice* (Cullompton, Devon: Willan Publishing, 2001).

[64] Cornish, D. B., and Clarke, R. V. (eds), *The Reasoning Criminal: Rational Choice Perspectives on Offending* (New York: Springer, 1986).

subjective perception of the risk of detection or punishment is more important than what it actually is. Those contemplating crime need to observe, or read, or hear about the pains actually suffered by others. In theory, if the public could be persuaded that the penalty had been inflicted, irrespective of whether it had or not, then that appearance alone would suffice and the actual infliction of pain would be unjustified. Of course, the activities of investigative journalists would be likely to uncover a total sham. It is, however, perhaps plausible that lesser punishments, suitably repackaged, could achieve the same deterrent effect as more severe ones. Effective publicity might be more important than the actual infliction of pain. In the case of severe penalties, it is sometimes said that their mere existence has a symbolic significance that has an intangible effect. Some countries, for example Belgium until quite recently, retained the death penalty but had not invoked it for many years. The mere existence of the penalty on the statute books was considered a sufficient deterrent.

General deterrence is commonly criticized on the grounds that it is neither effective nor morally acceptable. Examining first the question of efficacy, it should be obvious that for deterrence to be legitimate its claim to deter must be proven. Gaining empirical evidence is problematic since it is difficult to separate out the precise impact of deterrence from other influences upon potential offenders' decision-making processes. Deterrence is predicated on the rational calculation of the offender, but those who need to be deterred most may be pathologically lacking in self-control, addicted to drugs or alcohol, suffering from mental disorder, relish risk tasking, or simply be impulsive. To the extent that prospective offenders are risk averse, it is the risk of being caught rather than the remote possibility of particularly unpleasant consequences that is more likely to play upon their minds. Presuming that potential offenders engage in rational calculation as to the risk of apprehension, conviction, and sentence, they are unlikely to foresee themselves as belonging to that small class of those who are ultimately punished.

There is also a danger that the punitive quality of deterrent penalties will tend, cumulatively, to have a brutalizing impact on the general public. This impact is likely to be directly correlated with the cruelty of the punishment. As Cesare Beccaria famously observed of the ultimate sanction: 'the death penalty cannot be useful because of the example of barbarity it gives men. . . . It seems to me absurd that the laws, which are expression of the public will, which detest and punish homicide, should themselves commit it.[65] To the extent that penalties are considered to be unjustifiably harsh, they are liable to provoke evasive tactics. Historically, it has been shown that where penalties are deemed overly severe, prosecutors are unwilling to charge or resort to charging lesser offences, juries are reluctant to convict, and judges are loath to impose the required sanction.[66]

A second, thornier issue is that of moral acceptability. Deterrence theory is open to several obvious abuses. There is nothing inherent within it to inhibit punishment of the innocent, or to prevent disproportionate sentences in order to inflict exemplary punishment on those convicted of crimes a society particularly wishes to discourage. For example, if securing maximum publicity deters most, then punishing well-known public figures who attract extensive media coverage is likely to be more efficacious than punishing the less well known. To punish politicians and pop stars more than their unknown counterparts uses the offender as a means to securing social ends and, as Lacey has observed: 'individuals may be sacrificed to this dominant purpose.'[67] A second moral objection is that deterrence theory does not specify how much pain is necessary to achieve reduction nor at what level the infliction of pain is justifiable. If it were possible to state with certainty that the death penalty was the surest means of securing general deterrence, might this not legitimize inflicting it in cases where it was really important to deter? One answer might be that to the extent that deterrence is guided by Utilitarian principles, the felicific calculus imposes limits on the infliction of pain. It might also be said to imply proportionality on the grounds that if one punished a lesser offence as severely as a more serious offence, there would be no disincentive not to commit the latter rather than the former: one might as well be hung for the proverbial sheep as for a lamb.

Individual deterrence

Unlike general deterrence, individual or special deterrence is not concerned with imponderable calculations about the wider public but only with deterring the convicted offender from reoffending. The degree of

---

[65] Beccaria, C., *On Crimes and Punishments* (New York: Marsiho Classics, 1996) 50. See also Hood, R., *The Death Penalty: A World-Wide Perspective* (Oxford: Clarendon Press, 1989) 120.

[66] On the myriad means by which the rigours of the Bloody Code were mitigated in eighteenth-century England, see Beattie, J. A., *Judicial Punishment in England* (London: Faber & Faber, 1990) 36–49.

[67] Lacey, N., *State Punishment: Political Principles and Community Values* (London: Routledge, 1988) 29.

punishment thus needs to be precisely tailored to what is known about the offender and what is likely to deter that particular individual. This requires that the court collect information about the character, history, circumstance, and offending in order to work out what level of penalty is needed to prevent a recurrence. If an offender persistently offends, individual deterrence suggests that since the penalty has patently failed in the past, it is necessary to increase the level of pain. It is partly this reasoning (but partly also the drive to incapacitation) that led to the introduction of two and 'three strikes' sentencing policies under the Crime (Sentences) Act 1997. These require that a life sentence be imposed on an offender convicted of a second serious violent or sexual offence; a minimum of seven years' imprisonment on an offender convicted of trafficking Class A drugs for the third time; and a minimum of three years' imprisonment on an offender convicted for a third time of domestic burglary.

Again, the theory can be subject to critical scrutiny on the grounds of efficacy and moral acceptability. There is little evidence that individuals subject to more severe sentences on deterrent grounds reoffend less than those subject to less severe ones (though very long sentences do appear to result in lower reconviction rates). Measuring reoffending is practically impossible, so studies tend to reply upon the uncertain proxy of reconviction records. Thus the offender who appears to have been deterred may simply have learned more sophisticated means of avoiding detection. Moreover, punishment itself has criminogenic side effects that run counter to its deterrent properties. The stigmatizing effects of conviction and punishment may increase the likelihood of reoffending because, so labelled, the offender finds it more difficult to succeed in honest society. The disruption to home life and loss of employment that attend custodial penalties; exposure to criminogenic influences within prison, and even while serving a community penalty, all increase the likelihood of reoffending. Very severe penalties may have brutalizing effects upon those subject to them. For example, the 'Short, Sharp, Shock'[68] regime of detention centres instituted for juvenile offenders in the early 1980s were intended quite literally to shock juveniles out of offending. But the regime of harsh discipline and military drill proved to be so brutalizing for both officers and boys that detention centres were abolished just six years later, in 1988.

On the question of whether individual deterrence is morally acceptable

---

[68] Under the Criminal Justice Act 1982. See Morris, A., and Giller, H., *Understanding Juvenile Justice* (London: Croom Helm, 1987) 121.

several objections arise, not least that setting the penalty by reference to the demands of deterrence may lead to inconsistency and unfairness. The utterly repentant offender, unlikely to repeat their crime, would not need to be punished however serious the offence for which they stand convicted, whereas the unrepentant offender who appears unlikely to change might attract a penalty greatly disproportionate to the present offence. Utilitarian principles again ought to provide some guard against excessive penalties. As does the requirement that for marginal deterrence to be effective there must be a clear ranking between offences because if the punishment is the same, an offender has no incentive not to commit a more serious offence. It will not, however, prevent the overall scale being set high since a deterrence-based scale, unfettered by any countervailing impulse to parsimony, will tend toward greater severity.

Rehabilitation

If the heyday of deterrence theory was the eighteenth century, rehabilitation can be traced back to the early and mid-nineteenth-century experiments with reformatory schools for juvenile offenders, like Mettray in France, and the birth of the model convict prisons, like Pentonville in England, based upon reformatory principles. The early twentieth-century writings of the Italian Positivist School,[69] founded by Cesare Lombroso and whose members included Enrico Ferri and Raffaele Garofalo, was arguably the first systematic attempt to enquire into the personal characteristics of offenders and to set out a new paradigm of punishment that rejected notions of criminal responsibility and proportionate punishment. Focusing on the pathology of offenders, it identified mental, physical, and moral characteristics that marked out the born and the habitual criminal. Although its more bizarre claims, for example concerning the atavistic physical characteristics of 'born criminals', were later subject to scientific scrutiny and criticism, it introduced the idea that punishment should be about making good the defects of those who offend. Arguably, more influential still was the rise of the new Liberalism and the considerable raft of reforms introduced in Britain in the years around the beginning of the twentieth century.[70]

Rehabilitation or welfarism remained prominent for much of the first half of the twentieth century and arguably reached its zenith in the

---

[69] Radzinowicz, L., and Hood, R., *The Emergence of Penal Policy in Victorian and Edwardian England* (Oxford: Oxford University Press, 1986) ch. 1.

[70] Garland describes these as instituting the 'modern penal complex': Garland, D., *Punishment and Welfare: A History of Penal Strategies* (London: Gower, 1985) 18.

1960s.[71] At its height, punishment was recast as a means of restoring the offender to good citizenship through programmes of training, treatment, counselling, psychotherapy, drug and even shock treatment. Rehabilitation seeks to change those aspects of the offender's personality, traits, views, lifestyle, and life chances that predispose them to crime and to develop such qualities, skills, and opportunities as might enable them to desist from offending. It relies heavily on the expertise of members of the 'psy-' professions, social workers, and educationalists who diagnose the causes of offending behaviour, and prescribe and implement reformative programmes in response. It has been particularly influential in respect of juvenile offenders who, unlike their adult counterparts, are considered both in need of moral education and particularly susceptible to its teachings.[72] Central to rehabilitation is penal optimism or faith in the ability of penal measures to bring about change. In determining the amount of punishment to be imposed, rehabilitation eschews proportionality as liable to deliver too much to the offender who is already rehabilitated or too little to the offender in need of further intervention. Instead the quantum of punishment is set by expert assessment of the needs of the offender and the success or failure of the reform measures applied. It follows that rehabilitation is characterized by considerable discretion both at the sentencing stage and, more particularly, in the implementation of penal measures.

Rehabilitation is based upon a series of premises which when subject to critical scrutiny look decidedly questionable. It assumes that delinquency always has causes which are discoverable and open to treatment; that if offenders are not treated they will get worse; and that treatment, even if coerced, is not punitive since it is doing the offender good. It overlooks the fact that much offending is opportunistic. It ignores evidence that, amongst juveniles especially, offending may represent no more than a passing phase out of which the majority will grow unaided. It fails to recognize that crime is not necessarily the product of pathology but may represent perfectly rational behaviour in the constrained circumstances in which the offender is placed. Moreover, despite claims that rehabilitation is about doing good, treatment programmes are often experienced by the offender as painful and unwelcome. From the perspective of desert theory, to the extent that these programmes are disproportionate to the gravity of the offence, they constitute an unwarranted burden upon the

---

[71] Radzinowicz, L., *Adventures in Criminology* (London: Routledge, 1999) ch. 3.

[72] Morris, A., and Giller, H., *Understanding Juvenile Justice* (London: Croom Helm, 1987) ch. 3.

offender. Women, in particular, are liable to be subject to intensive treatment for relatively minor offences, particularly if they are considered to
be in 'moral danger' or at risk to themselves or their dependants. In some
cases, the treatment dictated by rehabilitation is considerably more intrusive and painful than that dictated by conventional punishment. If the
only criterion of success for rehabilitation is preventing reoffending then,
in some cases at least, diversionary tactics or legitimate alternatives to
delinquent behaviour might equally succeed.

The most questionable assumption underlying rehabilitation is that it
is effective in reforming people's behaviour. A primary difficulty is fixing
criteria by which the offender can be considered reformed. Reconviction
rates provide information only about those who have been caught and
successfully prosecuted. They tell nothing of those who have evaded
detection. For those who have been convicted, reconviction rates do not
indicate the type of offence they have gone on to commit. Should those
treated for a serious sexual or violent crime, now convicted of a minor
property offence be regarded as a success or a failure of the treatment
regime? A proper measure might be a test of the offender's improved
moral or social health, but how does one judge if an offender is now a
better person? However reliable the quality of reconviction data or
sophisticated the statistical analysis, this basic ambiguity about what constitutes success leaves rehabilitation exposed to shifting climates of penal
optimism. A now infamous article by Martinson, that began with the
question 'what works?' and concluded dramatically that 'nothing works',
sparked a decline of penal optimism in the 1970s.[73] Martinson's refuta-
tion of rehabilitation has since been challenged by studies that highlight
the difficulties of assessing efficacy and suggest that some forms of treatment, adapted to the specific needs of certain types of offender, do
work.[74] The rise, collapse and rekindling of faith in the rehabilitative ideal
would seem more to have to do with changing political climate, therefore,
than to reflect conclusive evidence of its failure or success.

The claim that rehabilitation is about doing good has been used to

[73] Martinson, R., 'What Works? Questions and Answers About Prison Reform' (1974)
Public Interest 22–54. In fact the article identified some successes and was swiftly followed
by a less publicized retraction by him.
[74] Maguire, J. (ed.), *What Works? Reducing Reoffending: Guidelines from Research and Practice* (Chichester: John Wiley & Sons, 1995); Vennard, J. *et al.*, *Changing offenders' attitudes
and behaviour: What works?* (London: HMSO, 1997); Rex, S., 'Beyond cognitive behaviouralism? Reflections on the effectiveness literature' in Bottoms, Gelsthorpe, and Rex (eds),
Community Penalties: Change and Challenges (Cullompton, Devon: Willan Publishing,
2003).

justify extensive intervention in the lives of offenders. In some countries, fixed-term sentences were replaced by indefinite treatment programmes, the length of which depended upon the progress of treatment. Judicial authority was thus subordinated to the expertise of doctors, psychiatrists, psychologists, and social workers and the offender released only when deemed cured. The decision to release depends upon the offender attaining contestable standards of normality. Deciding upon the nature of these standards, how they should be applied, and at what point the offender should be deemed to have attained them gives the state extensive paternalistic powers over the individual, who may not accept the therapeutically derived conception of normality imposed upon them. Research has shown that women offenders are particularly likely to be judged abnormal, or even mentally ill, for their failure to conform to conventional social norms or notions of sexual propriety.[75] Given that treatment depends on the nature of the pathologies identified and is directed toward the characteristics of the individual, rehabilitation is liable to impose disparate sentences on those convicted of like offences.

How grave one judges this potential problem of fairness to be will depend upon the weight one gives to considerations of proportionality and consistency. If one sees punishment as inherently entailing blame and pain, then it is difficult to justify decoupling the penalty from the blameworthiness of the conduct that invited it. If one views rehabilitation as displacing the impulse to censure and sanction, then inconsistency and disproportionality might be considered less problematic. But one would have to be sure that no such blame or pain was in fact entailed before these concerns dissipate entirely. The sceptically minded might be inclined to concur with the conclusion drawn by von Hirsch and Maher: 'The most dangerous temptation is to treat the treatment ethic as a kind of edifying fiction, that if only we cared—and minister treatment to offenders as a sign of our caring—a more human penal system will emerge . . . Such thinking is a recipe for failure.'[76]

Incapacitation

Incapacitation is at least as old as the prison and in part underpinned earlier, more brutal penalties such as amputation. Today, as Zimring and

---

[75] Allen, H., *Justice Unbalanced: Gender, Psychiatry and Judicial Decisions* (Milton Keynes: Open University Press, 1987); Heidensohn, F., *Sexual Politics and Social Control* (Buckingham: Open University Press, 2000).

[76] von Hirsch, A., and Maher, L., 'Should Penal Rehabilitationism be Revived?' in von Hirsch and Ashworth (eds), *Principled Sentencing: Readings on Theory and Policy* (Oxford: Hart Publishing, 1998) 32.

Hawkins observe, incapacitation enjoys 'dominance by default'.[77] Critical academic attention to other consequentialist rationales of punishment has undermined faith in deterrence and rehabilitation. Incapacitation, by contrast, has attracted little academic interest, allowing it to rise to prominence relatively unscathed.

A striking feature of incapacitation is that it is based upon no assumptions about human character or capacity for change. Incapacitation makes no claim to be able to reform or cure or deter the offender. Its more modest aim is to restrict the offender's liberty, movements, or capacity to do wrong. Nor is incapacitation concerned only with responding to harm done, but with preventing that which has yet to occur. It seeks to protect the public from future harms by trying to identify those who pose a serious risk of reoffending and restraining them in such a way as to minimize this risk. This is most usually done by containing individuals so as to ensure that they cannot reoffend for the period of their sentence, or by otherwise limiting their capacity to offend.[78]

Incapacitation asserts a common right to the presumption of security in person and property, and imposes upon the state a duty to protect against foreseeable threats to security. In pursuit of this protection, it is prepared to impose penalties longer than those that are proportional to the offence and it favours penalties with incapacitative potential. Incarceration is the most obviously incapacitative penalty for serious offenders. For example, the mandatory life sentence for murder and the use of the life sentence in respect of other serious offences serves not only retributive but also incapacitative purposes: release of the offender depends on the risk they are deemed to pose and their continued liberty depends on good behaviour. But lesser penalties can also have an incapacitative effect, for example disqualification from driving for drunken drivers, or curfews imposed on those convicted of public order offences. Alongside deterrence, incapacitation is clearly central to such penalties, as are ideas about the dangerousness of offenders and society's need to be protected from them.[79]

If the primary purpose of incapacitation is to reduce future risk, then it

---

[77] Zimring, F. E., and Hawkins, G., *Incapacitation: Penal Confinement and the Restraint of Crime* (New York: Oxford University Press, 1995) 3.

[78] See Floud, J., and Young, W., *Dangerousness and Criminal Justice* (London: Heinemann, 1981) and the special issue of the *British Journal of Criminology* (July 1982) on dangerousness, esp. Bottoms, A. E., and Brownsword, R., 'The Dangerousness Debate after the Floud Report' (1982) 22 *British Journal of Criminology* 229–54.

[79] Pratt, J., 'Dangerousness and Modern Society' in Brown and Pratt (eds), *Dangerous Offenders: Punishment and Social Order* (London: Routledge, 2000).

is unclear why its remit should be confined to known offenders. Arguably anyone who can be shown to pose a serious risk to society should be restrained.[80] Incapacitation, seen this way, becomes less a rationale for punishment than a ground for instituting social quarantine with conditions no more punitive than is necessary to restrain. Against the right to quarantine stands the countervailing right of citizens to be presumed harmless until they have, by their action, forfeited this right. On this account, only proven offenders are legitimate targets for incapacitation, whilst those who reoffend forfeit any residual right to be presumed harmless.

Incapacitation is open to serious criticism on both empirical and moral grounds. First, it presumes that it is possible to identify with sufficient certainty those who are likely to reoffend. Yet surveys reveal a very high 'false positive' rate in prediction attempts. One British study showed that nine out of ten serious sexual offenders thought by the Parole Board to pose a high risk were not reconvicted of a sexual offence within four years of their release.[81] This very high rate of false positives reveals the propensity of the Parole Board to overestimate risk and the limited ability of experts to predict with certainty. Given the difficulty of predicting who poses a serious risk of reoffending, the potential of incapacitation to reduce risk is questionable. Moreover, short of capital punishment, incapacitative penalties cannot claim to remove, but only displace or postpone, risk. The prisoner may not pose a threat to the wider population but continues to do so to his fellow inmates.[82] In all but a tiny number of cases, the offender will eventually be released. Long incapacitative sentences delay reoffending and very long sentences do appear to reduce reconviction rates, though it may be that desistance results from ageing. But the difficulties of returning to life in society may also increase the likelihood of reoffending when the prisoner is eventually released. The gain of short-term protection must, therefore, be weighed against exacerbating future risk.

Incapacitation is also open to a number of ethical objections. First, it determines the quantum of punishment not by reference to the offence

---

[80] Wood, D., 'Dangerous Offenders, and the Morality of Protective Sentencing' (1988) *Criminal Law Review* 424–33 at 426.

[81] Hood, R. *et al.*, 'Sex Offenders Emerging from Long-Term Imprisonment: A Study of Their Long-Term Reconviction Rates and of Parole Board Members' Judgments of Their Risk' (2002) 42 *British Journal of Criminology* 371–94.

[82] Few would be prepared to argue that by virtue of their sentence, prisoners have lost all rights to protection. On the prevalence of violence in prisons see Edgar, K. *et al.*, *Prison Violence: the Dynamics of Conflict, Fear and Power* (Cullompton, Devon: Willan Publishing, 2003).

but according to indicators of future risk (typically the offender's previous criminal record, their social situation, character, and prospects). Reference to these other factors may result in a penalty well beyond that which is deserved for the present offence alone.[83] Given the difficulty of predicting which offenders pose a future risk to society, imposing incapacitative sentences may extend restraint unjustly. Secondly, even if it were possible to predict risk with absolute certainty,[84] it might be objected that the rights of the individual should not be overridden in pursuit of the majority interest. The strength of this objection depends upon the gravity of the crime predicted and might be outweighed by the risk of a very serious crime reoccurring. Thirdly, given that the public tend to overstate their collective need for protection and demand punitive sentences well beyond those justified by risk, we should be wary of permitting future risk to dictate present punishment. It is not surprising that defining at what level of seriousness and certainty the risk should be before incapacitation becomes justifiable has been the subject of much philosophical discussion.[85]

Despite these objections, as Zimring and Hawkins observe, incapacitation lies behind, and provides the dominant justification for, the massive increase in the prison population. Every serious crime committed by a known offender is portrayed as a failure of incapacitation and, in a crude sense, it is. Populist politicians and journalists play upon the enormous intuitive appeal of incapacitation in their common assertion that only when dangerous predators are locked up can decent people sleep soundly in their beds at night. The practical difficulty of determining who is and who is not dangerous remains.

Restorative justice

It is questionable whether restorative justice should be considered a theory of punishment at all since it does not seek to justify punishment and is critical of punitive responses to offending. Rather, restorative justice seeks to make good the harm done and in so doing to shift attention from the culpability of the offender to the harms suffered. In contrast to earlier

---

[83] Honderich, T., 'On Justifying Protective Punishment' (1982) 22 *British Journal of Criminology* 268–75; von Hirsch, A., 'Selective Incapacitation: Some Doubts' in von Hirsch and Ashworth (eds), *Principled Sentencing: Readings on Theory and Policy* (Oxford: Hart Publishing, 1998) 125.

[84] For an illuminating fictional treatment of this possibility see Dick, P. K., *Minority Report* (London: Gollancz, 2002).

[85] Zimring, F. E., and Hawkins, G., *Incapacitation: Penal Confinement and the Restraint of Crime* (New York: Oxford University Press, 1995) ch. 4 reviews this literature.

theories it recognizes the harm not only to the victim but also to the offender and his or her friends and family; to the social relationship between offender and victim; and to the wider community. There is no single theory of restorative justice. Rather restorative justice (or RJ as it is commonly known) is a convenient umbrella term for a variety of related theories concerned with the restoration of the offender, victim, and community. Other terms used in broadly the same sense include community justice, positive justice, reintegrative justice, reparative justice, relational justice, and transformative justice but the term restorative justice increasingly prevails.[86]

Contemporary restorative justice has its roots in earlier experiments in mediation and reparation carried out in the 1970s and 1980s. These experiments sought to resolve disputes without recourse to the criminal courts and to divert offenders from punishment by allowing both victim and offender to retain control and voice their grievances under the supervision of a mediator. Advocates of mediation questioned the presumption that responding to crime is the preserve of legal authority and saw the state as having usurped the historic right of the victim to seek recompense for harm done. The central premise was that crimes are disputes whose resolution is a matter for offender and victim or, to put it another way, that the original parties should retain control over their property in the dispute.[87] By providing for mediation between victim and offender or encouraging the offender to pay compensation to the victim for their injuries, it also furnished the opportunity to make good.[88] Aside from material loss, it recognized that crime entails loss of security. In order to restore the victim's sense of security, it encouraged offenders to account and apologize for their conduct.

Another important root of restorative justice lies in growing knowledge and concern about victims of crime. The development of the sub-discipline of victimology generated many quantitative and qualitative research studies on victims that furnished new data on the emotional, psychological, physical, and material effects of crime.[89] These data,

---

[86] Marshall, T., *Restorative Justice: An Overview* (London: Home Office, 1999) 7; Braithwaite, J., *Restorative Justice and Responsive Regulation* (Oxford: Oxford University Press, 2001) 11.

[87] Christie, N., 'Conflicts as Property' (1977) 17 *British Journal of Criminology* 1–15.

[88] Davis, G., *Making Amends: Mediation and Reparation in Criminal Justice* (London: Routledge, 1992).

[89] For an overview of research on the impact of crime see Zedner, L., 'Victims' in Maguire, Morgan, and Reiner (eds), *The Oxford Handbook of Criminology* (3rd edn, Oxford: Oxford University Press, 2002) 428–32.

effectively mobilized by a burgeoning victims' movement,[90] led to demands for reduced reliance on punitive disposals aimed solely at the offender and greater recognition of the needs and interests of victims. As an early proponent of victims' interests, Barnett argued, 'Justice consists of the culpable offender making good the loss he has caused . . . Where once we saw an offense against society, we now see an offense against an individual.'[91] The logic of this approach demanded a shift in attention from the larger social interest in punishment, and from the culpability of the offender, toward the right of the victim to receive recognition, information about the progress of the case, compensation, and support.

If the growth of mediation and reparation and of victimology furnished its foundations, contemporary restorative justice derives much of its inspiration and political credibility from models of community justice in use in traditional cultures, particularly the indigenous peoples of North America and New Zealand. Native American sentencing circles, indigenous Canadian peacemaking processes, and Maori justice have inspired experiments in family group conferencing, restorative conferencing, restorative cautions, and community conferencing. In contrast to its forebear mediation, restorative justice replaces bi- or tripartite resolution with conferences involving all those deemed to have an interest, however tangential. The concept of conferencing is central to restorative justice, as we can see in the United Nations' definition of restorative justice as a process 'in which the victim, the offender and/or any other individuals or community members affected by a crime participate actively together in the resolution of matters arising from the crime'.[92]

One difficulty in identifying the central premises of restorative justice is that the theory takes many forms, each with its own foundations and orientation. Certain core characteristics can, however, be identified. Fundamental is the idea of stakeholder deliberation, namely that 'all the parties with a stake in a particular offence come together to resolve collectively how to deal with the aftermath of the offence and its

---

[90] In Britain, Victim Support and in America, National Organization for Victim Assistance (NOVA) are the main organizations. There are a proliferating number of small organizations such as the Zito Trust, Support After Murder and Manslaughter (SAMM), Victim's Voice, and Justice for Victims. Many of these are high-profile lobby groups actively campaigning for victims' rights.

[91] Barnett, R., 'Restitution: A New Paradigm of Criminal Justice' (1977) 87 *Ethics* 279–301 at 287–8.

[92] United Nations, *Draft Declaration on Basic Principles on the Use of Restorative Justice Programmes in Criminal Matters* (New York: UN, 1999).

implications for the future'.[93] The stakeholders thus determine what restoration means in any particular context. The problem is that this pragmatic definition gives little indication of the values that the process should espouse. Core values commonly agreed upon by advocates include mutual respect and consensual participation by all parties, understanding and forgiveness on the part of the victim, and moral learning, responsibility, and penitence on the part of the offender. The importance of accountability is a late but important addition to these core values and one that poses particular problems in the context of the informal, closed conferences that are the hallmark of restorative justice.[94]

The aims of restorative justice are similarly broad ranging and tend to be characterized by extraordinary ambition.[95] Restorative justice, it is claimed, simultaneously restores the harm done to victims, reintegrates the offender into civil society, restores and rebuilds the community, and reduces crime.[96] It is arguable, however, that evaluating restorative justice in terms of its aims and outcomes misses its essential characteristic: concern with the process itself. The important feature of restorative justice is arguably less what it ultimately achieves, or even aims to achieve, than the manner in which it seeks to do so. Incorporation of the victim as a central player in the response to crime, antipathy to coercion, promotion of dialogue, reparation, reconciliation, and constructive solution stand in striking contrast to the censure and sanction model of traditional penal theory.

This said, restorative justice can and has been subject to criticism. A primary issue is its claim to displace the existing paradigm of punishment. Although its lack of penal character is part of its appeal, retributivists object that restorative justice fails to provide adequate justification for the burdens it nonetheless imposes nor does it supply any mechanism for guarding against disproportionality.[97] To the extent that it aims to make

---

[93] Tony Marshall quoted in Braithwaite, J., *Restorative Justice and Responsive Regulation* (Oxford: Oxford University Press, 2001) 11.

[94] Roche, D., *Accountability in Restorative Justice* (Oxford: Oxford University Press, 2003).

[95] Zehr, H., *Changing Lenses: A New Focus for Criminal Justice* (Scottdale, Penn.: Herald Press, 1990); Braithwaite, J., 'Principles of Restorative Justice' in von Hirsch, Roberts, and Bottoms (eds), *Restorative Justice and Criminal Justice: Competing or Reconcilable Paradigms?* (Oxford: Hart Publishing, 2003) 1.

[96] Braithwaite, J., *Crime, Shame and Reintegration* (Cambridge: Cambridge University Press, 1989). See also the claims made by the contributors to Strang, H., and Braithwaite, J. (eds), *Restorative Justice and Civil Society* (Cambridge: Cambridge University Press, 2001).

[97] von Hirsch, A., Ashworth, A., and Shearing, C., 'Specifying Aims and Limits for Restorative Justice: A "Making Amends" Model?' in von Hirsch, *et al.* (eds), *Restorative Justice and Criminal Justice: Competing or Reconcilable Paradigms?* (Oxford: Hart Publishing, 2003) 30–1.

good the harm done, it might be said to provide the rationale for the enforcement of civil, but not criminal, liability. Likewise, in focusing on the harm done to the victim, restorative justice has a tendency to ignore the public nature of the wrong done and, in effect, to privatize it. Whether society's interests are served by restoring the victim alone is doubtful: take for example the case of the serial drink driver who runs over a forgiving victim. Even if restoration is extended to the wider community of stakeholders, this may not satisfy the legitimate public interest.

In its focus on harm, restorative justice tends also to ignore the offender's culpability, traditionally thought to be the basis of criminal liability and hence of punishment.[98] Moreover, reorientation around responses to harm makes little sense in respect of attempts, conspiracies, conduct crimes (such as careless driving), precursor offences (such as possessing firearms), and other offences where no harm has yet been caused. Likewise reorientation toward the victim provides little guidance on to how to deal with the mass of victimless offences or those to which the victim is acquiescent, such as drug dealing. Practical difficulties also arise in assessing the harm done and the measure of restoration needed to make good. However, at least in respect of compensation payments, it should be remembered that tort law deals daily with such assessments in respect of civil damages. In sum, its critics charge that restorative justice cannot effectively challenge the prevailing paradigm of punishment and should be regarded as no more than ancillary to it.

A second line of criticisms pertains to the claim of restorative justice to serve the interests of victims. The chief danger is that victims may be used to promote ends that have little to do with their interests, a phenomenon described by Ashworth as 'victim prostitution'.[99] Although consent is an important restorative value, victims may be, or feel, pressured to participate in conferences that impose further burdens upon their time and goodwill. Far from feeling restored by their participation, victims may suffer psychological costs from meeting their offender and having to talk about the offence and its impact again. Victims may feel burdened by responsibility for their offender's fate and so feel obliged to cooperate or to accept an apology even when they doubt its sincerity. And they may

---

[98] Ashworth, A., 'Punishment and Compensation: Victims, Offenders and the State' (1985) 6 *Oxford Journal of Legal Studies* 86–122 at 97.

[99] Ashworth, A., 'Victims' Rights, Defendants' Rights and Criminal Procedure' in Crawford and Goodey (eds), *Integrating a Victim Perspective within Criminal Justice* (Aldershot: Ashgate, 2000) 186.

feel obliged to offer forgiveness when they feel none. No wonder that a small but significant minority of victims report feeling worse after involvement in a restorative justice conference.[100]

In respect of the offender, it might be objected that restorative justice offers insufficient protection for defendants against abuse of process. The common resort to existing criminal justice officials, often the police, as facilitators of restorative justice conferences has a tendency to import their professional agendas, undermine impartiality, and lead to abuse of power.[101] Defendants' rights may also suffer from the lack of procedural safeguards, failure of adherence to due process values, and lack of access to legal advice. Restorative justice advocates might reply that it is unnecessary to retain these protective features under a model that is dedicated to diversion from pain and reintegration into civil society. However, the potential for intrusive and disproportional burdens upon the defendant, for example where the victim is vengeful, would seem to call for greater regard for due process, fairness, and proportionality.

Overall it has been suggested that the multiple, vague goals espoused by restorative justice render it difficult to assess or control, or to call it to account, and that the demands of fairness, consistency, and clarity require a single overarching rationale by which the scope and ambition of restorative justice might be subject to limits.[102] To all these criticisms, restorative justice advocates retort that they are born of undue pessimism, or an unwillingness to think beyond the conventions of the punishment paradigm. Roche, for example, argues persuasively that safeguards built in to the restorative justice process effectively replace due process rights with 'deliberative accountability'.[103] To insist upon formal process rights is a simple failure of understanding.

---

[100] As even advocates of restorative justice acknowledge: Braithwaite, J., 'Restorative Justice: Assessing Optimistic and Pessimistic Accounts' in Tonry (ed.), *Crime and Justice: A Review of Research* (Chicago: Chicago University Press, 1999) 22.

[101] Hoyle, C., and Young, R., 'Restorative Justice: Assessing the Prospects and Pitfalls' in McConville and Wilson (eds), *The Handbook of Criminal Justice* (Oxford: Oxford University Press, 2002) 540–2.

[102] von Hirsch, A., Ashworth, A., and Shearing, C., 'Specifying Aims and Limits for Restorative Justice: A "Making Amends" Model?' in von Hirsch, Roberts, and Bottoms (eds), *Restorative Justice and Criminal Justice: Competing or Reconcilable Paradigms?* (Oxford: Hart Publishing, 2003).

[103] Roche, D., *Accountability in Restorative Justice* (Oxford: Oxford University Press, 2003) 238.

THE POSSIBILITY OF SYNTHESIS

We have set out the various justifications of punishment as distinct and unrelated partly because this is how they appear in the literature. Academics tend to espouse and promote the superiority of one theory, to distinguish and disparage others. This tendency has the effect of polarizing theories and setting them up as presumptively incompatible. By examining each of these justifications in turn, we have similarly risked exaggerating their distinctiveness and independence. One defence might be that punishment inevitably reflects competing values that can only be upheld by a variety of different philosophical models. But in penal practice this may result, as Ashworth has observed, in theories being treated as analogous to the menu in a cafeteria from which sentencers may pick and choose according to whim, personal taste, or 'common sense'.[104] This cafeteria approach is commonly justified upon the grounds that justice is best served by appositeness to the individual case. But it carries with it the cost of creating a system of punishment characterized by inconsistency, incoherence, and possible injustice between like cases. In setting forth multiple justifications for punishment but providing no criteria for ranking them, the Criminal Justice Act 2003 might be charged with adopting just such a cafeteria approach.

Whether characterizing justifications of punishment as separate menu items is entirely accurate is another matter again. First, the rationales for punishment exist in their pure form only within the pages of academic texts and rarely survive in practice as discrete entities. Penalties imposed under one rationale may incidentally fulfil other aims or satisfy other principles. For example, public pressure to impose harsh, deterrent punishment may be mitigated by legal requirements of proportionality. And whilst the principle of proportionality may limit the quantum of punishment, the penalty itself may nonetheless fulfil rehabilitative or restorative aims. Even within academic writing, proponents of a given theory often recognize that their favoured model is impure in the sense that it can accommodate more than one justification. So, for example, desert theorists like von Hirsch recognize that hard treatment not only satisfies the requirement of proportionality but also supplies prudential reasons to desist, commonly known as individual deterrence.[105] He and other desert theorists also concede that, provided the constraints of desert are satisfied

---

[104] Ashworth, A., *Sentencing and Criminal Justice* (3rd edn, London: Butterworths, 2000) 62.

[105] von Hirsch, A., *Censure and Sanctions* (Oxford: Oxford University Press, 1993) 13.

in determining how much to punish, ulterior purposes may be pursued within these limits. Similarly, reparation and rehabilitation have a capacity to censure, as well as punitive qualities that may satisfy the desert principle of proportionality. There is thus more commonality amongst the various justifications for punishment than might first appear. What these examples suggest is that considering the various justifications of punishment as discrete and distinguishable items on a menu misrepresents what might better be seen as a smorgasbord of justifications.

Secondly, even within the academic literature there is no lack of interest in the possibility of reconciling different philosophical justifications for punishment and creating synthetic or hybrid models. H. L. A. Hart famously argued that we should distinguish between the *general justifying aim of punishment* and the *principles of distribution*. He concluded that it is perfectly consistent to advance Utilitarianism (for example, the protection of society) as the justifying aim of punishment but to limit this by reference to 'retribution in distribution' that requires that punishment should only be of an offender for an offence.[106] Other writers have suggested that although there are tensions between the rationales, it would be mistaken to see them as entirely distinct or irreconcilable.[107] Even the most stalwart defenders of particular theories acknowledge the possibility of exceptional departures from the model;[108] whilst others concede more routine relaxation of the demands of a particular model. Norval Morris, for example, espouses 'limiting retributivism' according to which proportionality furnishes outer limits within which resort may be had to other principles in order to determine the exact penalty.[109] This approach suggests that the requirements of any single justification might better be seen as prima facie claims that may be trumped by claims of greater urgency. These various hybrid or synthetic models can be and have been subject to sophisticated criticism.[110] Nonetheless, they do suggest that it

[106] Hart, H. L. A., *Punishment and Responsibility* (Oxford: Oxford University Press, 1968) 9.

[107] Zedner, L., 'Reparation and Retribution: Are They Reconcilable?' (1994) 57 *Modern Law Review* 228–50; Cavadino, M., and Dignan, J., 'Reparation, Retribution and Rights' (1997) 4 *International Review of Victimology* 233–53.

[108] Robinson, P., 'Hybrid Principles for the Distribution of Criminal Sanctions' (1987) 82 *Northwestern Law Review* 19–42.

[109] Morris, N., 'Desert as a Limiting Principle' in von Hirsch and Ashworth (eds), *Principled Sentencing: Readings on Theory and Policy* (Oxford: Hart Publishing, 1998).

[110] von Hirsch, A., *Censure and Sanctions* (Oxford: Oxford University Press, 1993) ch. 6; Hudson, B., *Understanding Justice: An Introduction to Ideas, Perspectives and Controversies in Modern Penal Theory* (Buckingham: Open University Press, 1996) ch. 4.

may not be necessary, or even desirable, to force a choice as between theories. Accepting the possibility of pluralism leads us to consider two very different ways forward for penal theory. One, broadly speaking, regards punishment positively, the other negatively. The first is communicative theories of punishment, the second abolitionist theories.

PENAL COMMUNICATION

Theories of penal communication recognize that punishment is an evil in need of justification but suggest that this may be found in the communicative power of censure backed up by hard treatment. One of the chief authors of penal communication theory is R. A. Duff.[111] He sees punishment as an opportunity for communicating with the offender, the victim, and wider society the nature of the moral wrong done. Punishment, argues Duff, is a necessary accompaniment to the declaratory function of the criminal law since failure to express a moral judgment about wrongdoing 'casts doubt upon the sincerity of my declaration that such conduct is seriously wrong'.[112] Communication is explicitly not a one-way process from the punisher to the punished but two-way: the object of punishment must be able to understand, internalize, and respond to that communication. Communicative theories such as Duff's thus suggest a way through the antinomies of retributivism and consequentialism. They respect the offender as a rational moral agent, acknowledge that hard treatment may be necessary to communicate censure adequately, aim to communicate not merely to condemn, convey a message proportionate to the offence, and yet pursue ends beyond the punishment itself, not least the reintegration of the offender back into the moral community. In these multiple aims we see the divide between backward- and forward-looking theories weaken and dissolve. Although most other theories do not place moral communication at the centre of their model,[113] it seems reasonable to assert, as Duff does, that 'any plausible theory must surely also hold that we are justified in punishing offenders only if they can be expected to understand their punishment as a justified response to their crimes'.[114]

---

[111] Duff, R. A., *Punishment, Communication and Community* (Oxford: Oxford University Press, 2001).

[112] Ibid. 28.

[113] Though, as we have seen, modern desert theory increasingly does: von Hirsch, A., *Censure and Sanctions* (Oxford: Oxford University Press, 1993) 9–11.

[114] Duff, R. A., *Punishment, Communication and Community* (Oxford: Oxford University Press, 2001) 198.

ABOLITIONISM

It is precisely because they doubt that offenders could be expected to consider their punishment as justified that Abolitionist theories offer an altogether more negative account of punishment. Starting from the presumption that punishment is an evil, abolitionism suggests that existing penal theories have been overly preoccupied with the question of how punishment can be justified and too little concerned with the logically prior question of whether it can be justified at all. As Duff wryly observes: 'If asked *why* we should abolish punishment, abolitionists might with some justice reply that the onus instead lies on their opponents to show why we should maintain it.'[115] Abolitionism thus challenges the assumption implicit in much penal theory that punishment can be justified and subjects it to varying degrees of critical scrutiny. *Partial abolitionism* acknowledges that some measure of punishment may be necessary for the most serious offenders but calls for a sharp reduction in reliance upon punishment beyond that minimum.[116] *Contingent abolitionism* argues that punishment as it is currently practised cannot be justified but acknowledges that a very different system of punishment might be.[117] *Radical or absolute abolitionism* avers that no system of punishment could ever be justified and calls for complete abolition of reliance upon punishment.[118] Some theorists posit abolition as a demand, others hold it as an aspiration toward a society free of conflict or capable of resolving it in other less painful ways. The various stances taken by different abolitionist theorists also dictate their response to existing penal institutions. Those who advocate radical abolition oppose any reform likely to shore up or strengthen existing penal institutions,[119] whereas contingent abolitionists focus rather on developing alternate, more legitimate, responses to crime or, as they would prefer, 'conflicts' or 'troubles'.[120]

---

[115] Ibid., 32.

[116] de Haan, W., *The Politics of Redress: Crime, Punishment and Penal Abolition* (London: Unwin Hyman, 1990) 203.

[117] Sim, J., 'The Abolitionist Approach: a British Perspective' in Duff, *et al.* (eds), *Penal Theory and Penal Practice: Tradition and Innovation in Criminal Justice* (Manchester: Manchester University Press, 1994).

[118] See, for example, Bianchi who proposes the replacement of the criminal process by a civil process of dispute resolution, although even he acknowledges that it would be necessary to create analogues of certain aspects of punishment: Bianchi, H., 'Abolition: Assensus and Sanctuary' in Duff and Garland (eds), *A Reader on Punishment* (Oxford: Oxford University Press, 1994).

[119] Mathiesen, T., *The Politics of Abolition: Essays in Political Action* (Oxford: Martin Robertson, 1974).

[120] Christie, N., 'Conflicts as Property' (1977) 17 *British Journal of Criminology* 1–15.

Abolitionism can be regarded as a pluralist theory not only because it comes in several varieties. It also shares both the retributivist's scepticism about consequentialist claims to achieve good through punishment and consequentialist doubts about the moral validity of inflicting pain solely to redress past wrongs.[121] By casting doubt both on the efficacy and on the legitimacy of punishment, abolitionism, whilst it does not unify, straddles the existing theories in its scepticism. Whether one is minded to accept the abolitionist view that punishment cannot be justified, or to side rather with those who see punishment as at worst a necessary evil, at best an institution capable of doing justice or achieving good, depends largely on one's assessment of the costs and benefits of punishment.

CONCLUSION

This chapter has considered punishment under three broad guises. First, it has explored the concept of punishment, its conditions, characteristics, and constitutive parts. Secondly, it has considered some of the more prominent sociological interpretations of punishment and its roles in social life. And finally, it has examined the prevailing justifications offered for this morally problematic state activity. Whilst theoretical and socio-logical accounts of punishment vary in their analysis of the role played by punishment, they tend to concur in their estimate of its importance. In the final chapter we will consider some new social theories that place a very different emphasis on the centrality of state punishment and suggest that it is increasingly being displaced by preventive and prudential pro-grammes located in the private quite as much as the public realm. They raise the startling possibility that state punishment may lose its present pre-eminence, a possibility that might cause us to reread all that has been said here in an entirely new light.

---

[121] Duff, R. A., *Punishment, Communication, and Community* (Oxford: Oxford University Press, 2001) 32.

4

Criminal Process

WHAT IS THE CRIMINAL PROCESS?

The criminal process has the character of a vast machine that grinds on relentlessly despite recurrent challenges to its efficacy and its legitimacy. Suspects are its raw materials, convicted offenders its official product. Although it is often characterized as being in crisis and although periodic scandals concerning the conduct of the police or the practice of prosecutors bring it into disrepute, the criminal process has an enduring authority. The editors of a major handbook on the criminal process observe: 'for policymakers in countries in social transition, the criminal justice process in England and Wales is often viewed as a model'.[1] Its status as an exemplar furnishes the criminal process with a sense of immutability that makes it difficult to conceive of any alternative. Yet it is by no means inescapable that a rule-bound process dedicated to the attribution of blame should follow evidence of wrongdoing.

An illuminating example of a very different response to wrongdoing is the establishment of the Truth and Reconciliation Commission in post-Apartheid South Africa. The Promotion of National Unity and Reconciliation Act 1995 held that the national priority was to establish as complete a picture as possible of the nature, causes, and extent of gross violations of human rights that had occurred during the period of Apartheid. The Act offered a complete amnesty to all those who made a full disclosure to the Commission. The granting of amnesties was consistent with its larger aim to determine the truth of what had occurred, not as a preliminary to prosecution, but so that the work of reconciliation could begin. The Act thus insisted: 'there is a need for understanding but not for vengeance, a need for reparation but not for retaliation'.[2] Of course it can be argued that the attempt to rebuild the nation in the aftermath of Apartheid is such a special case that it has only limited relevance for

---

[1] McConville, M., and Wilson, G. (eds), *The Handbook of the Criminal Justice Process* (Oxford: Oxford University Press, 2002) 1.

[2] No. 34 of 1995: Promotion of National Unity and Reconciliation Act 1995.

thinking about responses to crime more generally. But, at the very least, it permits us to see that other responses, even to grave wrongs, are possible. A more germane example may be found in the Zwelethemba Model: namely the development since 1998 of 'Peace Committees' in Zwelethemba, a poor black community near Cape Town. These Peace Committees engage local community members to help resolve disputes by convening gatherings of the interested parties who decide how to reduce the likelihood of a recurrence and so 'build peace'. The Zwelethemba Model of communal dispute resolution is proposed by Johnston and Shearing as a possible alternative to the formal state domination and retrospective penal orientation of traditional criminal justice processes.[3] Our interest in it here is less as a normative model (though it has attractions) than as an example of a very different means of responding to wrongdoing.

Restorative justice initiatives similarly seek to minimize the accusatory and adversarial aspects of the criminal justice process by substituting forums that are dedicated rather to resolution and reintegration. Restorative justice initiatives have developed across the world in Australia, Canada, New Zealand, and South Africa, as well as Britain. Typically they are intended to involve offenders, their families, victims, other interested members of the community, and a facilitator (often a youth justice coordinator, social worker, or police officer). The group discusses the offence, the circumstances underlying it, its effects on the victim, and how relationships have been affected by it. The principal purpose is to share information and, collectively, 'to formulate a plan about how best to deal with the offending'.[4] Although this brief summary presents a somewhat idealized account of endeavours that are often less than optimal in practice,[5] it is clearly the intention of restorative justice initiatives to pursue an entirely different approach to offending behaviour.

That there should be a criminal process at all is an assumption that might appear harder to challenge. But anthropological studies of

---

[3] Johnston, L., and Shearing, C., *Governing Security: Explorations in Policing and Justice* (London: Routledge, 2003) 151–60; Roche, D., 'Restorative Justice and the Regulatory State in South African Townships' (2002) 42 *British Journal of Criminology* 514–33.

[4] Morris, A., and Maxwell, G., 'The Practice of Family Group Conferences in New Zealand' in Crawford and Goodey (eds), *Integrating a Victim Perspective within Criminal Justice* (Aldershot: Ashgate Dartmouth, 2000) 209.

[5] See discussion in Chapter 3. For an example of the working of restorative justice in practice see Hoyle, C., Young, R., and Hill, R., *Proceed with Caution: An Evaluation of the Thames Valley Police Initiative in Restorative Cautioning* (York: York Publishing Services, 2002).

pre-literate societies reveal that it is perfectly possible for society to exist without any formal system of policing or criminal process.[6] What triggers the development of the criminal process is another question. Is it, as Durkheimian analysis would suggest, that the increasing complexity of society calls forth formal mechanisms by which to resolve disputes? Is the trigger, rather, the development of social and economic divisions that both foster crime and render informal communal policing inadequate to the task of maintaining order? Or is it, as Marxian analysis would pro-scribe, the development of class divisions that foster state-dominated processes, which in turn function as agents of class control? Rather than thinking of the criminal process as a natural response to crime, we might better conceive of it as one of an array of possible responses to wrong-doing that range from complete inaction through mediated resolution to lethal retaliation. Alongside these examples, the retrospective drive of the criminal justice process to prosecute past wrongs looks a good deal less inexorable. The present form and functions of the criminal process might be better understood as contingent on the particularities of its historical evolution than the result of grand design.

Even among formal, prosecution-led criminal justice processes there are major differences between adversarial (or accusatory) and inquisitorial systems. In the adversarial system the criminal process takes the form of a contest between prosecution and defence. The parties' purported, though rarely achieved, goal is to play out this struggle in the drama of the trial. Here competing versions of the events are pitted against one another in oral combat. By contrast the inquisitorial system, common in much of continental Europe, has the quality of a journey along which evidence as to both innocence and guilt is collected. This enquiry after the truth is overseen, in theory at least, by an examining magistrate or prosecutor. In the course of the investigation, the evidence is accumulated in a dossier, upon the basis of which the judge decides which witnesses to call. The paper record takes the place of the principle of orality and the search for the truth replaces the struggle between competing accounts.

The differing assumptions behind the adversarial and inquisitorial systems generate quite different approaches to basic elements in the criminal process.[7] For example the decision to prosecute is subject to

---

[6] Schwartz, R. D., and Miller, J. C., 'Legal Evolution and Societal Complexity' (1964) 70 *American Journal of Sociology* 159–69.

[7] Damaska, M., *The Faces of Justice and State Authority* (New Haven: Yale University Press, 1986); Langbein, J. H., and Weinreb, L., 'Continental Criminal Procedure: Myth and Reality' (1977) 87 *Yale Law Journal* 1549–69.

wide discretion in the adversarial system. But it is in principle mandatory in an inquisitorial system like that in Austria, in cases where there is prima facie evidence of illegality.[8] Plea bargaining and the entering of guilty pleas are common features of the adversarial process but, theoretically at least, inadmissible in the German inquisitorial system. More fundamentally still, the adversarial and inquisitorial systems might be said to embody different conceptions of truth, how it is best established, and the prominence it should be given. The centrality accorded to fact finding in the inquisitorial model is offset in the adversarial system by a countervailing concern that there be sufficient safeguards against abuse of power by state officials. Thus whereas the inquisitorial model places considerable trust in state officials to search after the truth, the adversarial model relies more heavily upon legal protections, defence lawyers, and limits on police powers to protect the individual from abuse.

The common tendency to set the adversarial and inquisitorial models up as ideal types obscures the specific qualities and failings of each system. There has been a long and inconclusive debate about the rival claims of the two systems to superiority.[9] Our purpose here is less to determine their respective merits than to draw attention to the variety of existing criminal processes in order that we may see the possibility of other forms and other ways of conceiving of that process.

Let us return then to our initial question, 'what is the criminal process?' Or better, let us divide it into three subsidiary questions: first, how should we think about the process? Secondly, what is its scope and nature? And in conclusion, what is it for? Answers to these questions tend to move uneasily between descriptive and normative statements about what the criminal process is and what it should be. Lying at the heart of criminal justice, the criminal process attracts considerable political and academic attention and has been subject to the scrutiny of penal theory, empirical research, and government commissions of inquiry upon which we shall draw in attempting to answer these three questions.

---

[8] This was formerly the case also in Germany under the *Legalitätsprinzip*: Leigh, L. H., and Zedner, L., *The Royal Commission on Criminal Justice: A Report on the Administration of Criminal Justice in the Pre-Trial phase in France and Germany* (London: HMSO, 1992) 41.

[9] A debate not entirely foreclosed by the confident claim in the introduction to one leading text that: 'it is a remarkable fact of modern times that the adversarial system of the common law is so manifestly in the ascendant and the inquisitorial system so clearly in retreat': McConville, M., and Wilson, G. (eds), *The Handbook of the Criminal Justice Process* (Oxford: Oxford University Press, 2002) 1.

MODELLING THE CRIMINAL PROCESS

Many scholars have constructed models in an effort to make sense of the criminal process, to identify its goals, and to assess its fulfilment of them. Model building is driven in part by the very complexity of the process and the difficulty of making sense of the mass of detailed operations it comprises without a larger frame of reference into which the minutiae can be made to fit. It is a moot point, however, whether models are the best way to understand the criminal process. It is often difficult to determine whether models are intended as analytical devices or as normative statements of ideals to which the process should aspire. The picture is complicated by the fact that even where the author of a model intended it as an analytical tool, this has proved no inhibition on others using it normatively and vice versa. Given that much of the criminal process involves the exercise of state power over individuals and intrusions against their liberties, it is not surprising that scholars are continually driven to ask whether and on what grounds these intrusions are warranted and how best they might be regulated. As with punishment, the impulse to justify is a constant feature of writing about the criminal process and it tends to intrude upon the prior task of understanding.

In order to assess the utility of model building we need to say a little about the dominant models and how they have been used. Probably the most enduringly influential models are those of due process and crime control developed by Herbert Packer in the 1960s.[10] In brief, the due process model characterizes the criminal process as an 'obstacle course'. It is replete with hurdles to prosecution employed by defence lawyers and the judiciary who are dedicated to upholding individual rights. Protecting the innocent; preventing abuse of power; and guarding against procedural impropriety are at least as important as convicting the guilty. Under the due process model, a factually guilty suspect would be allowed to walk free rather than allow the state to rely upon illegally obtained evidence. This insistence upon propriety and legality is essential in order to ensure that the police are constrained and that the moral authority of the process is upheld. It is clear, however, that Packer doubts the morality of the very ends that the process seeks to attain and he questions, in particular, the morality of punishing the disadvantaged and the poor.

The crime control model, by contrast, characterizes the criminal pro-

---

[10] Packer, H. L., *The Limits of the Criminal Sanction* (Stanford, Calif.: Stanford University Press, 1968).

cess as an 'assembly-conveyor belt down which moves an endless stream of cases' operated by the police and prosecutors for the creation of guilty pleas and convictions.[11] The primary purpose of the criminal process under the crime control model is to establish factual guilt and to this end the police are restrained only insofar as it is necessary to ensure that evidence is admissible. The process is dedicated to maximizing convictions and doing so at speed on limited resources. Given the slow, cumbersome operation of the court, the police are entrusted with high levels of discretion to pursue suspects and extract confessions. The risk of false confessions and wrongful convictions is tolerated provided it is not so common as to bring the system into disrepute and so diminish its deterrent effect.

These two models have had lasting influence upon thinking about the criminal process and have become terms of art in and outside academic writing. Yet as Roach, for example, observes: 'Packer's models were reflective of the time and place in which they were written. It is an open question how applicable Packer's models are outside of the United States of the 1960s.'[12] Aside from the question of continuing applicability, there is also the problem of how these models have been understood and employed by subsequent academic writers. They have typically been read as dichotomous models setting out antimonies between which there is a perpetual and irresolvable tension. We are invited to subscribe either to due process or to crime control, as if a stark choice between the two is necessary. Yet it is clear that Packer did not intend the models as polar opposites, indeed he insisted that the ideology underlying each model should not be read as the converse of the other.[13] Rather, he saw them as sharing a common commitment to law enforcement and a belief that there should be some limits to the power of officials. The difference between them lies in the relative priorities accorded to each rather than any absolute divergence.

Quite another reading of the two models is that they are not so much in tension as mutually interdependent. In a wonderfully provocative phrase, McBarnet concludes 'due process is *for* crime control'.[14] By this she

---

[11] Ibid. 158.

[12] Roach, K., 'Criminal Process' in Cane (ed.), *The Oxford Handbook of Legal Studies* (Oxford: Oxford University Press, 2003) 777.

[13] Packer, H. L., *The Limits of the Criminal Sanction* (Stanford, Calif.: Stanford University Press, 1968) 163.

[14] Emphasis in the original: McBarnet, D., *Conviction: Law, the State, and the Construction of Justice* (London: Macmillan, 1983) 156.

means that deviation from the rhetoric of legality and justice is institutionalized in the law itself as follows:

The rhetoric of justice requires incriminating evidence as the basis for arrest and search; the law allows arrest and search in order to establish it. Justice requires that no one need incriminate himself; the law refuses to control the production of confessions and allows silence as a factor in proving guilt. Justice requires equality; the law discriminates against the homeless, the jobless, the disreputable. Justice requires each case be judged on its own facts; the law makes previous convictions grounds for defining behaviour as an offence and evidence against the accused. Justice places the burden of proof on the prosecutor; the law qualifies the standard and method of proof required and offers the prosecutor opportunities for making a case which the accused is denied.[15]

In short, the law does not adhere to its self-declared ends. Although it purports to be about upholding justice, it is formulated so as to allow officials to pursue crime control goals under the rhetorical cover of due process. Whilst McBarnet's analysis is challenging, it may be that she overstates the case. She dismisses both the due process constraints incorporated in the law and, simultaneously, the degree to which the rhetoric of law is also for crime control.

It is also doubtful whether it makes sense to set due process and crime control as polarities. Central to Packer's characterization of crime control is its commitment to speed so that the guilty are processed and convicted as rapidly and efficiently as possible. This he compares to the deliberate and cautious pace of due process. But as Ashworth observes, 'delays are also a source of considerable anxiety and inconvenience, and occasionally prolonged loss of liberty, to defendants. A properly developed notion of Due Process would surely insist that there be no unreasonable delay'.[16] If efficiency and speed are as important characteristics of due process as crime control then an important distinction between the two models disappears.

Packer's models continue to hold considerable sway despite these and other criticisms levelled at them. Building models in order to render the process intelligible, or at least manageable, has obvious attractions. King has added a further four models to Packer's two, namely, the medical model, the bureaucratic model, the status passage model, and the power model, to describe the ways in which the process variously seeks to

---

[15] Ibid. 154.
[16] Ashworth, A., *The Criminal Process: An Evaluative Study* (2nd edn, Oxford: Oxford University Press, 1998) 28.

rehabilitate, manage, denounce, and dominate suspects and offenders.[17] He conceives of these models as a means both of testing the evidence and of evaluating the success of the process in promoting its own purported goals. Roach likewise sees the utility of models as lying principally in their ability to offer positive descriptions of the process and to furnish normative statements about the values to which it should aspire. He also shares King's preference for multiple models on the grounds that they legitimately account for different aspects of the systems' operation. Developing multiple models has the virtue of overcoming the tendency of single models to force the divergent and often contradictory elements of the criminal process into a monolithic schema.

Roach regards Packer's models as outdated principally because they predate victimization studies and the rise of victims' rights movements and in consequence have nothing to say about the role of the victim in the criminal process. In their place he proposes two models: the 'punitive model of victims' rights' and the 'non-punitive model of victims' rights'.[18] The former he describes as a roller-coaster ride toward punishment, in a constant state of crisis as it pits the rights of victims and potential victims against the due process rights of the accused. The non-punitive model of victims' rights he portrays 'as a circle which symbolizes successful crime prevention through family and community-building and successful acts of restorative justice'.[19] The future of the criminal process depends, for Roach, on which model prevails. Inclined to optimism, he concludes, much as Packer did in respect of the due process model 35 years before, that the non-punitive model could reduce reliance on the criminal sanction.

Others have abandoned model building in favour of developing principles and values that do, or ought to, underpin the pre-trial process.[20] The evaluative or principled approach has the advantage of furnishing a theoretical framework that is explicitly normative rather than descriptive. But it has also been promoted as superior to model building as a means of identifying what the criminal process is about. Morgan, for example, describes Ashworth's evaluative approach as more 'nuanced, subtle and multi-dimensional' than models which tend to reduce the world to black

---

[17] King, M., *The Framework of Criminal Justice* (London: Croom Helm, 1981) 13.

[18] Roach, K., 'Four Models of the Criminal Process' (1999) 89 *Journal of Criminal Law and Criminology* 671–716.

[19] Ibid.

[20] Most notably, Ashworth, A., *The Criminal Process: An Evaluative Study* (2nd edn, Oxford: Oxford University Press, 1998) 29.

and white.[21] By adopting an explicitly normative frame, the principled approach also provides standards by which to judge present practice and to prescribe reform. This said, it is sometimes difficult to determine when the principles under discussion are derived from those already intrinsic to the criminal process and when they reflect ideals to which the criminal process should aspire. Slippage between the two creates an uneasy tension between descriptive and normative theorizing. Where the principles are clearly set out, however, they may furnish an important normative complement to the explanatory power of model building. Instead of seeing model building and the development of principles as competing approaches to the criminal process therefore, we might better see them as fulfilling distinct but compatible functions.

THE ROLE OF RULES

Determining the scope and nature of so vast a machine as the criminal process is a daunting prospect. One common and entirely defensible approach is to focus on key decisions made in the course of the process— decisions to arrest, to detain, to remand, to bail, decisions relating to plea bargaining and as to mode of trial. Focusing on these decisions has the advantage of reducing an otherwise impossibly complex web of human agency to manageable proportions. It has the advantage also of imposing a chronological framework that follows through from the moment of first contact with criminal justice officials to the trial itself. And it has the power to reveal both the overall momentum of the process and the very different considerations at play at each point within that process. To focus upon decisions runs the risk, however, of accepting the present structure of decision making as immutable. It tends to reify current arrangements in such a way as to make it difficult to question their very existence. It also runs the danger of envisaging the criminal process as a machine that runs itself without recourse to external resources and having little to do with human agency. In this section, we will focus instead upon the rules that structure the criminal process and, in the section which follows, on the agents charged with implementing them. This approach seems to hold out a better prospect of understanding the criminal process as the product of human endeavour rather than a series of abstracted decisions.

---

[21] Morgan, R., 'The Process is the Rule and the Punishment is the Process' (1996) 59 *Modern Law Review* 306–14 at 309.

No account of the criminal process can ignore the centrality of rules. Read one way, rules serve as a fetter upon the exercise of highly coercive state powers which, if not so constrained, would profoundly erode civil liberties. Inhibitory rules relating to policing place limits upon the power of the police to stop, detain, and interrogate suspects. Rules proscribe certain forms of action, oblige officials to justify and account for their conduct, and penalize those who transgress. How far these legal requirements are effective in limiting impropriety is another question and it can happen that rather than imposing effective controls, purportedly restrictive rules instead promote adaptive behaviour. Criminal justice agents simply tailor conduct rendered illegal by inhibitory rules to accord with the new permitted forms. The capacity of rules to control conduct varies: some rules are more easily stretched, bent, or evaded than others. Rules requiring reasonable grounds for suspicion before arrest or the satisfaction of public interest criteria before prosecution, for example, are open to elastic interpretation if they are not closely circumscribed. Rules that stipulate their parameters tightly are less open to evasion. For example, prosecutors can only proceed in respect of offences laid down by statute or common law.

Much depends upon context. The degree of fit between professional culture and legal rules, the relative ease of evasion, and the costs of detection all govern how closely rules are regarded. Where the dominant professional culture holds that certain groups within the population are commonly dishonest; that securing important ends overrides other interests; or that loyalty to colleagues trumps devotion to duty then adherence to rules is attenuated. Where this is combined with plentiful opportunities for avoidance, low risk of detection, or paltry penalties, then rules are liable to be honoured more in the breach than in their adherence. Given that discipline for breach is ordinarily imposed upon the police by police, the costs of non-adherence may not be sufficient to deter. These observations apply most obviously to policing, but continue through the criminal process to trial and disposal. Within the public forum of the courtroom, where interested and knowledgeable observers can scrutinize every move, opportunities for deviance are limited. Prior to trial, however, lack of transparency permits greater discretion. For example, determining which case will fall before which judge is the duty of listing officers whose decisions are subject to little scrutiny and unlikely to be penalized. Listing officers may, or may not, assign cases to particular judges according to their known proclivities,[22] but rules intended to govern their conduct are

[22] Ashworth, A. *et al.*, *Sentencing in the Crown Court, Occasional Paper 10* (Oxford: Centre for Criminological Research, 1984) 56–9, 64.

likely to have limited impact on this important facet of the criminal process because their activities are so hidden from scrutiny.

Unsurprisingly, criminologists (professionally interested in deviance) have been more interested in the ways that criminal justice professionals subvert the rules than in the rules themselves or their power to induce conformity. As McBarnet observes: 'the law in law enforcement got lost in the fascinating analysis of human action; formal rules got lost in the unending informal methods of avoiding or redefining them; the intentions behind the law got lost in the unintended consequences of its operation; explanation got lost in micro-sociological description and indignant demystification'.[23] Certainly human agents are important in implementing and subverting legal rules, but without first analysing the role of rules, it is impossible to understand the framework within which they act. Nor, strikingly, has the power of law to induce compliance caught the criminological imagination to the same degree as its capacity to foster deviance.[24]

The cynic might be tempted to wonder whether, even where law appears to bind most tightly upon the agents of criminal justice, it is a mistake to ascribe it any centrality. That same cynic might reject the conventional view of the criminal process as bound by substantive and procedural rules that its officials are expected to enforce, uniformly and with minimal discretion. Instead of seeing law as a primary determinant of what happens in the criminal process, Smith, for example, argues rather that 'very little of the shape of policing or of its detailed texture can be understood as deriving directly from rules enshrined in law'.[25] Yet he does not deny entirely the importance of law in framing and influencing practice, acknowledging that 'the broad structure of the system of which the police are part—the system of law and administration of justice—has an enormous influence ... in shaping policing practice'.[26] Choongh, on the other hand, is sceptical of the importance of rules to the police. Far from being bound by legal rationality in the construction of

[23] McBarnet, D., 'False Dichotomies in Criminal Justice Research' in Baldwin and Bottomley (eds), *Criminal Justice: Selected Readings* (Oxford: Martin Robertson, 1978) 26.

[24] Though see Tyler, T., *Why People Obey the Law* (New Haven: Yale University Press, 1990); Hawkins, K., *Law as Last Resort: Prosecution Decision-Making in a Regulatory Agency* (Oxford: Oxford University Press, 2002) ch. 8.

[25] Smith, D. J., 'The Framework of Law and Policing Practice' in Benyon and Bourn (eds), *The Police: Powers, Procedures and Proprieties* (Oxford: Pergamon Press, 1986) 85–6; Smith, D. J., and Gray, J., *Police and People in London* (Aldershot: Gower, 1983).

[26] Smith, D. J., 'The Framework of Law and Policing Practice' in Benyon and Bourn (eds), *The Police: Powers, Procedures and Proprieties* (Oxford: Pergamon Press, 1986) 86.

cases, the police, he contends, are for much of the time singularly uninterested in the rules that would allow them to establish legal guilt.[27] As we shall see further below, Choongh's analysis of policing and the pre-trial process is such as to consign legal rules to the status of near irrelevance in many cases.

The danger of accounts that describe the criminal process as the product of human agency alone is that they may underplay the power of law and of legal ideology to constrain and direct human behaviour. Of course criminal justice agents deviate from and subvert the law, they allow their professional culture, political beliefs, prejudices, and personal interests to intrude. But they also adopt and internalize legal ideology, the language of law, and its goals to a striking degree. Recognizing the centrality of legalism and the rule-bound nature of the criminal process is essential if we are to avoid caricaturing it as a set of rules from which human actors routinely deviate.

As we have already observed, one of the failings of the due process model is that it accepts the rhetoric of rules uncritically. Slippage between their purported aims and their realization in practice is laid at the door of human agency. When rules of procedure and evidence fail to protect the innocent, secure civil liberties, or inhibit malpractice, failure is commonly ascribed to the subversive activities of the police and the inadequacies of the prosecution service. This account assumes that the content of law matches its rhetoric and that only human interference thwarts its fulfilment. Focusing on the content of rules reveals another truth: that they safeguard interests other than those officially proclaimed and that they have purposes much closer to actual outcomes than at first appears.[28] Apparent perversions of justice reveal themselves as permitted or even sustained by the law itself. Understood in this way, the rhetoric of legal ideology conceals other values and purposes.

This leads us to the alternative view that law is in large measure permissive or empowering. The legal framework of criminal justice furnishes a series of resources or opportunities to which criminal justice professionals have recourse in pursuing their allotted functions. On this view, legislation that purports to curb abuses of police powers might better be seen as a package of potent means for exercising that power. Although it is framed in such as way as to limit and constrain, in fact it allows the

[27] Choongh, S., *Policing as Social Discipline* (Oxford: Clarendon Press, 1997) 14.
[28] McBarnet, D., *Conviction: Law, the State, and the Construction of Justice* (London: Macmillan, 1983) 3.

police to stop, to restrain, to detain, to question, to search, to arrest, and to put cases forward for prosecution. A good example is the ostensible time constraints upon the detention of suspects under the Police and Criminal Evidence Act (PACE) 1984, which actually allow the police to hold suspects up to these limits. Often provisions are deliberately vaguely defined so as to increase their flexibility, as a resource that the police can adapt and apply at will.[29] Another example is the Regulation of Investigatory Powers Act 2000, introduced to provide police with new legal powers ostensibly within a human rights framework. Far from restraining, prohibiting, or sanctioning, laws such as these may better be viewed as permissive or, as Sanders and Young would have it, enabling rules.[30] How officials choose to exercise the discretionary powers furnished by these enabling rules determines the shape and direction of the criminal process.

The need to hold these constraints and resources in balance is one of the most difficult tasks for the lawmaker. Too many constraints and the process is frustrated, too ready resources and the civil liberties of the defendant are endangered. Maintaining this balance is complicated by the fact that constraints at one point in the process are liable to squeeze the exercise of discretion to another point entirely and create unforeseen results elsewhere. The image of balance, though pervasive, is perilous since it fails to stipulate what is being balanced, what interests are included or excluded, and what weight is being assigned to particular values or interests.[31] More grievously still, it assumes that a balancing is possible where in the case of certain fundamental rights no derogation or 'balancing away' is permissible. The image of balance is complicated further by the fact that some rules, which purport to be permissive, are in fact designed to bring the law into line with existing practice and are thus better read as legitimizing rules.[32] Still others, for example those concerning police powers to stop and search people on the street, appear to be inhibitory but in fact introduce no new or no effective constraint and are more accurately described as presentational rules.[33]

Although some rules fit only one of the descriptions inhibitory, enabling, legitimizing, or presentational, most embrace more than one

---

[29] Smith, D. J., 'The Framework of Law and Policing Practice' in Benyon and Bourn (eds), *The Police: Powers, Procedures and Proprieties* (Oxford: Pergamon Press, 1986).

[30] Sanders, A., and Young, R., *Criminal Justice* (London: Butterworths, 2000) 73–5.

[31] Ashworth, A., *The Criminal Process: An Evaluative Study* (2nd edn, Oxford: Oxford University Press, 1998) 30.

[32] Sanders, A., and Young, R., *Criminal Justice* (2nd edn, London: Butterworths, 2000) 74.

[33] Smith, D. J., 'The Framework of Law and Policing Practice' in Benyon and Bourn (eds), *The Police: Powers, Procedures and Proprieties* (Oxford: Pergamon Press, 1986) 89.

function and may operate in different ways at different times. Furthermore, law's influence varies at different stages in the process. At some junctures, law is relatively developed and exerts a strong delimiting force. At others, individuals appear to act with almost unfettered discretion. This might matter less if, where the rules run out, there were other effective sources of restraint and other means to accountability but often there are none.[34]

THE ACTORS IN THE CRIMINAL PROCESS

It should by now be clear that even if one thinks of the criminal process as principally rule bound, the rules are mediated by human actors. Establishing who the actors are and what roles they perform is more complicated than might at first appear. The police have iconic status and their actions and misdemeanours rarely escape the public eye but the workings of prosecution agencies attract little scholarly or public attention. The work of defence lawyers is studied and understood still less, despite its obvious importance in adversarial systems. So too are the boundaries of the criminal process uncertain. A narrow account of the criminal process might include only its formal institutions and officials; whereas a more expansive one would embrace the media who report its workings, the public whose decision to report crimes is the most common prompt to prosecution, and the host of non-criminal bodies that act as informants, police, prosecutors, or, as in the case of the insurance industry, the very engine to enquiry.[35]

Our account, like most, focuses on the official agencies of the criminal justice system. But it is arguable that this is to tell a partial story that distorts both the extent and the character of policing and prosecution. It excises from the picture the continuing existence and proliferation of non-state actors accorded policing functions. For example, historically, the park keeper, the bus conductor, train guard, and even the school caretaker fulfilled important policing functions alongside their primary tasks. These secondary agents of social control have declined markedly in

---

[34] An interesting experiment to introduce new mechanisms of accountability is the use of restorative justice conferencing as a means of responding to complaints against the police: Hill, R. *et al.*, *Introducing Restorative Justice to the Police Complaints System: Close Encounters of the Rare Kind* (Oxford: Centre for Criminological Research, 2003).

[35] Ericson, R., and Haggerty, K., *Policing the Risk Society* (Oxford: Oxford University Press, 1997); Ericson, R., Doyle, A., and Barry, D., *Insurance as Governance* (Toronto: University of Toronto Press, 2003).

number since the post-war period but may once have played as important a role in everyday policing as the formal state police.[36] The extent to which private agents employed by commercial companies have replaced them is a matter of some controversy to which we will return in the final chapter. But it is doubtful whether it makes sense to talk of policing without some reference to the many thousands of employees of private security organizations who work as guards, bouncers, patrolmen, security truck drivers, private detectives, and installers and operators of alarm and CCTV systems.[37] Even within the criminal process proper, private agents guard courts, escort prisoners, and patrol public buildings. Other important policing and prosecution functions are fulfilled by regulatory and investigative agencies charged with tax collection, environmental control, health and safety, customs and immigration controls. Likewise local authorities are responsible for licensing premises, enforcing local by laws and regulations, and, increasingly, developing and delivering local community safety programmes. Private citizens also fulfil important policing duties as special constables, neighbourhood watch coordinators, members of citizens' patrols, and as participants in community-based crime prevention programmes. This list is certainly not complete but it suffices to give some sense of the wider cast of actors engaged in policing and prosecutorial activities.

One difficulty in expanding our account of the criminal process to incorporate this larger array of actors is that studies of their operation as agents of the criminal process are only beginning to appear.[38] This difficulty notwithstanding, as we go on to focus upon the role of the formal police and prosecutors in the criminal process, we need to hold in view the wider context of policing and prosecutorial activities in which official agents of the criminal process operate.

THE POLICE

The public police forces are undoubtedly the most prominent and arguably the most powerful actors in the criminal process. So much can be

[36] Jones, T., and Newburn, T., 'The Transformation of Policing? Understanding Current Trends in Policing Systems' (2002) 42 *British Journal of Criminology* 129–46 at 142.

[37] Johnston, L., *The Rebirth of Private Policing* (London: Routledge, 1992); Johnston, L., and Shearing, C., *Governing Security: Explorations in Policing and Justice* (London: Routledge, 2003).

[38] Hawkins, K., *Law as Last Resort: Prosecution Decision-Making in a Regulatory Agency* (Oxford: Oxford University Press, 2002); Hobbs, D. *et al.*, *Bouncers: Violence and Governance in the Night time Economy* (Oxford: Oxford University Press, 2003).

said about them that the police duly fill entire books[39] and journals. What follows here is an appraisal of some analytical frameworks by which to explore their role within the criminal process. Given the controversial nature of policing and its capacity for abuse, it is all but impossible to maintain an analytical approach that does not continually revert to critical evaluation. Whilst we will attempt to concern ourselves primarily with its nature and quality, it is questionable whether it is possible, or even desirable, to force a separation between descriptive and normative accounts of policing.

CITIZENS IN UNIFORM

Conventionally, the police have been thought of as citizens in uniform, empowered by virtue of their office to act as any good and responsible citizen would. This view of the police as community representatives working with and for the community they serve has a long history. It derives, in part at least, from the distinction drawn between the state-imposed policing of continental systems and the supposed derivation of the British Bobby from communal self-policing. The historical accuracy of this characterization is doubtful and perhaps less important than its capacity to capture a different world-view of who the police are and whence their authority derives. Perhaps the heyday of the citizen model of policing was the post-war period when the popular television character Dixon of Dock Green epitomized the ideal of the policeman as model citizen. This television series now evokes an era when the police were respectful of those they served and in turn commanded respect themselves.[40] In the post-war period of consensus, the police enjoyed an aura of legitimacy that purportedly permitted them to maintain order without asserting their authority more aggressively. But we should be clear that this depiction caricatures the police just as it cosily caricatures the quiescent, homogenous, and well-ordered society over which they supposedly ruled.

The introduction of the patrol car in the 1960s led to a rapid decline in the number of police on foot patrol. Whereas foot patrols had provided ready opportunities for casual social interaction with the public and

---

[39] Reiner, R., *The Politics of the Police* (3rd edn, Oxford: Oxford University Press, 2000); Morgan, R., and Newburn, T., *The Future of Policing* (Oxford: Oxford University Press, 1997); Dixon, D., *Law in Policing: Legal Regulation and Police Practices* (Oxford: Clarendon Press, 1997).

[40] Loader, I., and Mulcahy, A., *Policing and the Condition of England* (Oxford: Oxford University Press, 2003) ch. 3.

cemented the police to their local beat, the patrol car encouraged them to drive around in search of action. In so doing, it forged a gulf between police officers and other citizens. Changes in social mobility, wealth distribution, and relations between citizens and the state have further eroded the consensus model of policing. Given that it is open to question how far conceiving of the police as citizens in uniform explains policing in any era, its ability to account for the police in today's more conflict-ridden and socially alienated society seems doubly questionable.

This said, its focus on the routine, commonplace aspects of policing is borne out by studies which reveal that the daily work of the police involves far more mundane activity, little connected with crime control, than one might expect.[41] As Felson wryly observes: 'police work consists of hour upon hour of boredom, interrupted by moments of sheer terror. Some police officers have to wait years for these moments'.[42] Determining which policing activities are really about crime control and which are about low-level order maintenance is complicated by the fact that though not obviously connected with crime, still less with its repression, they may nonetheless reduce social tensions or conduce to crime prevention. Giving directions to tourists, telling the time to those without watches, or passing the time of day with the elderly, the lonely, or the homeless do not appear to be crime control activities. But they may serve to reduce the social marginalization that feeds crime and fosters the sense of social inclusion that may inhibit it.

Here of course we risk falling into the trap of slipping from an analytical frame into a normative one. Unsurprisingly, the notion of police as citizens in uniform has been invoked as a normative guide to what policing might or should be. As such, it forms the basis, albeit an ill-defined one, for models of community policing that seek to reintegrate the police into often alienated communities and charge them with the task not of imposing but of inducing order through partnership and consensus. Developing good relations with local citizens; understanding the diverse circumstances, cultures, and concerns of those they police; and seeking to solve their problems are central priorities of community policing. Community policing has the potential to improve relations between police and those they police, to change police culture and police practice. But its ethos of problem solving and trust building conflicts with the dominant police culture wedded to action and fighting crime. In

---

[41] Reiner, R., *The Politics of the Police* (3rd edn, Oxford: Oxford University Press, 2000) 112.

[42] Felson, M., *Crime and Everyday Life* (3rd edn, London: Sage, 2002) 4.

consequence, it tends not to be regarded as real policing, suffers from low status and low priority, is poorly defined and inadequately monitored. It is also most difficult to implement in those inner city areas where the need to improve police relations with the community is greatest. The prospects for community policing thus depend in large part on the prevailing political climate; the priority accorded to building consensus over crime control; and the structural conditions of possibility.

LEGAL ACTORS UPHOLDING THE RULE OF LAW

Formally, the police are state agents who derive their power to intervene in people's lives by virtue of their office and the laws that license and circumscribe their daily activities. Colloquially, the police are often described as officers of the law, a tag that acknowledges the source of their operational powers in statute and subsidiary laws.[43] Police chiefs like to present their forces as agents of the law operating under the very constraints that characterize Packer's due process model. Their legitimacy rests upon adherence (or at least the appearance of their adherence) to legal rules. And their actions are warranted only to the extent of those powers granted them by law for the purposes of establishing a case that will be subject to the critical scrutiny of the court. But the designation 'officer of the law' suggests an unproblematic relationship between law and action that is hardly borne out by what we know of police practice. Research on policing commonly reveals the daily working practices of the police to be so far removed from the legal framework within which they theoretically operate that there is a strong temptation to assume that they derive from different sources of authority entirely. For example, despite the requirement that the police must have reasonable suspicion before stopping individuals on the street, in their classic survey of policing in London, Smith and Gray could find no such ground in one-third of cases.[44]

Two alternatives sources of influence upon policing stand out: the power to exercise discretion and the influence of cop culture. First, the exercise of discretion pervades policing at every level from the development of national and local force policies to the decisions made by individual officers on the street or in the police station. Yet the exercise of

[43] Not least the Police and Criminal Evidence Act (PACE) 1984, the codes of practice thereunder, and the Police Reform Act 2002.

[44] Smith, D. J., 'The Framework of Law and Policing Practice' in Benyon and Bourn (eds), *The Police: Powers, Procedures and Proprieties* (Oxford: Pergamon Press, 1986); Smith, D. J., and Gray, J., *Police and People in London* (Aldershot: Gower, 1983).

discretion by the police can be seen not as an abrogation from law but as an essential facet of its fair enforcement. A similar claim could be made of the working practices of other agents of the criminal process (defence lawyers, prosecutors, probation officers, magistrates, and judges). Only by exercising discretion can they apply laws fairly and reasonably: without discretion the application of the criminal law would be overbearing, burdensome, and excessively costly. Indeed, it is arguably the need to husband the scarce resources of police time and manpower that drives much discretionary decision making. Discretion is invited too by the very nature of the criminal law, laws of procedure, and evidence. Even where the legal provisions are tightly formulated, determining whether there are reasonable grounds for suspicion, whether the offender has the prescribed guilty mind, or whether the evidence is sufficient to satisfy the public prosecutor requires that the police officer exercise discretion at every turn. To this extent it can be argued that discretion is not at variance with, but an essential element in, the application of law. Without it every minor misdemeanour would result in prosecution. Seen another way, however, every exercise of discretion constitutes a departure from the strictures of legalism. Given that there is almost invariably a considerable power imbalance between the police and those subject to their discretion, the potential for abuse is always present. The exercise of power beyond, behind, or between the formal rules results in policing practice that is often far from that which the law prescribes.

Like discretion, professional culture sometimes seems more determinative of what the police do than the laws that ought properly to guide them. The distinctive character of cop culture, as it is commonly known, derives from the fact that the police work closely together and often in conflict with their surrounding community. Thus isolated they come to share strongly held beliefs about the nature of policing and those they police. Police culture has been the subject of extensive empirical research.[45] This reveals that the police are characterized by a strong sense of mission, by a common desire for action (in the face of the routine, mundane reality of much police work), by their cynicism concerning

---

[45] In studies too numerous to mention. See overview in Bowling, B., and Foster, J., 'Policing and the Police' in Maguire, Morgan, and Reiner (eds), *The Oxford Handbook of Criminology* (3rd edn, Oxford: Oxford University Press, 2002); Chan, J., 'Changing Police Culture' (1996) 36 *British Journal of Criminology* 109–34; Hoyle, C., *Negotiating Domestic Violence* (Oxford: Clarendon, 1998); Waddington, P. A. J., 'Police (Canteen) Sub-Culture: An Appreciation' (1999) *British Journal Of Criminology* 287–309.

human nature, by attitudes of constant suspicion, and by generic political, moral, and social conservatism. Most problematically, male domination of policing generates a shared sense of machismo that exacerbates the tough, aggressive aspects of their role, and engenders sexism, homophobia, and racism.[46] Add these cultural traits to the considerable scope for discretion discussed above and it is hardly surprising that police studies consistently report extensive evidence of bias and discrimination in policing practice.[47] Targeting of people of colour plays a prime part in the overrepresentation of ethnic minorities, in particular of Afro-Caribbeans, in the criminal process. It results in the overuse of police powers of surveillance, stop and search, and arrest, and the use of racist language, oppressive interview techniques, and excessive force in the policing of ethnic minority populations. Racism lies behind one of the most important working rules[48] of the police, namely that 'suspiciousness' can be determined by the suspect's appearance or behaviour or presence at a particular time or place. The fact that suspects are young or wearing particular types of clothes or are simply considered by the police to be incongruous (a black youth in a predominately white area or driving an expensive car, for example) is enough to satisfy this particular working rule.[49]

Thinking about policing as a cultural practice is productive insofar as it reveals the extent to which prior assumptions, organizational goals, and working practices determine police behaviour.[50] There are dangers in this approach, however. First, Hoyle suggests that we should distinguish between cop culture and canteen culture. The latter is the form of talk, replete with bias and prejudices, indulged in by police officers in the privacy of their station, but which Hoyle argues does not necessarily influence policing: ' "Canteen culture" allows officers to articulate their

[46] Bowling, B., *Violent Racism: Victimization, Policing, and Social Control* (Oxford: Clarendon Press, 1998).

[47] The Macpherson Enquiry (following the death of the black teenager, Stephen Lawrence) infamously concluded that institutional racism is endemic in the police: Macpherson, W., *The Stephen Lawrence Enquiry: Report of an Enquiry by Sir William Macpherson of Cluny* (London: HMSO, 1999). On research on racism in the police, see Phillips, C., and Bowling, B., 'Racism, Ethnicity, Crime and Criminal Justice' in Maguire, Morgan, and Reiner (eds), *The Oxford Handbook of Criminology* (3rd edn, Oxford: Oxford University Press, 2002) 593–7.

[48] McConville, M., Sanders, A., and Leng, R., *The Case for the Prosecution: Police Suspects and the Construction of Criminality* (London: Routledge, 1991) 26–8.

[49] Quinton, P., Bland, N., and Miller, J., *Police Stops, Decision-making and Practice* (London: HMSO, 2000) vi.

[50] Classic accounts include: Banton, M., *The Policeman in the Community* (London: Tavistock, 1964); Skolnick, J., *Justice without Trial* (New York: Wiley, 1975).

fears, and vent their frustrations and anger. But neither *causes* them to behave in a certain way when dealing with members of the public, nor corresponds with their actual practice.'[51] If this is so, then the distinction between cop and canteen culture is important in differentiating between what the police say and what they do.[52] The second danger is that cop culture is commonly portrayed as static and unchanging, whereas it is influenced by changes in law, in policy, and in the larger society from which the police are recruited. It is by no means necessary, therefore, that in focusing on the cultural determinants of police practice we should accord law little or no role at all.[53] Instead of distinguishing between 'law in the books' and the realities of policing practice, we might better see law and police culture as interactive. Legal rules, like other rules, are an important part of the context in which culture is formed. Thus, despite the evident importance of discretion and cop culture to the practice of policing, we need not abandon the idea that the police are legal actors. The exercise of discretion and the influence of professional culture upon policing might require rather that we reconceive what law is and how it operates in practice.

WARRIORS IN THE FIGHT AGAINST CRIME

The notion of the police as citizens in uniform or officers of the law has been overlaid by the self-presentation of the police as warriors in the fight against crime. Increasingly distanced from those they police, some officers think of themselves as upholding the thin blue line against social collapse. The imagery of war and of militarism is a central feature of this perspective. It shares certain characteristics of the crime control model in characterizing policing as the pursuit of the guilty whose convictions must be sought even at the cost of infringing due process rights. Legal regulation of the police is regarded as an unwarranted fetter on their ability to pursue criminals. But the warrior model goes further still in suggesting that illegal police practices are justified as a necessary evil in the fight against rising crime. Sanders and Young characterize this perspective thus: 'only the police know what it is really like "out there". If the naïve, well-meaning, respectable majority knew what it was like, they would not

---

[51] Hoyle, C., *Negotiating Domestic Violence* (Oxford: Clarendon Press, 1998) 75.

[52] Waddington, P. A. J., 'Police (Canteen) Sub-Culture: An Appreciation' (1999) *British Journal of Criminology* 287–309.

[53] Dixon, D., *Law in Policing: Legal Regulation and Police Practices* (Oxford: Clarendon Press, 1997) 13 ff.; Chan, J., 'Changing Police Culture' (1996) 36 *British Journal of Criminology* 109–34.

make police officers work with one hand tied behind their backs.'[54] The imagery of a war on crime has the effect of casting offenders, suspects, and entire social and, more particularly, ethnic groups as the putative enemy whose every move is regarded with suspicion and whose very presence in public space is seen to require justification. The effect is both to isolate and alienate the police from those they police and to promote social exclusion of those targeted by the police as a means to crime control.[55] A common effect of this frame is to encourage policing styles that are proactive, aggressive, and that favour the use of force over negotiation or attempts to dissipate conflict. It tends also to focus on certain types of police activity: undercover surveillance, detective work, and special operations such as those by drug squads. Thinking about the police as warriors highlights the use of high-tech gadgetry and specialist weaponry (arms, firearms, protective clothing, shields, and armoured vehicles). It focuses attention too on the policing of certain kinds of crime: the public order policing of riots and other disturbances, the targeting of drug dealing, and crackdowns on certain kinds of anti-social behaviour.

Of course it is not only the police who conceive of themselves as warriors. Politicians, the media, partisan groups, and lobbyists together foster this conception of policing. This perspective thus serves not only as a way of analysing what the police do but also as a force for legitimizing certain kinds of police behaviour and for privileging certain kinds of police work, in particular, special operations against perceived threats to public order or safety.

AGENTS OF SOCIAL DISCIPLINE

The classical models of the criminal process with which we began characterize police behaviour as dynamic or anticipatory. At each stage the police anticipate the demands of the next stage so that suspects are stopped and searched with a view to arrest; arrest is carried out with a view to charging; interrogation seeks to elicit evidence that will provoke a guilty plea or provide the basis for prosecution. In sum, the police act at every stage with one eye towards the authoritative legal resolution of the suspected offence. Quite another reading of the role of the police is that they are agents of social discipline[56] or practitioners of punishment

---

[54] Sanders, A., and Young, R., *Criminal Justice* (2nd edn, London: Butterworths, 2000) 76.

[55] Bowling, B., and Foster, J., 'Policing and the Police' in Maguire, Morgan, and Reiner (eds), *The Oxford Handbook of Criminology* (3rd edn, Oxford: Oxford University Press, 2002) 984.

[56] Choongh, S., *Policing as Social Discipline* (Oxford: Clarendon Press, 1997).

within the process itself.[57] Understood this way, the police are less interested in seeking resolution through the law, still less through the courts.
They see themselves not as the start of a continuing legal process
(whether crime control conveyor belt or due process obstacle course) but
rather as its common end point. Detention in the police station is not the
trigger of the process; rather, it is considered an end in itself or a site of
social discipline. Social discipline, according to Choongh, is the
imposition of 'summary punishment through illegal detention'.[58] Its
principal objectives are: 'maintaining authority, extracting deference,
reproducing social control and inflicting summary punishment'.[59]
According to this model, the police see their role primarily as disciplinary: meting out judgments about the moral worth of those they deem to
threaten respectable society. Whether those in police custody have committed a crime or not is less important than the threat their behaviour (or
even demeanour) is deemed to pose to authority. The police regard themselves as prime authority figures and seek to neutralize this threat by
asserting their power over those who challenge it. This assertion of police
authority thus has less to do with responding to or preventing crime than
communicating the relative power relations between the police and the
policed.

This interpretation of policing furnishes several illuminating possible
explanations for central conundrums within the criminal process. One is
that it helps to explain the very small numbers of cases that proceed to
trial. A goodly proportion of those cases falling out of the process do so
for lack of evidence or because they fail to satisfy public interest requirements. Beyond these, however, are the many cases that have not failed but
arguably were never intended for trial. These are the cases subject to
police resolution within the police station, which in Choongh's analysis
are 'from the outset . . . treated as *police* cases rather than as *criminal*
cases'.[60]

Interpreting policing as social discipline also provides a partial explanation for the repeated reappearance of the same suspects within the police
station. If those detained are not so much suspects of particular crimes as

---

[57] Feeley, M., *The Process is the Punishment: Handling Cases in a Lower Criminal Court*
(New York: Russell Sage Foundation, 1979).
[58] McConville, M., and Mirsky, C., 'Guilty plea courts: A social disciplinary model of
criminal justice' (1995) 42 *Social Problems* 216–34 at 217 ff.; Choongh, S., *Policing as Social
Discipline* (Oxford: Clarendon Press, 1997) 174.
[59] Choongh, S. op cit., 41.
[60] Choongh, S., 'Policing the Dross: A Social Disciplinary Model of Policing' (1998) 38
British Journal of Criminology 623–34 at 625.

members of designated target populations, deemed to threaten the authority of the police, it is hardly surprising that the same names appear again and again. According to Choongh, 'Policing is based upon a social disciplinary model of justice when the police, rather than investigating specific individuals whom they have reasonable suspicion to believe have committed specific offences, choose instead to use their powers to control or punish communities, families or individuals.'[61]

Let us explore the applicability of this model to core police activities. Stop and search becomes less a tool by which the police discover crime than a means by which they control those categorized as belonging to suspect populations. The requirement of reasonable suspicion, although intended as a fetter or inhibition on police abuse of this power, is so poorly defined as to allow the police considerable leeway to stop those they choose. This raises the unanswerable question of how far policing is reactive to reasonable suspicions of law-breaking behaviour and how far it is proactive. Do the police seek out trouble, for example by baiting people on the streets with the hope of provoking abusive reactions or violent confrontations which legitimize the full use of their powers? Certainly research provides some evidence that the police actively seek out confrontation because they feel that they are not being offered sufficient respect or because they wish to assert the authority of their office over those they police.[62]

Likewise, detention in the police station may be seen less as a mechanism for restraining suspects prior to interrogation than as an act of discipline in and of itself. The imbalance of power within the police station is such that 'the legal position amounts to a negation of the presumption of innocence'.[63] According to this perspective, innocence or guilt is almost an irrelevance in a scenario that is not about determining the truth but about asserting authority. Put another way, detention is a means of imposing control, of extracting deference, of reducing those detained to a position of absolute submission. Accordingly, at least some of those held in police stations are better seen not as suspects in the usual sense but as detainees, whose detention is part of an ongoing conflict between the police and particular subgroups within the population.

Interrogation is traditionally seen as essential to the construction of the case in that it provides the police with the means to elicit, at first hand,

---

[61] Choongh, S., *Policing as Social Discipline* (Oxford: Clarendon Press, 1997) 222.

[62] McConville, M., and Shepherd, D., *Watching Police, Watching Communities* (London: Routledge, 1992) 149.

[63] Choongh, S., *Policing as Social Discipline* (Oxford: Clarendon Press, 1997) 208.

information about the commission of an offence. But according to the logic of social discipline, interrogation is better understood as a means by which the police can exert their authority. Research evidence suggests that confession evidence is important in a small and declining proportion of cases.[64] Nonetheless, interrogations are carried out as a matter of routine, irrespective of whether prosecution is contemplated or confession evidence is necessary to the construction of the case. Confession evidence may be less essential to the preparation of the case for the prosecution, therefore, but rather a ground for legitimizing the disciplinary activities of police within the station.

Finally, police cautioning looks very different under the social discipline model. Conventionally, cautioning is lauded as a means by which less serious offenders (particularly juveniles) can be diverted from the unduly punitive and stigmatizing effects of the full criminal process whilst suffering an apposite and deterrent admonition for ill-conduct. But cautioning can be seen as a system of summary justice which rides roughshod over due process considerations and dispenses even with the legitimizing ritual of the trial to allow the police wide powers to punish those who may or may not be legally guilty. Cautioning (like other forms of diversion such as pre-trial restorative justice conferences) relies wholly on the confession of the accused to permit punitive intrusions that may in future have important ramifications for repeat offenders.

The social discipline model cannot provide a complete explanation of policing. If it did, then logically one would not expect any case to go to trial. Instead it offers a partial explanation of some aspects of policing or, perhaps, suggests a parallel or shadow system of policing that serves police-defined goals rather than the formal one of prosecution. This shadow system intersects with the formal process and is parasitic upon the powers of investigation and detention conferred upon the police in the name of law enforcement. Most importantly, it raises the question of whether one should think of the process as implying progression toward an end at all.

SYSTEMS MANAGERS

The two preceding models of police as warriors in the fight against crime and as agents of social discipline cast the police in a highly politicized role. Quite another way of looking at the role of the police in the criminal process is as systems managers engaged in an essentially bureaucratic task

[64] Ibid. 130–2.

that is neutral as to its orientation and ultimate goals.[65] Understood this way, the criminal process is less about fostering social order, upholding the rule of law, fighting crime, or imposing discipline than about the efficient management of a bureaucratic system. As key workers within this system, the police are primarily concerned with its internal efficiency. They do not work toward securing convictions but instead measure their success by reference to process-based performance indicators. Their central priorities are ensuring efficiency, economy, achieving performance targets, responding to the requirements of audit, and satisfying standards of service delivery and consumer satisfaction.[66] Systems-based mechanisms of accountability, it is argued, explain more about the day-to-day practice of policing, than larger, loftier, or indeed grubbier police motives. The test of performance is not a particular outcome but any outcome achieved according to predetermined standards of efficiency and economy. An investigation that results in 'no further action' is quite as much a success as that which results in a conviction, provided the relevant performance indicators are met in its pursuit.

Thinking about the police as systems managers also has implications for understanding their relationships with one another and with other actors in the criminal process. Ensuring the smooth running of the bureaucratic machine may have greater priority than fulfilling the ascribed roles of prosecutor and defence formally essential to the adversarial process. It should come as no surprise to learn that police and duty solicitors have warmer and friendlier relations than their ostensibly oppositional roles might suggest. Minimizing conflict and maintaining good working relations is important to the efficient discharge of both parties' daily duties. To challenge every breach of protocol by the police would not be conducive to the defence solicitors' continuing working relations within the police station nor would it conduce to an easy working life. As Cape reports: 'the main research finding was that defence lawyers generally said little or nothing in police interviews and rarely intervened to protect their clients' interests'.[67] Likewise for the police, cooperation by defence solicitors and a willingness to turn a blind eye to minor improprieties are

---

[65] King, M., *The Framework of Criminal Justice* (London: Croom Helm, 1981) 104.

[66] Loader, I., and Sparks, R., 'Contemporary Landscapes of Crime, Order, and Control: Governance, Risk, and Globalization' in Maguire, Morgan, and Reiner (eds), *The Oxford Handbook of Criminology* (3rd edn, Oxford: Oxford University Press, 2002) 88; Jones, C., 'Auditing Criminal Justice' (1993) 33 *British Journal of Criminology* 187–202.

[67] Cape, E., 'Assisting and Advising Defendants Before Trial' in McConville and Wilson (eds), *The Handbook of the Criminal Justice Process* (Oxford: Oxford University Press, 2002) 109.

important lubricants to the smooth running of the bureaucratic machine and, as such, are likely to be rewarded in future interactions. For both parties, the effective processing of cases eases the burdens of their respective jobs. A system that is formally adversarial is informally characterized more by collusion than by conflict.

It is arguable that the bureaucratic tendencies of policing have increased under the growing imperatives of managerialism. Managerialism or the 'audit explosion' is a political move to increase 'economy, efficiency, and effectiveness' in public life through the mechanism of audit. The increasing role of the Audit Commission in matters of criminal justice is just one manifestation of the growth of this culture. In prioritizing so-called key performance indicators (KPIs) as the standards by which the police are judged, the audit culture challenges the primacy of legalism. Drives towards efficiency or getting results may prove stronger than those toward going by the book. As a consequence, tensions inevitably arise between formal rule-following and performance-orientated behaviour designed to satisfy the exigencies of the audit.[68]

Central to the audit culture is the idea that the police should be responsive to consumer demand. By emphasizing the service nature of policing, this culture encourages local communities to be more demanding and to insist upon greater local accountability, for example, through consultative committees. Whether in practice this has any appreciable impact upon the way the police operate is another question entirely, not least because a parallel trend toward more centralized control undermines the ability of the police to respond to local demand. Further, the imperatives of managerialism mean that financial controls trump all other obligations, even to consumers of police services.

OTHER WAYS OF THINKING ABOUT POLICING

These various interpretations of policing are by no means exhaustive. Other obvious frames of analysis include conceiving of the police as a frontline emergency service whose primary role is not to fight crime but to respond to public calls for assistance, only a small proportion of which are crime related. Another is to conceive the police as a low-level peace-keeping force engaged in routine negotiations and dispute resolution between warring neighbours and other rival factions. In addition to these functional roles, the police fulfil an important symbolic role as cultural

---

[68] Power, M., *The Audit Society: Rituals of Verification* (Oxford: Oxford University Press, 1997).

icons.[69] Their distinctive uniforms, the bizarre anachronism of their domed helmets, and the flashing blue light of the speeding police car carry huge symbolic capital. It is not by chance that many little boys own a policeman's helmet and chase around the playground catching robbers. The police represent important authority figures whose looming presence in our childhood understanding of the world scarcely diminishes as we grow up. Today, an increasingly important conception of the police is as risk managers.[70] Understood in terms of risk, policing is less about detecting crime, constructing cases, or pursuing the truth than about managing an unruly population situated permanently outside civil society. This approach starts from the pessimistic premise that crime is not eradicable and that the criminal process can have little purchase on controlling crime. In place of the traditional retrospective orientation of policing as response to past offences, the management of risk requires that the police focus their efforts on preventing future offences. The work of the police is thus concerned less with establishing the legal guilt of juridical subjects than with the management of suspect populations. We shall return to explore this last characterization of the police as risk managers in our final chapter.

The diversity of police roles probably precludes the possibility that any single frame could adequately account for its variety. We have said little about policing as public order maintenance, state security service, investigative detective agency, still less about the increasingly important realm of trans-national and international policing. Instead of seeking to force these roles into one model or trying to reconcile different accounts with one another, we might do better to recognize that since policing is subject to constant shift and change, multiple models better account for the complexity of who the police are and what they do.[71]

THE POLICED

These different ways of thinking about policing suggest some interesting insights into the subject of those they police. The frame of analysis we adopt largely determines how we analyse those subject to policing and

[69] Loader, I., and Mulcahy, A., *Policing and the Condition of England* (Oxford: Oxford University Press, 2003).

[70] Ericson, R., and Haggerty, K., *Policing the Risk Society* (Oxford: Oxford University Press, 1997).

[71] King, M., *The Framework of Criminal Justice* (London: Croom Helm, 1981) 13.

their role within the criminal process. Just as prevailing models of policing wax and wane, so too do those relating to suspects.

If historically the predominant model for thinking about the police was as citizens in uniform, it followed that those subject to policing differ from those who police them only in that they happened not to wear uniform nor be burdened by its special responsibilities. Conceiving police officers as citizens in uniform did not place them above those they policed. The subjects of policing, as **equal citizens**, stood squarely alongside the police and expected to be served by them. Insofar as the police are thought of principally as legal actors upholding the rule of law, then those they police are juridical subjects protected by law and assumed innocent until proven guilty, as suspects whose rights are to be protected throughout the process. Thinking of suspects as juridical subjects has the undoubted advantage of emphasizing the extensive legal protections that apply to those stopped and searched, arrested, interrogated, or held in police custody. It draws attention also to the legal responsibility of the police to abide by the limits upon their powers and the vital role of defence lawyers in ensuring that these limits are observed. From this perspective, debate about the need to achieve a balance between police powers and suspects' rights sets up a false opposition that casts suspects into the role of victims of police powers rather than, as they ought properly to be, subjects of legal investigation but also of legal protection.

In practice, the basic human rights enshrined in the European Convention on Human Rights and incorporated into English law under the Human Rights Act 1998 are not central to the purpose of the criminal process;[72] are not conscientiously upheld by the police; and may not even be known to the suspect. The right to contact the outside world, the right to silence, and the right to legal advice are all routinely ignored, delayed, or denied to those in police custody.[73] The protections ostensibly offered by the tape recording of interviews can be undermined by the continuing practice of conducting informal interviews en route to the station to 'establish a rapport' or soften up the suspect in advance of the formal interview.[74] The duty of the custody officer is to uphold suspects' rights within the police station but their weak structural position and their need

---

[72] Ashworth, A., *The Criminal Process: An Evaluative Study* (2nd edn, Oxford: Oxford University Press, 1998) 65–6.

[73] Cape, E., 'Assisting and Advising Defendants Before Trial' in McConville and Wilson (eds), *The Handbook of the Criminal Justice Process* (Oxford: Oxford University Press, 2002) 109.

[74] Field, S., 'Defining Police Interviews' (1993) 13 *Legal Studies* 254–63.

to maintain working relations with colleagues limits their willingness and ability to do so. Vulnerable suspects, particularly the young, the mentally disordered, and the physically disabled, are a particular responsibility of the custody officer who is supposed to furnish them with an 'appropriate adult'. But identifying those in need of such protection is haphazard.[75] Lack of specialist mental health training among police surgeons leaves many of those with mental health problems unidentified. Where an appropriate adult is provided, lack of training undermines their effectiveness. In sum, the protection of legal rights falls far short of that which the conception of the suspect as juridical subject dictates.

Part of the explanation for these derogations is that, insofar as the police conceive of themselves as warriors in the fight against crime, those they police come to be seen as **enemy combatants** to be captured and defeated. Thinking of policing as a form of warfare tends also to imply suspension of normal safeguards, legitimated by the 'extraordinary' conditions of war. The enemy is deserving of no special treatment but can expect to suffer the full rigours that a state of emergency requires. Where criminals and others subject to policing are cast in the role of the enemy, they too are prone to be subjugated with little regard for their individual rights. The War on Drugs, begun in America and latterly imported to Britain, exemplifies the way in which drug users and drug pushers have been cast into this enemy combatant role.[76] Typically, stereotyped as black, impoverished inner city dwellers, they are all too readily sensationalized as posing a particular threat to social order.

Conceiving the police as agents of social discipline has the more damaging effect still of casting those they police into an irredeemable **underclass or outcast group** unworthy of respect or the accordance of basic rights. With this group deemed to stand outside citizenship, the police feel little compunction in denying suspects the dignities warranted by respectable members of society. According to Choongh's ethnographic research, the police regard those they police as the 'dross', the 'scum', the 'toe-rags' who fail to show the deference due to their office.[77]

---

[75] Peay, J., 'Mentally Disordered Offenders, Mental Health, and Crime' in Maguire, Morgan, and Reiner (eds), *The Oxford Handbook of Criminology* (3rd edn, Oxford: Oxford University Press, 2002) 758.

[76] Sheptycki, J., 'The Drug War' in Sheptycki (ed), *Issues in Trans-national Policing* (London: Routledge, 2000). South, N., 'Drugs, Alcohol and Crime' in Maguire, Morgan, and Reiner (eds), *The Oxford Handbook of Criminology* (3rd edn, Oxford: Oxford University Press, 2002) 927–8.

[77] Choongh, S., 'Policing the Dross: A Social Disciplinary Model of Policing' (1998) 38 *British Journal of Criminology* 623–34 at 628.

If, instead, we think of the police as systems managers, those subject to policing may play little role other than as **auditable subjects** in a system that has less interest in their guilt or innocence than in processing them efficiently and speedily. To the extent that they have the capacity to hinder its smooth running by failing to comply with the demands laid upon them, by insisting upon upholding their rights in a manner that retards its progress, or complaining, those subject to policing are but grit in the machine.

Insofar as the police are increasingly playing the role of risk managers, those they police come to be understood not as individuals suspected of any given crime but as members of a **generically suspect population**. As Feeley and Simon observe, 'this does not mean that individuals disappear in criminal justice. They remain, but increasingly they are grasped not as coherent subjects, whether understood as moral, psychological or economic agents, but as members of particular sub-populations and the intersection of various categorical indicators.'[78] Actuarial calculations of risk target those belonging to a particular economic class, sub-culture, racial minority, or youth cohort. Simply belonging to one of these groups is sufficient grounds to be regarded as a legitimate target for police intervention irrespective of any legal wrongdoing or the suspicion thereof. The young, the poor, and members of ethnic minority populations are most typically subject to this policing by typology.

These various models characterize those subject to policing as its unwilling, passive subjects who can do nothing other than hope to get out of the station as fast as possible. But given that the vast majority of suspects reappear again and again, it could be argued that the relationship between the police and the policed is characterized not only by conflict but also by continuing, common dependence. Although the police are clearly in a position of superior power, they are at least partially dependent upon those they police to cooperate to achieve mutually acceptable ends. Police clear-up rates require that suspects confess, that they ask for multiple other offences to be taken into consideration, that they provide information about other suspects, and that they agree to act as conduits of information (or 'grasses') to individual police officers about other past or future crimes. Such cooperation, if one can call it that, is essential to the daily working life of the police, not least in making plea

---

[78] Feeley, M., and Simon, J., 'Actuarial Justice: The Emerging New Criminal Law' in D. Nelken (ed), *The Futures of Criminology* (London: Sage, 1994) 178.

bargaining possible.[79] Seen this way, the police and those they police are **co-dependent regulars**, engaged in recurring rounds of confrontation and negotiation. Though this characterization may overstate their mutual dependence and though it certainly underplays the evident power imbalance at the heart of policing, it captures certain aspects of the process not reflected in the analytical frames discussed so far. Many of those who are subject to policing time and time again become old hands at the game, they are well known to the police, and they know those who detain and interrogate them. Familiarity may breed contempt but it also fosters an awareness of the rules of the game and a certain ease or fluency in handling the undeniably unhappy situation of finding oneself subject to the criminal process again. With the threat of coercion hanging heavily over them, suspects' willingness to respond to informal warnings, to show appropriate deference, to take advice, or to exhibit remorse play no small part in determining the process that follows.

VICTIMS IN THE CRIMINAL PROCESS

The role of victims in the criminal process was once scarcely a subject of criminal justice scholarship. Little regarded other than as sources of information about suspects and possible offences, and as sources of evidence for the prosecution case, victims were the forgotten actors in the criminal process. That position has changed radically over past decades and it is fair to say that victims are now significant players in their own right.

We can think about the role of victims in the criminal process in several ways. First, ironically, crime victims are often **victims of the criminal process**. Insensitive questioning by the police, inadequate provision of information, delays, or unexplained decisions by prosecutors to discontinue cases entail further suffering for victims. At worst, the impact of the criminal process is tantamount to 'secondary victimization', whereby victims are as traumatized by their treatment within the criminal process as by the initial crime that triggered it.[80] Failure to recognize the burdens placed upon victims can lead them to withdraw from the criminal process and limit its ability to pursue cases effectively.[81] As the first point of

---

[79] McConville, M., 'Plea Bargaining: Ethics and Politics' (1998) 25 *Journal of Law and Society* 562–87.

[80] Maguire, M., and Pointing, J. (eds), *Victims of Crime: A New Deal?* (Milton Keynes: Open University Press, 1988) 11.

[81] Hoyle, C., and Sanders, A., 'Police Response to Domestic Violence: From Victim Choice to Victim Empowerment' (2000) 40 *British Journal of Criminology* 14–36.

contact with the criminal justice system, the police play probably the most important role in shaping the victim's experience. Whilst initial levels of satisfaction with the police are generally high, these tend to decline steadily as the case progresses.[82] Dissatisfaction arises from police failure to keep victims informed, perceived inefficiency, unhelpfulness, or unfairness. Disillusionment is a product, therefore, of a progressive feeling that the police do not care and persist in regarding victims as no more than potential sources of information.

A second way of thinking about victims is as a **political tool**. That victims have become such a focus for political concern may be related to the profound and growing sense of disillusionment across the political spectrum with the ability of the criminal justice system to do anything about crime. By contrast, concern for the victim promises relatively easy, high public relations benefits. A more sinister reading of political interest in the victim is also possible. Garland, for example, sees the victim as a political tool in the cause of punitivism. He writes: 'the interests of the victim and offender are assumed to be diametrically opposed: the rights of one competing with those of the other in a zero sum game. Expressions of concern for the offender and his needs signal a disregard for the victim and her suffering.'[83] To the extent that the police are seen as warriors in the fight against crime, it is on behalf of victims, past and prospective, that they claim to do battle. This trend is only exacerbated by some victims' lobby organizations which politicize victims' interests as being in conflict with those of offenders.[84] More generally victims have been invoked as potent rhetorical devices or symbolic tools to lever up punitiveness, to become what Ashworth calls 'victims in the service of severity'.[85] In Britain, if not in America, these punitive tendencies have been countered to some degree by the restorative justice lobby. Restorative justice is predicated on the need to redress the harm done by crime to the victim, society, *and* the offender. But it is arguable that in restorative justice, quite as much as in punitive policies, the victim is a political tool

---

[82] Newburn, T., and Merry, S., *Keeping in Touch: Police–Victim Communication* (London: HMSO, 1990).

[83] Garland, D., *The Culture of Control: Crime and Social Order in Contemporary Society* (Oxford: Oxford University Press, 2001) 180.

[84] For example, Mothers against Drunk Drivers (MADD) in the USA or Justice for Victims in the UK.

[85] Ashworth, A., 'Victims' Rights, Defendants' Rights and Criminal Procedure' in Crawford and Goodey (eds), *Integrating a Victim Perspective within Criminal Justice* (Aldershot: Ashgate, 2000) 186.

for pursuing purposes that have more to do with restoring offenders than with the interests of victims.[86]

Yet another way of thinking about victims is as users or **consumers of the criminal process**. The reliance of the criminal justice system on the victim has proved a powerful bargaining tool in the recognition of victims' interests. The culture of managerialism with its emphasis on service designates consumer satisfaction as a key performance indicator for officials of the criminal process. Cast in the role of consumer, victims are encouraged to demand better information about the progress of 'their' case and insist that their views are obtained and considered when key decisions are made in respect of bail, remand, diversion, and the like. Innovations designed to meet the consumer demands of victims abound; of which two introduced by the Victim's Charter 1996 will serve as illustrations: the so-called 'One Stop Shop' and Victim Personal Statements. The One Stop Shop initiative attempted to overcome the difficulties faced by victims in obtaining information from several different sources throughout the case. It introduced a single point of information, available to victims of more serious crimes, to ensure that they had ready access to intelligence about its progress.[87] Victim Personal Statements invite the victim to state what physical, financial, psychological, social, or emotional effects the offence had on them or their family.[88] In theory this information is then used in making decisions about prosecution, bail, and, later in the process, sentencing. Read one way, these statements are an unobjectionable means of expanding the historic role of victim as source of information. Read another way, they are a dangerous sop to victims' interests. As critics note, they create false expectations about victims' ability to direct their case and have the potential to foster disparities in decision making dependent on the personal views of individual victims.[89] And although defendants argue that they have a therapeutic value for victims, research has shown that only a minority of victims wanted to give

---

[86] A claim borne out by the fact that victim attendance at restorative justice conferences, restorative cautions, and youth offender panels is very low: Hoyle, C., 'Securing Restorative Justice for the "Non-Participating" Victim' in Hoyle and Young (eds), *New Visions of Crime Victims* (Oxford: Hart Publishing, 2002) 105.

[87] Hoyle, C. *et al.*, *Evaluation of the 'One Stop Shop' and Victim Statements Pilot Projects* (London: Home Office, 1999).

[88] Home Office, *The Victim Personal Statement Scheme* (London: Home Office, 2001); Erez, E., and Rogers, L., 'Victim Impact Statements and Sentencing Outcomes and Processes: The Perspectives of Legal Professionals' (1999) 39 *British Journal of Criminology* 216–35.

[89] Sanders, A. *et al.*, 'Victim Statements—Don't Work, Can't Work' (2001) *Criminal Law Review* 447–58.

such a statement and of those that did only a third felt better as a result.[90] A final interpretation of victims is as **bearers of rights** within the criminal process.[91] Although there is much talk of victims' rights, it is less clear upon what legal basis they are founded. The Victim's Charter, which is the chief statement of victims' interests in Britain, has no legal status and cannot be said to furnish rights in any meaningful sense. And it is significant that the report of the Justice committee, *Victims in the Criminal Justice System*,[92] uses the language of standards and of 'legitimate expectations' rather than rights. The European Convention on Human Rights (ECHR), incorporated into English law through the Human Rights Act 1998, lacks any clear statement of victims' rights, though articles relating to the protection of life, liberty, and security of the person may be invoked in relation to victims.[93] It is arguable that, as yet, such rights as victims enjoy rest principally on the acknowledged reliance of the criminal process upon their participation. In an attempt to elaborate a theory of victims' rights, Roach contends that, whilst a punitive model pits victims' rights against those of defendants, a non-punitive approach might focus instead upon crime prevention, compensation, and restorative justice.[94]

PROSECUTORS

By contrast to the police, prosecution is relatively under-researched and the subject of far less scholarly debate, so our observations on the role of prosecutors necessarily have a more tentative air.[95] As with the police, we can conceive of the role of prosecutors in several ways. In what follows

---

[90] Hoyle, C., Morgan, R., and Sanders, A., *The Victim's Charter: An Evaluation of Pilot Projects. Home Office Research Findings No. 107* (London: Home Office, 1999).

[91] Fenwick, H., 'Procedural "Rights" of Victims of Crime: Public or Private Ordering of the Criminal Justice Process?' (1997) 60 *Modern Law Review* 317–33.

[92] Justice, *Victims in Criminal Justice: Report of the Justice Committee on the Role of Victims in Criminal Justice* (London: Justice, 1998).

[93] Ashworth, A., 'Victims' Rights, Defendants' Rights and Criminal Procedure' in Crawford and Goodey (eds), *Integrating a Victim Perspective within Criminal Justice* (Aldershot: Ashgate, 2000) 188–9.

[94] Roach, K., 'Four Models of the Criminal Process' (1999) 89 *Journal of Criminal Law and Criminology* 671–716 at 706–13.

[95] Keith Hawkins's magnificent work on prosecution decision making in the Health and Safety Executive is full of insights for thinking about prosecution more generally. Hawkins, K., *Law as Last Resort: Prosecution Decision-Making in a Regulatory Agency* (Oxford: Oxford University Press, 2002). There is no comparable study of the Crown Prosecution Service.

we try to tease out both the various roles they perform, the different interpretations that may be made of their place within the criminal process, and how these change over time.

Historically, prosecution in England was at first a private responsibility and then primarily a duty of the police, though the most serious cases became the responsibility of the Director of Public Prosecutions. It was only with the establishment of the Crown Prosecution Service in 1985 that a separate national prosecution agency came into being.[96] The creation of an independent national body of prosecutors charged with responsibility for reviewing all police decisions to prosecute raises the immediate question of what relationship prosecutors have to the police and to the courts and, crucially, what it is that prosecutors do. The Crown Prosecution Service is but the most important of a number of bodies charged with prosecutorial functions. Alongside its work, there are many other non-criminal governmental agencies with investigatory and prosecutorial duties in respect of specific areas such as taxation, health and safety, the environment, and factories. Only by distinguishing between the differing philosophies and working practices of these various prosecutorial bodies does the range and variety of prosecution become clear.

LEGAL ACTORS

Conceiving of prosecutors as legal actors bound by statute and by the strictures of their respective codes suggests an entirely formal role with little scope for discretion. Yet even in those jurisdictions where prosecution is ostensibly mandatory under the so-called 'legality principle', it is not clear that discretion is obliterated altogether.[97] Prosecution in Germany, for example, used to adhere to the principle that prosecution is mandatory if there is prima facie evidence of a crime. But departure from this principle is evidenced by the fact that prosecutors continued to have leeway to determine whether or not the evidence was sufficiently robust. Evidence as to the existence of plea bargaining, especially in respect of commercial crimes, undermined the legality principle further still. Other jurisdictions, such as France, unite elements of both legality and permitted discretion. In other, so-called 'opportunity systems', such as England, prosecutorial discretion within specified limits is officially permitted.

---

[96] Under the Prosecution of Offences Act 1985, following the recommendations of the Royal Commission on Criminal Procedure (the Philips Commission).

[97] Leigh, L. H., and Zedner, L., *The Royal Commission on Criminal Justice: A Report on the Administration of Criminal Justice in the Pre-Trial phase in France and Germany* (London: HMSO, 1992) 57–78.

Although it is said that England has moved toward a legal presumption in favour of prosecution, increases in the rate of discontinuance suggest that discretion still constitutes an important characteristic of the system. Given that the official function of the prosecutor is to undertake legal review of the file, this exercise of discretion hardly constitutes a departure from legalism. In short, prosecutors in opportunity systems are arguably no less legal actors than those in legality systems.

A greater difficulty in determining the extent to which prosecutors in England are legal actors is that the Code guiding them is framed in such broad and vaguely defined terms as to offer little concrete guidance.[98] This Code sets out two tests by which prosecutors are to determine whether or not to proceed: these are the sufficiency of evidence test, namely that the evidence must be such that there is a realistic prospect of conviction, and the public interest test, namely that it must be in the public interest to proceed. The difficulty with these tests is that they invite largely subjective evaluation or, more problematically still, intuition on the part of prosecutors. Prosecutors, operating as strictly legal actors, might be expected to interpret the sufficiency of evidence test as an inquiry into the intrinsic merits of the case. But it is no surprise to learn that the test is commonly interpreted as a pragmatic or predictive enquiry—how is the court in practice likely to respond to the evidence available? Given the pressure to avoid 'cracked cases', a prosecutor's main concern is whether or not the evidence will stand up in court. This anticipatory decision making results in considerable variation in practice, leading to what has been called 'justice by geography'.

The public interest test is more amorphous still, since the criteria by which desistence from prosecution is licensed are described in the form of illustrative examples rather than developed principles or full-blown guidelines. Further, the very wording of the public interest test tends to import non-legal considerations into the process. The test states: 'in cases of any seriousness, a prosecution will usually take place unless there are public interest factors tending against prosecution which clearly out-weigh those tending in favour.'[99] Thus worded, the test creates a pre-sumption in favour of prosecution that replaces the earlier stipulation that prosecution should continue only if the public interest required it. In

---

[98] Crown Prosecution Service, *The Code for Crown Prosecutors* (London: CPS, 2000).
[99] See discussion in Ashworth, A., and Fionda, J., 'The New Code for Crown Prosecu-tors: Prosecution, Accountability and the Public Interest' (1994) *Criminal Law Review* 894–903 at 899; Daws, R., 'The New Code for Crown Prosecutors: A Response' (1994) *Criminal Law Review* 904–9 at 907.

practice, the test can be read in such a way as to license discontinuance of less serious cases on grounds of cost rather than legal criteria alone.[100] Behind the published Code, prosecutors operate according to more detailed guidelines set out in a five-volume 'Prosecution Manual',[101] but it is difficult to assess the extent to which they limit prosecutorial discretion. Further, the principle of constabulary independence, which extends to all police and prosecutorial bodies, has the effect of protecting prosecutors from any external interference concerning their decision making or, to put it more critically, of rendering them singularly unaccountable. The establishment of an independent inspectorate charged with undertaking regular reviews of the working of the prosecution service is a significant move toward remedying this lack of accountability.[102]

HANDMAIDENS OF THE POLICE

Although the establishment of an independent prosecution service was designed explicitly to introduce external review of police decision making, prosecutors remain largely dependent upon the police. The police make the initial decision whether to prosecute or not, and if they decide not to prosecute there is no possibility of review by the prosecution service. Only once the initial police decision to prosecute has been made does the file pass to the CPS. Prosecutors thus depend on files compiled by the police with a particular goal in mind. As Sanders observes: 'cases being prosecuted are usually shaped to appear prosecutable; the facts to support this are selected, and those that do not are ignored, hidden, or undermined'.[103] The facts that tend against prosecution may appear only at trial, in advance of which prosecutors have little way of knowing what has been suppressed or missed out. The fact that the prosecution service has historically been under-resourced, and consequently finds it difficult to retain high-quality staff, only exacerbates their position of structural dependence on more experienced police officers whose decision to prosecute they rarely gainsay. In cases such as rape, domestic violence, and child abuse, this may result from legitimate reliance upon the expertise of specialist police officers who have interviewed the witness and are best

---

[100] Sanders, A., 'Prosecution Systems' in McConville and Wilson (eds), *The Handbook of the Criminal Justice Process* (Oxford: Oxford University Press, 2002) 157.

[101] CPS Guidelines are being put on the Internet at <http://www.cps.gov.uk>.

[102] Her Majesty's Crown Prosecution Service Inspectorate (HMCPSI) was established under the Crown Prosecution Service Inspectorate Act 2000.

[103] Sanders, A., 'Prosecution Systems' in McConville and Wilson (eds), *The Handbook of the Criminal Justice Process* (Oxford: Oxford University Press, 2002) 158.

able to judge their credibility or capacity to stand up in court.[104] Whatever the relative experience and status of individual police officers and prosecutors, the fact that the decision to prosecute has already been made by the police creates a major structural obstacle to discontinuance. As Sanders concludes: 'at present, the CPS is not so much a decision-*maker* . . . as a decision-*reverser*'.[105]

The limited ability of prosecutors to assess and challenge the evidence is only exacerbated by the use of summaries of interviews by the police. Pressure from prosecutors had resulted in the use of summaries being largely eradicated. However, pressure to 'fast-track' minor cases destined for the magistrates' courts within twenty-four hours of charging returned prosecutors to the position of reliance upon summaries. This reliance arguably undermines the principle of equality of arms that should be at the heart of the adversarial process. It reduces prosecutors to a position of dependence in which their role is presumptively to endorse but rarely to challenge decisions already made. Although, technically, prosecutors are entitled to reverse police decisions to prosecute, the momentum of the prosecution inhibits their capacity to do so.[106] To the extent that conviction rates are used as performance indicators, the momentum toward prosecution is difficult to resist (though it is partially assuaged by the countervailing concern to avoid weak cases failing at trial). The need to maintain good working relations with the police operates as a further inhibition on their ability and their willingness to challenge police decisions.

In an attempt to pre-empt the prosecution momentum that naturally builds up after the police decide to prosecute, prosecutors have been introduced into police stations. The hope was that appropriate legal advice given at an early stage would reduce the number of inappropriate recommendations to prosecute and wrong offences charged. Whilst there are obvious benefits, not least to the accused, in cases being reviewed at an early stage, the paucity of evidence available to prosecutors at the pre-charge stage is such that the advice offered is 'as likely to reflect a prosecutor's hunch, intuition, even wishful thinking, as it is to reflect evidential considerations or the application of a trained legal mind'.[107]

---

[104] Morgan, J., and Zedner, L., *Child Victims: Crime, Impact, and Criminal Justice* (Oxford: Oxford University Press, 1992) 122.

[105] Sanders, A., op. cit. 158.

[106] Baldwin, J., 'Understanding Judge Ordered and Directed Acquittals in the Crown Court' (1997) *Criminal Law Review* 536–55 at 551.

[107] Baldwin, J., and Hunt, A., 'Prosecutors Advising in Police Stations' (1998) *Criminal Law Review* 521–36 at 535.

Furthermore, having committed themselves to one position at such an early stage, prosecutors may find it difficult to review or retract their earlier decision later on without losing face. The introduction of Criminal Justice Units in the wake of the Glidewell Report on the Crown Prosecution Service recommends that police and prosecutors should work together to determine the charge. Given the concern that prosecutors have failed to establish sufficient independence from the police, it is perhaps curious that this innovation will likely foster closer working relations between police and prosecutors.

In sum, although there is a dearth of research on prosecution analogous to the studies of policing referred to earlier in this chapter, it would appear that cultural constraints and the impact of structural factors upon decision making are at least as important in respect of the work of prosecutors as of the police.

COMPLIANCE OFFICERS

The prosecution orientation of the Crown Prosecution Service stands in stark contrast to the tendency of other agencies to seek compliance through less coercive means. For those regulatory agencies engaged in the policing of health and safety, environmental regulations, and tax laws, the rarity of prosecution is such that Hawkins describes recourse to law as a 'last resort'.[108] Although the majority of the violations at issue are relatively minor, a considerable minority are not. Sanders points out that each year some 500 people die at work, thousands die from occupational diseases, and some 18,000 suffer major work-related injuries, in most of which cases the employer was in breach of the criminal provisions of the Health and Safety Act 1974.[109] Despite their gravity, prosecution is the preferred outcome in only a tiny proportion even of those cases.

Instead, inspectors seek to ensure compliance with the regulations through a varying mixture of 'persuasion, advice, and education, through to more formal and punitive approaches such as the issuing of

---

[108] Hawkins, K., *Law as Last Resort: Prosecution Decision-Making in a Regulatory Agency* (Oxford: Oxford University Press, 2002); see also Hutter, B., *The Reasonable Arm of the Law? The Law Enforcement Procedures of Environmental Health Officers* (Oxford: Clarendon Press, 1988); and Richardson, G., Ogus, A., and Burrows, P., *Policing Pollution: a Study of Regulation and Enforcement* (Oxford: Clarendon Press, 1982).

[109] Sanders, A., 'Prosecution Systems' in McConville and Wilson (eds), *The Handbook of the Criminal Justice Process* (Oxford: Oxford University Press, 2002) 159. Compare these figures with the fact that there are fewer than 1,000 official homicides per year.

improvement or prohibition notices'.[110] These informal measures short of prosecution rely heavily upon the expertise and negotiating skills of the enforcer. The threat of prosecution remains in the background as a powerful device for concentrating the minds of the regulated on the need to comply but it is not invoked unless the violations are extremely serious. Even persistent violations are generally regarded as problems to be solved by negotiation with the violator rather than offences to be punished. Indeed, non-compliance is regarded as a familiar, even natural condition, such that inspectors expect to discover violations during factory visits or environmental audits. Their attitude to individual violations varies according to their professional assessment or characterization of organizations as persistent 'cowboys' or as generally 'cooperative', even if in practice prone to violation.

The importance of cooperation is such that Hawkins observes: 'In a symbiotic relationship, bargaining between the two sides with competing interests becomes central to the enforcement of regulation.'[111] In part this arises because the enforcers are reliant upon companies to inform them about violations, to foster an internal culture of compliance, and to police their own employees day to day. Factory inspectors, for example, recognize that instrumental compliance (complying in order to avoid detection and punishment) is only one basis upon which conformity with the law is secured. Enforcers also adduce principled compliance (whereby companies comply because they think it is right to do so); self-interest (in which the economic or commercial benefits of complying prevail); and simple custom as contributing to law-abiding behaviour. Accordingly, relying upon instrumental coercion alone is regarded as inappropriate to the task. The decision to prosecute is tantamount to an admission that all other avenues have failed. It is also a declaration of hostilities in a field that relies heavily upon amicable negotiation and continuing good relations.

A more critical reading of the tendency of non-police/CPS agencies to seek compliance is possible. Sanders argues that the propensity of non-police agencies not to prosecute can be explained as much by reference to the fact that their resources are inadequate compared to the police; that collusive relationships result in inspectors being 'captured' by the interests of those they are supposed to regulate; and finally, that they are caught on the horns of an economic dilemma, namely that if industries

---

[110] Hawkins, K., *Law as Last Resort: Prosecution Decision-Making in a Regulatory Agency* (Oxford: Oxford University Press, 2002) 42.

[111] Ibid. 280.

are regulated too rigorously the costs of compliance will cause them to fail. In contrast to the prosecution-prone practices of the CPS against the disadvantaged and the poor, those subject to compliance strategies are typically relatively wealthy: the owners of factories or commercial companies, and middle-class businessmen. The strikingly divergent policies of different prosecution agencies thus raise questions about equality of treatment and social justice.[112]

OTHER WAYS OF THINKING ABOUT PROSECUTION

We have considered just a few ways of thinking about prosecution. Others are clearly possible.[113] Prosecution serves an important expressive function in making a moral statement about the law and the costs of its violation. It furnishes an opportunity for the formal restatement of norms and the occasion to reinforce the moral boundaries of socially acceptable behaviour in the manner described by Durkheim. By signalling that wrongdoing will be subject to prescribed legal processes, it serves as a possible deterrent to potential violators and as an assurance to the law-abiding that the public interest will be protected. It provides the state with the occasion to affirm its right to regulate wrongdoing and to pursue wrongdoers to the criminal courts. It acts as a retrospective affirmation of the actions of the police in pursuing wrongdoers and so confers legitimacy upon the police. And it serves the prospective function of making possible the public determination of wrongdoing in the criminal court. In both its backward- and forward-looking orientations, prosecution epitomizes the dynamic character of the criminal process.

Whilst prosecution can be seen as a ritual affirmation of the power and duty of the state to uphold the law, it can also be read as an intensely practical device for resolving ambiguities in the law, assessing the weight and veracity of evidence, and weighing the counterbalancing interests of public, victim, and defendant. The uncertainty surrounding these contested areas opens up a considerable space for prosecutorial scrutiny, evaluation, and assessment that is, of necessity, characterized by high levels of discretion or 'professional expertise'. That this discretion arises in respect of decisions that are of relatively low visibility gives considerable power to prosecutors. However, as we have already observed, their

---

[112] Ashworth, A., 'Developments in the Public Prosecutor's Office in England and Wales' (2000) 8 *European Journal of Crime, Criminal Law and Criminal Justice* 257–82 at 265.

[113] See Hawkins, K., *Law as Last Resort: Prosecution Decision-Making in a Regulatory Agency* (Oxford: Oxford University Press, 2002) 416–24 upon which the following observations draw heavily.

structural relations with the police and their ultimate accountability to the courts act as checks upon this discretionary power.

Just as we characterized the police as systems managers, so too prosecution can be seen as an operational system burdened with the organizational demands of efficiency and accountability. As Ashworth observes: 'The annual reports of the CPS are written in the language of Voltaire's Dr Pangloss, giving the impression of a public service which is achieving most of its targets, is at the forefront of innovation in the criminal justice system, and has no significant problems.'[114] In practice the prosecution service is a subject of continuing critical scrutiny. Decisions to prosecute must make sense not only in respect of the formally published criteria of sufficiency of evidence and public interest, but in respect of the prosecution service itself. Given the vagaries of the courts, every decision to prosecute places both the individual's and the organization's reputation for winning cases on the line. Insofar as the organization feels itself under fire, the risk of a case cracking at trial may disincline prosecutors to pursue potentially weak cases even where other grounds for prosecution are strong.[115] More generally, prosecutors seek to make decisions consistent with the larger policy imperatives of their organization. These are made known to prosecutors through internal bureaucratic rules, statements, guidelines, and codes, as well as less clearly stipulated forms of practice.[116] These policy imperatives may create pressures to derogate from law by obliging prosecutors to have regard for popular concern about particular crimes, by encouraging them to meet internal efficiency standards or to pursue career incentives. But policy can also be read as the means by which legislative intent is translated into practical action. Read this way, policy is less a derogation from law than the way in which laws are clarified and their implementation made possible. Whether prosecutorial decision making is actually consistent with larger organizational policy depends also, among other factors, on the success with which policy decisions are broadcast to those charged with implementing them, the practicalities of implementation, and the resources available to do so.

---

[114] Ashworth, A., 'Developments in the Public Prosecutor's Office in England and Wales' (2000) 8 *European Journal of Crime, Criminal Law and Criminal Justice* 257–82 at 261.

[115] Though there is evidence to suggest that prosecutors continue manifestly weak cases in the hope that the defendant will plead guilty at trial: Baldwin, J., 'Understanding Judge Ordered and Directed Acquittals in the Crown Court' (1997) *Criminal Law Review* 536–55 at 543.

[116] For example, the proposals concerning the efficiency and effectiveness of case preparation in the report of Sir Ian Glidewell: Glidewell, I., *The Review of the Crown Prosecution Service: A Report* (London: HMSO, 1998).

Within the criminal process, prosecution is but a moment, albeit a critical one. It is the moment at which the merits and demerits of progressing to the rarely reached apogee of the criminal trial are weighed up. Discussing the decision to prosecute by health and safety officials, Hawkins describes this moment as one of 'transformation':

important boundaries are crossed with the decision to prosecute. Private troubles become public affairs . . . the mode of law enforcement switches abruptly from private bargaining, in which compromise outcomes are not only possible but regarded by enforcers as desirable, to public adversarial debate, in which legal justice is delivered in a binary verdict of guilty or not guilty.[117]

Further important consequences follow on the decision to prosecute: the possibility of an informal negotiated solution is abandoned; determining the legal guilt of the subject trumps other considerations; evidentiary and procedural demands take over; and the prosecution faces the hazardous challenge of persuading the criminal court that their case is made out. Control over the outcome of the case is largely ceded to those who determine guilt in court, be it magistrates or judge and jury. In short, in deciding to prosecute prosecutors takes a gamble upon which their very reputations are at stake.

CONCLUSION

In our concluding section we will consider briefly the purpose of the criminal process. We have strayed on to this topic repeatedly in this course of the chapter for the very reason that it is almost impossible to talk about what the actors in the criminal process do without slipping into discussion of why they do it. We have considered the ways in which the police uphold the criminal law, wage war on the criminal enemy, impose social discipline on, or serve their fellow citizens. We have likewise considered the role of prosecutors as legal actors, as handmaidens to the police, and have examined their attempts to induce compliance by more powerful miscreants. And we have considered the role of both police and prosecutors as systems managers motivated by quite other priorities and imperatives.

Whilst thinking about the criminal process in terms of its agents has obvious advantages in making concrete the complexity of its operation, in concluding this chapter let us take a moment to think about the process in

---

[117] Hawkins, K., *Law as Last Resort: Prosecution Decision-Making in a Regulatory Agency* (Oxford: Oxford University Press, 2002) 422.

its totality. Although the term criminal process is generally used to describe those formal activities of the criminal justice system that lie between the commission of an offence and trial, only a minority of crimes invoke any formal response by the criminal justice system. More rarely still does an offence result in the entirety of the criminal process being played out. The trial is the purported but only rarely reached endpoint of the criminal process. The striking and oft-quoted finding that only 2.2 per cent of known offences result in a conviction should alert us to the marginal quality of the trial.[118] Since reporting by the public is by far the most common means by which offences come to the attention of the police, and since less than half of offences are so reported, the criminal process does not even stir into action in the majority of cases. Even when an offence is reported, in just less than a quarter of cases (24.3 per cent) is it formally recorded by the police. There are many good reasons why reports of crimes are not recorded: the witness or victim may withdraw their report; the offence may be too trivial; evidence of its occurrence may be too slight to warrant prosecution; or it may not correspond to any existing category of criminal offence. Only 5.5 per cent of known offences are then cleared up by the police, even though 'cleared up' is a broadly defined category including those which are simply marked up as 'no further action' (NFA). A mere 3 per cent of offences result in a caution or conviction and, as we have already observed, a bare 2.2 per cent result in a conviction.

What we should make of the statistics on attrition is a subject of considerable controversy. Read one way, they suggest that the criminal process is neither a conveyor belt nor even an obstacle course.[119] It is rather a filter by which social problems are sorted into those that are amenable to legal adjudication and those that are not. The image of the filter has the advantage of making very clear the limitations of the crim-inal justice process as a device for sorting and translating social action into predetermined legal categories and reducing the murky facts of social life to legally relevant evidence. By these means, deviance is rendered amenable to legal knowledge and control. To shift the metaphor only slightly, we might describe actors in the criminal process as

---

[118] 'Known offences' are the number of offences committed as measured by the British Crime Survey: Home Office, *Information on the Criminal Justice System in England and Wales: Digest 4* (London: HMSO, 1999) 29.

[119] Though these statistics might be read as giving greater credence to the due process model than that of crime control since one might expect the latter to secure convictions in a greater percentage of cases.

laboratory technicians engaged in a process of legal distillation that removes the crime or conflict from the context in which it occurred and extracts the offender from their social-economic circumstances. In this process, evidence becomes the factual substance by which socially problematic behaviour is made legal knowable. The criminal process deliberately removes from consideration the complexities of social conflict, economic deprivation, passion, and hatred. It seeks to reduce the criminal event to a legal abstraction amenable to categorization and judgment in the court of law. Unhappily its ability to do so is contested in the poignant theatre of misery played out daily in the criminal courts, to say nothing of the more dramatic moments of murder trials.

Read another way, the statistics on attrition evidence the failure of the criminal justice system to respond effectively to those crimes reported to it: the so-called 'justice gap'. The police commonly adduce attrition rates as evidence that the balance between their powers and suspects' rights is tilted unfairly, even fatally, against them. But they can also be read as evidence of the effectiveness of the criminal process in diverting from prosecution less serious cases or those amenable to less socially and financially costly forms of resolution. The role of diversion in the criminal process is an important means of mitigating the stigma or labelling effects of prosecution. Accompanied by formal reprimands or warnings, it can serve the purposes of censure in less serious cases. This said, where cautions are used not as an alternative to prosecution but when there is insufficient evidence to prosecute then the danger of net-widening arises. The variable use of diversionary devices such as reprimands, warnings, and cautions according to the age, class, gender, and ethnic background of the suspect raises further questions about the probity of decisions to divert.[120] The fact that whilst arrest rates have risen over past decades, prosecution rates have fallen suggests a growing shift away from formal procedure toward what Hillyard and Gordon term informal justice:

there has been a radical shift in power away from a formal, open and public system of justice towards an informal and closed system. There has been a significant displacement of the court as the site of decision-making to a range of bureaucratic sites—the police station, the CPS and, in the case of juveniles, committees of social welfare experts.[121]

---

[120] Walker, C., and Wall, D., 'Imprisoning the Poor? TV Licence Evaders and the Criminal Justice System' (1997) *Criminal Law Review* 173–86.

[121] Hillyard, P., and Gordon, C., 'Arresting Statistics: the Drift to Informal Justice in England and Wales' (1999) 26 *Journal of Law and Society* 502–22 at 521.

In this shift, informal negotiation prevails over formal public rituals, and professional judgments over legal formalism with the result that, as Hillyard and Gordon observe, ' "a day in court" is now a privilege of a minority drawn into the system'.[122]

Perceptive students will see opening up before them a yawning gap between the Kantian imperative that the last guilty man not go unpunished and the practical reality that neither he nor some 96 per cent of those before him will face conviction and sanction. Whilst tabloid headlines scream that villains are getting away with their crimes, there is much in this chapter to suggest that, for the very many who face it, the process is indeed the punishment.[123]

[122] Ibid. 522.
[123] Feeley, M., *The Process is the Punishment: Handling Cases in a Lower Criminal Court* (New York: Russell Sage Foundation, 1979).

5

Court

WHAT IS THE COURT?

It is possible to reduce the criminal court to a few key characteristics: an independent judge applies pre-existing legal norms, after adversary proceedings, to achieve a dichotomous decision as to the rightness of one party and the wrongness of the other. Where there is a conviction, the judge then embarks upon a process of sentencing by which the penalty is determined and handed down. Whilst this prototype of the court captures something of its essence and might serve as a benchmark for measuring deviance from the ideal, as Shapiro wryly observes: 'if we examine what we generally call courts across the full range of contemporary and historical societies, the prototype fits almost none of them'.[1] As we shall see in the following section, he contends that the court is better captured by the idea of the triadic dispute resolution. Accepting the centrality of dispute resolution does not pre-empt the possibility of other roles however. In what follows we elaborate a series of frames for analysing what the court is, what it does, and to what ends before going on to examine the law and practice of sentencing.

PLACE OF DISPUTE RESOLUTION

We have already commented on the centrality of dispute resolution to the purposes of criminal justice. In all but the most simple or nomadic societies (where disputants can resolve their differences by wandering off in opposite directions), some mechanism for dispute resolution evolves. That mechanism typically involves the disputing parties calling upon a third party to help them achieve a solution. Indeed, Shapiro contends: 'so universal across both time and space is this simple social invention of triads that we can discover almost no society that fails to employ it. And from its overwhelming appeal to common sense stems the basic political

---

[1] Shapiro, M., *Courts—A Comparative and Political Analysis* (Chicago: University of Chicago Press, 1981) 1.

legitimacy of courts everywhere.'[2] Fundamental to the very possibility of resolution is not only that the two disputants consent to the intervention of the third party but also that they consent to the norms or laws according to which resolution is sought. In simple societies it might be possible for the parties to determine the norms and to identify the third party personally. In more complex societies, it proves convenient to substitute formal law and the office of an intermediary to whom all are deemed to consent by virtue of their membership of that society. It is in this assumed consent both to the norm and to the office of the third party that the binding authority of the decision resides.

Whilst the notion of the triad may capture the 'courtness' of courts, in practice it manifests itself in many different permutations and forms of dispute settlement. The criminal court stands at one end of this continuum of possibilities, as the most formal and coercive manifestation of the triad. In order to appreciate the extreme position and particular characteristics of the criminal court, let us reflect briefly upon the less coercive forms of triadic dispute resolution that lie along this continuum.

The least formal, least authoritative form of the triad is the go-between. The go-between may hold an assigned office or arise as an ad hoc but convenient intermediary who moves back and forth between the disputants. The role of the go-between is not usually to resolve the dispute, indeed the possibility of resolution continues to reside in the hands of the parties themselves. Rather, the go-between is a conduit for communication, a means of distancing the parties from one another and minimizing hostilities in order that they may arrive at a resolution themselves. In practice, more power adheres to this office than its name implies, the go-between is also an interpreter who can render the position of each side in such a way as to facilitate or impede resolution. Those acting as go-between prior to and at the early stages of the criminal process may fulfil this function to resolve disputes before formal proceedings begin. As we have seen, much of the work of the police entails such intervention, commonly in petty and readily resolvable disputes.

Further along the continuum, the mediator may fulfil a more openly participatory role in resolving the dispute. Again it is not the mediator's function to impose a resolution. By providing a forum for communication, by bringing the parties together, and by making constructive proposals, mediation overtly contributes to the resolution of disputes. The mediator plays a more active role than the go-between, reminding the

[2] Ibid.

parties of the norms by which they have agreed to abide, trying to persuade them to agree, and, where persuasion fails, even resorting to threats. The hope is that the very fact that the proposal comes from a neutral third party may increase its likelihood of acceptance by both parties. Mediation has also been used in family group and restorative justice conferences to bring interested parties together to try to resolve disputes.

Arbitration sits a little further along the continuum. Arbitrators are engaged to arrive at a resolution made in accordance with pre-determined norms. Typically, though not invariably, their decision is binding upon the parties. Even where the decision is binding, however, the aim of arbitration is generally to arrive at a resolution agreeable to both parties. This may be because it is important to maintain continuing relations between the parties. Where there is little to choose between the legitimacy of the claims made by the two parties, it may be that a wholly partisan resolution would lack moral authority. The resolution is typically made in accordance with legal norms and, though the hope is that it will be acceptable to both parties, it may be virtually imposed. Research on some restorative justice conferences and, more particularly, restorative cautioning panels suggests that, in practice, the police may act more like an arbitrator than a mere intermediary.[3]

Adjudication is the final stop on this continuum of increasing formalization and coercion. Adjudicators are not chosen by the parties but derive their authority by virtue of their office and the laws they uphold. Consent is, therefore, no longer important since the decision is imposed, generally irrespective of the wishes of those involved. Typically adjudicators have the power to back up unpopular decisions by organized forces of coercion, such as the police or prison. Represented by lawyers who speak for them, the parties are thrown to the periphery of the proceedings. Indeed, as Christie observes of the criminal trial: 'the one party that is represented by the state, namely the victim, is so thoroughly represented that she or he for most of the proceedings is pushed completely out of the arena, reduced to the triggerer-off of the whole thing.'[4] According to Christie, by assuming responsibility for prosecution, the state usurps the place of the victim and denies their property in the dispute altogether. Given that crime is a public wrong, however, an

---

[3] Young, R., and Goold, B. J., 'Restorative Policy Cautioning in Aylesbury' (1999) *Criminal Law Review* 126–38.

[4] Christie, N., 'Conflicts as Property' (1977) 17 *British Journal of Criminology* 1–15 at 3.

alternate view is that the state, qua representative of the public, has every right to assert its proprietary interest over that of the victim.

As a place of adjudication, the court stretches the notion of the triad to its very limits. The court as a place of dispute resolution is unbalanced both by the assertion of the binding authority of the law and by the power of the judge over the disputants. If they are to regard the resolution as just, each party must be persuaded of the neutrality of the laws and the impartiality of the judge.[5] It is hardly surprising that losers are generally disinclined to regard judgments against them as neutral, impartial, or just. As Shapiro concludes: 'Contemporary courts are involved in a permanent crisis because they have moved very far along the routes of law and office from the basic consensual triad that provides their essential social logic.'[6] It is difficult to see how the criminal court, as presently constituted, could be other than coercive. Recognizing its fraternity with less coercive forms of resolution, however, is an important reminder of a core purpose all too often obscured in contemporary practice. It is a moot point whether the positive qualities of dispute resolution could plausibly be restored to the criminal court or whether they are better pursued in other arenas entirely.

TRIAL AND CONFLICT

A major difficulty is that over time the triadic origins of the criminal court as a place of dispute resolution have been overlaid by confrontation and combat. The adversarial logic of the court is that only one side can win. The exoneration of the defendant is simultaneously a loss for the prosecutor, their witnesses, and the victim (if there is one). The vindication of the victim is likewise necessarily a defeat for the defendant. As Shapiro observes: 'when the third decides in favour of one of the two disputants, a shift occurs from the triad to a structure that is perceived by the loser as two against one. To the loser there is no social logic in two against one. There is only the brute fact of being out-numbered.'[7] This brute fact is made more brute still because the trial today is constituted as a forum where legal gladiators challenge one another in a contest whose outcome must be fatal to one party. As Rock observes:

Truth in the English criminal justice system is won dialectically and agonistically. Trials involve adversaries and adversity, defeats and victories, winners and losers.

[5] Tyler, T., *Why People Obey the Law* (New Haven: Yale University Press, 1990).

[6] Shapiro, M., *Courts—A Comparative and Political Analysis* (Chicago: University of Chicago Press, 1981) 8.

[7] Ibid. 2.

They pivot around serious allegations presented by their champions as wholly true and by their opponents as almost wholly false. At stake are very grave matters of liberty and confinement, accusation and vindication, reputation and veracity, matters which passionately concern defendants and defence witnesses, victims and prosecution witnesses.[8]

It is no surprise that the court evokes strong emotions in all its players since they find themselves in the structural situation of winning or losing everything. These emotions reveal themselves most clearly in the vicious exchange that is cross-examination. Cross-examination, by its very nature, obliges each side to call into question the moral probity of the other. Success relies upon one side persuading the magistrate or jury that their version of events is true and that that of their opponent is false. Self-evidently, that end is more readily achieved if the character of a defendant or witness can be successfully impugned. The result is that it is not merely the facts of the case that are on trial but the moral standing of all those involved. Thus the role of the prosecutor is not only to call into question the veracity of the defendant's claim to innocence but to debase his very character. It is for this reason that Garfinkel described the trial as a degradation ceremony.[9] Of course if the case results in an acquittal, that serves as a powerful exoneration, whatever went on before. Garfinkel's analysis might profitably have been extended to witnesses and victims who appear as witnesses since all those who take the stand face a similar risk of being humiliated. As Rock observes:

The work of defence counsel in cross-examination is substantively the same as that of the prosecution. It is to make witnesses appear so inconsistent, forgetful, muddled, spiteful, or greedy that their word cannot safely be believed. Victims and defendants, prosecution and defence witnesses alike face accusations of mendacity, impropriety, and malice. . . . The outcome is that the trials are among the most charged of all secular rituals. They are infused with feelings which threaten continually to erupt.[10]

Despite its organization around conflict, the trial holds within it more positive possibilities. For the accused, the trial might serve as a means to

---

[8] Rock, P., 'Witnesses and Space in a Crown Court' (1991) 31 *British Journal of Criminology* 266–79 at 267.
[9] Garfinkel, H., 'Conditions of Successful Degradation Ceremonies' (1956) 61 *American Journal of Sociology* 420–4; though on the ethical dilemmas faced by barristers, see Temkin, J., 'Prosecuting and Defending Rape: Perspectives from the Bar' (2000) 27 *Journal of Law and Society* 219–48.
[10] Rock, P., 'Witnesses and Space in a Crown Court' (1991) 31 *British Journal of Criminology* 266–79 at 267.

tell their story, to be heard, and even to be exonerated. For the victim, the court might be a place of vindication, of catharsis, or of closure. But the dual aspect of the court as a place of exoneration for the defendant or of vindication for the victim cannot be maintained simultaneously. As it is presently constituted the court is a forum in which one side must lose. It is an open question whether, if it were possible to reject the brutal logic of victory and defeat, less costly forms consistent with the place of the court on the continuum of dispute resolution might be evolved.

RITUAL

Quite another reading of the criminal trial is as a place of ritual and spectacle. The court and the trial process remain perhaps the most public, most publicized aspect of criminal justice. The imposing architecture of the courthouse is designed to declare law's authority. As a public edifice, the courthouse is often centrally situated and well signed to its neighbouring community both by the grandeur of its architecture and by prominent symbols of authority. As Rock observes, the turrets, crenellations, and pinnacles of the Victorian Crown Court was designed to 'engender a feeling of awe and respect in the public'.[11] The towering statute of Justice herself high above the Central Criminal Court (the Old Bailey) is a prime example of the use of symbolism by the criminal court. It is perhaps less clear that modern courthouse design, being more functional and less exuberant, can compete with such clear symbolism. The interior design of the courtroom, and particularly its use of space, is also designed to convey certain symbolic messages to the public. Traditionally, the panelled interior, the raised bench of the judge, and the railed dock for the defendant all send out signals as to the role and status of the proceedings and its participants. Modern courtroom design may dispense with some of the more archaic trappings but it is careful to preserve the symbolic power of its layout.

Legal actors with their archaic gowns, antiquated wigs, and stilted, formalized forms of speech communicate their exclusive purchase on the rarefied corpus of knowledge that prevails within the court. The combined effect is designedly intimidating. So too are proceedings within the courtroom, conducted in accordance with arcane rules of highly stylized ritual. The rising of the assembled company at the entrance of the judge; the calling and swearing in of witnesses; and the dramatic

---

[11] Rock, P., *The Social World of an English Crown Court: Witness and Professionals in the Crown Court Centre at Wood Green* (Oxford: Clarendon Press, 1993) 202.

exchange that is cross-examination are all designed to proclaim the gravity and authority of the proceedings. The deliberate pace and formalized temporal routines further underline the majesty of the court's proceedings.

The public is invited into the courtroom, as observers in the public gallery, as witnesses in the box, as jurors, and via the agency of court reporters whose scribbled notes form the basis of countless column inches and news reports. As Garland has observed 'Even in the lower courts, where crimes are mundane and the sentences routine, there is a ritual evocation of the symbols of justice and an implied address to the watching public.'[12] Indeed, the implied presence of public observers even when there are none is an important fiction in satisfying the old rubric that justice must not only be done but be seen to be done. The 'seeing' here is not a passive activity. As actual, distant, or fictional observers, the public represent that moral community in whose name justice is dispensed and according to whose moral precepts sentences are determined. By these various means society is deemed to participate in the ritual of the courtroom. The experience of family courts in some jurisdictions has been that authority and legitimacy breaks down when proceedings are less public and less formal. In this light, the trial is a public performance that is as much about imposing social order upon the larger world outside the court as upon those within its walls.

In so characterizing the court, there is a danger that we appear to suggest that the signals sent out invariably succeed in evoking respect for law and the authority of its legal actors. In practice, the ritual of the court provokes very mixed reactions in its multiple audiences. Divisions of class, race, age, and gender counter the court's claim to authority and justice. As a consequence, its operation may appear coercive, partial, and unjust, and its decisions evoke not respect but indignation and even fury. Perceptions of bias, particularly against members of ethnic or religious minorities, are a source of particular concern.[13]

In case it is thought that challenges to the symbolic authority of the court are a recent phenomenon born of a multi-cultural and multi-faith society, it is illuminating to reflect upon the role of the court in the

---

[12] Garland, D., *Punishment and Modern Society: A Study in Social Theory* (Oxford: Oxford University Press, 1990) 70.

[13] Interestingly, a recent study of ethnic minority court users suggests that perceptions of racial bias appear to be less widely held than in the past: Hood, R., Shute, S., and Seemungal, F., *Ethnic Minorities in the Criminal Courts: Perceptions of Fairness and Equality of Treatment* (London: Lord Chancellor's Department, 2003).

eighteenth century, about which there is a wealth of historical research.[14] Our received image of the eighteenth-century court as a majestic spectacle inducing deference through the exercise of judicial mercy has been profoundly shaken by King's vivid evidence of the difficulties faced by assize judges in controlling courtroom crowds. In capital cases, in particular, the crowds were powerful actors who brought pressure to bear upon judge, jury, and prosecutors alike to secure merciful outcomes in all but exceptional cases. One colourful example, cited by King, will suffice to illustrate the power of the crowd. In 1800, after convicting a young boy for a capital offence, one Judge Hotham recorded: 'The scene was dreadful on passing sentence and to pacify the feelings of a most crowded court, who all expressed their horror . . . by their looks and manners, after stating the necessity of the prosecution . . . I hinted something slightly of its still being . . . open to clemency.'[15] That this counter-theatre of the crowd had the power to gainsay all the pomp and ceremony that surrounded the assize judge's declaration of the death sentence and induce him to mercy dents a hole in the notion that the courts, at any time, hold unassailable symbolic power.

The elaborate rules of procedure that surround the workings of the court might be seen as a means not only of ensuring due process, but of subjecting all those involved to their considerable discipline. Together, rules of procedure and of evidence, the formality of proceedings, and the careful management of space both within and outside the courtroom[16] serve to ensure that, for the most part, trials are controlled events and that the potential for subversion of law's authority is contained.

LEGAL INSTITUTION

The importance of the court as an emblematic legal institution is yet another reason why the origin of the court as a forum for dispute resolution has been obscured. The legal role of the court is open to several interpretations. First, the criminal court is a coercive legal instrument. Through its offices the state may hold its subjects guilty of wrongdoing, may censure and pass sentence upon them. The activity of judging

---

[14] Hay, D., 'Property, Authority and the Criminal Law' in Hay *et al.* (eds), *Albion's Fatal Tree: Crime and Society in Eighteenth Century England* (London: Allen Lane, 1975); Gatrell, V., *The Hanging Tree: Execution and the English People, 1770–1868* (Oxford: Oxford University Press, 1994); King, P., *Crime, Justice and Discretion in England, 1740–1820* (Oxford: Oxford University Press, 2000).

[15] King, P. op. cit., 255. See also ch. 10, 'Rituals of Punishment'.

[16] Rock, P., 'Witnesses and Space in a Crown Court' (1991) 31 *British Journal of Criminology* 266–79.

furnishes the occasion for making authoritative statements of legal norms and for restating the rules in order to make clear the entitlements and, more particularly, the obligations of the citizen. The two activities are more closely related than may at first appear since the assertion of legal authority is simultaneously a means of asserting power over the citizen: 'once they enter the drama of criminal court proceedings, real concrete persons and their disputes are transposed into "a peculiar juridical reality, parallel with the real world" '.[17] The defendant is cast as a legal actor and, unless it is proven according to arcane rules otherwise, is assumed to be a rational actor. The rational actor is deemed to be responsible and free to exercise his or her will unfettered and equally with all others. The realities of structural inequality, of class, gender, or race discrimination, of constraints or barriers to the exercise of free will are barely acknowledged. According to Pashukanis, therefore, 'the criminal court is not only an embodiment of the abstract legal form', it is also 'a weapon in the immediate class struggle'.[18] It is not necessary to adopt the Marxian analysis of class struggle to be impressed, nonetheless, by the efficiency of the court in divorcing those subject to its power from the socio-economic context in which their alleged offences occurred. Indeed, key legal principles such as equality before the law presume a fictitious parity at odds with the realities of defendants' lives. The principle of equality is upheld as central to the legitimacy of law but, in ignoring structural inequality and in maintaining the legal fiction of free will, it serves rather to reinforce the repressive nature of the court.

A second, more benign reading is that the criminal court is a key institution in the relationship between citizen and the state but one that has the power to protect as well as to condemn and sanction. The citizen charged with crime is in a peculiarly vulnerable position in relation to the state. As Honoré observes, 'one way of protecting the suspected criminal is by dividing the stages in criminal procedure between different bodies'.[19] By separating the powers of the state in this way, these powers can be both limited and regulated. Honoré goes on to argue: 'State powers should be sliced up, and the slices should be able to keep a check on one another.' The institution of the criminal court can be read as just such a slicing up. Just as we observed above that prosecutors are intended to act as a check upon the decisions of the police, so the judge in court has the

---

[17] Garland, quoting Pashukanis: Garland, D., *Punishment and Modern Society: A Study in Social Theory* (Oxford: Oxford University Press, 1990) 112.

[18] Cited Garland, D., op. cit. 113.

[19] Honoré, T., *About Law* (Oxford: Clarendon Press, 1995) 83.

power to rule whether the prosecution has produced sufficient evidence or not. And in the Crown Court the jury, in theory, represents another institutional check upon state power. Whether, in practice, the jury is an effective check is said to be less important than its symbolic power to stand as such in the minds of ordinary people. But jury trials are not the norm. Only just over 1 per cent of defendants are tried by jury in the United Kingdom and although juries may sometimes prevent wrongful conviction, given the tiny number of cases in which they are instrumental, their power to do so is very limited.

A third aspect of the criminal court is as a legal forum for declaring the criminal law. In this sense the criminal court can be seen as a linchpin of criminal justice: as the procedural link between crime and punishment. It is the authoritative institution for the clarification, declaration, and development of the criminal law. We have already observed how the criminal law is mediated through the criminal process. In court this process of translating statute and common law into 'law in action' continues apace. Even after the decision to prosecute has been ratified by the prosecution, many decisions intervene to determine the manner and form of the charge that the defendant will ultimately face. Decisions as to bail, mode of trial, and listings procedures, which determine in which court the case will be held, influence the application of the criminal law in practice. About the important phenomenon of plea bargaining we will have more to say below.

Despite the distinction commonly drawn between the substantive criminal law and the 'adjectival' laws of procedure and evidence, it is arguable that these latter laws are equally central to understanding how crime is constructed within the criminal court. As Lacey and Wells observe: 'these rules set out what may or may not count as evidence, whom it may be given by and about, what form it may take, who may hear it, to what standard an issue must be proved and by whom, when an issue may be withdrawn or introduced and a host of other elements crucial to the conduct of the trial'.[20] By extending our conception of the criminal law to include both doctrinal and adjectival laws we can better understand how law is in practice articulated in the daily working of the criminal trial.

INSTRUMENT FOR TRUTH FINDING

Rules of procedure and evidence are also important in another central function of the criminal trial, namely truth finding. It is often argued that

---

[20] Lacey, N., and Wells, C., *Reconstructing Criminal Law: Text and Materials* (3rd edn, London: Butterworths, 2003) 96.

the adversarial trial is less committed to finding the truth than its inquisitorial counterpart. Finding the truth is deemed to be closer to the heart of the inquisitorial model because the primary obligation upon all those involved is to pursue all evidence as to guilt or innocence. By contrast in the adversarial trial, truth is sought by pitting two opposing accounts against each other in a battle to see which best persuades. Each side is charged with the duty (not always discharged with vigour) of scrutinizing the other's account for weaknesses and challenging the veracity of their story in public. It is arguable that this method of truth finding is likely to be more effective than one in which a judge must pursue the truth unaided by these opposing stories. Indeed, a commonly observed danger of the inquisitorial system is that the judge may become prematurely convinced of one version of events without giving full consideration to alternative possibilities. Rapidly persuaded of the defendant's guilt, the judge may overlook evidence as to their innocence. The medium of advocacy, by contrast, is said systematically to test whether an account is capable of more than one interpretation. In setting forth their opposing accounts as polar positions and in cross-examining witnesses in order to expose the weaknesses of their stories, the advocates endeavour to 'reveal to the tribunal which witnesses can be relied upon and which can be cast aside'.[21] Of course this is an idealized account. Much depends also upon the skill of the advocate and the quality of the witnesses. The art of advocacy is a highly refined one whose very best practitioners may manage to persuade in the face of the facts. And a weak, inarticulate, or unwilling witness may cause a case to founder whatever its merits.[22] The duty of the judge to sum up the evidence before a jury may temper these problems but cannot eliminate them entirely.

The battle that is the adversarial trial is wrought about with procedural safeguards which sometimes act as inhibitions upon the finding of truth. The rules as to exclusion of evidence, for example, are a powerful tool for the protection of the defendant against abuse of state power but they may inhibit the discovery of the truth. Although truth finding is central to the adversarial process, therefore, it is balanced against other considerations, not least maintaining the integrity of the system. The prosecution case will succeed only if it can demonstrate convincingly in public that the defendant is guilty according to the full panoply of rules of procedure and

[21] Solley, S., 'The Role of the Advocate' in McConville and Wilson (eds), *The Handbook of the Criminal Justice Process* (Oxford: Oxford University Press, 2002) 312.

[22] Sanders, A., *et al.*, *Victims with Learning Disabilities* (Oxford: Centre for Criminological Research, 1997).

evidence. The truth sought in the criminal trial is a particular juridical species of veracity therefore. As Zuckerman observes: 'The doctor, the scientist, the journalist, and the historian are also interested in finding the truth about facts, yet each of these adopts different procedures to that end. The procedure that each follows is influenced by the purpose for which the investigation is carried out and by the conditions under which it is conducted.'[23] Seen this way, the search for truth becomes inseparable from the procedural constraints under which it is pursued and in turn these are determined by the very purpose of the enquiry.

   In the criminal court, the purpose of the enquiry is to discover whether or not the defendant is guilty of the offence or offences charged according to the law, both substantive and adjectival. The presumption that the defendant is innocent until proven guilty means that it is not enough for the prosecution merely to cast doubt upon the defendant's innocence; it must prove that the defendant is guilty beyond all reasonable doubt. The particular kind of truth with which the court is concerned, therefore, is instrumental to the purpose of conviction. In pursuit of this ulterior goal, those in court must carve out that arena of facts germane to the defendant's guilt, reconcile differing accounts of what occurred, and call upon witnesses to recollect events long past or which they might rather forget. The difficulties in so doing might seem insuperable were it not for the remarkable fact that in the majority of cases the court is indeed persuaded 'beyond all reasonable doubt'. As McBarnet observes: 'The philosophical problem of how one reproduces "reality" thus becomes a sociological one: how is it that in such a situation of ambiguity, conflict, subjectivity, fading or moulded memories, the judges of the facts can so readily find themselves convinced beyond all reasonable doubt?'[24] Her brute answer is that the prosecution does not even attempt to reproduce reality, still less seek truth. It represses and denies the difficulties involved and devotes itself instead to constructing an account of the facts sufficiently persuasive to convince the court of the defendant's guilt and so to secure a conviction. If the prosecution fails, the defendant will be acquitted. Whatever the audience within or outside the court may think of the outcome, an acquittal is a defining moment of legal exoneration. Should the prosecution succeed, their reward is not merely a professional victory, and in a sense the validation of their case, but also the conviction of the defendant. The

[23] Zuckerman, A. A. Z., *The Principles of Criminal Evidence* (Oxford: Oxford University Press, 1989) 1.
[24] McBarnet, D., *Conviction: Law, the State, and the Construction of Justice* (London: Macmillan, 1983) 12.

moment of conviction is a decisive one in the criminal trial precisely because it is then that the defendant undergoes a dramatic, and only rarely reversible, change of status. At that time, the defendant becomes a convicted offender subject to the sentence of the court.

It is to sentencing that we now turn. In the remainder of the chapter we will explore the scope, form, and role of sentencing, the sources of its legal authority, and the difficulties and the tensions it entails.

FORUM FOR ALLOCATING PUNISHMENT

Many of our observations thus far pertain to trials that are contested. Yet a very high proportion of cases are not disputed. Around 60 per cent of defendants in the Crown Court and over 80 per cent of defendants in the magistrates' courts plead guilty.[25] Whether they do so because they expect to be convicted anyway, because they hope for a sentence discount, or as a result of systemic pressures imposed upon them varies from case to case. These statistics lead Sanders and Young to tag the criminal process a system for 'the mass production of guilty pleas'.[26] The guilty plea renders redundant the dispute-resolving, conflict-airing, and truth-finding aspects of the trial. Indeed, it is to this end that plea bargaining is promoted. A contested trial is a lengthy and necessarily expensive endeavour. The guilty plea cuts these costs dramatically, saves court time, and spares the witnesses the burden of cross-examination. Its effect is to reduce the role of the court to a forum for allocating punishment alone.

Of course, the allocation of punishment, or sentencing, is a common feature of all trials, whether contested or not. Sentencing is a multifaceted phenomenon capable of multiple readings. If conviction is a moment of condemnation, sentencing is its refinement and elaboration. Sentencing communicates both to the offender and to the wider public the precise measure of condemnation and the consequences that attend it. In this sense it may be seen as a communicative device for delivering authoritative statements of societal disapproval. This condemnation is most powerful in respect of the particular wrongdoing in the instant case, but sentencing also sends out messages about larger issues of norms, morals, and social expectations. Extending well beyond the legal categories of crime with which it daily deals, sentencing proclaims, or purports to proclaim, where authority lies in society; how order is maintained and by whom; who or what constitute threats to that order; how these threats

---

[25] Sanders, A., and Young, R., *Criminal Justice* (2nd edn, London: Butterworths, 2000) 396.
[26] Ibid., ch. 7; McConville, M., *et al.*, *Standing Accused* (Oxford: Clarendon Press, 1994).

should be regarded and how they should be met. Increasingly, it also proclaims the pre-eminence of legal ideology, not least by reference to ideas of contract and breach, of duties and rights, of fairness, equality, and justice.

For the communicative power of sentencing to achieve its goals it must be authoritative. For sentencing is the symbolic means of upholding the dignity of the criminal law. In passing sentence the magistrate or judge demands that law be respected and makes clear that those who do not show such respect can expect to be punished. It is not by chance that the declaration of sentence is often attended by homilies on the authority of the law and the duty of the court to uphold it. Nor is it fortuitous that sentences are handed down with deliberate formality of language, intonation, and demeanour. This self-conscious gravitas is not only intended to impress the full majesty of the law upon the offender but speaks also to a wider audience beyond the courtroom. Conveyed by the daily jottings of the court reporters, the message of the sentence extends to potential offenders, victims, and the public at large. Newspapers, radio, and television carry reports of sentences, of judges' comments upon passing sentence, of their implications, and of reactions to and criticisms of them. Media commentary amplifies (and in amplifying may also distort) the message of the sentence, maximizing its impact and inviting public debate that amplifies it further still. Sentences which depart from that expected commonly provoke controversy about their appropriateness and the implied message they convey about the gravity of the offending behaviour, the culpability of the offender, the character of the victim, and so on. Controversial sentencing decisions may provoke anger and inflict pain, but they also furnish an opportunity for public discussion of the limits of accepted behaviour and for the clarification of norms. The lenient sentence given to a woman who responds to years of physical abuse by killing her husband, for example, provides the occasion for clarifying societal views of both culpable homicide and domestic violence.[27]

Sentencing is also a means of dividing up the labour of judging. If conviction is the moment at which guilt is attributed, sentencing is the point at which the appropriate penalty is determined. In setting the penalty, the sentencer transforms criminal law from a merely declaratory statement about wrongdoing into a potent means of censuring and sanctioning the offender. As Ashworth has observed, 'it is sentencing, largely,

[27] Wells, C., 'Battered women syndrome and defences to homicide: where now?' (1994) 14 *Legal Studies* 266–76.

that gives criminal law its bite'.[28] Determining which penalty should be handed down is a complex exercise. Depending upon the particular philosophy of punishment to which the sentencer subscribes and the constraints of present sentencing legislation, it may entail making several enquiries before a sentence can be arrived at. These include determinations as to the gravity of the offence in order to ensure proportionality; or, in the case of consequentialist sentences, enquiries into the prevalence of the offence or the degree of public concern about it; the offender's state of mind, their penitence or lack of remorse; their background, personal, social, or financial problems; or assessments of the risk they pose to themselves, the victim, or the wider public. To this extent, sentencing is also an information-gathering exercise, though the amount and nature of the information gathered varies widely from case to case. The requisite information in hand, the sentencer sets about deciding the precise measure of pain, the appropriate treatment regime, the strictures or requirements that the sentence should entail. This may be satisfied by a single penalty but the multiple demands made upon the sentence often require that a more complex package is put together which in turn places multiple demands upon the offender subject to it.

Sentencing requires, of course, that there be a subject so sentenced: the offender in the dock. At the point of sentence, perhaps more than at any other in the criminal process, the offender is held up as an autonomous agent whose assumed free will and moral responsibility legitimate, even demand, this calling to account. In sentencing, the court acknowledges the offender's capacity to make moral choices. If these choices contravene the limits of morally acceptable behaviour as enshrined in the criminal law, then the logic of individualism requires the court to respond through the medium of the sentence. To do otherwise, it is said, would be disrespectful of the moral autonomy of the individual. Passing reference may be made to background and circumstances but it is the moral responsibility of the individual that is centrally at issue. All that is known about the social and economic causes of crime, all that is elsewhere acknowledged about the political character of criminalization is, at the point of sentence, suppressed. Although, provisions for mitigation may erode the fiercely abstract individualism of sentencing and permit some elements of the context of the crime to be acknowledged, they are little more than a palliative. Mitigation may condone reduction of sentence in

---

[28] Ashworth, A., *Principles of Criminal Law* (4th edn, Oxford: Oxford University Press, 2003) 20.

acknowledgement of human frailty, cooperation with the police, or remorse by the offender but the courts have difficulties taking effective account of larger social considerations or economic circumstance.[29] Their chief difficulty is that the very *raison d'être* of sentencing remains perched upon the precarious edifice of abstract individualism in blunt denial of the social character of crime.

We turn now to consider the formal legal, principled, and informal, factual, cultural, and other bases of sentencing. The legislative and judicial constraints upon sentencing cannot readily be separated from the principles that underlie it, nor the informal influences that inform and direct the individual decision. They are presented separately here as a matter of convenience. In reality these various influences and sources of law interweave (and form tangles and knots) to make up the complex tapestry that is sentencing practice.

THE FORMAL SOURCES OF SENTENCING LAW

Magistrates and judges, in passing sentence, are apt to announce dutifully 'the law requires'. This reference to law's authority reinforces the important fiction that the sentencer is but a tool of the community and exercises power only in accordance with its will expressed through the law. This avowed deference sits oddly with powerful images of judicial independence and authority. It is perhaps because the passing of sentence represents one of the most violent expressions of state power over the lives of its citizens that sentencers seek to justify their actions by reference to forces beyond their individual will.

The legal sources that frame and direct the sentencing decision are more numerous and more contradictory than those operating at earlier stages in the criminal process. Legislation is an increasingly important means by which Parliament establishes the formal framework of sentencing law by setting out the respective powers of magistrates' and Crown Courts to impose penalties. It is also the means by which Parliament exerts authority over the sentencing process by imposing restrictions upon the judicial exercise of discretion. Legislation seeks to limit discretion by laying down maximum sentences for almost every offence, specifying the terms of penalties, and restricting the use of orders. These restrictions, many and varied as they are, leave much scope for judicial

---

[29] Hudson, B., 'Mitigation for Socially Deprived Offenders' in von Hirsch and Ashworth (eds), *Principled Sentencing: Readings on Theory and Policy* (Oxford: Hart Publishing, 1998).

discretion, though mandatory penalties, once rare, are an increasingly important feature of sentencing legislation.[30]

At its best, legislation stands as an attempt by Parliament to articulate a set of principles, a coherent framework, or even an overarching grand plan for sentencing. The Criminal Justice Act 1991 was widely hailed as a landmark in sentencing reform. In laying down clear principles upon which sentencing should be based and in specifying the criteria for sentencing, the Act was an unprecedented attempt to reform sentencing practice in England and Wales. But the difficulties of reform are evidenced by the hostile reception it received at the hands of sentencers who questioned the constitutionality of legislative influence over them. Yet less far-reaching and coherent sentencing legislation may amount to little more than piecemeal tinkering with elements of the sentencing system in response to specific pressures.[31] It may be driven by policy imperatives or larger political problems,[32] or be no more than a proactive electioneering device designed to win votes.[33] At its worst, legislation may be little more than a reactive response to public disquiet or moral panic.[34] The Criminal Justice Act 2003, for example, sets out half a dozen purposes, each pointing in different directions, and bearing all the hallmarks of an attempt to please several different constituencies simultaneously.

Successive governments have manifested an increased willingness to develop, refine, and alter sentencing policy and the rate of legislative change seems to speed up with each passing year. In a bid to reduce the confusion caused by the proliferation of sentencing laws, legislation was passed to consolidate that which went before, but the rate of change is such as to render this out of date almost as soon as it was enacted.[35] This expansion of legislative activity reflects a conspicuous politicization of sentencing. The sentencing bill is a powerful pronouncement of the

---

[30] The Crime (Sentences) Act 1997 introduced mandatory and prescribed minimum sentences. Arguably it marked a turning point in the willingness of Parliament to impose such sentences upon the courts.

[31] The Criminal Justice Act 1993 was arguably such a measure in that it sought to undo unpopular elements of the 1991 Criminal Justice Act such as the Unit Fine.

[32] The Criminal Justice and Public Order Act 1994, for example.

[33] The Crime (Sentences) Act 1997 springs to mind.

[34] The Crime and Disorder Act 1998 might be cited as an example here. The Anti-Social Behaviour Act 2003 is another.

[35] The Powers of the Criminal Courts (Sentencing) Act 2000 brought together provisions from the Criminal Justice Act 1991, the Crime (Sentences) Act 1997, and the Crime and Disorder Act 1998. Some provisions were almost immediately overtaken by the Criminal Justice and Court Services Act 2000. The Criminal Justice Act 2003 dramatically altered the picture yet again.

political will of the ruling party and reflects the determination by government to direct, and in recent years continually to re-direct, the practice of the courts, even at the risk of alienating sentencers.[36]

Judges have long since attempted to develop their own sources of guidance and self-restraint, latterly through the medium of guideline judgments. Guideline judgments derive from judicial decisions at appellate review.[37] They attempt to set out in some detail the framework within which judges should sentence a specific offence and indicate what considerations should be taken into account.[38] The judgments are intended to be binding upon the lower courts and have been regarded as such by magistrates and judges. As Ashworth observes: 'This method of guidance seems to have caused less judicial opposition . . . probably because it has been developed *by* judges *for* judges.'[39] Clearly the role of the appeal courts in setting precedents relies on the reporting of decisions so that they are widely known to the lower courts, and no doubt the development of information technology has facilitated publicity.[40] Whether as a consequence of the greater accessibility of appellate decisions, or a change in judicial mentality, or both, guideline judgments have become an increasingly important part of the judicial repertoire.

There have been limits, however, on the influence of guideline judgments. First, guidelines can only be issued if a case comes to the Court of Appeal. Secondly, historically, only the most serious offences went to appeal so guidelines concerned only the length of custodial sentences. The resulting judgments offered little guidance on the types of case

---

[36] The government's decided taste for change is evidenced by the commissioning of the Auld Report (Home Office, *Review of the Criminal Courts in England and Wales* (London: Home Office, 2001)) and the Halliday Report (Home Office, *Making Punishments Work: Report of a Review of the Sentencing Framework for England and Wales* (London: Home Office, 2001)); by the Government White Papers *Criminal Justice: The Way Ahead* (2001) and *Justice for All* (2002); by the introduction of the Criminal Justice Act 2003 and the Anti-Social Behaviour Act 2003; and Carter, P., *Managing Offenders, Reducing Crime: A New Approach* (London: HMSO, 2003) and the government response to the Carter review, Home Office *Reducing Crime—Changing Lives* (London: Home Office, 2004).

[37] Appeals follow two routes: appeal by the offender against severity of sentence was introduced in 1907 and appeal by the Attorney-General against undue leniency in 1988. The Court of Appeal has developed guideline judgments since the 1980s.

[38] For example, the Court of Appeal's landmark guideline judgment on sentencing of drugs offences in *Aramah* (1982) 4 Cr App R(S) 407 (subsequently revised in *Aroyewumi* (1995) 16 Cr App R(S) 211); on the sentencing of rape, *Billam* (1986) 1 WLR 349 and on causing death by reckless driving, *Boswell* (1984) 6 Cr App R(S) 257.

[39] Ashworth, A., 'Sentencing' in Maguire, Morgan, and Reiner (eds), *The Oxford Handbook of Criminology* (3rd edn, Oxford: Oxford University Press, 2002) 1094.

[40] Even before the impact of the Web, cases were widely reported: in *Criminal Law Review* since 1954, and in *Criminal Appeal Reports (Sentencing)* since 1979.

typically coming before magistrates and the mass of middle-range and less serious cases heard in the Crown Courts. Thirdly, guidance as to sentence tended to focus on the most serious incidence of each type of offence and as such diverged markedly from the common ranges of sentences for that crime.[41] The result is that guideline judgments tended to be out of line with levels of sentence commonly handed down in the trial courts. Accordingly, it is not surprising that their impact has been somewhat modest in guiding everyday sentencing practice. Finally, since each guideline judgment focuses on a particular offence, there has been little opportunity to develop an overall framework capable of ensuring consistency among different offences.

Despite their shortcomings, guideline judgments offer a politically acceptable means by which the senior judiciary could steer their junior colleagues and achieve greater coherence in sentencing. The Sentencing Advisory Panel[42] was set up to assist the Court of Appeal by researching and considering the bases for sentencing of particular offences and recommending guidelines. Since the establishment of the Sentencing Advisory Panel, the Court of Appeal has been obliged to notify it before setting down guideline judgments. The Panel then researches and considers the relevant area of law and reports back to the Court of Appeal. But again because the Sentencing Advisory Panel provides advice only in respect of a given offence, it cannot assist in elaborating a comprehensive framework across offences.

Ashworth has long advocated the setting up of a sentencing council bringing together sentencers, lawyers, other criminal justice professionals, and academics to keep sentencing practice under review and to offer coherent packages of authoritative guidance.[43] A sentencing council would allow for the sharing of expertise, experience, and information among criminal justice professionals and the presence of magistrates would ensure relevance to the working practices of the lower courts. His ideas are followed remarkably closely in the setting up of a Sentencing Guidelines Council,[44] which will receive reports from the Sentencing Advisory Panel and set guidelines within which judges and magistrates

[41] The development of the Attorney-General's Reference since 1988 has, if anything, intensified this emphasis on top-of-the-range offences: Shute, S., 'Prosecution Appeals Against Sentence: The First Five Years' (1994) 57 *Modern Law Review* 745–72.

[42] Established under the Crime and Disorder Act 1998 s.81.

[43] Ashworth, A., *Sentencing and Penal Policy* (London: Weidenfeld & Nicolson, 1983) 447–451.

[44] Under the Criminal Justice Act 2003 s. 167. See <http://www.sentencing-guidelines.gov.uk>.

will have discretion to decide upon cases. The establishment of the Sentencing Guidelines Council represents a radical change from previous practice and sentencers will be obliged to take into account its guidelines or give reasons for departing from them.

There are, however, several problems entailed in sustaining such a dialogue. First, the Home Secretary's power to usurp the Council by imposing mandatory sentences in Parliament is likely to be seen by the judiciary to compromise its independence. Secondly, given the centrality of the judiciary in sentencing, if judges oppose the imposition of strictures then they can very substantially undermine any guidelines imposed upon them. If judges are to be won over they must be fully involved in setting the guidelines (though ideally not allowed to dominate this process); the proposals made must be workable in practice; and the judges must be persuaded or educated into accepting the guidelines as a 'Good Thing'. That leaves open the question of whether guidelines per se are a good thing. On the positive side, as Tonry observes, they have the capacity to make sentencing 'more consistent, transparent, and predictable; . . . reduce the scale of racial, ethnic and gender disparities; . . . provide a tool for the management and control of state resources devoted to punishment of offenders and . . . make judges more accountable for their decisions about citizens' liberties'.[45] On the other hand, as he goes on to note, in aiming to treat all like cases alike, guidelines may fail to acknowledge significant differences between cases and so create injustice. It is fair to say that the English model permits greater discretion than that permitted under the US federal guidelines. Nonetheless, balancing consistency with the demands of justice in the individual case is perhaps the most difficult challenge for the setting of sentencing guidelines. The lack of any clear overriding rationale for sentencing in the English system does nothing to assuage this difficulty.

THE ROLE OF PRINCIPLES

The role of principles in sentencing is similarly complex. It is questionable whether we should see them as the criteria by which the state infliction of pain is justified and the legitimate quantum of pain determined; as the articulation of the philosophy by which sentencers make their decisions; as a matter of academic debate but of little relevance to

---

[45] Tonry, M., 'Setting sentencing policy through guidelines' in Rex and Tonry (eds), *Reform and Punishment: The Future of Sentencing* (Cullompton, Devon: Willan Publishing, 2002) 101.

sentencers; or, most cynically, as a means by which to dress up decisions reached by altogether different criteria. A more complex question still is the relationship between sentencing principles, the statutory framework, and the judicial guidelines discussed so far. Following, Dworkin, we might say that principles stand behind and inform the legal rules, that they may endorse or, more importantly, license departure from a rule, and that they can be weighed against one another in the case of conflict.[46]

Ideally, principles act as a constraint on the pursuit of the rationales of punishment described in Chapter 3. They limit, for example the temptation to impose harsh sentences in the hope that they will deter or in order to mirror exactly the severity of the most heinous crime. And they limit highly differentiated sentencing tailored exactly to the interests of the victim or the rehabilitative needs of the offender. The principles of sentencing are not constant but change over time, flourish, and decline, according to shifts in the values that they reflect. As Ashworth observes: 'it would be extravagant to claim that there is a settled core of these principles and policies. . . . The reality is that they form a fluctuating body at different stages in penal history, and are invoked selectively as the tides of penal politics ebb and flow.'[47] Though the invocation of a principle may genuinely reflect its political ascendancy, it may signify no more than the bald attempt to revive old, or launch new, grounds for sentencing entirely. Let us turn to some principles presently in play.

The principle of respect for human dignity acts as an important limiting constraint upon penalties that are degrading or inhumane. It effectively outlaws certain types of penalty altogether. Respect for human dignity is central to the prevailing rights culture.[48] It prohibits inhumane or degrading treatment or punishment;[49] it also prohibits unwarranted intrusion upon rights to privacy, religious freedom, freedom of expression, and freedom of assembly. What we regard as inhumane or otherwise intrusive upon basic rights is not fixed however. Penalties involving bodily punishment or the infliction of physical pain are, in the West at least, generally deemed unacceptable. Penalties that impact upon the mind rather than the body tend to be more readily accepted. The widespread practice of administering mind-altering psychotropic drugs (the 'liquid

---

[46] Dworkin, R., *A Matter of Principle* (Oxford: Oxford University Press, 1985) ch. 3.

[47] Ashworth, A., *Sentencing and Criminal Justice* (3rd edn, London: Butterworths, 2000) 79–80.

[48] Introduced by the European Convention on Human Rights Art.3 and incorporated into English law under the Human Rights Act 1998.

[49] Article 3 European Convention on Human Rights. See discussion in Ashworth, A., op. cit. 79.

cosh') to recalcitrant prison inmates provokes little outrage compared to the use of physical restraints. Our sensibilities as to what constitutes an affront to human dignity are culturally specific and vary over time according to prevailing concerns and values.

The principle of equality has powerful determinative force in sentencing and is often invoked by sentencers resisting pressure to impose a particularly light or unusually harsh sentence. But the principle embraces dual, sometimes irreconcilable, imperatives. It requires that offenders enjoy equality before the law and that the penalties that they suffer are of equal impact. The first of these demands that irrespective of class, wealth, sex, or race, offenders should be treated equally. Wealthy offenders should not be allowed to buy their way out of imprisonment nor should middle-class offenders be treated differently on the grounds of their particular sensibilities. The principle of equality before the law is challenged, however, by those cases where equal treatment would have differential impact: for example the mother responsible for rearing a young family, or the offender who will lose a hard-earned job if imprisoned. The difficulty is how to respond compassionately in these cases without risking discrimination against those without children or jobs. A complication is that differential sentencing, howsoever justified, may be a cover for unwarranted discrimination. Although equal impact might dictate the same sentence as equality before the law in some cases, there are others in which equality of impact will stand in direct conflict. To achieve parity of impact in the imposition of fines, for example, it is generally necessary to impose a heavier fine on the rich offender than the poor for the same offence. The obvious difficulty with varying sentences in this way is that it creates the appearance of unequal treatment, an appearance that is readily manipulated by the writers of newspaper headlines.[50]

The principle of parsimony suggests that since punishment involves inflicting pain, it should be used as sparingly as possible. As a general principle this requires that penalties should be minimally intrusive in the lives of offenders, though this may lead to conflicts with the demands of desert, deterrence, incapacitation, and so on. Practically it would dictate

---

[50] The attempt under the Criminal Justice Act 1991 to achieve equality of impact through the device of unit fines was undermined by newspaper headlines expressing outrage at the apparent inequality of imposing heavy fines upon middle-class offenders whilst unemployed offenders 'got off' with minimum penalties. The proposed introduction of 'Day Fines' is a welcome revival of the idea of variable fines Carter, P., *Managing Offenders, Reducing Crime: A New Approach* (London: HMSO, 2003).

that the penalty imposed should be the least burdensome possible and that more intrusive penalties should be resorted to only if it can be shown that the lesser penalty would not suffice.[51] Imprisonment, as the most severe penalty, should be employed only when it can be shown that lesser penalties have been considered and deemed insufficient. Parsimony employed as a delimiting principle in individual cases is liable to raise problems of equity as between offenders, however, since it may dictate a lesser penalty for one offender than another, even where seriousness of the offence is the same.

The principle of economy recognizes that the state has limited funds and that money spent on punishment could well be spent on health or education or other social goods. Since punishment is a drain on precious resources, the principle of economy demands that the least expensive option is preferred. Again there is a danger that this principle will conflict with others. Economy might suggest that the cheapest response to the most serious offences is capital punishment but economic considerations cannot be allowed to trump the demands of humanity. Economy in the use of social resources is here in direct conflict with parsimony in the infliction of pain. In general, however, the cheapest penalties tend to be the least intrusive and to marry, rather than conflict, with the demands of parsimony.

How far these principles act as a delimiting force on the daily deliberations of sentencers is a moot point. The vocabulary of principle is often invoked to justify a particular sentencing decision and may indeed have been a determinative factor in reaching that decision. It may, on the other hand, amount to no more than the *post hoc* rationalization of decisions arrived at by common sense, intuition, or prejudice. It is also questionable whether these principles can invariably be safely considered legal principles. Economy, for example, may be such a principle or it may, more cynically, be a cover for altogether less lofty managerialist concerns to satisfy the auditors by showing value for money. Read this way, principles become little more than window-dressing for decisions driven by policy considerations. This is not to deny the potential of principles to act as a powerful constraint upon sentencing decisions, only to alert us to the need to be sure that it is principle and not some baser motive at work.

---

[51] This principle is endorsed in the Magistrates' Courts Sentencing Guidelines, see Wasik, M., and Turner, A., 'Sentencing Guidelines for the Magistrates' Courts' (1993) *Criminal Law Review* 345–56 at 350.

INFORMAL INFLUENCES UPON SENTENCING

Beyond the formal structures and direction provided by legislation, precedent, guidelines, and principles there are a number of more informal sources of sentencing law. Recognizing the limited relevance of Court of Appeal judgments to the everyday practice of the lower courts, the Magistrates' Courts Sentencing Guidelines are issued to guide magistrates.[52] They are not legally binding but provide magistrates with guidance as to appropriate sentences for the mass of motoring and many non-motoring offences. The Guidelines represent a significant step toward structuring decision making, curbing maverick magistrates, and so limiting inconsistency between benches. This said, their lack of binding authority would appear to limit their ability to control magistrates' sentencing decisions in practice.

Other informal sources of influence upon magistrates include training from local training officers, usually justices' clerks, who operate under the general supervision of the Department for Constitutional Affairs. Local liaison judges[53] are also an important source of guidance to magistrates. These judges may develop strong relationships with local magistrates and exert a powerful influence over them. Whether their influence is in fact authoritative is open to question. Such judicial guidance relating to legislation or appeal court judgments clearly is authoritative, but beyond this it is not clear that judicial influence or advice is binding. Although local liaison judges have the potential to increase consistency between magistrates' benches, a maverick judge may, by his influence, exacerbate discrepancies between areas.

Another informal source is the National Mode of Trial Guidelines issued by the Lord Chief Justice to proffer guidance to magistrates on mode of trial decisions. Although not strictly a guide to sentencing, these have important implications given the very different sentencing powers available at Crown and magistrates' court level. Again this form of guidance is not legally binding but seeks to reduce inconsistencies between magistrates' courts in their decision as to mode of trial. Finally, the Judicial Studies Board, established in 1979, provides courses for newly

---

[52] On the introduction of these guidelines see Wasik, M., and Turner, A., 'Sentencing Guidelines for the Magistrates' Courts' (1993) *Criminal Law Review* 345–56. The latest edition of the Magistrates' Courts Sentencing Guidelines is 2004.

[53] Crown Court judges appointed to oversee a particular area, speaking at magistrates' conferences and training sessions.

appointed judges, including district judges, refresher courses for experienced judges, and advice on the training of lay magistrates. It thus provides an important conduit by which sentencers, and especially judges, learn about legislative developments and appeal court decisions on sentencing.

FACTUAL BASES FOR SENTENCING

In theory, during a trial all the relevant details of a case are recounted aloud in court. In contested cases, by the end of the trial the whole story should have been told and the sentencer be armed with the information necessary to decide upon sentence. Unfortunately, however, the broad definition of offences under English law means that finding an offender guilty will not necessarily provide adequate guidance as to the seriousness of the particular offence. Moreover, information sufficient to prove guilt does not always encompass all those facts relevant to sentencing. For example, sentences are varied to take into account mitigating and aggravating factors, many of which may not have arisen at trial. The general principle is that the judge must pass sentence in accordance with the version of the facts consistent with the verdict.[54] It is as if, in order to maintain the authority of the law, one truth must inform both conviction and sentence.

Where defendants plead guilty or are found guilty in their absence, as occurs in a staggering 94 per cent of cases in the magistrates' courts and around 60 per cent of cases in the Crown Court, no evidence will have been heard. Here the court arrives at a sentence by hearing the prosecution outline the case and make any ancillary applications (for example, for compensation) and the defence offer any plea in mitigation. Problems arise where there is a significant difference between the facts alleged by the prosecution and those asserted by the defence. In contested cases, judges may order a pre-sentence hearing[55] and hear either evidence or submissions from both sides in order to reach their own conclusions as to the truth of events. Around these 'Newton hearings' a considerable case law has developed concerning rules of procedure and evidence, in an attempt to ensure fairness to both sides in determining the facts.

Pre-sentence reports provide the courts with detailed information

---

[54] Ashworth, A., *Sentencing and Criminal Justice* (3rd edn, London: Butterworths, 2000) 308.

[55] Known as 'Newton hearings' after the case of *Newton* (1983) 77 Cr App R 13.

upon which to base the sentence.[56] Presented in standard format, they are formally intended neither to offer a plea in mitigation, nor to make recommendations as to sentence but rather to provide relevant information. The pre-sentence report must not usurp, nor appear to usurp, the role of the sentencer. They include information about the nature of the offence, the offender, the risk they pose, and suggestions as to sentence. Since their introduction the advance and retreat of the influence of pre-sentence reports has reflected tensions between the rival authority, ethos, and outlook of different professional groups within the criminal justice system, not least between the competing claims of judicial independence versus the expertise of other criminal justice professionals.

What influence, if any, an offender's previous criminal record should have upon the sentencing decision has also been a matter of controversy. Should the fact that an offender has committed similar offences in the past or failed to comply with previous penalties have any bearing on sentencing or not? Here again, previous record has, over the past decade or so, been ruled in and out and back into play when determining sentence. The exclusion and reinsertion of the offender's criminal history into the sentencing decision reflects both a struggle for dominion over the courtroom and a struggle of prevailing ideologies. The current position is that information as to previous convictions is contained within an 'antecedents statement' and that the court is required to consider each recent and relevant previous conviction as an aggravating factor.

Tensions about which information, conveyed by whom, should inform the sentencing decision arise also in respect of victims of crime. Evidence as to the impact of the crime on the victim has traditionally been thought beyond the remit of a process primarily orientated around the culpability of the offender. However, the victims movement has promoted the idea that evidence as to the physical, material, or psychological harms suffered by victims should be considered in sentencing. In the United States, Victim Impact and Victim Opinion Statements are used to inform and to give the victim some say over the sentencing process. In Britain Victim Personal Statements[57] were deliberately so named in order to distance them from the American model of giving the victim a say in sentencing. Indeed, British sentencers are directed not to take into account any views as to sentence that might be expressed by the victim. Despite their

---

[56] Introduced under the Criminal Justice Act 1991, they replaced social enquiry reports and were originally made mandatory prior to passing custodial and more serious non-custodial sentences.

[57] Discussed in the previous chapter.

limited remit, the role of these statements in the sentencing process has been the subject of heated debate.[58] Proponents argue that these statements should inform assessment of the seriousness of the offence and hence the appropriate level of sentence.[59] They are also said to enable the criminal justice system to respond more sensitively, to ensure protection and appropriate compensation. They are also used at other stages in the proceedings, for example in relation to bail decisions, to home leave from prison, and to release on licence. Victim personal statements are said to allow the victim to be heard in court and to receive public acknowledgement. Against these claims it is countered that to invite victims to report their suffering risks giving them undue influence over the process and creates problems of fairness and consistency. In practice it appears that victim personal statements seldom influence sentencing decisions. It is unclear whether this is a product of resistance by criminal justice professionals or because they are 'misconceived in principle and unsatisfactory in practice'.[60]

THE ROLE OF DISCRETION

We already observed that the bite of law is far from uniform throughout the criminal process. At certain points, law is relatively developed and exerts a strong delimiting force on the operations and processes of the system. At others, individuals and agencies act with relatively unfettered discretion. Sentencing is just such a point, prompting Frankel to describe it as 'a wasteland in the law'.[61] Judges passing sentence enjoy a degree of latitude markedly at odds with the close adherence to procedural safeguards expected earlier in the criminal process. Lacey notes 'a usually unnoticed strangeness of our system. This is that much has traditionally been made of the requirement of responsibility and due process safeguards at the conviction stage, but this is followed by a sentencing process

---

[58] For a wide-ranging consideration of the issues by a leading sceptic see Ashworth, A., 'Victim Impact Statements and Sentencing' (1993) *Criminal Law Review* 498–509. See also Sanders, A., *et al.*, 'Victim Statements—Don't Work, Can't Work' (2001) *Criminal Law Review* 447–58.

[59] Erez, E., 'Who's Afraid of the Big Bad Victim? Victim Impact Statements as Victim Empowerment and Enhancement of Justice' (1999) *Criminal Law Review* 545–56; Erez, E., and Rogers, L., 'Victim Impact Statements and Sentencing Outcomes and Processes: The Perspectives of Legal Professionals' (1999) 39 *British Journal of Criminology* 216–35.

[60] Sanders, A., *et al.*, op. cit.

[61] Frankel, M., 'Lawlessness in Sentencing' in von Hirsch and Ashworth (eds), *Principled Sentencing: Readings on Theory and Policy* (Oxford: Hart Publishing, 1998) 226.

replete with discretion and lacking both procedural safeguards and a coherent rationale'.[62] Of course, this is not everywhere the case. In the United States, the federal sentencing guidelines band types of offence and assign to each band a presumptive sentence.[63] The grid gives judges such limited discretion to vary the sentence that it might be described as sentencing by computer.

By contrast in England and Wales, until relatively recently, the sparseness of the legislative framework, combined with the weak authority of judicial precedent, permitted lower court judges a degree of latitude markedly greater than that pertaining in the pre-trial process. One hypothesis is that the more open and more subject to public scrutiny the process, the less need there is for the constraint of rules. Policing, especially as carried out in the relative privacy of the police station, lacks the transparency and self-conscious need for justification that characterizes the activities of the courtroom. Adherence to principles of legality in the police cells is sought through the imposition of rules circumscribing every minute decision. By contrast in the courtroom, public scrutiny acts as an effective fetter against abuse. But this cannot be a complete explanation. The sentencing stage is free from regulation even by comparison with the trial, a difference that cannot be explained by reference to transparency alone. An alternative hypothesis, therefore, is that the imperatives of due process demand only the protection of the innocent. Once the offender has been found guilty, such protection is deemed obsolete and the discretion of the sentencer is given full sway.

Magistrates and judges enjoy considerable discretion as to the choice of sentencing aim, to assessment of the seriousness of the offence, to the admission of mitigating and aggravating factors, and to the choice of penalty. Discretion is founded upon the immensely powerful, though arguably mythical, notion of judicial independence: a notion that in most countries requires only that government should not interfere in the individual case. In England it has been inflated, at least in the minds of the judiciary, to suggest that any attempt by government to influence sentencing is unconstitutional. Despite the doubtful validity of this extreme

[62] Lacey, N., 'The Territory of Criminal Law' (1985) 5 *Oxford Journal of Legal Studies* 453–62 at 460.
[63] Account is taken of previous record (or 'criminal history score') and aggravating or mitigating factors: von Hirsch, A., 'The Project of Sentencing Reform' in Tonry and Frase (eds), *Sentencing and Sanctions in Western Countries* (New York: Oxford University Press, 2001) 207.

interpretation of judicial independence, it has acted as an important bulwark against legislative attempts to limit or structure judicial powers of sentencing. Twentieth-century law reform has, if anything, given greater sway to judicial discretion through the replacement of highly specific, if chaotic, crime categories with a smaller number of rather broadly defined offences. Judges have fiercely resisted attempts to structure sentencing as constituting unwarranted interference in their role. Even where structures have been erected they leave sentencers with considerable latitude to determine exactly how any given sentence should be implemented. Given that discretion plays such an important role, let us consider the factors that inform its exercise.

Common sense is probably the most elusive yet most often cited element of sentencing discretion. It is particularly beloved of magistrates.[64] The assertion that a decision derives from common sense makes the unassailable claim that the sentence is both proper and obvious to all right-thinking people. Yet it defies rational explanation and as such relieves sentencers of the uncomfortable burden of having to give reasons for their decision. The parallel assertion made more often by judges that 'experience demands' is likewise a means of evading more detailed explication.[65] For although it is expected that sentencers should explain the thinking behind their selected sentence, in practice they rarely do. That which passes for explanation is more often an occasion for comment on the prevalence or harmfulness of the offence, or an excuse for further admonishing the offender. Even in those instances where sentencers are required by law to give reasons, they quickly develop formulaic responses readily adaptable to differing situations but which explain nothing. This lack of proper explanation may be seen as no more sinister than a convenient shorthand employed by hard-pressed officials. A less benign interpretation is that to offer proper explanations would reveal the sentencer to be constrained by legal strictures at just that moment when they purport to be the very embodiment of law. The moment of sentencing has an important, dramatic impact that might be lost in the intricacies of justifying one penalty over another or cataloguing the factors taken into account in mitigation or aggravation. This is not to excuse reference to common sense as a substitute for explanation but rather to reveal its power as an evasionary tactic. Presented as an objective good, common

---

[64] Parker, H., Sumner, M., and Jarvis, G., *Unmasking the Magistrates* (Milton Keynes: Open University Press, 1989) ch. 4.

[65] Ashworth, A., *et al.*, *Sentencing in the Crown Court, Occasional Paper 10* (Oxford: Centre for Criminological Research, 1984) 27–8.

sense is, of course, shaped by the complex of beliefs and attitudes held by the individual sentencer.

Sentencers' views on the aims of sentencing, on the nature and causes of crime, and on the role of the court together form an over-arching framework within which they make decisions. More specific views about the type of crime, its causes, gravity and prevalence, aggravating and mitigating factors, and the efficacy or appropriateness of particular penalties inform the individual case. The general and the particular intermingle in determining the choice of sentence. For example, sentencers who think that crime is caused by disadvantage and lack of education may be more inclined to give community rehabilitation orders (formerly probation orders) with requirements as to training than those who consider crime to be the product of individual pathology. Or again, a sentencer who observes a crime becoming prevalent in their area, and who believes in the efficacy of deterrence, may impose a harsher sentence than would normally be warranted in the hope of discouraging others. Whereas other sentencers, less persuaded by the efficacy of deterrence or more bound by considerations of justice in the individual case, would be constrained to impose no more than a proportional sentence.

A third factor informing the exercise of discretion is court culture. The views of individual sentencers tend to be mutually reinforcing with the result that particular Crown Court centres or magistrates' benches grow to share similar assumptions about the rationale behind or appropriateness of any given sentence. In medium-sized courthouses especially, the development of greater homogeneity of approach tends to reinforce sentencing practices so that they appear self-evidently the only 'right' way. Much has been written about the canteen culture of the police station but it is less often observed that judges, dining daily together, also develop a shared outlook and beliefs.[66] Magistrates may be less prone to this homogenizing influence, coming together only intermittently and being exposed to the influences of their professional and other lives. Being lay people, however, they are particularly susceptible to the influence of the professionals: the local liaison judge or the court clerk. Magistrates, in

---

[66] Possible evidence of this is provided in Hood, R., *Race and Sentencing* (Oxford: Oxford University Press, 1992) which found that judges sitting in Dudley Crown Court were significantly more severe on black defendants than those sitting in other court centres throughout the West Midlands. See particularly ch. 12. This marked local variation, not explicable by other factors, suggests the mutual reinforcement of discriminatory attitudes in the Dudley court.

their over-eagerness to appear magisterial, embrace that which they are told constitutes the law and, lacking legal education, may be less well equipped to question what they are told. Court clerks can thus be a powerful influence upon the culture of magistrates' courts, even though their official role is merely advisory.

A more controversial element in this complex of factors is the influence of the demographic background of sentencers on their attitudes to crime and punishment. The fact that nearly three-quarters of judges went to public school and Oxford or Cambridge universities, that they tend to be middle-aged, or older, white, middle-class, and male are likely to be influential factors in determining their outlook. How far these demographic characteristics inhibit judges from understanding the socio-economic disadvantages of many of those appearing before them; how far they lead judges to revere certain values, not least the protection of property, over others; or to identify more sympathetically with middle-class, middle-aged white offenders than with the poor, young, or members of ethnic minorities requires further systematic research. One difficulty is that although there have been a number of studies of the sentencing practices of magistrates,[67] attempts to conduct similar studies into the attitudes and reasoning practices of judges have proved very difficult to carry out.[68]

Such evidence as we have suggests that there are considerable disparities both among different areas and in the sentencing of different types of offender. Hood's landmark study of racial discrimination found that when all other factors had been accounted for there was a 5 per cent greater probability of a black offender being sent to prison than a white offender.[69] Likewise a study of gender discrimination by Hedderman and Gelsthorpe found considerable variations between the sentencing of men and women, not least because magistrates tend to regard women

---

[67] Hood, R., *Sentencing in the Magistrates' Courts* (London: Tavistock, 1962); Hood, R., *Sentencing the Motoring Offender* (London: Heinemann, 1972); Flood-Page, C., and Mackie, A., *Sentencing Practice: an examination of decisions in magistrates' courts and the Crown Court in the Mid-1990s, Home Office Research Study No. 180* (London: HMSO, 1998).

[68] Ashworth, A., *et al.*, *Sentencing in the Crown Court, Occasional Paper 10* (Oxford: Centre for Criminological Research, 1984) Their pilot study produced a number of preliminary findings about judicial attitudes; not least that judges regarded social security fraud as a much more serious crime against the public interest than 'tax fiddling': 24–5.

[69] Hood, R., *Race and Sentencing* (Oxford: Oxford University Press, 1992) 198. This finding was not replicated in a later Home Office Study: Flood-Page, C., and Mackie, A., *Sentencing Practice: an Examination of Decisions in Magistrates' Courts and the Crown Court in the Mid-1990s, Home Office Research Study No. 180* (London: HMSO, 1998) xii.

offenders as 'troubled' rather than 'troublesome'.[70] Although overall women received more lenient sentences than men, the picture in respect of individual penalties was more complicated, varying according to the perceived appropriateness of the penalty to women offenders. They conclude that the particular brand of common sense to which magistrates have recourse when sentencing women is a 'gendered common sense'.

The influence of public opinion on sentencing decisions is similarly difficult to assess. In sentencing, judges commonly deploy statements like 'public opinion demands' to suggest that they do no more than reflect popular sentiment. Given the relative isolation of many judges from popular culture and attitudes, it is open to question how much they know of what the public wants[71] or whether they simply project their views on to some unknown blank canvas public. More cautious reference to 'informed public opinion', 'right-thinking members of the public', or 'decent members of society'[72] suggest a smaller constituency with a special claim to influence. In purporting to express public opinion, judges may express their own opinions conveniently rendered authoritative by reference to this wider community. Alternatively, it may be that they do no more than proclaim what they consider the public ought to think. The much-quoted observation of James Fitzjames Stephen that 'the sentence of law is to the moral sentiment of the public in relation to any offence what a seal is to hot wax' is graphically suggestive of this inverse relationship.[73] Whether judicial decisions reinforce social standards and community solidarity, or are the very motor of them, is not clear. Even where apparent fluctuations in sentencing appear to reflect public outcry, as for example after the murder of the toddler James Bulger in 1993, it is extremely difficult to distinguish the influence of public opinion from other possible causal factors. Moreover, the very idea that there is a homogenous public view seems doubtful given the cultural diversity of modern society.

Although judges insist that the legitimacy of their decision making resides in reflecting public opinion, research evidence suggests that the

---

[70] Hedderman, C., and Gelsthorpe, L., *Understanding the Sentencing of Women: Home Office Research Study No. 170* (London: HMSO, 1997) viii.

[71] Roberts, J. 'Public Opinion and Sentencing Policy' in Rex and Tonry (eds), *Reform and Punishment: The Future of Sentencing* (Cullompton, Devon: Willan Publishing, 2002) 22.

[72] Ashworth, A., *et al.*, *Sentencing in the Crown Court, Occasional Paper 10* (Oxford: Centre for Criminological Research, 1984) 31–2.

[73] Quoted in Garland, D., *Punishment and Modern Society: A Study in Social Theory* (Oxford: Oxford University Press, 1990) 58.

public are systematically ignorant of current sentencing practice.[74] There is also evidence that whilst the public generally consider the courts too lenient, they tend to underestimate the severity of current court practice. When sentencers declare themselves obliged to increase severity in order to maintain public confidence, therefore, the better solution might be more effective communication and explanation of sentences rather than any change in practice.[75] Whether reference to public opinion is a genuine attempt to gauge what the public would condone or no more than a justificatory device for the exercise of state power remains open to question.

Attempts made at widely separate intervals to constrain judicial discretion have been met with strong resistance. The stubborn defence of judicial independence, the resilience of courthouse culture, and the continued reference to local or regional characteristics, all powerfully repel external attempts to impose consistency. Seen one way, this conflict reflects legitimate tensions in the proper allocation of competences; seen another way it is sheer obduracy on the part of a powerful club. On the first view, whilst Parliament may be best placed to classify offences according to their relative seriousness, only sentencers can observe and make judgments about the defendant before them. While Court of Appeal judgments may be the surest way to rectify maverick decisions, judicial training and Magistrates' Courts Guidelines more closely reflect and inform daily sentencing practice. Seen this way, direction, guidance, and the exercise of judicial discretion draw upon relevant sources of expertise and render the final decision a cooperative venture. A second, more cynical view is that by preserving maximum discretion judges display their power. In the face of all the legal strictures, constraints, and guidelines that now abound, sentencers remain remarkably immune to external attempts to constrain their exercise of discretion. It may be that Norrie is right, therefore, to suggest that 'the indeterminacy of the sentencing stage is not just the product of the determinacy required at the conviction stage. It is also the result of the setting loose of the contradictions inherent within the historical and ideological project that is the criminal law.'[76] In short, when the legal strictures of conviction

---

[74] Hough, M., and Roberts, J., *Attitudes to Punishment: Findings from the British Crime Survey. Home Office Research Study No. 179* (London: HMSO, 1998).

[75] The Halliday Report (2001) recommended that the Home Office consider ways of increasing public knowledge about sentencing. One result is Chapman, B., Mirrlees-Black, C., and Brawn, C., *Improving Public Attitudes to the Criminal Justice System: The Impact of Information. Home Office Research Study No. 245* (London: HMSO, 2002).

[76] Norrie, A., *Crime, Reason and History: A Critical Introduction to Criminal Law* (London: Weidenfeld & Nicolson, 2001) 231.

are slackened, giving rise to greater discretion for sentencers, the complexities and inconsistencies of sentencing have full reign.

CAN DIFFERENTIAL TREATMENT BE JUSTIFIED?

There is now good evidence of differential patterns of sentencing in respect of race, gender, and class. In the main, these differences do not reflect any distinction drawn in sentencing law but result rather from the exercise of discretion by sentencers. In some cases the effect of discretion is largely benign. For example, in the case of female offenders, it is often claimed that chivalry on the part of sentencers leads to more lenient sentences, at least for those women who conform to expectations of their gender role.[77] The data are complicated by the fact that the numbers of women sentenced by the courts are so small, the patterns of offending and the levels of severity so different compared to men as to undermine the use of aggregate statistics to compare sentencing patterns. To the extent that differential patterns of sentencing can be determined, the question then arises whether this is indicative of improper discrimination by sentencers or not. The answer depends in part upon what allowances for difference we are prepared to concede and what degree of uniformity we expect. As Gelsthorpe and Hedderman reflect, 'what exactly does fairness consist of in this context?' They conclude that fairness resides less in uniformity of sentencing outcomes than in consistency of approach to the sentencing decision.[78] Given the differences in the types and gravity of offences committed by women, in their social position, and familial responsibilities, it may be that we should expect sentencing outcomes for women to be different. The difficult question then is how to permit recognition of legitimate differences in the needs and responsibilities of female offenders (most obviously as primary carers of children) without allowing these differences to feed the very stereotypes that underpin illegitimate discrimination. In short, we should be wary of accepting gendered differences in sentencing as unproblematic or justified even where they result in more lenient penalties.

More problematic is differential treatment of offenders from ethnic

---

[77] Demeanour, behaviour in court, status, and conformity with role stereotypes were all cited by magistrates as factors taken into account in determining sentences for women: Hedderman, C., and Gelsthorpe, L., *Understanding the Sentencing of Women: Home Office Research Study No. 170* (London: HMSO, 1997) Part II 'Magistrates' explanations of sentencing decisions'.

[78] Ibid. 55. This approach was endorsed in the Halliday Report 2001.

minority backgrounds. Where differential treatment is the result of bias or prejudice—what Hudson terms bluntly 'malign discrimination'[79]— there can be no difficulty in condemning it as damaging to the defendant and to the legitimacy of the system as a whole. The picture is complicated, however, by the fact that discrimination may occur at earlier stages in the criminal justice process: in policing, in prosecution, in plea bargaining, and even in the writing of pre-sentence reports.[80] Racism is also endemic in wider society, adversely affecting the life chances and employment prospects of black people and exacerbating factors associated with offending. As Faulkner observes: 'members of ethnic minority groups are more likely than the rest of the population to live in poor areas, be unemployed, have low incomes, live in poor housing, have poor health and be victims of crime. Higher rates of criminality are only to be expected.'[81] The importance of Hood's study lies in that he controlled for extraneous factors in order to single out racial differences that could not be explained by anything other than discrimination.[82] His finding that, at least in some courts, black people are sentenced more harshly as a result of malign discrimination poses a major challenge to the sentencing system. In the light of this evidence, it is curious that there has been relatively little attention by government to the problem of racism in sentencing.[83]

Evidence as to discrimination leaves open the question of when and under what conditions differential treatment is justified. In posing the enormously difficult question of how one does 'justice to difference', Hudson concludes that ' "equality" is not necessarily sameness'.[84]

---

[79] Hudson, B., 'Doing Justice to Difference' in Ashworth and Wasik (eds), *Fundamentals of Sentencing Theory* (Oxford: Clarendon Press, 1998) 224.

[80] Bowling, B., and Phillips, C., *Racism, Crime and Justice* (London: Longman, 2002) 176–9.

[81] Faulkner, D., 'Taking account of race, ethnicity and religion' in Rex and Tonry (eds), *Reform and Punishment: The Future of Sentencing* (Cullompton, Devon: Willan Publishing, 2002) 65.

[82] Hood, R., *Race and Sentencing* (Oxford: Oxford University Press, 1992); see also discussion in Phillips, C., and Bowling, B., 'Racism, Ethnicity, Crime and Criminal Justice' in Maguire, Morgan, and Reiner (eds), *The Oxford Handbook of Criminology* (3rd edn, Oxford: Oxford University Press, 2002) 600–2.

[83] The Race Relations (Amendment) Act 2002, which imposes upon public authorities a duty not just to avoid discrimination but also to promote racial equality, does not apply to sentencers. The Halliday Report (2001) has very little to say about race and sentencing. See discussion in Faulkner, D., 'Taking account of race, ethnicity and religion' in Rex and Tonry (eds), *Reform and Punishment: The Future of Sentencing* (Cullompton, Devon: Willan Publishing, 2002).

[84] Hudson, B., 'Doing Justice to Difference' in Ashworth and Wasik (eds), *Fundamentals of Sentencing Theory* (Oxford: Clarendon Press, 1998) 249.

Instead, she argues that sentencing should be gendered and 'racialized' to take account of differences between the sexes and between ethnic minorities. If it were possible to formulate some means to take account of legitimate difference, this might also provide the basis for introducing 'categorical leniency' so that offences associated with poverty might be regarded as less serious than those not correlated with economic circumstance. Hudson's proposals mirror those made by Tonry for 'social adversity mitigation',[85] which would license sentencers to have regard to the particular difficulties faced by impoverished, unemployed, and otherwise disadvantaged offenders. Although these proposals have some attraction, deciding which differences and difficulties should be taken into account, and in what measure, is politically contentious and problematic in practice.

Given the lack of systematic regard given to legitimate considerations of difference in respect of gender, race, and class, it seems less than obvious that the category of young offenders should have attracted an entirely separate sentencing system. And yet the distinct theory, law, and practice of juvenile justice is developed to a degree that stands in striking contrast to the sentencing of women, black people, or the poor. Part of the explanation may be that young people have long been considered different to a degree that other offenders have not.[86] The differential sentencing system for young offenders has a long history resting upon the recognition of their particular social and moral situation.[87] First, the very young are so lacking in the capacity to understand right and wrong that they stand outside criminal liability altogether.[88] Secondly, even when youngsters attain an age at which they can be held responsible, their capacity for making informed moral choices is still inadequate and their comprehension of other people's interests remains undeveloped. To the extent that sentencing is predicated upon the moral responsibility of the

---

[85] Tonry, M., *Malign Neglect* (New York: Oxford University Press, 1995) 170.

[86] The nineteenth-century reformer Mary Carpenter was influential in establishing the principle that juveniles should be treated differently in the interests of their particular welfare needs: Carpenter, M., *Juvenile Delinquents: Social Evils, their Causes and their Cure* (London: Cash, 1853).

[87] The Reformatory School movement, of which Carpenter was a leading protagonist, first established specialist institutions for children in the mid-nineteenth century. The Children Act 1908 set up the juvenile court with specific instructions that it should take account of the child's welfare in any disposition it made.

[88] The age of criminal responsibility is now set at 10. For a critical account of the abolition of *doli incapax* for 10–14-year-olds under the Crime and Disorder Act 1998 see Zedner, L., 'Sentencing Young Offenders' in Ashworth and Wasik (eds), *Fundamentals of Sentencing Theory* (Oxford: Clarendon Press, 1998) 170–1.

offender, therefore, juveniles as a class have a claim, on grounds of capacity, to be treated more leniently. Further, to the extent that youngsters enjoy less than equal status and less than a full share of rights, it is questionable whether they should be held strictly to account for their actions. If they enjoy reduced benefits should they bear the full burdens of citizenship?

These different ways of thinking about the bases of juvenile responsibility have diverse implications for sentencing: for example, whether there should be a generalized discount for youth or individualized treatment according to personal circumstances. If notions of responsibility provide the initial grounds for differential treatment, it is arguable that historically it is penal welfarism that has shaped the distinctive character of juvenile justice. Welfarist ideology cast youngsters as inadequate or disadvantaged people in trouble. As such they were the proper subject of caring intervention by a paternalist state rather than punishment. At its best, welfarism recognized that some sections of society, particularly the young, need greater protection. But although welfarism justified intrusion into young offenders' lives on the grounds that it was in their best interests, at its worst it subjected them to intrusive treatment programmes, justified indeterminate sentences, and sanctioned prolonged incarceration on the grounds that reform was best secured by removing them from the corruptions of their home environment.

The decline of faith in the rehabilitative ideal in the 1970s put in question the maintenance a differential system of juvenile justice. The growth of just deserts as the dominant rationale of punishment raised further difficulties in seeking to apply a theory predicated upon individual autonomy to youngsters whose capacity for moral agency was in doubt.[89] Von Hirsch, suggests one solution in the form of a categorical (as opposed to individualized) discount based upon 'a special "tolerance" for juveniles'.[90] This partial tolerance is based not on grounds of lesser culpability but upon recognition of the fact that adolescence is a time of testing the limits during which period of natural experimentation youngsters will inevitably make wrong moral choices. Partial tolerance is necessary, therefore, to encourage the young to learn to make correct moral choices.

Yet another further difficulty resides in reconciling the demands of equality before the law with the principle of equality of impact. Whilst

---

[89] Ibid. 169–75.
[90] von Hirsch, A., 'Proportionate Sentences for Juveniles: How different than for adults?' (2001) 3 *Punishment and Society* 221–36 at 233.

equality before the law requires that, to the extent they can be held responsible, youngsters should be punished as adults, equality of impact requires the court to consider whether the burdens of punishment do not fall more heavily on the young. One solution lies in Duff's suggestion that we should distinguish between formal proportionality and the 'substantive appositeness of "match" or "fit" between the particular substantive punishment and this particular crime and this particular criminal'.[91] This approach would lead to more individualized sentences than von Hirsch, for one, is prepared to contemplate. Instead von Hirsch argues for a categorical assessment of penal 'bite' based upon the degree to which a penalty impinges upon the interests of juveniles as a class in enjoying schooling, a nurturing environment such as that of the family, exposure to adequate role models, and the development of ties and friendships. He argues: 'these are not mere preferences, but real interests: a young person should have such resources in order to mature adequately and have a good life. Punishments are thus more onerous for adolescents because of the way they compromise these kinds of interests.'[92] This line of argument thus provides the grounds for a blanket reduction of punishment for juveniles in recognition of the greater burden it imposes upon them.

Desert theory claims an intuitive connection between wrongdoing and punishment. An alternative view is that in many cases concerning juveniles non-intervention would be preferable.[93] First, it is argued that delinquent behaviour amongst the young is too common to be regarded as abnormal or deviant. Statistics show that offending is very common in the late teens but then drops away rapidly into adulthood without any intervention. Secondly, many offences committed by the young are 'status offences' or trivial delinquencies that do not attract attention when committed by adults. Finally, persuading young offenders to enter a moral community they have yet to join may be more appropriate and productive than punishment. These considerations have been the driving force behind many more recent developments in youth justice.[94] The espousal of reintegration as the model of youth justice in international

---

[91] Duff, R. A., 'Penal Communications: Recent Work in the Philosophy of Punishment' (1996) 20 *Crime and Justice: A Review of Research* 1–97 at 62.

[92] von Hirsch, A., *op. cit.* 228.

[93] van Bueren, G., 'Child-Oriented Justice: An International Challenge for Europe' (1992) 6 *International Journal of Law and the Family* 387–99 at 388.

[94] Newburn, T., 'Young People, Crime, and Youth Justice' in Maguire, Morgan, and Reiner (eds), *The Oxford Handbook of Criminology* (3rd edn, Oxford: Oxford University Press, 2002) 559–71.

law,[95] the development of restorative justice conferencing, and of restorative cautioning panels[96] for young offenders, all reflect a new approach to young offenders that tends to pre-empt the sentencing stage by diverting them from the system beforehand. Yet alongside diversionary measures, an increasingly punitive attitude to young offenders legitimates early and increasingly intrusive intervention on the grounds of 'nipping crime in the bud'.[97] We shall have more to say about these measures in the following chapter.

CONCLUSION

In this chapter we have explored several divergent ways of thinking about the court and all that occurs within its walls. We have considered the court as a place of dispute resolution; as a place of trial and conflict; and as a site of symbolism and ritual. We have observed its simultaneous operation as a coercive legal instrument; as a means of asserting, and of checking, the power of the state over the individual; and as a forum for declaring the criminal law. The trial lies at the heart of the criminal process yet has attracted less academic interest than the pre-trial process and sentencing stage that adjoin it. The trial can be seen as an institution for fact finding; though the truths in which it deals are a peculiar kind of juridical reality. Its conclusion is the moment of acquittal or conviction, a decisive turning point in the criminal process. In the case of conviction, the court becomes a forum for the allocation of punishment. Sentencing is characterized by a high degree of discretion, the exercise of which is rendered fraught by the multiple, competing demands placed upon those who hand down the penalties. It is to these penalties that we now turn.

---

[95] van Bueren, G., op. cit.

[96] Crawford, A., and Newburn, T., *Youth Offending and Restorative Justice: Implementing Reform in Youth Justice* (Cullompton, Devon: Willan Publishing, 2003).

[97] Muncie, J., 'A new deal for youth?: early intervention and correctionalism' in Hughes, McLaughlin, and Muncie (eds), *Crime Prevention and Community Safety: New Directions* (London: Sage, 2001).

6

Financial and Community Penalties

THE PLACE OF FINANCIAL AND COMMUNITY PENALTIES IN THE PENAL ORDER

In contrast to the processes of trial and sentencing, punishment takes place away from the public gaze. As we saw in the previous chapter, the staging of the trial is designed for public consumption. The moment of sentence is the dramatic high point upon which public interest and debate centres. Thereafter, the penal process largely disappears from view and it is almost an act of faith that the sentence is actually carried out. For the most part, the public have little idea where, how, or with what consequences sentences are realized. Implemented quietly and without flourish, their form, content, duration, and purposes remain obscure.

Even at the post-trial stage, there are important distinctions to be made between the symbolic capital of custodial and non-custodial sentences. Custodial institutions, with their high walls, massive entry doors, and numerous visible security devices signal to the outside world their power and purpose. Most people have a mental image of the prison, even if they have never been inside one, for prisons are the stuff of novels, television dramas, and films. Their drama and symbolism capture the public imagination and designedly so. By contrast, discharges, financial, and community penalties remain relatively unknown. The work of the probation service takes place in unremarkable buildings that offer few hints to the public of their purpose. Few could conjure up the inside of a probation office, still less describe the workings of most community penalties. Nor is this failure of interest and understanding confined to the general public. Sentencers know, or think they know, what prison is. By contrast, some may never visit nor seek to understand the array of financial and community penalties to which they daily sentence the vast majority of offenders.

This lack of symbolic moral force is problematic. Having no institutional presence and sending out no powerful signals, community penalties, in particular, fail to offer concrete assurance of delivering punishment. As a consequence, misgivings arise about their penal value and their ability to fulfil the aims of punishment.[1] The prison clearly deprives the offender of liberty, income, and normal contact with their family and friends. By contrast, the burdens imposed by community penalties, though myriad, are indistinct and poorly understood. To the extent that community penalties claim to serve other purposes, not least to reform or rehabilitate, doubts also arise about their effectiveness.

Continued attempts by penal policymakers and some politicians to displace the centrality of the prison have failed to weaken its powerful hold over the popular imagination. The vocabularies used to describe other penalties reveal this. The labels 'alternatives to custody' or 'non-custodial penalties' were once used to signal the 'poor cousin' status of those punishments which were not prison but which were in place of, and, by implication, lesser than. So labelled, these penalties were subject to sustained scrutiny and criticism. Were they really alternatives to custody or only to each other, did they reduce reliance on imprisonment, or simply replicate its features outside the prison walls? The subsequent re-labelling of these orders as community penalties sought to displace the prison as the pre-eminent penalty that all others must emulate.[2] Similarly, Americans adopted the term 'intermediate sanctions' to denote non-custodial penalties more severe than fines and compensation in the hope of stressing that these penalties occupy a legitimate middle ground in the penal order.[3]

Whether these linguistic shifts are sufficient to endow what in Britain are presently labelled community penalties with credibility and independent status is open to doubt. Raynor describes community penalties as 'the slippery fish'[4] in recognition of their contested, fluid, and imprecise nature. In the pages of the popular press, imposition of a community sentence is commonly portrayed as a failure to punish; community rehabilitation (formerly probation) is condemned as a 'let-off'; and community punishment (formerly community service) is deemed a benefit rather than a detriment at times when work is scarce. Sentencers

---

[1] Home Office, *Making Punishments Work: Report of a Review of the Sentencing Framework for England and Wales* (the Halliday Report) (London: Home Office, 2001) vi.

[2] This linguistic shift was first introduced in the White Paper preceding the Criminal Justice Act 1991 with the explicit intention of decentring the prison. Home Office, *Crime, Justice and Protecting the Public* (London: HMSO, 1990) 18.

[3] Tonry, M., *Sentencing Matters* (New York: Oxford University Press, 1996) ch. 4.

[4] Raynor, P., 'Community Penalties: Probation, Punishment, and "What Works"' in Maguire, Morgan, and Reiner (eds), *The Oxford Handbook of Criminology* (3rd edn, Oxford: Oxford University Press, 2002) 1168.

are sensitive to such misgivings and are increasingly prone to take refuge in the decisive punitiveness of a custodial sentence.[5] Government, too, has shown itself to be ambivalent: at one moment promoting community penalties as appropriate for less serious crimes, and insisting that they are 'rigorous and demanding',[6] at another declaring that 'they are still not viewed as being sufficiently punitive'.[7] This political ambivalence further confuses the penal message sent out about community penalties and perpetuates a lack of clarity about what place they occupy in the penal order.

Whereas financial penalties recognize relationships between offender and state (fines) and between offender and victim (compensation), community penalties invoke yet another player, the community. The role of community has been the subject of much debate.[8] Attention has focused upon the ambiguity of the concept of community and the peculiarities of its meaning in respect of punishment. It is questionable whether the community is involved primarily as a beneficiary (of the reparative efforts of the offender or the wider benefits of crime reduction); as an institution through which punishment is administered; or as no more than the location in which penalties take place.[9] Nor is it clear whether community penalties are intended to recognize the state's responsibility towards its citizens, to encourage self-help, to promote citizen cooperation, or to incorporate the community within state governance. A complicating factor is that the term community has multiple normative connotations. During the heyday of welfarism, recourse to community implied a rejection of centralized state control, the promotion of informal justice, and the pursuit of social reconstruction. More recently its appeal seems to have lain more in the relative economy of community-based measures and the covert transfer of responsibility for punishment from state to citizens that it condones.

This blurring of the line between the punitive functions of state agencies and lay or voluntary initiatives has been recognized by Cohen in his

---

[5] Hough, M., Jacobson, J., and Millie, A., *The Decision to Imprison: Sentencing and the Prison Population* (London: Prison Reform Trust, 2003).

[6] Home Office, *Crime, Justice and Protecting the Public* (London: HMSO, 1990) 18 ff.

[7] Home Office, *Making Punishments Work: Report of a Review of the Sentencing Framework for England and Wales* (the Halliday Report) (London: Home Office, 2001) vi.

[8] Lacey, N., and Zedner, L., 'Discourses of Community in Criminal Justice' (1995) 22 *Journal of Law and Society* 301–25; Crawford, A., *The Local Governance of Crime: Appeals to Community and Partnership* (Oxford: Clarendon Press, 1997); Hughes, G., and Edwards, A. (eds), *Crime Control and Community* (Cullompton, Devon: Willan Publishing, 2002).

[9] Nelken, D., 'Community Involvement in Crime Control' in, N. Lacey (ed), *Criminal Justice* (Oxford: Oxford University Press, 1994) 247–77.

powerful identification of the dangers associated with too ready recourse to community penalties.[10] 'Punishment in the community', Cohen argues, 'widens the net' by expanding networks of social control and diffusing surveillance. It pulls more people into the system and it 'thins the mesh' by subjecting them to more intense intervention. The combined effect is greater 'penetration': the system of social control extends ever more deeply into society, augmenting existing control mechanisms (most notably the prison) rather than acting as alternatives to them. This critical perspective has been widely adopted by criminologists who have developed ever more pessimistic accounts of community penalties. The logical conclusion of their work is an 'impossibilist' stance that deplores imprisonment, sees community penalties as extending rather than diminishing the scope of social control, and offers no hope for reform.

Early critics doubted whether this nihilism was justified by the extent and nature of recourse to community penalties. They argued that community penalties had not been extensively used and, to the extent that they were used, this was in lieu of prison rather than in addition to it.[11] On the whole, they argued, most community penalties are less punitive, less destructive of people's lives, cheaper, more flexible, and more readily adapted to the particular needs of the offender. And the most commonly used of all, the fine, has little by way of the disciplinary qualities associated with the net-widening thesis.[12] At the time, these observations appeared as sobering counterblasts to Cohen's bleak vision, but it is arguable that his predictions are now rapidly coming true. The fine is in decline whilst the use of more intrusive community penalties has increased. Moreover, the introduction of curfews, electronic tagging, drug testing and treatment orders, and other forms of surveillance all increase the danger of net-widening.

THE LEGAL FRAMEWORK

The legal framework of financial and community penalties specifies only the outer delimiting parameters of each penalty, leaving very wide scope for variation. Guidance, appellate and other, which abounds in respect of

---

[10] Cohen, S., *Visions of Social Control* (Cambridge: Polity Press, 1985) 42–4.

[11] McMahon, M., ' "Net-widening": Vagaries in the Use of a Concept' (1990) 30 *British Journal of Criminology* 121–49 at 141.

[12] Bottoms, A. E., 'Neglected Features of Contemporary Penal Systems' in Garland and Young (eds), *The Power to Punish: Contemporary Penality and Social Analysis* (London: Heinemann Educational Books, 1983) 176–7.

custodial sentences, is thin. Moreover, whereas financial penalties are specified and exacted by the court, community penalties are implemented by non-legal professionals. Although the court has powers to specify certain aspects of these orders, in most cases the detailed content and implementation are left to the discretion of probation officers, social workers, educationalists, and therapists. As a consequence, the court has little oversight of what is practised in its name. Seen one way this is an appropriate allocation of expertise, seen another it represents a surprising limit on the powers of the courts.

Various moves have been made to augment the judicial role, for example by enabling sentencers to specify in detail the content of the order, requiring probation officers to keep sentencers more closely informed as to the progress of their supervision, and introducing greater judicial oversight of the implementation of orders.[13] All these proposals might be seen as indicating a lack of confidence in the ability or willingness of non-legal actors to design sufficiently 'demanding' penalties, to enforce them vigorously, and to return offenders to court on breach for re-sentencing. The proposals call into question the traditional distinction made between allocation and delivery of punishment by extending judicial authority beyond the doors of the courtroom.

The introduction and enforcement of National Standards for Supervision in the Community[14] takes this juridification of penalties further. Primarily a mechanism of audit, the National Standards provide for monitoring and internal review to ensure that predetermined standards for the implementation of community penalties are met. Presented as a technique of good management designed to ensure consistency in enforcement, the National Standards are a covert means both of extending juridical power and of strengthening the punitive quality of penalties. The presumption behind these standards appears to be that rigorous enforcement is an unequivocal good and that departure from the penalty laid down by the court is generally unwarranted and undesirable. The

---

[13] Judicial oversight was first mooted in the 1988 Green Paper: Home Office, *Punishment, Custody and the Community: Green Paper* (London: HMSO, 1988) 14, but later dropped. It was revived in the 1995 Green Paper: Home Office, *Strengthening Punishment in the Community* (London: HMSO, 1995) and again by the Halliday Report which proposed that courts should develop a 'sentence review capacity': Home Office, *Making Punishments Work: Report of a Review of the Sentencing Framework for England and Wales* (the Halliday Report) (London: Home Office, 2001) vii.

[14] National Standards were first introduced in 1992. They have been intermittently reviewed and revised. A new version was published in 2000: Home Office, *National Standards for Supervision in the Community* (London: Home Office, 2000).

standards thus value uniformity and consistency of implementation over and above the claims of individual circumstance. They also exhibit a lack of regard for the authority of the probation service and a desire to render it more accountable by requiring that judges and magistrates are kept informed as to both the content and the outcome of the sentence. Although the National Standards are designed to increase judicial and public confidence, they may do so at the cost of greater punitiveness.

Community penalties permit deeper intrusions into the lives of offenders and impose greater infringements of their liberty than do financial penalties. In recognition of this and in an attempt to limit their use, a threshold to their use has been introduced. Sentencers may consider imposing a community penalty only if, in the opinion of the court, the offence is 'serious enough to warrant such a sentence'.[15] This apparently stringent restriction is somewhat undermined by the fact that the level of gravity that might be deemed 'serious enough' is left unspecified. Having established that the offence is sufficiently serious to warrant a community sentence, the court must select a penalty that is commensurate with it.[16] The danger is that careful consideration of these issues is overborne by the looming shadow of the prison. Von Hirsch calls this the 'anything-but-prison' fallacy: that 'an individual cannot complain about how he is being punished if something still nastier could have befallen him'.[17] The fact that community penalties are generally less nasty than imprisonment should not blind us to their capacity to be unwarrantedly punitive, intrusive, or degrading.

A second important restriction is that in selecting a community sentence, the court must be satisfied that the penalty is 'the most suitable for the offender'.[18] Again it is unclear upon what grounds such a judgment should be made. 'Suitable' is an elastic term whose meaning varies according to the perspective and purpose of the sentencer. For example, some regard community punishment as unsuitable for those who are unemployed on the grounds that it constitutes a benefit. By contrast others regard it as particularly suitable for the unemployed on the grounds that it furnishes work discipline and training, makes good use of

---

[15] Initially introduced under Criminal Justice Act 1991 s.6(1), now Criminal Justice Act 2003 s. 148(1).

[16] Criminal Justice Act 2003 s. 148(2)(b): 'the restrictions on liberty imposed by the order must be such as in the opinion of the court are commensurate with the seriousness of the offence, or the combination of the offence and one or more offences associated with it.'

[17] von Hirsch, A., *Censure and Sanctions* (Oxford: Oxford University Press, 1993) 81.

[18] Originally, Criminal Justice Act 1991 s.6(2), now Criminal Justice Act 2003 s.148(3)(a).

their time, and restricts opportunities for wrongdoing. A further difficulty is the lack of guidance as to what the court should do where the most suitable penalty would impose burdens that exceed the demands of proportionality. Given that the legal requirements of proportionality and suitability inevitably sometimes conflict, one suggested solution is that the most suitable order should be selected only if it does not impose a more onerous burden than that justified by the seriousness of the offence. Allowing proportionality to trump all other considerations at least has the merit of placing a strict limit on any temptation to employ tougher penalties than the offence demands. The Criminal Justice Act 2003 introduces a new generic Community Order, which will replace all the existing community penalties described in this chapter, by combining 12 possible requirements within a single order.[19] Sentencers will be free to combine any of the 12 requirements, which largely replicate existing provisions under new names ('unpaid work requirement', 'activity requirement', 'programme requirement', etc.). There is no limitation on sentencers combining all 12 requirements should they see fit, though this would clearly impose considerable burdens upon an offender so sentenced.

THE PENALTIES

In turning to the penalties themselves, our primary purpose is less to provide detailed descriptions than to enquire into their role and nature.

DISCHARGES

The least severe penalty a court can impose is an absolute discharge. It is rarely imposed and then mainly only in respect of the least serious of offences; it makes no requirements of the offender; and it imposes no restrictions upon future conduct. Given that the likelihood of a case resulting in a purely nominal penalty is one of the grounds for discontinuance of prosecution, it might be asked whether absolute discharges should ever occur.[20]

Conditional discharges differ in that they insert the condition that the offender must commit no further offence during the period specified by the discharge (up to three years). If the offender is reconvicted, then the court is entitled to sentence the offender not only for the new offence but

---

[19] Criminal Justice Act 2003 s.177.

[20] Accordingly, Ashworth describes absolute discharges 'as "failures" of the prosecution system': Ashworth, A., *Sentencing and Criminal Justice* (3rd edn, London: Butterworths, 2000) 265.

also for that which gave rise to the original conditional discharge. The essence of the conditional discharge is 'a threat or warning' or 'sword of Damocles' which hangs over the offender for the period of the penalty.[21] Sitting at the bottom of the tariff, discharges jostle with financial penalties for sentencers' attention in respect of the least serious offences. Curiously, the two types of penalty could not be more dissimilar. The conditional discharge inflicts little immediate pain but maintains a long-term disciplinary presence in the offender's life: almost the exact obverse is true of financial penalties.

FINANCIAL PENALTIES

Despite the importance of financial penalties, curiously little attention has been paid to their underlying rationale or role. The language of discipline which was developed principally to account for imprisonment[22] has come to dominate our talk about punishment, yet it has little reson-ance in respect of the most commonly used penalty, the fine. Arguably we need a distinct vocabulary to talk about financial penalties.

It may be helpful to begin by examining the points of similarity and difference between the two main financial penalties, fines and compensa-tion orders. Both order the offender to pay a specified sum. Both regard any debt owed to society or to the victim as having been discharged upon payment. For the offender it may well make little difference whether the recipient is the Treasury or the person they have harmed. We do not know whether offenders perceive and experience the two penalties differ-ently. The impact on the offender of the two orders is very similar: money is demanded, paid, and the debt extinguished. As such both may be said to fit neatly Bottoms' description of juridical punishments: the punish-ment is precisely stipulated and once it is discharged, the offender returns to full society as a 'requalified subject'.[23] Beneath these surface similarities, however, the two forms of payment rest on divergent philosophies.

The fine

The fine is primarily a punitive device, inflicting the pain of financial deprivation upon an offender in satisfaction of wrongdoing. Its bite is

---

[21] Ibid. 266.

[22] Following Foucault's analysis in Foucault, M., *Discipline and Punish: The Birth of the Prison* (Harmondsworth, Middlesex: Peregrine, 1979).

[23] Bottoms, A. E., 'Neglected Features of Contemporary Penal Systems' in Garland and Young (eds), *The Power to Punish: Contemporary Penality and Social Analysis* (London: Heinemann Educational Books, 1983) 176–7.

designed to deter the individual from further wrongdoing. Properly publicized, it may also deter others. It is endowed with little by way of reparative content (except in the attenuated sense that it obliges the offender to repay society) and purports neither to cure nor to reform. Despite these limited goals (or perhaps because of them), the fine is the presumptive penalty and one of the most frequently ordered by the courts.

The fine has a number of curious qualities not shared by other penalties. First, it is the only penal sanction for which the offender can (and routinely does) get someone else to bear the burden. There is no prohibition against others, for example family or friends, paying fines on behalf of the offender and thus suffering the punishment in their place. Indeed, in respect of young offenders, it is assumed by the courts that it is the parents who will pay and it is their means that the courts take into account in setting the amount. Secondly, the fine relies more heavily upon the cooperation of the offender than do other penalties. Whilst other penalties require some degree of offender cooperation, offenders can refuse to pay a fine in a way that they cannot, for example, decline to be imprisoned. Setting the terms of the fine routinely involves negotiations with offenders, for example to allow them time to pay. Thirdly, in practice fining allows offenders to trade with the criminal justice system. Provisions for default, for example, allow offenders to choose to exchange their liberty or their time for the fine itself. Whilst further punishment may follow from breach of other sanctions, in respect of the fine non-compliance is so endemic as to be a constitutional part of the penalty itself. Those who fail to pay may be unable to do so or lead such chaotic lives that non-payment is not a reasoned decision. However, research suggests that many offenders make a rational decision whether or not to pay according to considerations of budget and their willingness to trade liberty for financial resources. It is for this reason that Peter Young dubs the fine an 'auto punishment' which the system permits offenders to administer themselves.[24]

The fine is commonly hailed as a success: flexible, readily calibrated to reflect the gravity of the offence, minimally intrusive, it is followed by fewer reconvictions than other penalties.[25] It requires little intervention by officials; it intrudes in the lives of offenders only in so far as it may

[24] Young, P., 'Putting a Price on Harm: The Fine as Punishment' in Duff *et al.* (eds), *Penal Theory and Practice* (Manchester: Manchester University Press, 1994).

[25] Although, as Bottoms has pointed out, offenders selected for fining tend to be those whose social and financial circumstances indicate a lower risk of reoffending. See discussion in Ashworth, A., *Sentencing and Criminal Justice* (3rd edn, London: Butterworths, 2000) 272.

entail financial hardship; and it demands no evidence of penitence or willingness to reform. In all these respects it accords closely with the demands of modern liberal desert theory. Sceptics might point out, however, that proportionality is founded here upon the questionable formulation of equivalence between an act of wrongdoing and a financial sum. It is not easy to say how much an act of vandalism or damage is worth, still less an assault or rape. Though the fine is readily calibrated, the appearance of proportionality does not stand up to critical scrutiny in every case. As Young observes, if we ask why a fine is an inappropriate punishment for rape the answer is not that it is too lenient but rather that it is the 'wrong kind' of punishment.[26]

Nor is it the case that the fine inflicts pain unproblematically. The same sum of money exacted from ten individuals may have a different impact upon each one depending upon their income, outgoings, financial status, or the value they attach to money. To achieve some measure of fairness among offenders, we might argue that the fine should be varied not only according to the gravity of the offence they have committed but also according to their relative wealth. Equality of impact can be achieved only if the amount fined is adjusted according to the financial means of the offender. And yet, recognition that offenders of differing means should be fined differentially has been vanquished by the claim that like offenders be treated alike. A £100 fine may be ten times more painful for the poor offender than for the rich, yet press and public appear to be more impressed by the seeming unfairness of fining a rich man ten times more for the same offence. One way to get around this problem is to allow courts to calculate the penalty according to penal units rather than in straight financial terms.[27] This allows the judiciary to take account of the financial means of the offender but to impose sentences that appear alike, without advertising the fact that where the offender is impoverished the penalty is correspondingly small. The unit fine system failed in Britain in the face of popular and judicial opposition. In its place, the present

---

[26] Young, P., op. cit.

[27] The Criminal Justice Act 1991 introduced a 'unit fine' scheme by which fines were calculated in terms of units whose value was varied between £4 and £100 according to the disposable income of the offender. Opposition arose in respect of the complexity of the scheme, the difficulty of calculating offenders' means fairly and accurately, and, above all, the comparatively high fines imposed on the wealthy (often middle-class motoring) offenders. In the face of opposition particularly from magistrates, the unit fine scheme was abolished under the Criminal Justice Act 1993. Despite this earlier failure, the reintroduction of income-related fines is proposed by the Carter Review: Carter, P., *Managing Offenders, Reducing Crime* (London: Home Office, 2004), <http://www.homeoffice.gov.uk/docs2/managingoffenders.pdf>.

statutory framework requires that the fine be set so as to reflect the seriousness of the offence.[28] Only as a subsidiary requirement should the court take into account other things including the financial circumstances of the offender. The ideology of legalism here privileges the principle of formal equality before the law ahead of equality of impact (which may require variation by offender). In practice, however, research evidence suggests that sentencers vary considerably in their willingness to take financial means into account.[29]

Fines that do not take account of the means of the offender are not merely unfair, they are liable to be unworkable in practice. Many people offend precisely because they are indigent, and to impose further financial burdens upon them may only compound the very problems that first led them into crime. Depriving people of money is not a self-evidently desirable or useful response to wrongdoing. It is less appropriate still where it imposes so great a burden as to push the offender into defaulting. The decline in use of the fine[30] reflects in part the unwillingness of sentencers to impose financial penalties on those unable to pay. It may also reflect their unwillingness to impose 'fair' fines where they would be so low as to appear derisory in the public mind.

In the absence of unit fines, other means are needed to temper the bite of fines so that they can be deployed without inviting frequent default. Extending the period allowed for repayment, forbearing to bring swift default proceedings against those in cases of financial difficulty, and recovering money directly from income support are all tactics that have been tried with varying degrees of success. A primary difficulty for the courts lies in differentiating between those who are genuinely unable to meet payments and those who are disinclined to do so. It was long the case that prison was the presumptive penalty on default with the result that fine defaulters represented about a fifth of those going into prison. These figures made for a vast revolving door through which large numbers of fine defaulters swung in and out of jail. The revolving door

---

[28] Criminal Justice Act 2003 s. 164.

[29] Flood-Page, C., and Mackie, A., *Sentencing Practice: an Examination of Decisions in Magistrates' Courts and the Crown Court in the Mid-1990s, Home Office Research Study No. 180* (London: HMSO, 1998) 53. The Magistrates' Courts, Sentencing Guidelines (London: Magistrates' Courts, 2004) seeks to impose a loose structure by setting three presumptive levels of fine for each offence to be selected by reference to the offender's disposable income.

[30] The proportionate use of the fine for indictable offences declined from 34 per cent in 1992 to 23 per cent in 2002: Home Office, *Criminal Statistics England and Wales 2002. Cm. 6054* (London: HMSO, 2003) 75.

imposed a massive bureaucratic burden, daily disruption to the life of the prison, and, for the offender, the experience of a penalty whose burdens were quite out of proportion with the gravity of their original offence. In recognition of this, new alternatives to custody for fine defaulters, namely community punishment and curfews, were introduced. These have had the effect of massively reducing the numbers of those entering prison 'by the back door' for offences which were not, in the first instance, sufficiently serious to merit a custodial sentence.[31]

Compensation orders

If the fine is primarily a transaction between offender and state, the compensation order takes as its focus the relationship between offender and victim. Like the fine, the compensation order often exacts money from those who are poorly placed to pay. By contrast to the fine, the compensation order is avowedly reparative, seeking to make good damage done by a payment of some financial equivalence.[32] Calculating the sum to be paid under a compensation order is a complicated and somewhat haphazard affair. Guidelines are generally based upon sums which would be awarded in civil courts and accordingly the compensation order may be seen as a means of securing civil ends through the criminal process, with little of the punitive or deterrent purposes attributed to the fine. Regarded this way, the compensation order is an anomaly in a system primarily orientated to responding to the culpability of the wrongdoer rather than the interests of the wronged.[33] Although compensation orders can only be made where damage or loss has been caused by the crime and are thus analogous to damages, they are not an exact mirror of their civil counterpart, and a criminal court may make a compensation order where there is no right of the recipient to sue in civil law. Nor are they intended to allow offenders to buy their way out of punishment, though other penalties may be reduced to enable a compensation order to be paid.

Seen another way, compensation fulfils the purposes of punishment in ways not dissimilar to other more orthodox penalties. It arises only in relation to criminal offences, is imposed as a consequence of criminal

---

[31] Under the Crime (Sentences) Act 1997. This led to a dramatic decline in the use of imprisonment on default from 22,469 in 1994 to 1,192 in 2002: Home Office, *Prison Statistics England and Wales 2002. Cm. 5996* (London: Home Office, 2003) 33.

[32] Compensation orders for 'loss, damage or injury' were introduced under the Criminal Justice Act 1972 and were established as an independent penalty under s. 35 of the Powers of the Criminal Courts Act 1973.

[33] Ashworth, A., 'Punishment and Compensation: Victims, Offenders and the State' (1985) 6 *Oxford Journal of Legal Studies* 86–122 at 97.

proceedings, after the finding of guilt and the accompanying stigma of conviction, and is a full sentence of the court. Since most victims do not have the time or resources to pursue civil claims, the compensation order generally extorts money from offenders that they would not otherwise have been required to pay and thus imposes upon offenders an additional burden. It takes precedence over the payment of a fine and may be ordered as the sole penalty. Failure to make payment leads to breach proceedings that may ultimately result in imprisonment. Together these factors endow compensation orders with a punitive dimension that has long been recognized. Jeremy Bentham (1748–1832) acknowledged this when he wrote 'exacted at the expense of the evil doer, compensation necessitates suffering: exacted in consideration of, and in proportion to, the evil done by him, that suffering, by the whole amount of it, operates as a punishment'.[34]

If the compensation order satisfies the central elements of punishment, how far does it fulfil its more immediate purpose of reparation? The restricted financial means of many offenders limits the ability of courts to impose compensation orders that properly reflect the harm caused. Accordingly, the compensation order is probably more important as a device for recognizing the harm done than as an effective means of making good. This said, it is far from clear that offenders acknowledge, still less accept, the reparative aspects of their sentence. Although in drawing the attention of offenders to the damage their actions have caused the compensation order may fulfil some educative role, there is no research evidence as to whether offenders think differently about the effects of their offence as a result. The compensation order is perhaps better seen as a means of acknowledging victims' losses than as a properly reparative device. Whether victims feel adequately repaired by the payment of compensation is similarly unclear. They have difficulty in suggesting what would be an adequate sum for compensation and recognize the practical necessity of taking the offender's means into account.[35] And yet victims evince markedly higher levels of satisfaction where compensation is ordered, consider it to be a proper sentence of the court, and share few doubts as to the appropriateness of locating compensation within the criminal justice process.

Despite both their lack of conceptual clarity and their relatively low

[34] Jeremy Bentham quoted in Wasik, M., 'The Place of Compensation in the Penal System' (1978) *Criminal Law Review* 599–611 at 601.

[35] Shapland, J., Willmore, J., and Duff, P., *Victims in the Criminal Justice System* (Aldershot: Gower, 1985) 139.

profile, compensation orders are an important penalty. Courts must consider making a compensation order in every case where they are empowered to do so and must give reasons where no order is made.[36] Although compensation orders are commonly made, their use has declined markedly.[37] Again, part of the explanation may be the requirement that the courts take into account the means of the offender both in deciding whether to make an order and in setting the sum to be paid. Guidelines require that the sum set be reasonable and that it can realistically be paid without undue hardship to the offender within a few years of the order. Inevitably, these requirements restrict the sum demanded, in many cases so significantly as to deprive the order of much of its reparative value. The tension here between the demands of fairness to victim and to offender is probably irresolvable.

COMMUNITY PENALTIES

As we noted above, the entire panoply of community penalties is to be replaced under the Criminal Justice Act 2003 by a single generic Community Order under which up to 12 separate requirements can imposed independently or in combination. Although the nomenclature changes, it may be that much that forms the essence of the existing orders will not change greatly in practice. The major change is that the new generic Community Order makes it possible to combine the different requirements in any number of permutations or, theoretically at least, all together.

Community rehabilitation orders—probation

Since its introduction at the start of the twentieth century, probation has proved to be extremely mutable, changing in response to prevailing penal ideologies. Born out of the voluntary efforts of nineteenth-century evangelical 'police court missionaries', probation was made a formal alternative to custody[38] and, as such, contributed to the reduction in the use of imprisonment in the first half of the twentieth century. As an order made in place of sentencing, historically the probation order could not be used for punitive purposes or combined with any penalty. The acknowledgement that probation restricts liberty and imposes conditions that might

---

[36] Criminal Justice Act 1988 s. 104.

[37] Just under 18,000 violent offenders received compensation orders in magistrates' courts in 1991 but fewer than 8,000 by 2001: Home Office, *Criminal Statistics England and Wales 2002. Cm. 6054* (London: HMSO, 2003) Table 4.21.

[38] Under the Probation of Offenders Act 1907.

properly be recognized as punitive led to demands that it be recognized as a sentence in its own right. As a result probation was made a full sentence of the court in 1991, it could henceforth be combined with other orders,[39] and it became subject to the National Standards. It has since been renamed a community rehabilitation order.[40]

The community rehabilitation order is simultaneously a command to offenders to offer themselves up for inspection, assessment, and correction and a mandate to the probation service to intervene in and to direct the lives of those subject to it. The order is sufficiently flexible to allow it to be repackaged in differing guises. The order places the offender under the supervision of a probation officer for a specified period of between six months and three years. Offenders are required to 'be of good behaviour' and lead an industrious life; inform the probation officer of any change in address or employment; and comply with instructions to report to the probation officer and receive visits from them at home. In addition, various conditions may be attached to the order pertaining to residence, participation in specified activities, attendance at a probation centre, psychiatric treatment, or treatment for drug or alcohol abuse (irrespective of whether the offence for which they were convicted was drug or alcohol related). They may also be subject to negative conditions such as forbearing from taking part in particular activities at specified times. This array of possible attachments to the order renders it flexible, so transforming its character that two orders may have little in common other than their name. The danger, however, is that the increasing attachment of conditions to community rehabilitation orders intensifies the potential for net-widening, permitting intrusions into offenders' lives in ways unrelated to the offence itself.[41]

The renaming of probation as a community rehabilitation order reflects its role as a rehabilitative device. It is predicated upon a penology that sees wrongdoing as principally the product of individual pathology; perceives human nature as infinitely malleable; and invests great faith in expert intervention. By identifying and responding to the faults and frailties of the offender, it seeks to transform their attitudes, habits, and

---

[39] Under the Criminal Justice Act 1991 s. 8. It could be combined with compensation, curfew, or a community punishment order in a 'community punishment and rehabilitation order'.

[40] Under the Criminal Justice and Court Services Act 2000.

[41] In 1992 26 per cent of orders had an additional requirement; by 2002 this figure had risen to 37 per cent: Home Office, *Probation Statistics: England and Wales, 2002* (London: Home Office, 2003) 7.

practices in ways that will resolve their problems and restore them to good citizenship. Curiously, during the post-war heyday of welfarism, when one might expect the rehabilitative potential of probation to have been most thoroughly explored, use of the order was in decline. In the 1970s a more modest ambit for probation was set out in the designation of the order as a means by which the welfare professionals of the probation service might 'advise, assist and befriend' the offender.[42] The decline of the rehabilitative ideal in the late 1970s further compounded the loss of faith in probation and its use fell to just 5 per cent of adult indictable offences in 1977.

Thereafter probation came to be seen principally as a means of diverting offenders from custody. By the 1980s it was increasingly transformed into a managerial device for supervising, regulating, and controlling those whose lives appeared most chaotic. This non-treatment paradigm suggested a more modest role for probation, seeking not to transform the offender but merely to exercise some constraint over their behaviour during the period of the order. In this latter guise, probation was less an engine of reform than a means of communicating and enforcing social obligations. Whilst this more modest goal increased probation's likelihood of success, it may also have denied it credibility in the eyes of sentencers (and the public) who baulked at probation officers speaking of their 'clients' in court and chafed at their seeming reluctance to bring offenders back before the court on breach. In the early 1990s, probation was, therefore, relaunched yet again as a primarily punitive means of obliging offenders to confront their offending behaviour, to recognize the effects of their offence upon victims, and to receive that measure of 'punishment in the community' dictated by the gravity of their offence. This change was mirrored also in a revealing rhetorical shift: those subject to the order were no longer to be known as 'probationers' but as 'offenders'.[43] The punitive demands of 'punishment in the community' required greater intrusion into the lives of offenders in the form of more stringent conditions, minute regulation, return to court for petty infractions of the order, and the certainty of further punishment for breach. This increase in the penal bite of probation was justified on the grounds that whereas it was once intended for first-time or relatively trivial

---

[42] A requirement incorporated into Schedule 3(8) to the Powers of the Criminal Courts Act 1973.

[43] In the amendments made to the Powers of the Criminal Courts Act 1973 by the Criminal Justice Act 1991.

offenders, it was now meant to be used increasingly for persistent and more serious offenders.

The revival of interest in the rehabilitative potential of community penalties during the 1990s renewed faith in the reformative power of community punishment. It has resulted in innumerable evidence-based initiatives and so-called 'pathfinder programmes' based upon cognitive behavioural research.[44] It is reflected also in a growing confidence within the probation service that certain kinds of intervention can have a significant impact on offending rates. Judged by breach rates, community rehabilitation orders have a high degree of success. Around three-quarters of orders are completed without breach. But the criteria by which one should judge success is a matter of continuing debate. For example, if an important facet of the order is a programme tackling alcoholism or drug abuse, then should it be achievement in this domain that is the criterion of success or simply the prevention of reoffending?

In practice, community punishment has probably always embraced various different philosophies simultaneously. Apparent transformations suggested by rhetorical shifts may well reflect changes in political discourse as much as changes in the working practices of the probation service. Disciplinary requirements and punishment for breach were key facets even at the height of the rehabilitative ideal. Its assistance and treatment aspects no doubt likewise survived the demise and revival of welfarism. Paradoxically, despite the rise of a populist rhetoric of punitivism, the use of custody for breach of community penalties has declined. The continuing multiplicity of possible penal purposes indicates a lack of clarity about its underlying rationale, leaving the probation service to fulfil several, possibly conflicting, goals and with little indication as to which, if any, should have priority. Given the failure of the Criminal Justice Act 2003 to indicate any priority among the several purposes it sets out for sentencing, it is doubtful whether these will suffice to clarify the goals of community rehabilitation.

Community punishment orders—community service

In requiring that the offender attend for work and complete the number of hours specified, the community punishment order revives the

---

[44] See overview in Raynor, P., 'Community Penalties: Probation, Punishment, and "What Works" in Maguire, Morgan, and Reiner (eds), *The Oxford Handbook of Criminology* (3rd edn, Oxford: Oxford University Press, 2002) 1186 ff. For a critical evaluation of their limits see Rex, S., 'Beyond cognitive behaviouralism? Reflections on the effectiveness literature' in Bottoms, Gelsthorpe, and Rex (eds), *Community Penalties: Change and Challenges* (Cullompton, Devon: Willan Publishing, 2003).

nineteenth-century conception of hard labour in modern, non-custodial form.[45] It is intended as a demanding sentence: a fact reflected in the change of name from community service to community punishment.[46] In addition to satisfying itself that the penalty is proportionate to the offence, the court must ascertain that the offender is suited to undertake work within the community and that appropriate work is available. The elasticity of the terms 'suitable' and 'appropriate' allow sentencers considerable discretion and may deny certain categories of offender where, for whatever reasons, they are deemed unsuitable, or the kind of work available locally is thought inappropriate. For example, certain kinds of heavy or rough work may not be thought suitable for female offenders. Difficulties also arise in providing childcare for women offenders, locating sufficient female supervisors, and avoiding sexual harassment of female offenders. Despite these difficulties the use of community punishment orders for women has grown, perhaps partly due to the declining use of the fine.[47]

Recognizing that the lives of many offenders are often disorganized and impulsive, the order may be tailored to the characteristics of the offender. This permits a degree of individualization that sits oddly against pressures toward consistency in sentencing. The logic applied is that if the order is unrealistic in its demands it is likely to set the offender up for further failure. The licence to vary orders also recognizes that the same penalty may make more severe demands upon one offender than another. Courts may specify anywhere between 40 and 240 hours of labour; work is generally carried out in the offender's spare time; and must be completed within a year. Where previously the offender's consent had to be obtained before a community service order could be imposed, this requirement was removed[48] partly on the grounds that it gave the impression that the court was subject to the whim of the offender.

---

[45] Community service orders were introduced in 1972 on a trial basis following the recommendation of Home Office, *Report of the Advisory Council on the Penal System: Non Custodial and Semi-Custodial Penalties* (London: Home Office, 1970) as a means of ensuring 'reparation to the community . . . bringing the offender into close touch with those members of the community who are most in need of help and support'. After trials in six areas, the order was introduced nationwide in 1975.

[46] Community Service Orders were renamed Community Punishment Orders under the Criminal Justice and Court Services Act 2000.

[47] Women receive one in eight of all such orders compared to one in eighteen a decade ago: Worrall, A., ' "What Works" and community sentences for women offenders' (2003) 53 *Criminal Justice Matters* 40–1.

[48] Under the Crime (Sentences) Act 1997.

The community punishment order embraces a number of divergent, even conflicting, penal purposes. It exacts some measure of reparation to the community, sometimes to the very person or persons who have been wronged. In carrying out their work, offenders are called upon to recognize the harm their offence has done both to their victim and to the wider the community. In some instances, their labours are directly orientated toward making good that damage or, more commonly, to doing work of general value to the community. This reparative effort may have the subsidiary effect of drawing offenders back into the community against which they have offended. Ordering offenders to work alongside volunteers to improve their local environment by redecorating community halls, play areas, and other communal buildings or to help disadvantaged, disabled, or elderly people within their community similarly has the potential to foster offenders' sense of involvement and to strengthen community ties. The strength of this reintegrative potential depends upon the nature of the work, the degree of alienation suffered by the offender, and the cohesiveness of the community. There would seem to be little prospect of reintegration where there is no effective community into which an offender might be reintegrated.

A second goal of community punishment is to rehabilitate by instilling labour discipline and perhaps even by introducing offenders to the rewards of hard work. The power of community punishment to inculcate work discipline by requiring regular attendance and rewarding hard labour varies from scheme to scheme and offender to offender. The rehabilitative potential of a few dozen hours of labour may be weak when set against a history of unemployment or a dearth of appropriate employment opportunities. But for many younger offenders it may be their first taste of employment and exposure to the world of work. Its disciplinary properties are further enhanced by the power to impose conditions concerning drunkenness, lack of effort, violent or aggressive behaviour, or other conduct likely to give serious offence.[49] Together these aspects of community punishment suggest the growing emphasis on discipline observed by Foucault and so deplored by Cohen in his net-widening theory, discussed above.[50]

Finally, and in contrast to the positive, forward-looking goals of

[49] As laid down by the National Standards. See discussion in Brownlie, I., *Community Punishment: A Critical Introduction* (London: Longman, 1998) 116.
[50] Foucault, M., *Discipline and Punish: The Birth of the Prison* (Harmondsworth, Middlesex: Peregrine, 1979); and Cohen, S., *Visions of Social Control* (Cambridge: Polity Press, 1985) 41–4.

reparation and reform, community punishment has a punitive function. Its penal bite is to be found in compulsory attendance, deprivation of free time, and the requirement of demanding labour. As Rex and Gelsthorpe observe, community punishment is a ' "fine" on time'.[51] The Home Office has long been careful to specify that 'it is not the intention that the activities carried out during a community service order[52] be made unpleasant in the expectation that this will deter either the offender or other potential offenders, but rather that they should be demanding in a number of ways'.[53] The line drawn deliberately avoids demeaning hard labour of the sort excluded by the European Convention on Human Rights and is a very far cry from the use of chain gangs in the USA and in the Northern Territory in Australia.[54]

Maintaining the line between decency and credibility has proved problematic. Community punishment is often said to lack sufficiently punitive and deterrent qualities to have credibility with the general public and, perhaps more importantly, the judiciary. The requirement that all community punishment orders must now comprise an element of manual work is one attempt to overcome this problem. Emphasis is placed on the punitive demands of hard labour over and above the reparative or rehabilitative potential of other forms of employment. Its change of name from community service to community punishment is no doubt a further attempt to make clear its punitive purpose and has served further to differentiate it from the community rehabilitation order. Yet these shifts in emphasis are only the latest in a series of role changes. Seen one way, this eclecticism constitutes one of the strengths of community punishment, reflecting its capacity for fulfilling diverse functions. Viewed more sceptically, it squeezes within one order an array of purposes that are set up to conflict.

Community punishment and rehabilitation orders

Community punishment and rehabilitation orders allow for the combination of community rehabilitation with community punishment orders.[55]

---

[51] Rex, S., and Gelsthorpe, L., 'The Role of Community Service in Reducing Offending: Evaluating Pathfinder Projects in the UK' (2002) 41 *Howard Journal of Criminal Justice* 311–25 at 311.

[52] Author's note: as it was then known.

[53] Home Office, *Crime, Justice and Protecting the Public* (London: HMSO, 1990) 18.

[54] Pratt, J., 'The Return of the Wheelbarrow Men; or, the Arrival of Postmodern Penality?' (2000) 40 *British Journal of Criminology* 127–45.

[55] They were first introduced under the Criminal Justice Act 1991 s. 11 as Combination Orders and were renamed community punishment and rehabilitation orders under the Criminal Justice and Court Services Act 2000.

The orders combine not less than 40 and up to 100 hours' community punishment with between one and three years' community rehabilitation. They may also be given with other penalties, including curfew orders, fines and compensation orders. By layering penalties one upon the other in this way, community punishment and rehabilitation orders increase the burden of punishment applied, subject to the general principle of commensurability. Their introduction was designed to create a demanding penalty towards the upper end of the tariff. They were initially aimed particularly at repeat property offenders whose offences are not sufficiently serious to justify custody but whose persistence is deemed to warrant some stiffer penalty than either penalty alone could provide. By satisfying the demand for tough and demanding penalties, such orders may serve to keep from prison those who might otherwise have received a custodial sentence. In multiplying the burdens placed upon offenders, however, they may simply increase the likelihood of breach. It has been feared that the community punishment and rehabilitation order constitutes all too exact an illustration of Cohen's 'denser nets' that signify 'an increase in the overall intensity of intervention with old and new deviants being subject to levels of intervention . . . which they might not have previously received'.[56] The fact that an increasing proportion of those sentenced to community punishment and rehabilitation orders (CPROs) are found to have breached their sentence would seem to support this contention. However, the picture is complicated by the countervailing fact that of those who are found to be in breach, the proportion sentenced to immediate custody has markedly declined.[57]

Curfew orders

The curfew order requires that an offender remain at home during specified hours.[58] It may therefore be characterized as a form of house arrest, designed to incapacitate offenders and prevent crime. Carefully targeted, it has the power to restrain offenders at precisely those moments when they are most likely to offend. By keeping them away from sources of

---

[56] Cohen, S., *Visions of Social Control* (Cambridge: Polity Press, 1985) 44.

[57] In 1998 25 per cent of those sentenced to a CPRO breached their sentence; this figure rose to 50 per cent in 2002. However, the proportion of those who breached their sentences and who were then sentenced to immediate custody fell from 29 per cent in 1998 to 19 per cent in 2002: Home Office, *Criminal Statistics England and Wales 2002*. Cm. 6054 (London: HMSO, 2003) Table 4.25.

[58] It was introduced under the 1991 Criminal Justice Act s. 12 (for between 2 and 12 hours for a period of up to six months) and made the subject of enabling legislation under the Criminal Justice and Public Order Act 1994. Its use was extended to fine defaulters under the Crime (Sentences) Act 1997.

temptation and places of risk, it has the potential to reduce opportunistic crimes like assaults after pub-closing hours or en route to and from football matches. Given that curfews can only be applied for limited periods, this incapacitative effect applies only where offending is to some degree time specific. It will not be effective against the offender whose crimes are no more likely to occur at night than during the day. Whether the curfew has qualities beyond its incapacitative effects is open to doubt.

It is only minimally punitive; the degree of public censure it conveys is slight; and the pain it inflicts relatively small—unless of course you happen to be a football fan whose order serves to prohibit attendance at the Saturday match or a young man denied the company of his mates at the local pub. For such offenders the penal bite of the curfew order may be deeper than at first appears. Nor does the curfew have any positive reformative effect. It does not address the problems that led to the offending behaviour and may leave the offender as likely to offend at its conclusion as before. Devoid of rehabilitative content, the curfew maintains control over offenders, in the name of risk reduction and protecting the public, but does little more.

Unsurprisingly, the curfew order has been the subject of intense academic and political debate. Seen positively, the curfew order imprisons only in the sense that it limits freedom and achieves a potentially effective form of restriction at relatively little personal, social, or financial cost. As with other community penalties, offenders remain in free society, avoid the contamination effects and stigma of imprisonment, and can maintain their home, their ties with family and friends, and their employment. They are restricted only during periods set by the court and are otherwise free to go about their life as usual. Moreover the order is extremely flexible in its application: it can be combined with other programmes, used at any stage in the penal process from pre-trial remand to parole, and readily altered to fit changing circumstances. It has the potential to reduce the prison population and to avoid the contaminating effects of sending offenders, particularly first offenders, to jail.

On the other hand, if the curfew order is applied to those who would otherwise have received a less restrictive form of penalty, it may widen the net of penalty. If applied to those who would not otherwise have been sent to prison, then the claim that it is less intrusive and less costly is defeated. Regarded negatively, the curfew can even be said to transform the offender's home into a prison. The venerated privacy of the home is undermined, state control intrudes, and the public–private divide is eroded. Moreover, the curfew impacts not only upon the offender but also on other members of the household, turning them into fellow inmates or even quasi-warders. The offender's family or friends have done nothing to warrant state intrusion but residing at the same address, they cannot escape its impact. Policing of the curfew order and the enforcement of compliance may invade their privacy quite as much as the offender's. More seriously still, curfew orders may lead to profound intra-familial tensions as a consequence of enforced confinement of the offender within the home. From the outset, family and child welfare organizations expressed grave concerns about the burdens curfews place on already strained familial relations, increasing the likelihood of domestic violence and child abuse. And family members themselves reported finding long curfews to be 'a definite strain' and 'sometimes a considerable source of friction'.[59] Despite these early misgivings and the mixed results of initial pilots, curfews were adopted nationwide.

Seen one way, the curfew order is a sensible, parsimonious means of dealing with non-dangerous offenders within the community. Seen another it is a gross invasion of personal freedom and a threat to civil liberties. As Ball and Lilly ask, 'Is home incarceration really a humanitarian reduction of social control, or is it further intrusion into private life under a humanitarian guise?'[60] Civil libertarian concerns are exacerbated by the fact that the curfew order is generally assessed in conjunction with its handmaiden, the electronic tag.

Electronic monitoring

Electronic monitoring, or 'tagging' as it is popularly known, is a device straight out of the comic books. Quite literally so, for the device was first developed by Judge Love of Albuquerque, New Mexico who got the idea from reading a Spiderman cartoon in which a villain tracked the hero by means of an electronic bracelet. Although it may take different forms, tagging is generally a band attached to ankle or wrist that transmits signals to a receiver located in a telephone within the home. If the tagged offender moves beyond a specified distance from the telephone, the signal is broken and the central computer alerted to a possible violation. The offender remains permanently tagged but the computer may be programmed to expect signals only during periods specified by the courts to coincide with a curfew.

[59] Mair, G., and Nee, C., *Electronic Monitoring: The Trials and their Results* (London: Home Office, 1990).
[60] Ball, R. A., and Lilly, J. R., 'Home Incarceration with Electronic Monitoring' in Scott and Hirschi (eds), *Controversial Issues in Crime and Justice* (London: Sage, 1988) 154.

Electronic monitoring provides a high degree of surveillance. And as technology advances, the possibility of tracking the offender outside the home or even observing his or her activities within it looms large.[61] In its current form it is relatively cheap to install and administer, and the technology is increasingly reliable.[62] Computers can record night-time violations making it unnecessary to staff the control room outside normal working hours. As an adjunct to the curfew order it enjoys all the benefits of that order whilst rendering it more effective. It does not rely upon the offender exercising high levels of self-discipline nor is it subject to the vagaries of discretion exercised by probation officers. Indeed, such faith does the Home Office have in the multiple uses of electronic monitoring, it claims it 'can provide a cheap and effective means of imposing tighter supervision on offenders; of imposing discipline on chaotic lives; of reintegrating offenders more effectively into society; and an inescapable means of detecting breaches of court orders'.[63]

Against these claimed advantages must be set a worryingly long list of problems and objections. First, electronic monitoring requires that the offender have a stable home address, that they have a telephone line, and that they can continue to meet the costs of its rental and that of the monitoring device. For the many offenders who fail to meet these basic criteria, electronic monitoring will not be possible and they are liable to be imprisoned instead, even though to do so breaches the principle of equal treatment. Secondly, it might be argued that electronic monitoring violates human rights in so far as the affixing of the tag invades bodily autonomy. The European Convention on Human Rights forbids 'degrading punishment' and protects the right to 'privacy'.[64] It is questionable whether having to wear a visible device on arm or leg does not contravene these provisions. A modern-day electronic equivalent to the ball and chain, the tag is, at the very least, a source of social stigma and may frustrate an offender's attempts to find employment. Thirdly, the tag

---

[61] Mair, G., 'Technology and the future of community penalties' in Bottoms, Gelsthorpe, and Rex (eds), *Community Penalties: Change and Challenge* (Cullompton, Devon: Willan Publishing, 2003).

[62] Early pilot schemes were plagued by technological problems that threatened to undermine the credibility of electronic monitoring altogether: Mair, G., and Nee, C., *Electronic Monitoring: The Trials and their Results* (London: Home Office, 1990). Later trials proved more successful: Mair, G., 'Technology and the future of community penalties' in Bottoms, Gelsthorpe, and Rex (eds), *Community Penalties: Change and Challenge* (Cullompton, Devon: Willan Publishing, 2003) 171.

[63] Home Office, *Joining Forces to Protect the Public—Prisons Probation: A Consultation Document* (London: Home Office, 1998) 8.

[64] Articles 3 and 8 respectively.

shames, but despite the claims of the Home Office cited above, it has none of the qualities of 'reintegrative shaming' promoted by Braithwaite and others.[65] It labels the offender but provides no means for constructive dialogue with the offender's community, for the expression of remorse, or for eventual reintegration back into civil society. A fourth objection is that electronic monitoring threatens to replace a highly effective form of supervision in the community by probation workers, with technological oversight. The effects of continual surveillance by a remote machine are not yet known, but it may be imagined that this form of observation is ultimately dehumanizing. Finally, the device, at least in its current form, is more limited in its ability to curb crime than its proponents care to admit. It allows the authorities to know where an offender is, not what he or she is doing. It does nothing to stop offending from or indeed within the home.

One curious ambiguity about both curfew orders and electronic monitoring is the question of who has oversight and responsibility for carrying them out. The Criminal Justice Act 1991 which introduced the order failed to specify this and the probation service was initially reluctant to fill the role. The government responded by contracting out the operation of electronic monitoring to private security firms, though the probation service remains responsible for taking action upon breach. Arguably, it is in part the unsatisfactory nature of this dual responsibility; opposition to the use of private security firms in a quasi-probation role; and the hostility of the probation service that has inhibited take-up of curfew orders with electronic monitoring.[66] Its future is less certain, though some observers have begun to speculate that 'electronic surveillance might in time become the dominant means of controlling sentenced offenders in the community'.[67]

Drug testing and treatment orders

These orders are simultaneously a disciplinary device and a treatment technique.[68] Although technically the offender must be willing to

---

[65] Braithwaite, J., *Crime, Shame and Reintegration* (Cambridge: Cambridge University Press, 1989) ch. 4.

[66] Though the numbers are increasing: 9,182 orders were made in respect of offenders over the age of 16 in 2002: Home Office, *Probation Statistics: England and Wales, 2002* (London: Home Office, 2003) 9.

[67] Whitfield, D., 'What Next: The Magic Bracelet?' (2000) 39 *Criminal Justice Matters* 24–5; Nellis, M., 'Community penalties in historical perspective' in Bottoms, Gelsthorpe, and Rex (eds), *Community Penalties: Change and Challenges* (Cullompton, Devon: Willan Publishing, 2003) 33.

[68] Introduced under the Crime and Disorder Act 1998, drug testing and treatment orders last between six months and three years.

undergo treatment, it is likely that consent is often induced by the fear of a more onerous penalty. This element of compulsion is at odds with what in essence is a medical regime. The orders are usually managed by specialist drug treatment agencies that work in partnership with the probation service. Their administration by multi-agency teams of probation officers, drug workers, psychologists, psychiatric nurses, psychiatrists, and doctors places medics in the invidious position of acting as both medical practitioner and police of those they treat. They may be imposed if the court is satisfied that the offender is a regular drug user who needs and is willing to receive treatment. Because the orders cannot be applied to alcohol abusers, they leave out a substantial population whose addiction is also highly correlated with crime.[69] The order provides for both treatment and regular testing to detect use of illicit drugs. Unusually, the courts are mobilized to enforce the order through regular court reviews that invoke the authority of the sentencer to induce compliance. Although the schemes tend to select low-risk users, the order nonetheless appears to be predicated upon a capacity for compliance that is beyond the scope of many drug users. As result many fail to present themselves for regular drug tests and those that do, test positive in the majority of cases.[70]

Given the very great difficulties involved, it remains open to doubt whether a penal order is an appropriate means by which to secure treatment and whether the likely prospect of imprisonment on breach is a helpful response to the predictable failure of drug users to comply.

Suspended sentence

The suspended sentence is an anomalous order, the use of which has declined dramatically and which is now hardly imposed by magistrates.[71] Its decline can be explained in part by the apparent illogicality of an order that imposes upon the offender a period of up to two years' imprisonment, which is then 'suspended'. The suspended sentence thus requires that the court deem the offence so serious that custody is appropriate, and then step back from imposing immediate custody—in effect letting the offender walk from the court without sanction—only to reactivate it should the offender reoffend during the prescribed period. In its defence,

---

[69] An oversight remedied in the generic community sentence introduced by the Criminal Justice Act 2003 s. 177(1)(j) which includes alcohol treatment among the 12 specified requirements that may be imposed.

[70] Home Office, *The impact of Drug Treatment and Testing Orders on offending. Home Office Findings 184* (London: Home Office, 2003).

[71] Use of the suspended sentence fell from 22,000 in 1992 to just 2,500 in 2002: Home Office, *Criminal Statistics England and Wales, 2002. Cm. 6054* (London: HMSO, 2003) 80.

it can, however, be argued that the suspended sentence has the potential to inflict a large measure of deterrence at very little cost (economic, personal, or social). Although the suspended sentence was introduced as a means of reducing the prison population, inadequate guidance as to when it was to be used, against whom, and the length of sentence to be imposed inhibited it from serving this purpose. The introduction of 'Custody Minus' under the Criminal Justice Act 2003 is an attempt to revive the suspended sentence and give it new credibility by imposing community requirements during the period of the suspension.[72]

ORDERS FOR YOUNG OFFENDERS

In addition to the penalties for adults so far outlined, there are a number of community penalties specifically targeted at young offenders. Youth justice is a particularly turbulent area of criminal justice policy and that of community penalties is no exception.

Supervision orders

The supervision order is the juvenile equivalent of a community rehabilitation order and shares the same aims of reform, preventing reoffending, and protecting the public from harm.[73] The requirement that the young offender make reparation can also be made a condition of a supervision order.[74] Significantly, supervision is principally carried out by the local social services department, arguably reflecting the more solidly welfarist orientation of this order. Under the National Standards, it is stipulated that the order aims 'to encourage and assist the child or young person in his or her development towards a responsible and law-abiding life, thereby promoting the welfare of the offender'. This welfarist orientation reveals itself practically in weekly meetings between offender and social worker to discuss personal problems such as training, employment, benefit claims, and housing.

A more intensive form of supervision arises in the form of the 'intermediate treatment order', or IT as it is commonly known. IT combines the characteristics of supervision with that of the more restrictive care order. Offenders subject to IT may be required to reside at a specific place for up to 90 days and must follow the instructions of their supervising

---

[72] Criminal Justice Act 2003 s. 189.

[73] Introduced under Children and Young Persons Act 1969 s.12, the supervision order may be imposed on young offenders between the ages of 10 and 18 for a period of up to three years. In practice periods of supervision tend to be for one or two years.

[74] Under the Crime and Disorder Act 1998 s. 71.

officer.[75] IT is thus designed to offer the courts an alternative to custody or care where earlier intervention has not succeeded. It is aimed at young offenders whose offences are more serious, and who might otherwise face custody if such a disposal were not available. The decline in use of custody for young offenders during the 1980s is generally credited to the expansion of IT. Although its use declined somewhat under the new punitivism of the 1990s, the Labour government signalled a new commitment to intensive community penalties for juveniles by setting up multi-agency Youth Offending Teams which serve as a 'one-stop shop' for all young offenders.[76]

The Intensive Supervision and Surveillance Programme (ISSP) is not a court order but can be attached as a condition of a supervision order, community rehabilitation order, or bail. It is targeted at persistent young offenders and combines intensive supervision with surveillance measures including electronic tagging, voice verification, and an intense programme of education, training, and reparation. The aim of ISSPs is to impose demanding programmes on repeat young offenders who might otherwise be at risk of custody. The danger, however, is that ISSPs may be imposed on those who were not at risk. Even in respect of those who were, the effect of loading them with such demanding programmes significantly increases the risk of breach and return to court.

Attendance centre order

The attendance centre order is part incapacitative, part punitive, and part therapeutic.[77] Under the order, a young offender can be required to attend a specified place for short periods of time up to a maximum of 36 hours. Usually this takes the form of three-hour periods at an attendance centre on Saturday afternoons when the local football team is playing at home. The young offender is thus kept out of trouble at a time of maximum risk, denied the pleasure of supporting his or her team, and given physical training and social skills classes.

Action plan order

The government introduced the action plan order as 'a short intensive programme of community intervention combining punishment,

---

[75] Conditions may be stipulated by the supervisor under Children and Young Persons Act 1969 s. 12 or, more rarely, by the court under a new Criminal Justice Act 1982 s. 12A.

[76] The Crime and Disorder Act 1998 s.39 imposes a duty upon local authorities to establish local youth offender teams.

[77] It was introduced for young offenders up to the age of 21 by the Criminal Justice Act 1948, and was designated a community sentence under the Criminal Justice Act 1991 s. 6.

rehabilitation and reparation to change offending behaviour and prevent
further crime'.[78] The action plan runs for a period of three months and
may impose requirements as to the offender's whereabouts and activities
during that time. The offender is placed under the supervision of a
specified officer (whether a probation officer, social worker, or member
of a youth offending team) and is required to follow the directions given
by that officer.[79] These requirements may include participating in
specified activities, attending meetings or an attendance centre, staying
away from particular places, complying with arrangements for education, making reparation (whether to individual persons or the community at large), and attending court hearings. The wide-ranging
nature of these provisions reflects both the eclectic array of purposes
the order is supposed to fulfil and also the intention that that the order
be tailored to the offender's individual needs. Before making the order,
the court must explain to the offender in ordinary language the effect of
the order, the proposed requirements, and the consequences of breach.
Clearly the intention is both to impress upon the offender how demanding the order is and to co-opt them in their own self-discipline. The
action plan order is designed to meet the perceived need for demanding
and credible community penalties. Whether, in practice, the order actually adds very much to the existing penal repertoire is, however, doubtful since its provisions largely replicate those available within existing
orders.

Reparation order

This order requires young offenders to make good to the victim, to someone otherwise affected by the crime, or to the community at large by
writing a letter of apology, apologizing in person, repairing harm done, or
doing other work for up to 24 hours. As with compensation orders, there
is a presumption in favour of making such an order and where the court
does not do so it must give reasons.[80] Reparation is made 'in kind', varying from a simple letter of apology to several hours per week of practical
activity that benefits an individual victim or the community at large.
Where the victim does not desire reparation, the court may order the
offender to make reparation to the community instead, for example, by
repairing damage or cleaning graffiti. The purpose is both to help young

---

[78] Home Office, *No More Excuses: A New Approach to Tackling Youth Crime* (London:
HMSO, 1997).
[79] Criminal Justice and Disorder Act 1998 s. 69.
[80] Crime and Disorder Act 1998 s. 67.

offenders to understand and address the consequences of their actions and to offer some practical recompense to the victim. The order is obviously restorative in its intent. However, it is arguable that its restorative ambitions are at odds with the generally punitive climate within which it operates.[81] If the reparation order is used primarily as a means of punishing offenders or forcing them to face up to their responsibilities then its ability to restore is limited. Several features of the order also place in question its restorative potential. First, although victim offender mediation is contemplated as one possible outcome of the order, the emphasis is on reparative action by the offender rather than upon the kind of constructive dialogue between victim and offender which research suggests is most likely to be restorative. Secondly, although the victim's consent has to be sought, that of the offender does not. Again, it is questionable whether coercion is consistent with restoration and, as Dignan points out, it is likely that reparation thus imposed will be perceived as punishment by the offender and be regarded as lacking sincerity by the victim.[82] Finally, there is a danger that these orders will result in the co-option of the victim in the shaming of the offender. Dignan suggests that the enthusiasm of some police for restorative justice derives from their perception that it is more demanding than conventional court-based processes. Without proper guiding principles and good practice standards, there is a danger that the reparation order will fail to fulfil the very high expectations of it proclaimed by politicians and promoted by the media.

Referral orders

If doubt has been cast over the restorative potential of the orders described so far, more positive interest has been evinced in referral orders.[83] Indeed Crawford and Newburn declare, 'of all New Labour's restorative youth justice initiatives, arguably the most significant . . . has been the creation of referral orders'.[84] The referral order is mandatory for

---

[81] The Crime and Disorder Act 1998 which introduced the reparation order also abolished the doctrine of *doli incapax* for 10–13-year-olds, introduced local child curfew schemes and anti-social behaviour orders, and extended provisions for imprisoning 'persistent' young offenders as young as 10 years old. See Dignan, J., 'The Crime and Disorder Act 1998 and the Prospects for Restorative Justice' (1999) *Criminal Law Review* 48–60 at 54.

[82] Dignan, J., op. cit. 55. Cynics might question how far consent by the offender, even if sought, is voluntarily given when the alternative is likely to be greater punishment.

[83] Referral orders were set up by the Youth Justice and Criminal Evidence Act 1999 and consolidated as ss. 16 and 17 of the Powers of the Criminal Courts (Sentencing) Act 2000.

[84] Crawford, A., and Newburn, T., *Youth Offending and Restorative Justice; Implementing Reform in Youth Justice* (Cullompton, Devon: Willan Publishing, 2003) 18.

10- to 17-year-olds who plead guilty and are convicted for the first time by the courts, unless the crime is so serious as to demand imprisonment, or the court orders an absolute discharge. The order refers the young offender to a youth offending panel (or YOP) and runs for between 3 and 12 months. The panel includes one member of a youth offending team, at least two community panel members, one or both parents of those under 16, the offender can also nominate an adult to act as a supporter, and various other people may be invited to attend. Thus comprised, the panel harks back to earlier mediation experiments in Britain and family-group conferencing initiatives, for example in New Zealand. A key primary duty of the panel is to formulate a contract with the offender.[85] This contract constitutes the term of the penalty at the end of which the offence is deemed to be 'spent'.[86] The work of the panel is officially governed by the principles of 'restoration, reintegration and responsibility'[87] and their meetings, which occur at intervals during the life of the order, are intended to provide a less formal context than the courts in which to facilitate restoration. Against the negative expectations of many commentators, Crawford and Newburn's assessment of their operation is promising: 'youth offending panels appeared relatively quickly to have established themselves as deliberative and participatory forums in which to address a young person's offending behaviour'.[88]

There are, however, a number of problematic aspects to the referral order. First, it provides young offenders with an incentive to admit their guilt safe in the knowledge that as soon as the contract is over they will no longer be burdened by a criminal record. Read one way this is a valuable way of reducing the stigma that might otherwise attach to first offenders and that might otherwise injure their employment prospects. Read more cynically, it is a means of speeding up the criminal process by inducing guilty pleas by the promise of the rapid return to a clean record. Secondly, where on a guilty plea the referral order is mandatory, the court is obliged to sentence for a minimum of three months even if it is of the view that a modest fine or conditional discharge would suffice. If the offender reoffends, the referral order is no longer available and so, paradoxically, for a second similar offence the court may impose one of these

[85] On the growing importance of contracts, see: Crawford, A., ' "Contractual Governance" of Deviant Behaviour' (2003) 30 *Journal of Law and Society* 479–505.

[86] For the purposes of the Rehabilitation of Offenders Act 1974.

[87] Home Office, *No More Excuses: A New Approach to Tackling Youth Crime* (London: HMSO, 1997) 32.

[88] Crawford, A., and Newburn, T., *Youth Offending and Restorative Justice; Implementing Reform in Youth Justice* (Cullompton, Devon: Willan Publishing, 2003) 131.

lesser penalties.[89] In order to evade the mandatory referral order in cases where it seems disproportionate, it seems likely that lawyers will advise their clients to plead not guilty and force a trial. Finally, even if the referral order holds out all the promise that Crawford and Newburn's study suggests, its operation in the larger climate of popular punitivism discussed above creates, at the very least, confusion. The orientation of other technically non-penal initiatives such as anti-social behaviour orders, child safety orders, child curfew schemes, as well as parental bind-overs and parenting orders is far from restorative. The resulting tensions and contradictions between policies that are reintegrative and those that tend toward social exclusion, between those that seek to restore and those that seek only to repress, do not permit of a confident or coherent assessment of the prospects for youth justice in the community.

THE MULTIPLE PURPOSES OF FINANCIAL AND COMMUNITY PENALTIES

The multiplicity of purposes ascribed to financial and community penalties places conflicting demands upon those called upon to implement them and generates no little confusion. In what follows, we revisit the main purposes of punishment outlined in Chapter 3 to explore whether and to what degree financial and community penalties can be said to fulfil them.

ENSURING PROPORTIONALITY

We have observed that a common charge against financial and community penalties is that they lack punitive bite, but a strong counter-argument is that proportionality can only be maintained if the relative seriousness of offences is matched by ranking penalties according to severity. A very grave offence may demand imprisonment but if this penalty is not used sparingly it becomes difficult to maintain any hierarchy of penalties. Financial penalties provide a convenient means of imposing clearly ranked penalties at the bottom of the scale. Further up the scale an appropriate measure of pain is provided by community penalties. Yet despite the fact that financial and community penalties furnish suitable punishments at the lower end of the tariff, in practice the political imperatives of ensuring that they are credible with sentencers and the

---

[89] Greenlow, J., 'Referral Orders: Problems in Practice' (2003) *Criminal Law Review* 266–8 at 267.

public has had the ironic effect of increasing the restrictions imposed on offenders' liberty. It is as if community penalties need to demonstrate their punitive qualities. The fact that the restrictions they impose are inherently punitive seems to be lost from view.

Part of the problem may be that the centrality of the prison has tended to focus calculations of proportionality on terms of months or years in prison. Whilst it is obvious that two years are more onerous than one, it is not immediately apparent how one should rank community penalties against each other. For example, is two years of community rehabilitation more or less onerous than 200 hours' community punishment? Assessing their relative severity is also hampered by the fact that, in serving diverse penal goals, these penalties do not neatly fit a theory dedicated to apportioning punishment.[90] The problem is not, however, insuperable. Some degree of proportionality could be achieved by ranking community penalties in broad bands according to their relative severity and allowing substitution between different penalties of comparable severity depending upon the particular goal to be attained in any individual case.[91] Employed in this way, proportionality could dictate the amount of punishment required, leaving sentencers free to determine the content of the penalty in pursuit of other purposes.

DETERRENCE

To the charge that community penalties are not credible punishments and that they lack the ability to deter, it can be argued that in differing degrees and through differing means, both financial and community penalties entail many of those deterrent effects that are the much-vaunted capital of the prison. Loss of free time is an essential element of community punishment and of attendance centre orders. Fines, by reducing spending power, restrict life choices. Even the compensation order extorts payments which, in the vast majority of cases, the offender would not otherwise be required to pay and can be seen as a potential deterrent. Restrictions on lifestyle, mobility, and choice of association may all be made conditions of community rehabilitation orders. The deterrent potential of financial and community penalties resides in the fact that

[90] Whilst academic critics of desert theory see this quality of community sentences as illustrating a weakness within desert theory, the Home Office has regarded it as a weakness in the penalties themselves. See respectively, Hudson, B., *Justice through Punishment: A Critique of the 'Justice' Model of Corrections* (Basingstoke: Macmillan, 1987) 136; Home Office, *Strengthening Punishment in the Community* (London: HMSO, 1995) 12.

[91] Wasik, M., and von Hirsch, A., 'Non-Custodial Penalties and the Principles of Desert' (1988) *Criminal Law Review* 555–72 at 559 ff.

their very variety makes it possible to target pains at the specific characteristics or habits of the individual offender. They can deliver these pains in the least onerous manner consistent with their purpose and they can do so very cheaply.[92] Arguably flexibility, parsimony, and economy are the very strengths of financial and community penalties over the prison. It can be argued, however, that to make deterrence a central purpose of financial or community penalties would be to deny and downplay other more positive purposes to which they might better be put.

REHABILITATION

Given the origins of community penalties in the post-war era of penal welfarism,[93] it should come as no surprise to discover that rehabilitation is one of their core rationales. Rehabilitation explains not only the development of community penalties; as the overarching rationale it framed their early organization and implementation as well. From the start, the possibility of treatment and even cure licensed considerable leeway in the delivery of community penalties. As Garland observes: 'the individualizing, indeterminate, and largely discretionary character of the correctionalist arrangements allowed the system's decision-makers extensive latitude in their treatment of convicted offenders.'[94] Yet even at the height of welfarism, different community penalties were accorded differing degrees of reformative potential. Even before its change of name to community rehabilitation, probation always had a greater rehabilitative content than community service (as it was then called). And the most frequently used of non-custodial sanctions, the fine, has at no point been seriously presented as a means of treatment or cure.

Faith in the power of penalties to reform was severely dented by research studies carried out in the 1960s that concluded, in Martinson's famous phrase, 'nothing works'.[95] This credo was quickly taken up in the United States by the media, academics, and practitioners despite the fact that Martinson's conclusions were circumspect and despite the fact that

---

[92] Whilst the prison costs £2,070 per person per month, community rehabilitation (probation) costs only £183 and community punishment (community service) £141. Figures from Home Office, *Information on the Criminal Justice System in England and Wales: Digest 4* (London: Home Office, 1999) 73.

[93] Though probation is, of course, much older, having its origins in the work of the nineteenth-century police court missionaries.

[94] Garland, D., *The Culture of Control: Crime and Social Order in Contemporary Society* (Oxford: Oxford University Press, 2001) 35.

[95] Martinson, R., 'What Works? Questions and Answers About Prison Reform' (1974) *Public Interest* 22–54; Lipton, D., Martinson, R., and Wilks, J., *The Effectiveness of Correctional Treatment* (New York: Praeger, 1975).

others quickly responded with studies suggesting that some penalties did work.[96] Although Garland describes the loss of confidence in rehabilitation as 'akin to a stock market crash',[97] outside America probation and community service thrived and even increased in proportionate use in the 'post-rehabilitative' period. Although community penalties are clearly susceptible to the changing political fortunes of rehabilitation, therefore, their implementation in practice is not invariably tied to that political agenda.

More recent research suggests a much higher degree of efficacy for community penalties than had been previously thought.[98] This revival of faith in rehabilitation has spawned a renewed interest in 'what works?' studies that revisit the reformative potential of interventionist programmes.[99] Raynor categorizes these research studies into psychological approaches, meta-analyses, and evaluations of structured programmes. He concludes: 'taken together these various strands of research carried an encouraging message: far from nothing working, it appeared that appropriate forms of supervision were capable of delivering reductions in offending of between 10 and 20 per cent, or even more in some cases.'[100] Effective dissemination of these findings[101] has spawned a large array of new evidence-based initiatives. Yet, despite the growing persuasiveness of the 'what works' research, community penalties struggle to maintain their credibility as rehabilitative orders. Pressure to impose ever-greater restrictions upon offenders, to implement penalties that are demanding, and to

---

[96] Gendreau, P., and Ross, R. R., 'Effectiveness of Correctional Treatment: Bibliotherapy for Cynics' (1979) 25 *Crime and Delinquency* 463–89. As indeed did Martinson: Martinson, R., 'New Findings, New Views: A Note of Caution Regarding Sentencing Reform' (1979) 7 *Hofstra Law Review* 242–58.

[97] Garland, D., *The Culture of Control: Crime and Social Order in Contemporary Society* (Oxford: Oxford University Press, 2001) 69.

[98] See discussion of the research evidence in McGuire, J., and Priestly, P., 'Reviewing "What Works": Past, Present and Future' in McGuire, J. (ed.), *What Works: Reducing Reoffending* (Chichester: Wiley, 1995) 7 f.; Vennard, J., Sugg, D., and Hedderman, C., *Changing Offenders' Attitudes and Behaviour: What Works?* (London: HMSO, 1997).

[99] For example, on the findings of the Pathfinder projects in community service see Rex, S., and Gelsthorpe, L., 'The Role of Community Service in Reducing Offending: Evaluating Pathfinder Projects in the UK' (2002) 41 *Howard Journal of Criminal Justice* 311–25.

[100] Raynor, P., 'Community Penalties: Probation, Punishment, and "What Works" ' in Maguire, Morgan, and Reiner (eds), *The Oxford Handbook of Criminology* (3rd edn, Oxford: Oxford University Press, 2002) 1183–6.

[101] Chapman, B., and Hough, M., *Evidence-Based Practice* (London: Home Office, 2000); McGuire, J., *Cognitive-Behavioural Approaches* (London: Home Office, 2000); Rex, S., Bottoms, A. E., and Wilson, S., *Accrediting Offender Programmes: A Process-Based Evaluation of the Joint Prison/Probation Services Accreditation Panel. Home Office Research Study No. 273* (London: Home Office, 2003).

target even those whose risk of reoffending is slight, all hamper the capacity of community-based programmes to reform. The pressure to maintain credibility has imposed strains also upon the probation service, caught between their original mandate to 'assist, advise, and befriend' their clients and their new obligations to manage offenders efficiently and effectively.[102]

INCAPACITATION AND MANAGING RISK

One of the major competitors to the rehabilitative purpose of community penalties is the growing compulsion to take account of risk. No penalty, short perhaps of manacles and leg irons, can stop reoffending. The power of the prison to incapacitate is also limited: it does so only for the term of the sentence and even then may only displace crime to within the prison walls. There are high rates of offending, particularly of violence, within all custodial institutions and yet equal concern is not always expressed for the inmates who suffer victimization inside.[103] Financial orders apart, community penalties generally place constraints over offenders for longer periods than comparable sentences of imprisonment. Curfew orders, conditions attached to community rehabilitation, and time spent doing community punishment all reduce opportunities for offending. In the case of community rehabilitation and community punishment, they may also reduce motivation for offending by engaging offenders in constructive activities or training programmes. In addition, some penalties explicitly seek to incapacitate. Curfew orders, especially with the additional requirement of electronic tagging, restrict the movement of offenders at those times of the day when they would otherwise be most likely to engage in criminal activities. Whilst the power of the prison to incapacitate clearly outstrips these orders, it is doubtful whether the exclusion and confinement of individuals is justifiable where the risks of reoffending are slight or the nature of the predicted crime less serious.

The rise of prudentialism or 'actuarial justice', with its increasingly sophisticated techniques for measuring risk,[104] has obliged those

---

[102] Wargent, M., 'The New Governance of Probation' (2002) 41 *Howard Journal of Criminal Justice* 182–200.

[103] Edgar, K., O'Donnell, I., and Martin, C., *Prison Violence: the Dynamics of Conflict, Fear and Power* (Cullompton, Devon: Willan Publishing, 2003).

[104] Feeley, M., and Simon, J., 'Actuarial Justice: The Emerging New Criminal Law' in Nelken (ed.), *The Futures of Criminology* (London: Sage, 1994); O'Malley, P., 'Risk societies and the government of crime' in Brown and Pratt (eds), *Dangerous Offenders: Punishment and Social Order* (London: Routledge, 2000); Loader, I., and Sparks, R., 'Contemporary Landscapes of Crime, Order, and Control: Governance, Risk, and Globalization' in Maguire, Morgan, and Reiner (eds), *The Oxford Handbook of Criminology* (3rd edn, Oxford: Oxford University Press, 2002).

administering community penalties to advert to risk and to take pre-
cautionary measures even in respect of less serious offenders. The
demands of risk assessment, together with the growing expectation that
probation services be accountable to their local communities, impose
considerable political pressure to ensure that those under supervision do
not reoffend. Risk thus licenses more intensive and more intrusive
community penalties, greater resort to technologies of control, and
resort to prudential considerations in the management of offenders. The
development of statistical risk-assessment systems using information
technology to calculate individual risk scores has further increased the
emphasis of community penalties on risk management.

RESTORATIVE JUSTICE

Restorative justice is another increasingly important role ascribed to
community penalties. Some financial and community penalties are
explicitly restorative and others are reparative in a more narrowly
material sense. The compensation order seeks to make good to the victim.[105] Community punishment orders oblige offenders to engage in
works that directly or indirectly make amends to the community. Other
penalties have more attenuated reparative qualities: fines for example
bring in a substantial income to the Treasury and, in so doing, might be
said to make some contribution to the general good. By contrast
imprisonment provides few opportunities for either reparation or restorative conduct and, ironically, may prevent the payment of compensation or
making amends in the very cases where the harms caused are most serious
and claims for compensation or redress are strongest.

The rise of restorative justice, in the sense of seeking to restore both
offender and victim, has tended to overshadow the earlier emphasis on
material reparation. It has increased most rapidly in respect of the many
community penalties available for young offenders. Reparation orders
and requirements to make reparation to the victim under action plan
orders are explicitly restorative. And yet the requirement that the reparation be commensurate with the seriousness of the offence suggests a
tension between restorative and punitive purposes. The conduct of youth
offending panels is governed by the principles of restorative justice, and
the panels seek to help young offenders to make good and to reintegrate

---

[105] Though the requirement that compensation orders be set with reference to the ability
of the offender to pay means that they rarely result in complete restitution: Zedner, L.,
'Reparation and Retribution: Are They Reconcilable?' (1994) 57 *Modern Law Review* 228–
50 at 235.

into society.[106] Indeed it can be argued that restorative justice is now the central purpose of community penalties for young offenders. Despite the claims of its proponents, it has yet to become the dominant rationale for community penalties for adults more generally.[107] And indeed, given the many problems identified in respect of restorative justice in Chapter 3, it remains open to question whether its larger-scale adoption would be an untrammelled good.

PENAL COMMUNICATION

A key difficulty faced by financial and community penalties is their capacity to convince the general public that they are proper punishments. The press has had a significant part to play in that their headline and leader writers commonly insist that the popular outrage provoked by crime is unlikely to be satisfied by anything less than prison. Research on public opinion and sentencing suggests that the public tend systematically to underestimate the severity of court sentences.[108] If the public were better informed, the courts could perhaps increase their use of financial and community penalties without risking public dissatisfaction. Research evidence suggests that it is possible to communicate effectively the nature of the strictures and burdens imposed by community penalties and by so doing to increase judicial confidence.[109]

Community penalties have a communicative function in a second sense: namely in conveying to offenders the nature of the wrong they have committed, in encouraging them to confront their offending behaviour, and in getting them to recognize the need to amend. Duff describes this enterprise as one of 'transparent persuasion'.[110] Where successful it allows offenders the occasion for what Duff terms 'secular penance'. He claims that community punishment 'constitutes a forceful public apology; . . . it provides an authorized, publicly recognized form in which an offender who has genuinely repented her crime can express that apologetic repentance to her fellow citizens . . . But it is also a means by

[106] Crawford, A., and Newburn, T., *Youth Offending and Restorative Justice; Implementing Reform in Youth Justice* (Cullompton, Devon: Willan Publishing, 2003) ch.4.

[107] Braithwaite, J., 'Restorative Justice' in M. Tonry (ed.), *Handbook of Crime and Punishment* (New York: Oxford University Press, 1998) 323.

[108] Hough, M., 'People Talking About Punishment' (1996) 35 *Howard Journal of Criminal Justice* 191–214.

[109] Hedderman, C., Ellis, T., and Sugg, D., *Increasing Confidence in Community Sentences: the Results of Two Demonstration Projects* (London: Home Office, 1999).

[110] Duff, R. A., *Punishment, Communication, and Community* (Oxford: Oxford University Press, 2001) 101.

which an offender who has not yet faced up to or repented her crime can properly be brought to do so.'[111] Whilst we might question whether the state has standing to impose this form of secular penance, we can nonetheless accept that community penalties have communicative potential, if only as a means of providing prudential reasons for desistence from wrongdoing.[112]

The multiplicity of purposes potentially fulfilled by financial and community penalties requires that we seek clarity about the specific goal any single penalty pursues. Demands that penal orders be effective are vacuous if the criteria by which efficacy is judged in any given case remain undefined. This is not to suggest that uniformity of purpose across penalties is necessary or desirable. One of the strengths of community penalties is their ability to fulfil many different goals. And despite claims that the fine is purely retributive, we have suggested that financial penalties also play multiple roles. Measuring effectiveness in respect of financial and community penalties therefore requires clear identification of sometimes disparate goals. As it stands, confusion reigns in the probation service as to which purpose predominates in any one penalty.

CONCLUSION

If the multiple possible roles of financial and community penalties are a positive advantage, they are also potentially hazardous. The many divergent demands placed upon the probation service have led to the 'creative mixing' of different requirements imposed upon offenders.[113] It seems probable that the possibility of combining the existing community penalties under the new single Community Order introduced by the Criminal Justice Act 2003 will exacerbate this tendency to intensify the requirements placed upon offenders. Indeed the tendency has already been identified as 'condition creep' or 'sentence stacking'. If the courts are tempted to add conditions under Community Orders, the increased burdens will increase the risk of breach. The creation of combined community and custodial sentences to be known as Custody Plus further adds to this trend of piling burden upon burden.[114] And the introduction of

---

[111] Ibid. 106.

[112] von Hirsch, A., 'Punishment, Penance, and the State: A Reply to Duff' in M. Matravers (ed.), *Punishment and Political Theory* (Oxford: Hart Publishing, 1999) 74.

[113] Bottoms, A. E., Gelsthorpe, L., and Rex, S. (eds), *Community Penalties: Change and Challenges* (Cullompton, Devon: Willan Publishing, 2003) 6.

[114] Criminal Justice Act 2003 s. 181.

Custody Minus likewise imposes new burdens in the form of requirements to be fulfilled in the community during the period of a suspended sentence.[115] Although these new sentences are intended to reduce reliance upon custody for less serious offenders, in every case, if offenders fail to comply with the conditions imposed, they are also liable to find themselves imprisoned on breach. Far from reducing reliance upon prison, therefore, they may increase it. The trend toward mixing and stacking of community penalties, of combining community and custodial sentences, together with new forms of technological surveillance and risk assessment, might properly revive our interest in Cohen's net-widening thesis. Sadly, it may transpire that he was even more far-sighted in his dystopic vision of community penalties than his early critics could predict. If his grim prophecies are not to transpire then the trick for proponents and practitioners of community penalties is to formulate a model that resists the temptation to believe that more is always better. Encouraging greater resort to juridical penalties like the fine, as a means of withstanding the proliferation of conditions, requirements, and technologies of control, might be a disarmingly simple way to start.

[115] Criminal Justice Act 2003 s. 189.

7

Prisons

If community sentences have been the subject of critical and correspondingly pessimistic analysis, that attracted by the prison is much bleaker. It is commonly assumed that, unless crime can be brought under better control by other means, there is no escaping the remorseless growth of the prison population; the continuing expansion of the prison estate; and greater reliance on private contractors to provide a prison system spiralling beyond the means of the public purse. The prison dominates our criminal justice system as the cardinal penalty, against which all other penalties must be assessed. Despite repeated efforts by penal policymakers, politicians, and lobbyists to displace the prison from its central position, it continues to have a powerful hold over our collective imagination. It is the prison that dominates political and public debate, media coverage, and, to a lesser extent, academic enquiry. It is as if it were impossible to imagine a penal system in which the prison did not exist as penalty of last resort. In this chapter we start by examining the origins of imprisonment in order to explore the role of the prison and to explain why it continues to be the dominant penalty of our criminal justice system.

WHY DOES THE PRISON PERSIST?

Our continuing reliance on the prison is a puzzle given that it is arguably more often a site of corruption and demoralization than reform; of marginal value in protecting the public;[1] and expensive compared to community sentences.[2] Given these multiple failures, the enduring dominance of this tired and manifestly malfunctioning institution demands an explanation. That many prisoners continue to be held in

[1] Morgan points out that only 0.3 per cent of offenders are caught, convicted, and imprisoned: Morgan, R., 'Imprisonment: a Brief History, the Contemporary Scene, and Likely Prospects' in Maguire, Morgan, and Reiner (eds), *The Oxford Handbook of Criminology* (3rd edn, Oxford: Oxford University Press, 2002) 1119. Though the more serious the offence, the greater is the likelihood of a custodial sentence ensuing.

[2] On the comparative costs of penal measures, see Chapter 6, n. 92.

crumbling Victorian jails, whose architecture reflects another time and penal philosophy entirely, only underlines the need to explain the persistence of the prison. Yet the prison as we know it is a relatively modern invention. Only in the nineteenth century did the abolition of judicial torture and the removal of the death penalty from public audience elevate imprisonment to become the dominant penal measure. At the same time, prisons themselves were transformed: though the extent and degree of this transformation is a matter of lively historical debate. The small, locally run, and often chaotic, prisons of the eighteenth century were increasingly overshadowed by the building of the vast, monolithic, centralized, and highly ordered penitentiaries of the nineteenth.[3] The traditional Whig interpretation was that this transformation reflected a triumph of humanitarian reform over barbarism.[4] The modern prison represented progress from chaos to order and from brutality to benevolent discipline. If only this were true, the Whig account alone might explain the persistence of the prison. But this benign interpretation does not withstand critical scrutiny if we observe that the modern prison, for all its purported commitment to reform, holds inmates in conditions that tend to brutalize rather than reclaim. In the following sections, we will ask what role the prison fulfils and why it persists despite a legacy of failure and heavy costs, both human and financial.

THE PRISON AS FACTORY

The social role of the prison has been of considerable interest to Marxist historians (though curiously not to Marx himself) who seek to establish the link between forms of punishment and the mode of production. Rusche and Kirchheimer suggest that continued use of the prison is directly related to changes in the labour market.[5] Prior to industrialization, life was cheap and capital and corporal punishment predominated. With industrialization, they argue, labour became valuable and the prison an essential tool in conserving and controlling the labour supply. When

---

[3] This transformation should not be overplayed. Local prisons continued in large numbers and reforms did not always have their intended impact upon local regimes: McConville, S., *English Local Prisons, 1860–1900: Next Only to Death* (London: Routledge, 1995).

[4] The designation Whig here refers to a particular brand of nineteenth-century optimism in the power of reform to secure progress toward an ever more civilized society.

[5] Rusche, G., and Kirchheimer, O., *Punishment and Social Structure* (New York: Columbia University Press, 1939). Although first published in 1939, this book became widely influential only after it was reprinted in 1968.

labour was scarce, use of the prison declined, when labour was plentiful, it increased. Melossi and Pavarini characterize the prison as a factory in which the recalcitrant poor could be put to work.[6] As such, they claim, it was a source of labour discipline essential to emergent capitalism. The principle of less eligibility required that conditions in prisons should be of a lesser standard than those enjoyed by the poorest workers outside. Designed to deter, the principle served as an additional means by which to induce conformity among honest workers.

The problem with this characterization of the prison is that it is both reductive and overly functionalist. It fits ill with historical fact and, as Cavadino and Dignan wryly note, 'it fails to explain the mechanisms linking an economic imperative with a penal practice. Capitalism needed the house of correction, and somehow it magically came into being as a result.'[7] In short, economic determinism fails precisely because it fails to provide any account of human agency.

More recent accounts provide a less deterministic account of the relationship between economic change and the role of the prison. In his consideration of the continuing close relationship between the prison and industrial capitalism, Christie contends that the classic problem of industrialization, namely that it creates a surplus and therefore potentially dangerous population, has not diminished. A 'crime control industry' has developed to resolve this problem by incarcerating the surplus population in ever-increasing numbers. Like all industries, the crime control industry is driven by commercial concerns that tend toward expansion. But Christie's account, unlike its predecessors, concedes that the burgeoning growth of the prison population, particularly in countries like Russia and the United States, is the result of choices.[8] Although economic conditions are powerful drivers, they could be resisted by the force of moral and political arguments and public and elite sentiment.

A SITE OF DISCIPLINE

A further set of explanations for the persistence of the prison resides in the so-called revisionist histories that challenge the Whig account of

[6] Melossi, D., and Pavarini, M., *The Prison and the Factory* (London: Macmillan, 1981).

[7] Cavadino, M., and Dignan, J., *The Penal System: An Introduction* (3rd edn, London: Sage, 2002) 64. Although public works were carried out by convict prisons from the mid-nineteenth century, there was little useful work in local prisons: McConville, S., *English Local Prisons, 1860–1900: Next Only to Death* (London: Routledge, 1995).

[8] Christie, N., *Crime Control as Industry* (London: Routledge, 1994) 15.

progress and reform with an altogether less benign reading.[9] The birth of the modern prison, they argued, was based upon an 'ambitious conception of power, aiming for the first time at altering the criminal personality. This strategy of power could not be understood unless the history of the prison was incorporated into a history of the philosophy of authority and the exercise of class power in general.'[10] Accordingly, their accounts drew links between the emergence of the prison and other total institutions dedicated to surveillance and control. Foucault, by far the most influential of these writers, saw the prison as part of a larger complex of disciplinary institutions or 'carceral archipelago'. 'Is it surprising', Foucault asks, 'that prisons resemble factories, schools, barracks, hospitals, which all resemble prisons?' His seminal work *Discipline and Punish: The Birth of the Prison* sees the birth of the modern penitentiary as reflecting a shift from corporal to disciplinary punishment. The prisoner is no longer the object of suffering but of correction; punishment is not of the body but 'of the soul'. Subject to a regime of surveillance, routine, and reform or 'normalization', the prisoner emerges a compliant, conforming, and useful member of society—a 'docile body'.

For Foucault, the quintessential disciplinary prison is the Panopticon. Conceived by Jeremy Bentham, the Panopticon was planned as a circular architectural structure in which all the cells are arranged around a central viewing tower that makes permanent and complete surveillance possible. Foucault proposes that the disciplinary power theoretically inherent in the 'total knowledge' made possible by the Panopticon is paralleled throughout modern society: 'one can speak of the formation of disciplinary society in this movement that stretches from the enclosed disciplines, a sort of social "quarantine", to an indefinitely generalizable mechanism of "panopticonism".'[11]

The evident failure of the prison to reform its inmates might appear to undermine claims as to its disciplinary power were it not reinterpreted by Foucault as a covert success. The prison was designed, he argues, not so

---

[9] Rothman, D., *The Discovery of the Asylum: Social Order and Disorder in the New Republic* (Boston: Little, Brown & Co., 1971); Foucault, M., *Discipline and Punish: The Birth of the Prison* (reprint, Harmondsworth, Middlesex: Penguin Books, 1982) (trans. Harmondsworth: Penguin, 1982, first pub. 1975, in French); Ignatieff, M., *A Just Measure of Pain: The Penitentiary in the Industrial Revolution, 1750–1850* (London: Macmillan, 1978).

[10] Ignatieff, M., 'State, Civil Society and Total Institutions: A Critique of Recent Social Histories of Punishment' in Cohen and Scull (eds), *Social Control and the State: Historical and Comparative Essays* (Oxford: Basil Blackwell, 1983) 77.

[11] Foucault, M., *Discipline and Punish: The Birth of the Prison* (reprint, Harmondsworth, Middlesex: Penguin, 1982) 216.

much to reform as to manufacture delinquents. Incarcerated and marginalized, the prison population serves as a threat by which to control the working classes. Delinquency validates the maintenance of a system of policing with the prison at its end. It justifies the surveillance, supervision, and domination of the working classes and it furthers this end by dividing the working classes against themselves. The revolving door of the prison, which sees recidivists return repeatedly to the prison, thus signifies not a failure of the regime but its very purpose. Read this way, the prison persists not despite its failure but because of it.

Foucault's ideas have profoundly influenced our understanding of the prison and its role in society. It is now almost impossible to think or write about the prison without reference to them. Unsurprisingly, they have also been sharply criticized. We have already enumerated more general criticisms of his account of penality in Chapter 3. With specific regard to the prison, his historical account has been faulted for overstating the transition from physical to carceral punishment:[12] corporal punishment did not disappear overnight nor did the reformed penitentiary replace it entirely. The changes Foucault observes were more erratic and less widespread than he admits. Secondly, he imputes penal reform solely to the impulses of social control[13] and ignores both humanitarian efforts made to reform the prison in the nineteenth century and also the limits of this reform process.[14] Thirdly, he generalizes from specific penal institutions (reformatories for young offenders) to extrapolate to the adult prison and from specific geographical locations (France) to make larger claims about developments that are less readily observable elsewhere. Finally, he concentrates on the instrumental role of the prison, as a technology of power, at the expense of its expressive aspects, namely the ways in which the prison signifies and shapes values. Whilst these criticisms dent the explanatory power of Foucault's thesis, they do not negate his larger, still powerful insights into why the prison should have persisted in the face of its own apparent failure.

---

[12] Spierenburg, P., *The Spectacle of Suffering* (Cambridge: Cambridge University Press, 1984).

[13] Ignatieff criticizes both Foucault's and his own earlier work, for relying upon a monolithic explanation of prison reform that does not fit with historical fact: Ignatieff, M., 'State, Civil Society and Total Institutions: A Critique of Recent Social Histories of Punishment' in Cohen and Scull (eds), *Social Control and the State: Historical and Comparative Essays* (Oxford: Basil Blackwell, 1983) 77–8.

[14] For example, see DeLacy, M., *Prison Reform in Lancashire, 1700–1850* (Manchester: Manchester University Press, 1986); Zedner, L., *Women, Crime, and Custody in Victorian England* (Oxford: Oxford University Press, 1991) 95.

THE PRISON AS IDEOLOGY

Whereas Foucault's account is premised upon the claim that the prison succeeds despite its apparent failure, Mathiesen takes the failure of the prison as his starting point.[15] Unequivocally declaring the prison a 'fiasco', he is concerned to explain the continuing pervasive 'ideology of prison'. According to Mathiesen, this ideology is a belief system that renders the prison 'meaningful and legitimate', despite its transparent failure. He identifies five distinct functions. These are, first, the **expurgatory function** by which the prison banishes and contains a portion of surplus or unproductive labour unwanted by late capitalism. By housing this population out of sight, the prison allows society to forget about the casualties of the economic system. Put another way, the prison imposes a form of internal exile upon those incarcerated within its walls. Terms of imprisonment grow longer and longer, subjecting those sentenced to them to enduring exile from civil society. Secondly, Mathiesen identifies the **power-draining function** that prevents this unwanted population from interfering further in the economic order. Both these functions recall earlier Marxian analysis of the economic functions of the prison. But Mathiesen goes further to observe that the power-draining function deprives inmates of power even within the prison. His latter observation is reminiscent of Goffman's insights into the characteristics of 'total institutions'.[16] Goffman identifies the mechanisms by which inmates are psychologically stripped or dispossessed of their identity as a process he labels the 'mortification of self'. Denied privacy and personal clothing, and reduced to a number, the prisoner is rendered a mere subject of the regime.

Thirdly, Mathiesen identifies the **diverting function** by which the prison focuses our attention on a limited array of crimes traditionally committed by the working classes and away from the socially and economically more harmful acts committed by those higher up the social scale. The prison is filled with those guilty of theft, offences against the person, and public order offences, whilst the crimes of the powerful such as white-collar crime, tax evasion, corporate and environmental crimes

[15] Mathiesen, T., *The Politics of Abolition: Essays in Political Action* (Oxford: Martin Robertson, 1974) 76–8; Mathiesen, T., *Prison on Trial: A Critical Assessment* (London: Sage, 1990) 137–9.

[16] Goffman, E., 'On the Characteristics of Total Institutions' in Cressey (ed.), *The Prison: Studies in Institutional Organization and Change* (New York: Holt, Rinehart, & Winston, 1961); Goffman, E., *Asylums: Essays on the Social Situation of Mental Patients and Other Inmates* (Harmondsworth, Middlesex: Penguin, 1970).

only rarely result in imprisonment. Closely allied to this is the **symbolic function** by which Mathiesen refers to the power of the prison to stigmatize its inmates. In so doing it allows the rest of the population to distance themselves morally from those who have been incarcerated. This function recalls Goffman's work on stigma as a means of labelling the lower classes as deviant or inferior in order to uphold a virtual middle-class ideal of itself.[17] The fact that the prison population is disproportionately composed of the young, the poor, and members of ethnic minority groups is a direct product of this stigmatizing function.

A final function, added by Mathiesen only later, is the **action function** by which prison is used to convince us that something is indeed being done about law and order. Read this way, the prison works less in the sense of reducing, still less curing, crime than in the more cynical sense of performing the political trick of persuading us that the government remains in control of a problem palpably beyond its power. Together, argues Mathiesen, these 'supportive' functions imbue the prison with sufficient positive ideological attributes to persuade us of the need for its continued existence. Countervailing evidence that the prison is ineffective is, he claims, consistently negated by a wide-ranging conspiracy of non-recognition and denial in the mass media, the professions, and even in research.

Mathiesen's identification of the hidden functions of the prison provides a powerful set of explanations for its persistence. There is a danger, however, that in so doing he too falls foul of assuming that because the institution persists there must be functions that it performs for those in power. This danger is only partially averted by his simultaneous acknowledgement that the prison fails according to all penal rationales.

AGENT OF CULTURAL PRODUCTION

Whereas these accounts stress the functional and the ideological aspects of the prison, a fourth interpretation of the prison is as an agent of cultural production. According to Garland, the institution of punishment relies upon a repertoire of rhetoric, symbols, and imagery by which it conveys its purposes to its various audiences.[18] Of all the penalties available to the courts, the prison has the most dramatic physical and moral presence. Although the offender, and the penal process to which he is subject, disappears from view behind the prison walls, the prison itself is

---

[17] Goffman, E., *Stigma* (Englewood Cliffs, NJ: Prentice-Hall, 1963).

[18] Garland, D., *Punishment and Modern Society: A Study in Social Theory* (Oxford: Oxford University Press, 1990) 17.

very visible. Its continual representation in paintings, novels, television drama, and film ensures that the prison is well known even to those who have never passed through its gates. Moreover, the lurid, and often damning, accounts of former inmates, visiting journalists, and the prison inspectorate regularly reveal to an avid audience the base and burdensome nature of life inside. Recurrent scandals of prison administration, periodic riots, and breakouts by prisoners also provide the occasion for external scrutiny. By these various means, this most closed of institutions opens up to the public gaze. As a result, public knowledge about the prison is a curious mixture of informed fact and fiction-inspired fantasy. For Garland, the prison, of all penal institutions, is the most important symbolic expression of the state, furnishing a constant, visible reminder of its power to use institutional violence against its citizens. As such, he argues, 'the prison is as much a basic metaphor of our cultural imagination as it is a feature of our penal policy'.[19]

Garland is not alone in noting that the imagery of the prison is powerfully expressive: its architecture has been designed to signal its custodial and punitive purposes to the outside world.[20] It was not by chance that, historically, prisons were typically situated in working-class areas whose inhabitants were thus daily reminded of the looming power of the state. The classic Victorian design with its crenellated walls, towering façades, and forbidding portcullis-like entrance persists as our popular image of the prison. It intentionally conveys a terrifying deterrent image that bears scant relation to the nature of the disciplinary regime inside. Modern prison buildings are more anonymous, functional, and secretive. Yet even here the watch towers, security cameras, searchlights, perimeter wires, and blank façades speak volumes of the authority of the regime and its capacity to control its hidden inmates. Through all its various representations, the prison has acquired a central place in our imagination as the final sanction against those who transgress our laws. Its persistence derives as much from its powerful symbolic meaning and moral significance as from its clearly limited utility as an instrument of reform.[21]

Also implicit in Garland's account is the suggestion that to ask why the

[19] Ibid. 260.

[20] See Evans, R., *The Fabrication of Virtue: English Prison Architecture, 1750–1840* (Cambridge: Cambridge University Press, 1982).

[21] It is striking that the abolitionist literature of the Netherlands and Scandinavia has little parallel in Britain: Mathiesen, T., *The Politics of Abolition: Essays in Political Action* (Oxford: Martin Robertson, 1974); de Haan, W., *The Politics of Redress: Crime, Punishment and Penal Abolition* (London: Unwin Hyman, 1990).

prison persists reflects a preoccupation with a problem that has been overplayed. The assumption of the failure of the prison focuses largely on its propensity to turn out recidivists. Yet like many other modern institutions, the prison is allotted complex and varied roles some of which inevitably entail social costs and some of which are pursued at the expense of others. To say that we have been too quick to assume the failure of the prison is not to offer an apologia but to acknowledge that the institution simultaneously pursues many goals and that to judge it by its failure to reform is to miss this point. An effective critique needs to challenge the prison in all its complexity. Quite apart from its reformative function, the prison is charged with depriving offenders of their liberty, excluding them from society, coercing compliance with court orders, and satisfying public desires for vengeance by punishing offenders in the most severe manner our society permits. In order to understand, and to challenge, the continuing centrality of the prison, we need to examine these various functions more closely. But we also need to be wary of falling into the trap of assuming that the prison must be functional or it would not have persisted.

Finally, we should not overlook the fact that the massive infrastructure of the prison estate represents a huge sunk cost that is too expensive to give up readily. Sunk costs alone will not explain our continued ideological commitment to the prison, still less the massive expansion of the prison estate nor the rapidly growing prison population. But sunk financial costs are also sunk political costs. The apparent inability of politicians and sentencers to resist the demands of popular punitivism may be driven by their unwillingness to acknowledge the failings of their own policies, of which over-reliance upon the prison must be one of the more grave. Understood this way, the persistence of the prison is a policy choice but a policy choice made in decidedly constrained circumstances. It is possible for politicians and sentencers to decide to reduce reliance upon the prison, as examples from both Germany and the Netherlands attest.[22] But, despite the demands of abolitionists, it is nowhere the case that this policy choice has gone so far as to end imprisonment. Quite the contrary, in most Western countries, political commitment to imprisonment is stronger than ever.

---

[22] Downes, D., *Contrasts in Tolerance* (Oxford: Clarendon Press, 1993); Feest, J., 'Reducing the German Prison Population' in Muncie and Sparks (eds), *Imprisonment: European Perspectives* (Hemel Hempstead: Harvester Wheatsheaf, 1991). In Britain, too, prison use declined after the First World War and some prisons were then closed.

THE PLACE OF THE PRISON IN THE PENAL ORDER

Given the centrality of the prison, we need a conceptual framework for understanding its place in the penal order. One obvious framework takes the form of triptych of functions: custody, coercion, and punishment. In this section we will examine these in turn before going on, in the following section, to explore the more detailed purposes ascribed to the prison by politicians, policymakers, and academics over time.

The prison functions as **custody** in the sense that it is used to hold those awaiting trial and punishment. Historically, this custodial function was probably the most important facet of imprisonment. Offenders were incarcerated awaiting punishment whether corporal punishment, capital punishment, or, from the late sixteenth century, transportation to the colonies. Until the late eighteenth century, this custodial use of the prison was more important than any inherent punitive purpose.[23] The prison was thus used not so much as punishment but until punishment.

Today, the purely custodial function of imprisonment applies most commonly in respect of remand. In 2003, those on remand constituted about one-sixth of the total prison population and nearly a quarter of the female prison population.[24] For those remanded awaiting trial, or already convicted but not yet sentenced (because awaiting a pre-sentence report or the results of medical or psychiatric enquiry), the prison is intended not to punish but simply to contain. Smaller numbers of would-be immigrants are also held in detention whilst enquiries are made or a decision reached as to their status. For these people, the prison is purportedly purely a place of containment. That it inevitably imposes punitive conditions not justified by this carceral requirement is a continuing source of political disquiet, and use of the prison, rather than some other lesser form of restraint, demands special justification.

Remand in custody is often defended as a means of ensuring the smooth running of the criminal process. Defendants may be remanded where the court has substantial grounds for believing that they cannot be relied upon to appear for trial; that they would commit an offence while

---

[23] Peter, E. M., 'Prison Before the Prison' in Morris and Rothman (eds), *The Oxford History of the Prison: The Practice of Punishment in Western Europe* (Oxford: Oxford University Press, 1995).

[24] Prison Reform Trust, *Briefing from Prison Reform Trust October 2003* (London: Prison Reform Trust, 2003).

on bail; or that they would obstruct the course of justice. Custody is defended as a means of protecting the public in the case of those accused of serious crimes and of protecting witnesses from harassment. All remand decisions entail weighing the probabilities of what defendants may do in the future against depriving them of liberty, even though they are assumed for the moment to be innocent. Defendants may also be remanded for their own protection; if there has been insufficient time for the court to obtain information to reach a decision; or if the defendant has previously breached bail. Those held on remand are permitted special privileges but in practice are often held in worse conditions and locked in their cells for longer periods than sentenced prisoners. Given that they have yet to be convicted of any crime, the poverty of conditions for remand prisoners is particularly open to objection.

Whether it is really necessary to remand in custody all those who are held is placed in doubt by the fact that a significant proportion of cases against those remanded are dropped or result in acquittals. Added to this, about half of all remand prisoners go on to receive community sentences, an outcome that raises questions about why they were remanded in the first place. That the outcome of the trial and sentencing may be affected by the fact of remand makes its extensive use even more questionable. Those held on remand have greater difficulty in preparing their defence, are more likely to plead guilty, less likely to be acquitted, and more likely to receive a custodial sentence than those remanded on bail.[25] Although many are held on remand for good reason, it would appear that use of the prison in this purely custodial function disadvantages those held in the outcomes they are likely to face in the criminal court.

The prison also has a custodial function in respect of sentenced prisoners who, in addition to punishment, may be held on the incapacitative grounds that imprisonment is the only means adequate to protect the public from the risk posed by the offender.[26] Where the offender poses a significant risk of serious harm, the extension of their prison term beyond that which is proportional may be authorized solely on incapacitative

---

[25] Cavadino, M., and Dignan, J., *The Penal System: An Introduction* (3rd edn, London: Sage, 2002; 82–9), Ruthven, D., and Seward, E., *Restricted Access: Legal Information for Remand Prisoners* (London: Prison Reform Trust, 1996).

[26] Under the Criminal Justice Act 2003 s.152(2): 'The court must not pass a custodial sentence unless it is of the opinion that the offence, or the combination of the offence and one or more offences associated with it, was so serious that neither a fine alone nor a community sentence can be justified for the offence.'

grounds.[27] As we saw in Chapter 3, this use of the prison as an incapacitative device is controversial. Quite apart from the difficulties of determining which offenders pose a risk and in what degree, it is arguable that where offenders are imprisoned for incapacitative purposes alone, the prison should resemble no more than a protective quarantine.[28] Any further diminution of their quality of life beyond that necessary to secure containment cannot be justified by the requirements of incapacitation alone.

A second core function of the prison is **coercion**. The prison is coercive in the sense that it is used against those who have failed to comply with an existing court order. Historically, many inmates were imprisoned for failure to pay fines and were released only when the debt was met. Up to the eighteenth century, about half the prison population were civil debtors. As Haagen observes, 'so many debtors went to prison that every defaulter must have understood only too well that he was in the power of his creditors'.[29] It is debatable how effective imprisonment was as a means of coercing repayment of debts and the historical records are not adequate to answer this question. One thing, however, is clear. It was not necessary 'to carry out the threat to imprison in order to coerce or control. As long as a debtor believed that his creditors might take such action, they did not need to do anything.'[30] In this sense, the coercive power of the prison lay as much in the threat of it being used as in incarceration itself.

Today fine defaulters and others in default of payments ordered by the court are commonly imprisoned either to compel payment or, more usually, in lieu of payment. Imprisonment is also now a statutory presumption for breach of community sentences. The prison is coercive in the sense that it either forces the offender to meet the obligations laid upon him or, again more commonly, impresses upon him the burden of non-compliance. The introduction of alternative community sentences as means of coercion for fine default has reduced reliance upon the prison but, if only symbolically, it is still an important means of pressing offenders to comply. Once the fine is paid, the coercive pressure is lifted,

[27] Provisions for the incapacitation of 'dangerous offenders' are laid down in the Criminal Justice Act 2003 ss. 225–9.
[28] Wood, D., 'Dangerous Offenders, and the Morality of Protective Sentencing' (1988) *Criminal Law Review* 424–33.
[29] Haagen, P., 'Eighteenth-century English Society and the Debt Law' in Cohen and Scull (eds), *Social Control and the State: Historical and Comparative Essays* (Oxford: Martin Robertson, 1983) 233.
[30] Ibid. 233–4.

and the offender released. Another potentially coercive use of the prison is for treatment purposes, most notably of mentally disordered offenders. Although prisoners technically have the right to refuse treatment, the institutional pressures, imbalance of power between those delivering and those receiving treatment, and the implied costs of refusal may all induce compliance in ways that are subtly, or not so subtly, coercive.

Punishment, the third function of the prison, dominates today, though it is a comparatively modern aspect of imprisonment. Only in the sixteenth century were the prototypes of the modern prison, the houses of correction, established. They were designed not simply to contain but also to reform and retrain prisoners into industrious habits. The earliest house of correction in Britain was probably the Bridewell in London founded in 1555. Inmates were set to work either for the benefit of the institution or for external private employers. Whether this emphasis on prison labour was principally reformative, as its proponents claimed, or whether it was designed to meet the growing demand of nascent capitalism for a disciplined labour force is, as we have seen, a matter of continuing debate. The emergence of the modern prison as a principally punitive rather than custodial institution occurred only during the late eighteenth century when growing disquiet at the overuse of capital punishment coincided with the outpouring of new treatises on the potential of the reformed prison to fill this penal gap.[31] Long terms of penal servitude in prison were introduced in the mid-nineteenth century as a substitute for transportation to the colonies.[32] The idea that a regime of silence or separation combined with hard labour, a spartan diet, and exposure to religious influence could reform even the most recalcitrant convict became widely accepted.

Today the great majority of prisoners are held under sentence of the court for an offence for which they stand convicted. Following Paterson's famous dictum, prisoners are officially sent to prison 'as punishment, not for punishment'. In theory, this means that the punitive element in a custodial sentence is furnished by the loss of liberty and the deprivations (such as loss of free movement, separation from friends and family, limited contact with the outside world, and loss of privacy) this inevitably

---

[31] Of which the most important was Howard, J., *The State of the Prisons* (Abingdon: Professional Books, 1777). See Morris, N., and Rothman, D. (eds), *The Oxford History of the Prison: The Practice of Punishment in Western Europe* (Oxford: Oxford University Press, 1995) chs 3, 4, and 5.

[32] Radzinowicz, L., and Hood, R., *The Emergence of Penal Policy in Victorian and Edwardian England* (Oxford: Oxford University Press, 1986).

entails. In practice, however, as the reports of successive Chief Inspectors of Prisons attest, additional punishment arises in the poor quality of living conditions, the lack of facilities for useful employment, and poor treatment by some staff. Moreover there is a continual tension between the principle that the punishment imposed by imprisonment should not extend beyond that which is inherent in the nature of the institution (not least the need to maintain control over the inmate population and prevent escape), and the countervailing pressures of popular punitivism. These pressures limit the ability of the Prison Service to eliminate the inhumane and degrading aspects of prison life and they render controversial any positive steps to improve prisoner welfare.[33] Politicians could resist this climate of popular punitivism but there are few votes in improving prison conditions and instead a policy of 'penal austerity' has been actively embraced.[34] Penal reform lobbyists have consistently argued that to subject prisoners to inhumane or degrading treatment is, quite apart from all other objections, counterproductive to the disciplinary purposes of the institution but this line of argument appears to have little popular appeal. The Labour government have sought to overcome this political problem by maintaining the public rhetoric of punitivism whilst promoting better education, health, offender behaviour programmes, and drug treatment programmes within prisons. The introduction of an 'Incentive and Earned Privileges' policy (by which prisoners earn privileges in return for good behaviour) is another example of an internal regime change at odds with the public rhetoric of punitivism.[35] The difficulty, however, is that this rhetorical tactic may prove fatal to internal reform. A climate of populist punitivism fosters tougher sentencing and leads to prison overcrowding which limits the ability of staff to implement positive regime changes.

Together the triptych of custody, coercion, and punishment provides a framework for thinking about the larger functions of the prison. We should be clear, however, that there is often some measure of disjuncture

---

[33] Pressure to make prison conditions 'tough' by banning televisions and radios, removing sports facilities, and introducing degrading uniforms are said to have popular approval in the United States. See Sparks, R., 'Prisons, Punishment, and Penality' in McLaughlin and Muncie (eds), *Controlling Crime* (2nd edn, London: Sage, 2001) 226–7.

[34] Sparks, R., 'Penal "Austerity": The Doctrine of Less Eligibility Reborn' in P. Francis (ed), *Prisons 2000: An International Perspective on the Current State and Future of Imprisonment* (Basingstoke: Macmillan, 1996).

[35] Bottoms, A. E., 'Theoretical Reflections on the Evaluation of a Policy Initiative' in Zedner and Ashworth (eds), *The Criminological Foundations of Penal Policy* (Oxford: Oxford University Press, 2003).

between these larger functions and those purposes pursued day to day by governors and staff inside. Although punishment may provide the primary external justification for sending an offender to prison, it furnishes little positive guidance for those in charge of daily life as to the nature, standards, or goals of the regime. The fact that, in principle, offenders are sent to prison as and not for punishment leaves open the question of what values the prison should espouse and what goals it should pursue.

THE CHANGING PURPOSES OF THE PRISON

Like its larger functions, the internal purposes of the prison are far from fixed. It comes as little surprise to discover that so troubled an institution as the prison should continually try to reinvent itself as policymakers, governors, and staff seek to make sense of or find fruit in the most unpromising of circumstances. In what follows, we will examine the changing purposes assigned to the prison over the past century or so. It is a moot point how much difference policy changes make in practice. For all their flourish, it is certainly not invariably the case that changes announced from above substantially alter the direction of life inside. In what follows we will observe the tensions between the purported purposes and the demands of life inside.

TREATMENT

The belief that prisons might be made places of reformation prevailed for much of the twentieth century. As far back as 1895, the Gladstone Departmental Committee on Prisons proposed that 'prison discipline and treatment should be more effectually designed to maintain, stimulate, or awaken the higher susceptibilities of prisoners, to develop their moral instincts, to train them in orderly and industrial habits, and whenever possible to turn them out of prison better men and women, both physically and morally, than when they came in'.[36] This welfarist or treatment model framed subsequent penal policy and was reflected also in the stipulation of the Prison Rules (1964) that prisoners be encouraged to lead 'good and useful lives' and that the regime promote 'self-respect' and the development of 'personal responsibility'.[37] These injunctions, formulated in the mid-1960s, fitted broadly with the welfarist philosophy of the time

---

[36] Quoted Radzinowicz, L., and Hood, R., *The Emergence of Penal Policy in Victorian and Edwardian England* (Oxford: Oxford University Press, 1986) 578.

[37] Prison Rules (SI 1964/388) rules 1 and 2. The latest, and substantially revised, Prison Rules were issued in 1999 as SI 1999/728.

by requiring that prisons become places of treatment and training. The aspirations set by these rules were clearly worthy: that the prison should become a place in which the causes of delinquency are addressed and the qualities of good citizenship imbued. The problem was that the rules themselves gave little indication of how these goals should, or could, be pursued.

Although the philosophy of welfarism set lofty aspirations for prison managers, in so doing it also sent out a message to sentencers that prisons could plausibly fulfil a positive purpose. The danger, observed by contemporary commentators, was both that sentencers would be attracted to make greater use of the prison and that they would persuaded to commit offenders for longer, or even indeterminate, sentences in the hope of achieving these admirable ends. In truth there was little that the prison could do to change the structural conditions of offenders' lives most implicated in their offending. Long-term poverty and limited employment opportunities, factors most closely correlated with risk of reoffending, could not be addressed effectively from inside. Although specially formulated programmes sought to address poor schooling, emotional problems, and drug and alcohol dependencies within the prison, there were severe limits to the ability of the prison staff to change the chronic conditions that had caused these problems in the first place. Moreover, imprisonment actually reduced inmates' chances of return to law-abiding lives. Quite apart from the stigma of imprisonment; severance from family and friends; the loss of homes and jobs; and, for long-term prisoners especially, the enormous difficulty of overcoming the dislocating effects of incarceration all combined to counteract any positive effects the regime may have had. The findings of empirical research; widespread industrial relations problems; and the pressure of a rising prison population combined to feed growing disillusionment with the efficacy of treatment.[38] Increasingly, the claim that the prison is a plausible place of reform was doubted. The claim that the reformative potential of imprisonment justifies incarceration looked more doubtful still.

POSITIVE CUSTODY

The demise of welfarism as a plausible goal for the prison created an ideological vacuum for those managing prisons and, in particular, for

---

[38] Most famously, Martinson, R., 'What Works? Questions and Answers About Prison Reform' (1974) *Public Interest* 22–54; Lipton, D., Martinson, R., and Wilks, J., *The Effectiveness of Correctional Treatment* (New York: Praeger, 1975); Brody, S., *The Effectiveness of Sentencing: Home Office Research Study No. 35* (London: HMSO, 1976).

probation and other welfare agencies working within them. Starting from
the premise that welfarism had promised more than the prison could
possibly provide, in 1979 the May Committee reconsidered the purposes
of the prison.[39] It concluded that faith in the treatment model was
exhausted but, fearing that the abandonment of all positive purpose
would reduce imprisonment to little more than human warehousing, it
insisted that a new mission for the prison be found. It proposed the goal
of 'positive custody', which was intended to be simultaneously 'secure
and yet positive'. Positive custody sought to promote self-respect and
stressed the obligation on the prison to prepare inmates for discharge. It
demanded that the prison should allow inmates to contribute to society as
positively as possible and, so far as security allowed, that the regime
should minimize the harmful effects of incarceration.[40] But beyond this it
did not articulate clearly in what respects the regime was to be positive.
The idea of positive custody was fiercely criticized by academics and
penal reform groups for its lack of content and its continued adherence to
the idea that prisons could serve positive purposes which might encourage courts to imprison more people and for longer periods than could
otherwise be justified.

HUMANE CONTAINMENT

King and Morgan immediately condemned positive custody as a rhetorical device that, like treatment and training, had 'no real meaning'.[41]
They proposed in its place the starkly realist objective of 'humane containment'. Recognizing that prisons were often places of inhumane containment, they had as their goal the setting of minimum standards to
which the prison could plausibly aspire. The idea of humane containment
was also a clarion call to parsimony in the use of the prison. If prisons
were acknowledged to do nothing more than contain, then their use could
only be justified where absolutely necessary. What constitutes 'necessary'
here was perhaps less clearly articulated but the message was clear
enough: 'imprisonment should only be used as a last resort . . . for the
minimum length of time consistent with public safety'.[42] The idea of
humane containment had implications also for the nature of the regime:

---

[39] Home Office, *Home Office Committee of Inquiry into the United Kingdom Prison Services*
(the May Committee) (London: HMSO, 1979).
[40] Ibid. 67.
[41] King, R. D., and Morgan, R., *The Future of the Prison System* (Aldershot: Gower, 1980)
29.
[42] Ibid. 34.

security should be of the minimum level necessary to safeguard the public, and conditions should otherwise be as normal as the fact of custody
allowed. For King and Morgan, the deliberately prosaic nature of their
blueprint had the merit of failing to capture the sentencer's imagination
and thus reducing the attractiveness of sending offenders to prison. For
their critics, however, it denied the prison any positive purpose beyond
the warehousing of its inmates.[43] The failure of either positive custody or
humane containment to provide a sufficient answer to the question 'what
are prisons for?' left a moral vacuum that the penal policy debates of the
1980s failed to fill.

SECURITY, CONTROL, AND JUSTICE

Only with the outbreak of major disturbances at Strangeways and many
other prisons in 1990 was there occasion for a fundamental reassessment
of the principles and purposes of imprisonment. The Woolf Inquiry that
followed suggested that the primary cause of the disturbances was the
widely shared sense of injustice among prisoners.[44] In turn Lord Woolf
set about determining how the requirements of justice might be met in
prisons in such a way as to render the regime legitimate in the eyes of
prisoners and to minimize the risk of future large-scale disturbances.

His report concluded that if stability was to be achieved three basic
requirements must be met: security, control, and justice.[45] The first two
of these emphasized the responsibility of the Prison Service to prevent
prisoners from escaping and from disrupting life within the prison. In
this they merely reiterated the longstanding obligation on prisons to
contain their prisoners and maintain good order within the institution.
The final requirement of justice was more radical in that it went beyond
the existing condition that prisoners be treated with humanity to articulate a series of procedural rights upon which prisoners might rely in
respect of all decisions affecting their treatment. Woolf recommended
that reasoned explanations be given for all decisions which adversely
affect individual prisoners and that fair procedures be instituted to deal
with prisoner grievances and indiscipline. If treated with justice,
reasoned Woolf, prisoners were more likely to regard the regime as

---

[43] 'it is a means without an end . . . it can only result in making prisons into human
warehouses': Home Office, *Home Office Committee of Inquiry into the United Kingdom Prison
Services* (the May Committee) (London: HMSO, 1979) paras 4.24 and 4.28.
[44] Woolf, L. J., *Prison Disturbances, April 1990* the 'Woolf Report' (London: HMSO,
1991) para. 9.24.
[45] Ibid., para. 19.

legitimate and less likely to resort to violent protest to resolve their grievances. The pursuit of justice was thus fundamental to the fulfilment of
the first two purposes of security and control. It would be easy therefore
to regard Woolf's promotion of justice as merely an instrumental means
of preventing the reoccurrence of riot and disorder: indeed Woolf
acknowledged 'the achievement of justice will itself enhance security and
control'.[46] But it is clear that he was concerned also with the substantive
injustice that results where prison conditions are degrading or inhumane
and where the procedural rights of prisoners are not respected.

It is striking that the key features of the Woolf Report—security, control and justice—are not purposes, in the sense of end goals, but rather
standards by which the legitimacy of internal regime may be judged. The
same climate that fostered the revival of desert theory would appear to
have denied not only sentencers but also policymakers the possibility of
formulating forward-looking aims for imprisonment. Whilst this had the
merit of denying sentencers the justification that a term of imprisonment
might serve positive ends, it risked reducing the penalty to little more
than the loss of liberty. Whether this is necessarily a bad thing is a matter
of debate. Claims that 'prison works' represent the antithesis of this
approach and, without spelling out in what possible sense it does work,
provide sentencers with too ready a justification, even an incentive, for
recourse to imprisonment.

MANAGEMENT

The question of penal purpose has been further sidelined by the rise of
managerialism as the prevailing ideological framework within which
penal policy is pursued.[47] Sparks observes two facets of managerialism
that have particular relevance to prisons:

First, there is the prevalent view that in order to become efficient the organization
must conform as fully as possible to 'good business practices' as these are held to
exist in dynamic private companies. Second, there is the view that management
itself is neutral with regard to the substantive goals of the system: these are
defined elsewhere in the political and judicial systems.[48]

The promotion of managerialism has thus withdrawn attention from the
question of larger purpose to focus instead on the minutiae of service

[46] Ibid., para. 14.43.
[47] James, A., and Raine, J. W., *The New Politics of Criminal Justice* (London: Longman,
1998) ch. 3, 'Managerialism and Criminal Justice'.
[48] Sparks, R., 'Prisons, Punishment, and Penality' in McLaughlin and Muncie (eds),
Controlling Crime (2nd edn, London: Sage, 2001) 238.

delivery, 'market testing', and auditable practices.[49] In particular, pre-occupation with the so-called 'three Es' (Economy, Efficiency, and Effectiveness) concentrated attention on the use of resources and the introduction of new management structures.[50] It conspicuously side-stepped the question of the ends to which the prison was supposed to be effective. The subsequent proliferation of aims, targets, Prison Service Standards, Key Performance Indicators (KPIs), and, most importantly, Treasury-imposed Public Service Agreements (PSAs) has not clarified matters greatly. The PSA identifies the purpose of imprisonment as the 'effective execution of the sentences of the courts so as to reduce re-offending and protect the public'.[51] Achievement of this extraordinarily wide-ranging remit is judged according to Key Performance Indicators 'which measure the success of the Prison Service in achieving high quality outputs within a framework of efficiency and economy'.

The picture is complicated by the fact that many different sets of standards and purposes are imposed by different bodies (the Home Office, the Treasury, the Prison Service itself) and, as a consequence, contain injunctions that conflict with one another. Little indication is given of priority between one standard and another, with the result that prison staff are left uncertain which to pursue first. To give just one example: the Director General of the Prison Service is required to submit annually to the Home Secretary for approval 'Prison Service *objectives* in support of Home Office *aims*, together with *key performance indicators* and *targets*' [emphasis added].[52] No indication is given of how these four separate sets of indicators are intended to interrelate or which has priority. Set centrally, they give insufficient regard to local conditions, particular problems within any given prison, or the unexpected exigencies that inevitably arise in daily prison life. The pressure to meet measurable indicia of performance or 'best value' distorts working practices and engages staff in a remorseless round of statistical compilation and form filling.

[49] Power argues that the primary focus of managerialism is less the practices of those under scrutiny but rather their systems for self-auditing: Power, M., *The Audit Explosion* (London: Demos, 1994) 33ff.; Power, M., *The Audit Society: Rituals of Verification* (Oxford: Oxford University Press, 1997).

[50] The review of management and staffing under the 'Fresh Start' initiative of 1987, the relaunching of the Prison Service as a semi-autonomous executive 'Prison Agency' in 1993, and the publication in 1994 of its first Business Plan and Corporate Plan were early features of this trend.

[51] Prison Service, *Prison Service Framework Document* (London: HMSO, 1999) 5, para.2.2.

[52] Prison Service website: <http://www.hmprisonservice.gov.uk/corporate/dynpage.asp? Page=1021>.

The administration of the Prison Service now resembles nothing so much as a business corporation. The Prison Service produces annual corporate plans and business plans. It produces quarterly prison performance ratings for individual prisons according to which each institution is 'benchmarked'. It does this according to 'cost performance and output data from the Weighted Scorecard, showing performance against key performance targets'.[53] Although centralized control is a key feature of managerialism, this corporate mentality and management style is by no means confined to the central administration, For example, as part of the 'Performance Recognition' programme, Prison Service staff are now rewarded for exceeding their performance targets by 'leisure vouchers or gifts from the corporate gift catalogue'.

Another key plank of managerialism is the imposition upon public services of conditions as closely resembling those of the market as possible. The Prison Service has been obliged to admit market forces in the tendering and contracting out of some prisons to private providers. Contracts for escorting prisoners between prison and the courts have also been awarded to private security firms. The ability of the Prison Service to mimic the open market is, of course, very limited: there are relatively few 'service providers' as competitors to the government agency and there are no real consumers (given that offenders themselves could hardly be designated as customers) to exercise market choice.[54] The most important effect of managerialism has been to replace an entirely publicly run prison system with a mixed economy of public and private provision. But in terms of influencing thinking about the purposes of the prison, managerialism has tended to divert attention to the calculable indicia of service delivery and away from qualitative questions about the very purpose of the regime. In this sense, managerialism might be said to signal the death of the question 'what is the purpose of imprisonment?'

It remains to be seen whether the recent revival of interest in 'what works' and the implementation of so-called 'research-based offending behaviour programmes' in prisons will succeed in formulating a more positive purpose for the prison.[55] This raft of programmes is typically based upon the cognitive behavioural model, which assumes that offending is best tackled by enhancing offenders' capacity to control their

---

[53] Whatever that might mean. Prison Service website: <http://www.hmprisonservice. gov.uk/corporate/dynpage.asp?Page=950>.

[54] These points will be explored further in relation to the privatization of prisons below.

[55] Liebling, A., 'The Uses of Imprisonment' in Rex and Tonry (eds), *Reform and Punishment: The Future of Sentencing* (Cullompton, Devon: Willan Publishing, 2002) 114.

behaviour. One of the stated objectives of the prison service is now to 'to reduce crime by providing constructive regimes which address offending behaviour, improve educational and work skills and promote law abiding behaviour in custody and after release'.[56] Efforts to meet these objectives may signal a shift toward more constructive regimes within prison. However, in their focus on behavioural modification, they do not generally deal with the very considerable problems offenders face outside, nor are they usually tied to throughcare on release. Whether the proliferation of accredited programmes in prisons is driven by a genuine revival of faith in rehabilitation or, more cynically, by the need to meet performance targets[57] is an open question. Since prison establishments compete in spending rounds for the resources to host accredited programmes and since their completion is a performance indicator for the purposes of audit, it could be that, here too, it is the culture of managerialism and the proliferation of targets that are the key drivers rather than genuine faith in the possibilities of rehabilitation.

THE PRISONERS

Who is subject to imprisonment depends in part upon the nature of the role or roles ascribed to it. To the extent that the prison is conceived as a place of reform, those sentenced to prison are deemed **suitable subjects of treatment**. Mental health problems are the most common characteristic of prisoners: 72 per cent of male and 70 per cent of female sentenced prisoners suffer from two or more mental health disorders. Neurotic and psychotic disorders are particularly common.[58] Self-harm and suicide are shockingly common but, despite this, provision for treatment is poor; there are shortages of mental health professionals working in prisons; and prison regimes do little to address the mental health problems of their inmates. Although many prisoners might more suitably be accommodated in hospitals where appropriate medical care and effective measures against self-harm and victimization can be administered, the

[56] Prison Service, *Prison Service Framework Document* (London: HMSO, 1999) 5.

[57] The Home Office Public Service Agreement, 2001–2004, Objective No. 10, reads: 'Reduce the rate of reconvictions: of all offenders punished by imprisonment or by community supervision by 5 per cent by 2004 compared with the predicted rate'.

[58] Unless otherwise indicated, all the statistics relating to prisoners in this section derive from Prison Reform Trust, *Briefing from Prison Reform Trust October 2003* (London: Prison Reform Trust, 2003). Of all sentenced prisoners, 40 per cent of males and 63 per cent of females have a neurotic disorder (over three times the proportion in the general population); 64 per cent of males and 50 per cent of females have a psychotic disorder.

available places are only a fraction of those needed.[59] As David Rose observes, 'for significant numbers of the most vulnerable and disturbed, prison has become a social service of last resort'.[60]

Many prisoners are persistent drug users or have alcohol problems. Around two-thirds of prisoners used illegal drugs and around a quarter of men and a third of women admit to using heroin or crack cocaine in the year before imprisonment.[61] Over half admit to having a drug dependency problem. For many of them, imprisonment is the first occasion upon which they have received any help with their drug problems. Likewise, heavy alcohol consumption is common amongst prisoners—around three-fifths of male and two-fifths of female prisoners admit to hazardous drinking habits. For both groups, prison brings the possibility of desistence and the prospect of help from one of the many detoxification and treatment programmes inside. This said, resources are presently available to meet only 30 per cent of the treatment needs of drug-abusing prisoners; treatment in the community for prisoners leaving custody is very limited; and drug use on release is very high.[62]

Another group of prisoners commonly considered suitable cases for treatment is women. Women still represent a small minority of prisoners but their numbers have risen rapidly over the past decade. By the end of 2003, there were 4,509 women in prison, an increase of 189 per cent over the previous decade. Many suffer from multiple mental health problems such as depression, anxiety, and phobias. The rate of self-harm and attempted suicide amongst women is disproportionately high. Around half of women prisoners are on medication such as anti-depressants or anti-psychotic medicines, the ready resort to which has been criticized as reflecting the tendency to treat women as mad rather than bad. This tendency was even more pronounced at the height of welfarism: for example the rebuilding of Holloway Prison for women in the late 1960s was predicated upon the assumption that 'most women and girls in custody require some form of medical, psychiatric or remedial treatment'.[63]

---

[59] The therapeutic prison Grendon Underwood stands out as a beacon of what is possible: Genders, E., and Player, E., *Grendon: A Study of a Therapeutic Prison* (Oxford: Oxford University Press, 1994).

[60] Rose, D., 'A boy eats his own flesh in desperation: the reality of life inside our juvenile jails' *The Observer*, 14 Dec. 2003.

[61] Ramsay, M., *Prisoners' Drug Use and Treatment: Seven Research Studies. Home Office Research Study No. 267* (London: Home Office, 2003).

[62] Ibid.

[63] Zedner, L., 'Wayward Sisters: The Prison for Women' in Morris and Rothman (eds), *The Oxford History of the Prison* (New York: Oxford University Press, 1995) 360.

This was at the very height of the treatment ideal and it is unlikely such a view would be voiced so unequivocally today. It remains to be seen whether the rebirth of the 'what works' movement and the proliferation of cognitive behavioural initiatives will serve to widen the remit of prisoners regarded as suitable cases for treatment.

The demise of rehabilitation as the dominant *raison d'être* of punishment has tended to reduce the prison to a place of containment. In consequence, those held in prison were increasingly regarded as fit only for internal exile. According to the containment model, prisoners have come to be seen as **an excluded people**. Prominent among them are the very many who come from economically deprived and socially disadvantaged backgrounds. Over two-thirds are unemployed at the time of imprisonment and of those who do have a job, two-thirds lose it on being imprisoned. Around a third of prisoners have no permanent accommodation prior to being sent to prison and one in twenty were sleeping rough. Prisoners are thus, in the main, economically and socially marginal, unemployed, and unemployable. Their incarceration only confirms and makes concrete their peripheral status. As Cohen observed, 'working class deviant behaviour is segregated away and contained: if the proles are threatening they can be "subjected like animals by a few simple rules" '.[64]

Members of some ethnic minority groups are also significantly overrepresented. Twelve per cent of prisoners are black, though they account for only 2 per cent of the general population, and their numbers are rising. Between 1999 and 2002, the total prison population increased by just over 12 per cent but the number of black prisoners grew by 51 per cent. These figures conceal a more complex picture of variance amongst different ethnic minorities. Those of Caribbean origin are significantly more likely to be imprisoned than those from Africa and, in respect of the Asian sub-continent, those from Pakistan are imprisoned at two and three times the rate of those from Bangladesh and India respectively.[65] Part of the explanation for the over-representation of some ethnic minorities is the very significant numbers of foreign nationals of black, South Asian, and Chinese origin imprisoned, often for drugs offences such as trafficking, which attract long prison sentences. Part of the explanation is that

[64] Cohen, S., *Visions of Social Control* (Cambridge: Polity Press, 1985) 234; see also Young, J., *The Exclusive Society: Social Exclusion, Crime and Difference in Late Modernity* (London: Sage, 1999) ch. 3.

[65] Source: Morgan, R., 'Imprisonment: a Brief History, the Contemporary Scene, and Likely Prospects' in Maguire, Morgan, and Reiner (eds), *The Oxford Handbook of Criminology* (3rd edn, Oxford: Oxford University Press, 2002) 1134.

some ethnic minority populations figure disproportionately in those subgroups most at risk of offending, namely the young, the unemployed, and the economically marginal. Racial discrimination is also an important factor: discrimination within the criminal process exacerbates this over-representation,[66] and once inside, racism amongst prison staff undoubtedly makes worse the experience of prison life.[67] The striking over-representation of black people in prison has prompted Wacquant to observe that the prison has become ever more like a ghetto whose inhabitants are 'undesirables' purged from the body politic: 'that makes the mission of today's prison identical to that of the classical ghetto, whose *raison d'être* was precisely to quarantine a polluting group from the urban body'.[68]

Dispiritingly, another group who reflect the warehousing tendency of the prison are the young. Over half those under 18 in custody have a history of being in care or of involvement with the social services and 45 per cent have been permanently excluded from school. These are children with a history of serious social exclusion, many of whom have previously been institutionalized, many with behavioural and mental health problems and poor educational attainment. That they also have serious drug and alcohol abuse problems[69] attests to the fact that those who might once have been deemed suitable cases for rehabilitative treatment outside the prison are increasingly contained within it.

The growing emphasis on security also has implications for the types of prisoner held. Increasingly, they are serious and violent offenders who are caricatured as **dangerous predators**. Because they are sentenced to longer terms of imprisonment than was previously the case they make up a larger proportion of the prison population. Over the period since the Second World War the prison population has transformed from one in which the majority of prisoners were serving short terms for property offences to one in which the majority are serving long sentences for violent, sexual, and drugs offences. Deemed to be exceptional risks, Category A prisoners are held under conditions of high security and dramatized in the media as dangerous offenders whose escape must be

---

[66] Hood, R., *Race and Sentencing* (Oxford: Oxford University Press, 1992).

[67] Genders, E., and Player, E., *Race Relations in Prisons* (Oxford: Clarendon Press, 1989).

[68] Wacquant, L., 'Deadly Symbiosis: When ghetto and prison meet and mesh' (2001) 3 *Punishment and Society* 95–134 at 112.

[69] Over half of 16–20-year-olds report dependence on a drug in the year prior to imprisonment. Over half of female and two-thirds of male inmates had a hazardous drinking habit prior to custody.

prevented at all cost.[70] The highly publicized scandals surrounding prison disturbances and prisoner escapes in the early 1990s led high-risk prisoners to be regarded as the proper subjects of a profound intensification of security from which we are only now seeing some slight retreat.

The epitome of the prison as security device is the American 'super-max' prison. The super-max is a model for holding the most 'dangerous prisoners in a state of near isolation through the use of electronic surveillance, specially designed cell units and blocks, and rigidly organized protocols for staff communication with inmates'.[71] In these prisons the inmates are reduced to total isolation in order to minimize their presumed capacity for harm. Because these inmates are construed as predators and dangerous beyond repair no attempt is made to do anything other than contain them. Indeed one of the documented consequences of this high-security regime is to exacerbate psychoses and behavioural abnormalities. But since many of those sentenced to life in the super-max prisons will die there, the regime has little concern for the violence it inflicts upon those so contained.

Finally, as a consequence of the growing culture of managerialism, it might be argued that prisoners are being reduced to little more than the data according to which **performance indicators** are met. Their behaviour and activities must be managed in order for anxious staff to demonstrate that their establishment is meeting prescribed targets. Prisoners become the subject of statistical returns upon which 'prison performance ratings' are determined, according to which each institution is then 'benchmarked', but they are otherwise of little moment.

CAN PRISONS BE LEGITIMATE?

A particular casualty of managerialism is the fact that its focus on the pragmatic and instrumental purposes of service delivery diverts attention from issues of justice and legal rights.[72] This tendency to de-juridify threatens the rule of law throughout the criminal process, but it has particular dangers for the prison, where regard for justice and respect for the apparatus thereof are essential to the protection of those who are

---

[70] Sparks, R., 'Risk and blame in criminal justice controversies: British press coverage and official discourse on prison security (1993–6)' in Brown and Pratt (eds), *Dangerous Offenders: Punishment and Social Order* (London: Routledge, 2000).

[71] Simon, J., 'The "Society of Captives" in the Era of Hyper-Incarceration' (2000) 4 *Theoretical Criminology* 285–308 at 300–1.

[72] On which see the landmark case *Raymond v Honey* [1983] 1 AC 1.

otherwise most vulnerable to abuses of power. The countervailing movement for prisoners' rights, and human rights more generally, slows but cannot entirely halt the path of the managerialist juggernaut, which tends to favour aggregate performance indicators over concern for individual justice. Despite the incorporation of the European Convention of Human Rights into English law under the Human Rights Act 1998, its potential to develop prisoners' rights jurisprudence has not yet been fulfilled. The formal existence of prisoners' rights is likely to have little impact in practice if the prevailing culture is inherently hostile or indifferent to their application. The relative paucity of prisoners' rights in Britain stands in striking contrast with countries like Germany, where the Constitutional Court has shown itself receptive to the influence of both the legal academy and the penal reform lobby; prisoners' rights are fully articulated; and the prisoner's legal status is clearly defined. Whilst English judges have made some strides to uphold and develop protections for prisoners, they have been restrained by their traditional deference to Parliament. As a consequence, their development of prisoners' rights appears 'partial and uneven' compared to those found in Germany.[73]

The absence of a developed prisoners' rights culture in Britain is all the more important given that the prison, as a total institution, places its inmates in a position of profound dependency upon prison staff for the provision of the basic necessities of everyday life. The situation of gross inequality in power is a permanent, structural feature of prison life.[74] In this context, how power is wielded and whether legitimacy is achievable at all become key questions.[75] Of course order could be maintained by coercion alone but this would be to accept the prison as a place of inhumanity, even brutality. To the extent that prisoners consider themselves subject to abuse of power they are liable to try to subvert, protest against, or overthrow the regime. The repeated occurrence of small-scale disturbance and full-scale riot is testimony to the continuing problem of legitimacy in prison. In order to establish if and how legitimacy can be

---

[73] Lazarus, L., *Contrasting Prisoners' Rights* (Oxford: Oxford University Press, 2004) ch. 7.

[74] Though it is possible to envisage an institutional regime in which power was more evenly distributed and indeed, experiments of this kind have been attempted from time to time, for example at the Special Unit, Barlinnie Prison in Scotland from 1973 to 1995, and at the resettlement prison, Blantyre House in Kent.

[75] Sparks, R., 'Can Prisons be Legitimate? Penal Politics, Privatization, and the Timelessness of an Old Idea' (1994) 34 *British Journal of Criminology* 14–28; Sparks, R., and Bottoms, A. E., 'Legitimacy and Order in Prisons' (1995) 46 *British Journal of Sociology* 45–62.

achieved we need to clarify what we understand by the term, how it is threatened by the conditions of prison life, and by what means it might be safeguarded.

THE CONCEPT OF LEGITIMACY

Legitimacy has been defined as arising where power is wielded in conformity with established rules, which are themselves justified by reference to beliefs shared by both the dominant and the subordinate groups, in such a way that the subordinate group consents to the power relation.[76] An analogous concept of legitimacy was indirectly espoused by Woolf when he argued that decent prison conditions make it more likely that prisoners will accept, albeit conditionally, the authority of their custodians.[77] Major breakdowns in order, such as occurred at Strangeways Prison and elsewhere in 1990, are cited as evidence of a larger crisis of legitimacy. But the use of the word crisis here suggests a temporary deficit in an otherwise justifiable and generally accepted regime. It fails to reflect the chronic adverse conditions that are a constant of prison life and the enduring illegitimacy of the prison in the minds of those subject to it.

That consideration of legitimacy in prisons has arisen principally in response to crises such as riots has had the unfortunate result that the issue is often addressed as a means to the attainment of order rather than as a matter of justice. This emphasis on the instrumental purposes of pursuing legitimacy has also excluded from consideration the question of whether legitimacy rests upon the perceptions of prisoners alone. Arguably the judgment of prison and probation staff, of outside observers, of political commentators, and of the general public is also important in establishing whether or not the prison has legitimacy. The need to answer to this wider audience complicates the matter: for as much as inmates regard the repressive and inhumane qualities of the prison as illegitimate, so the populist view is inclined to condemn the prison as overly liberal, lenient, or even lax. Calls by politicians for greater penal austerity reflect and foster this latter view and diminish the chances of creating a regime that will be accepted by those subject to it.

THE STRUCTURAL CONDITIONS OF IMPRISONMENT

Legitimacy in prisons is undermined by an array of factors some of which are structural; some determined by the priorities set by

---

[76] Beetham, D., *The Legitimation of Power* (London: Macmillan, 1981) 16.

[77] Woolf, L. J., *Prison Disturbances, April 1990* (the 'Woolf Report') (London: HMSO, 1991) para. 9.37.

policymakers; and some of which result from the arbitrary exercise, and abuse, of power by prison staff. Of the first of these, the conditions of imprisonment are arguably the most intractable. The poverty of prison conditions and the long-term problem of overcrowding are closely inter-related factors that threaten the legitimacy of any prison regime. Poor prison conditions arise principally from the inadequacies of the dilapi-dated and old buildings in which many prisoners are held. Successive prison inspectors have condemned as squalid and unacceptable the living conditions in many of the prisons they visit. Prisoners who are locked in cramped cells with inadequate sanitary facilities for up to 23 hours a day are unlikely to regard as anything but illegitimate the power wielded over them.

The woeful quality of the buildings that house many prisons is exacer-bated by the problem of overcrowding, itself caused by the steady increase in the prison population in the post-war period (from 11,000 in 1938 to 75,000 in 2004). Expansion of the prison estate has not kept pace with this increase, with the result that there is generally insufficient accommodation of the appropriate type available. The categorization of inmates into different risk categories A to D (which dictates whether they be held in open, closed, or dispersal prisons) together with the need to provide remand, local, women's and young offender accommodation means that the global amount of 'certified normal accommodation' (CNA) available gives little indication of the usable space available. Over-crowding often requires that two or even three prisoners must share cells built for one. As a consequence, they live in cramped and often squalid conditions.[78] It also frequently means that the repair or decommissioning of dilapidated buildings must be postponed, thus exacerbating the squalor in which prisoners live. The temporary use of police cells, former military establishments, and boats often inflicts even worse conditions on those accommodated in them.

Overcrowding has implications beyond the impoverishment of the physical conditions in which prisoners are held. It necessitates the trans-fer of prisoners around the system from overcrowded institutions to those that have surplus space. The practice of transfer is disruptive: it is dis-locating for inmates, often taking them far from family and friends; it disturbs both the internal life of the institution and any attempt to

---

[78] In 2003, 85 of the 138 prisons in England and Wales were overcrowded and over 16,000 prisoners were doubling up in cells designed for one: Prison Reform Trust, *Briefing from Prison Reform Trust October 2003* (London: Prison Reform Trust, 2003).

develop a sustained programme of education, treatment, or training. Overcrowding also restricts opportunities for these activities, since excess numbers place severe pressures on space, facilities, and staffing. The expansionist policies pursued by successive governments have resulted in overcrowding becoming a durable feature of imprisonment with little prospect for its end. The steeply rising curve of the prison population is presented as a fact of modern life. If it were recognized instead as the product of deliberate policy decisions rather than a species of uncontrollable organic growth, then overcrowding too might become a more central topic in discussions of legitimacy.

To the problems caused by prison conditions and overcrowding must be added the poverty of the daily regime suffered by many prisoners. Perhaps the most important aspect of this is the difficulty of providing purposeful activities with which inmates might fill their days, whether in work, training, education, treatment for drug or alcohol problems, or other forms of therapy. Such work as is provided in prisons is often dull and repetitive manual labour which does little to give inmates any sense of constructive purpose, still less to equip them with skills which might improve their chances of employment on release. Educational opportunities vary enormously from prison to prison but are commonly the first item to be cut when financial or staffing resources are under pressure.[79] Most problematically, education and treatment within the prison have to compete with the countervailing demands and interruptions of daily prison life, against which they have low priority. In sum, the impoverished daily regime, inadequate living conditions, and limited opportunities for work, education, or treatment to which most are subject leaves prisoners bored, frustrated, and resentful of an institution where schoolrooms lie empty and workshops unused. Despite increasing expectations placed upon prisons to put their establishments to positive uses, the structural conditions of imprisonment continue to militate against their attainment.

COMPETING PRIORITIES

The priority given to security and control of prisoners over that of justice also has profound ramifications for the legitimacy of the prison. External

---

[79] The low priority accorded to education is indicated by the fact that, despite the very low levels of educational attainment and poor literacy rates among prisoners, the Prison Service spends on average £1,185 per annum per prisoner, less than half the average cost of secondary school education (£2,590): Prison Reform Trust, *Briefing from Prison Reform Trust October 2003* (London: Prison Reform Trust, 2003).

pressure to organize prisons so as to minimize all chance of escape, together with the internal imperative to ensure good order on a daily basis, has established the twin goals of security and control as the pillars of prison policy. Successive escapes by high-risk prisoners have stimulated intense political concern and led to enquiries, the principal agenda of which has been to identify and eliminate security risks.[80] That prisoners are, as a consequence, categorized according to the assessment of their risk to security on reception and that the type of penal establishment to which they are then allocated should be determined by this categorization is testimony to the resulting dominance of security. Whilst security is clearly important in the case of high-risk prisoners, it tends to subordinate all other considerations (of prisoner's needs for training or treatment, of the desirability of maintaining contact with home and community, of preparing prisoners for release) to its demands. The effect has been to focus debate upon such issues as whether it is more effective to concentrate high-risk prisoners in one or two special maximum security establishments or to disperse them into high-security prisons throughout the system. The adoption of the policy of dispersal had the effect of greatly intensifying the security arrangements imposed on all inmates in prisons where those deemed to be high risk are held. The priority given to security, particularly within the dispersal prisons, but also throughout other establishments, has led to increased perimeter fortifications, limits on movement within the prison, and restrictions on association and other communal activities. The effect of these changes has important ramifications for legitimacy. The failure to maintain a reasonable balance between security and humanity undermines the prisoners' sense that they are being dealt with fairly and instead generates a sense of unwarranted oppression and restriction of basic freedoms.

The primary focus of security on preventing escapes from the prison has also tended to overshadow the problem of control—that is, maintaining order within the prison. The issue of control has dual and divergent implications for legitimacy. If emphasis on order maintenance overrides all other considerations, it is likely to undermine legitimacy by imposing an unduly repressive regime based on physical force and segregation. If,

---

[80] Home Office, *Report of the Inquiry into Prison Escapes and Security by Admiral of the Fleet, the Mountbatten of Burma* (the 'Mountbatten Report') (London: HMSO, 1966); Woodcock, J., *The Escape from Whitemoor Prison* (the 'Woodcock Report') (London: HMSO, 1994); Woolf, L. J., *Prison Disturbances, April 1990* (the 'Woolf Report') (London: HMSO, 1991); Learmont, J., *Review of Prison Service Security in England and Wales and the Escape from Parkhurst Prison* (the 'Learmont Report') (London: HMSO, 1995).

on the other hand, insufficient attention is paid to order maintenance, then the inmates are liable to exploit opportunities for exercising control with the resultant danger that bullying, extortion, protection rackets, and summary justice occur.[81] For the most part, it is the former, repressive outcome that is most prevalent. The historic reliance on force to subdue inmates and prevent disorder has persisted in the use of specially trained squads to quell outbreaks of disorder; the use of 'control and restraint' techniques based upon martial arts; and of old-fashioned physical restraints such as handcuffs, body belts, and ankle straps. Segregation in individual 'strip cells', punishment blocks, larger 'special units', 'closed supervision centres', and, more recently, 'special security units' have all been used as means of temporary and longer-term control. The last of these, used for inmates who pose an 'exceptional escape risk',[82] impose conditions that are restrictive and cramped and subject inmates to intense security, closed visits, and strip-searches before and after every visit. The Prison Rules (1999, as amended) include the power to remove a prisoner from association where this is desirable for the 'maintenance of good order and discipline'.[83] Those subject to this rule are generally segregated in their cells on the punishment block for 23 hours a day and without access, therefore, to work, education, or recreation. Segregation under this power is categorized as an administrative procedure in pursuit of good order, though it is very punitive in effect.

A further technique for maintaining order, and one that is greatly resented by those subject to it, is that of transferring disruptive prisoners from one prison to another.[84] The Woolf Report condemned the disruption and dislocation caused by transfer, the uncertainty it engendered, and the fact no reasons were given before the transfer was carried out.[85] In order to overcome the sense that power was being wielded arbitrarily and capriciously, new procedures were introduced designed to limit recourse

---

[81] Sparks and Bottoms observed a striking example of this at Long Lartin prison where the laxity of control from above left vulnerable inmates prey to such dangers: Sparks, R., and Bottoms, A. E., 'Legitimacy and Order in Prisons' (1995) 46 *British Journal of Sociology* 45–62 at 57; Edgar, K., O'Donnell, I., and Martin, C., *Prison Violence: the Dynamics of Conflict, Fear and Power* (Cullompton, Devon: Willan Publishing, 2003).

[82] Cavadino, M., and Dignan, J., *The Penal System: An Introduction* (3rd edn, London: Sage, 2002) 185.

[83] For example, in the case of sex offenders or other vulnerable prisoners.

[84] Under the Management Strategy for Disruptive Prisoners set out in Instructions to Governors 28/93, the transfer of prisoners is authorized in the 'interests of good order and discipline'.

[85] Woolf, L. J., *Prison Disturbances, April 1990* (the 'Woolf Report') (London: HMSO, 1991) para. 9.34.

to transfers, to require governors to take the decision to transfer upon reasoned grounds, and to ensure that prisoners are given reasons within 24 hours of the transfer. The giving of reasons is clearly a step towards ensuring greater legitimacy in the minds of prisoners, but the failure to provide for adjudication or appeal places equally clear limits on this move. The result, as Morgan observes, is that: 'prisoners can still be and are transferred in large numbers, without explanation, to prisons relatively distant from their homes in order better to distribute prisoner numbers within the prison estate, or as an administrative control measure'.[86]

No aspect of the legitimacy of the prison weighs more heavily upon prisoners than the possibility of release from custody under supervision before the end of their sentence or, as it is formally known, parole. Discretionary parole constitutes a second sentencing of the prisoner based upon an assessment of their progress in prison.[87] Progress here relies upon a potentially contradictory assessment of both rehabilitation and risk. Its origins lie in the rehabilitative 'ticket of leave' system instituted for convicts transported to the colonies at the end of the eighteenth century. Parole has long been defended as an effective means of reducing the risk of reoffending by providing a bridge back into the community for those released early and under supervision. But parole has always been open to other uses and subject to competing priorities.

At times of prison overcrowding, parole is a convenient management tool or safety valve for releasing prisoners and so easing prison conditions. Used this way it is also a covert means of limiting the time actually served without publicly reducing sentence lengths. As an engine of control within the prison, parole is used as a reward for good behaviour or, more potently, as a disciplinary device against recalcitrant inmates. Used for control purposes, parole represents the assertion of executive discretion over the sentence of the court. It is small wonder that when parole is used either to manage numbers or to control the inmate population, individual prisoners feel aggrieved to find their prospects of early

---

[86] Morgan, R., 'Imprisonment: a Brief History, the Contemporary Scene, and Likely Prospects' in Maguire, Morgan, and Reiner (eds), *The Oxford Handbook of Criminology* (3rd edn, Oxford: Oxford University Press, 2002) 1128.

[87] After serving half their sentence, prisoners sentenced to less than a year are eligible for automatic unconditional release; those sentenced to less than four years are eligible for automatic conditional release (conditional in the sense that they are released on licence under supervision); and those sentenced to four years or more are subject to discretionary conditional release. The introduction of Custody Plus under the Criminal Justice Act 2003 s. 181 replaces these provisions for release by a licence period subject to conditions.

release determined less by their own conduct than by administrative priorities.

Increasingly, these various uses of parole are overshadowed by its usage as a tool of security: as a means of risk management or protecting the public. The assertion of risk as the primary criterion for release is controversial not least because risk assessment by members of the Parole Board is extremely haphazard. A study by Hood and Shute found that 'members appeared to overestimate the degree of risk posed by many prisoners, as indicated by the actuarially-calculated risk of reconviction score'.[88] Their follow-up study of released serious sex offenders went on to reveal that 'nine out of ten of those thought to pose a "high risk" were not reconvicted of a sexual offence within four years of their release'.[89] The tendency to overestimate risk is perhaps not surprising in the context of a larger political climate of populist concern about 'sexual predators' and dangerous offenders more generally. Where offenders have committed a type of crime that provokes strong popular emotion or where their individual case is notorious, early release from prison is debarred less on the grounds of any objective assessment of risk than as a means of political indemnity by a Parole Board that is increasingly risk averse. Ill-founded parole decisions result in the liberty of prisoners being unnecessarily restricted. They may also expose the public to unwarranted risk.

THE EXERCISE OF POWER OVER PRISONERS

The daily exercise of power within the prison by governors and staff is also central to the pursuit of legitimacy. However poor the physical conditions of imprisonment and however resented the priorities pursued by the Prison Service, the prisoners' perception of the regime is determined principally by the quality of treatment they receive from prison staff. Where staff are seen to be fair and reasonable in their relationship with inmates, then the other inadequacies of the regime may be tolerated more readily.[90] Where, on the other hand, staff exercise power in ways that are

---

[88] Hood, R., and Shute, S., *The Parole System at Work: Home Office Research Study No. 202* (London: HMSO, 2000) xvii.

[89] Hood, R., and Shute, S., *Reconviction Rates of Serious Sex Offenders and Assessments of their Risk* (London: HMSO, 2002) 1.

[90] A study by Sparks and Bottoms found that in the case of Albany Prison a highly restrictive regime with stringent controls, which might otherwise have been regarded as illegitimate by inmates, was rendered tolerable by the fairness and amenableness of the staff: Sparks, R., and Bottoms, A. E., 'Legitimacy and Order in Prisons' (1995) 46 *British Journal of Sociology* 45–62 at 56. See also Tyler, T., *Why People Obey the Law* (New Haven: Yale University Press, 1990).

arbitrary or oppressive, prisoners develop a strong sense of injustice. More damaging still are serious abuses of power in the form of psychological brutality, racial insult, physical violence, or sexual assault. The frequency of such abuse is impossible to measure given the secrecy that surrounds it and the enormous obstacles to prisoners succeeding in bringing complaints against staff. The imbalance of power, the likelihood that staff will be believed over the word of an individual inmate, the danger of overt or more subtle reprisals all inhibit their success. In general only the most serious forms of abuse come to light, whilst low levels of arbitrary or oppressive behaviour daily undermine the legitimacy of the prison in the minds of its inmates.

Transparency of decision making is perhaps most important in respect of decisions made against prisoners, especially those which adversely affect their liberty. The initial security classification, and any reclassification made subsequently, determine in which establishment prisoners serve their sentence and profoundly affect their experience of life in prison. The prison disciplinary system permits staff to exercise a still greater degree of power over inmates, and its procedural fairness is vitally important for their perception of legitimacy. Prison governors can refer criminal conduct to the police but in practice the governor or deputy typically deal with lesser crimes and other non-criminal disciplinary offences internally.[91] The governor has the power to impose a wide array of penalties ranging from a simple caution to forfeiture of privileges, exclusion from association, stoppage of earnings, or confinement to the cell. Though the effect of disciplinary proceedings may be to impose worse conditions, due process safeguards are inadequate and difficult to invoke. The place of disciplinary proceedings within the prison places prisoners in a position of structural dependency, reliant for redress upon the very people whose possible abuse of power they wish to challenge. The independence and impartiality of the governor is likely to be compromised by managerial considerations, by the overriding need to maintain good order within the prison, by prior knowledge of the parties involved, and by the perception among prisoners that staff testimony will be believed over their own.

Grievance procedures are central to the pursuit of justice in prison.

---

[91] Important revisions were made to the power of governors to impose discipline in *Ezeh and Connors v United Kingdom* (2002) 35 EHRR 28. The Prison (Amendment) Rules 2002 (SI 2002/728) rule 53A takes away the governor's power to award 'additional days' and gives this power to an independent adjudicator. See Lazarus, L., *Contrasting Prisoners' Rights* (Oxford: Oxford University Press, 2004) ch. 5.

Historically, prisoners could take complaints to the Boards of Visitors,[92] to the governor, to the Prison Service, to an MP or the Home Secretary. All decisions taken under the Prison Rules could also be challenged through the courts by means of judicial review.[93] But prisoners lacked confidence in the internal grievance procedures to resolve their grievances impartially. And seeking redress outside the prison required a degree of confidence and resources that most prisoners lacked. The ability of most prisoners to pursue the daunting, expensive, and time-consuming undertaking of seeking judicial review severely limits its use in practice. The judiciary have substantially increased their intervention in prison life over the last thirty years and prison disciplinary proceedings stands out as one of the areas in which prisoners' rights have been most fully developed.[94] Protection of legal correspondence and access to justice are other areas in which there has been significant judicial intervention. And yet, there are still large areas of prison administration over which judges are disinclined to assert supervision. Despite the much vaunted introduction of the Human Rights Act 1998, the judicial record on prisoners' rights in England remains partial and equivocal.[95]

As an autocracy in a democratic polity, the prison is in perpetual need of legitimation. The panoply of threats to legitimacy discussed so far might be read as suggesting that it is constitutionally incapable of achieving it. For abolitionist writers like Mathiesen, de Haan, and Sim the impossibility of the prison achieving legitimacy renders all efforts at reform worthless and points only toward abolition of the institution itself.[96] Indeed, for committed abolitionists, reform is positively hazardous in that it provides an opportunity for prison authorities to claim legitimacy where none exists. This is not to say that abolitionists advocate the complete eradication of the prison; most accept that imprisonment

---

[92] An independent body of lay volunteers, mainly made up of local dignitaries, charged with responsibility for hearing complaints from prisoners and reporting any abuse of prisoners.

[93] *R v Deputy Governor of Parkhurst, ex p Hague* [1992] 1 AC 58.

[94] The most important early case is probably *R v Board of Visitors of Hull Prison, ex p St. Germain* (1978) 1 QB (CA) 425.

[95] Lazarus, L., *Contrasting Prisoners' Rights* (Oxford: Oxford University Press, 2004).

[96] Mathiesen, T., *The Politics of Abolition: Essays in Political Action* (Oxford: Martin Robertson, 1974); Mathiesen, T., *Prison on Trial: A Critical Assessment* (London: Sage, 1990); de Haan, W., *The Politics of Redress: Crime, Punishment and Penal Abolition* (London: Unwin Hyman, 1990); Sim, J., 'The Abolitionist Approach: A British Perspective' in Duff *et al.* (eds), *Penal Theory and Practice: Tradition and Innovation in Criminal Justice* (Manchester: Manchester University Press, 1994).

will continue to remain necessary for a small number of very dangerous offenders. But even if we are not inclined to advocate abolition, the apparent intractability of the legitimacy deficit might prompt us to question whether uncritical acceptance of the prison as a customary response to crime can be defended.

REFORMING THE PRISON

We have seen that the principal threats to legitimacy in prisons share a common theme: that is, they all create the perception that power is being wielded in a way that lacks humanity and justice. The pursuit of humanity requires that prisoners are held in decent accommodation with access to basic facilities; that the conditions and routine are as normal as the demands of security and control allow; and that the staff are subject to adequate controls over their exercise of power. The pursuit of justice is arguably more problematic. It requires not only substantive accordance with agreed standards of fairness, adequate safeguards, and means of challenge in respect of all decision making within the prison, especially disciplinary and grievance procedures, but also that prisoners perceive these to be fair.

The question of how best to set about reforming prisons absorbs the energies of prison lobby organizations and pressure groups,[97] think tanks, successive committees of enquiry, independent enquiries, as well as government and academic researchers. On a day-to-day basis, the critical role of the **Chief Inspector of Prisons**[98] has had considerable impact, not least because successive incumbents in this office have not held back from filing damning reports of failing prisons and making swingeing criticisms of prison staff. It is, however, possible that the confrontational style adopted by the Chief Inspectors has inhibited cooperation from those who are the subject of attack. It is also questionable whether criticism alone suffices to give direction to those running prisons as to the standards they should maintain. Articulating enforceable minimum standards or criteria for prison conditions might be a more positive way of raising

---

[97] The Howard League for Penal Reform founded in 1921 is the oldest of these. More recently founded lobby organizations include the National Association for the Care and Resettlement of Offenders (NACRO), Justice, the Prison Reform Trust, Liberty, and the Penal Affairs Consortium (a grouping of 40 diverse organizations).

[98] Established in 1980 in accordance with a recommendation of the Committee of Enquiry into the United Kingdom Prison Services (the May Committee). See <http://www.homeoffice.gov.uk/hmipris/hmipris.htm>.

standards than condemning prisons as 'degrading' and 'unacceptable'.[99] The publication of an annual report of the Prison Service, of annual Prison Statistics, of Corporate and Business Plans (all of which are readily accessible on the Prison Service website)[100] aid transparency and so increase accountability. It is notable, however, that key information is not, or more significantly no longer, made available within these publications, causing Morgan to regret that 'some aspects of policy are reported in so limited a manner that it arguably serves to obfuscate the degree to which progress is being made'.[101]

The inadequacies of the disciplinary and grievance systems are somewhat mitigated by the institution of the **Prisons Ombudsman**[102] as a source of independent oversight, a site of recourse for prisoners unhappy with their treatment in prison, and final arbiter once all internal appeal procedures[103] have been tried and exhausted. The Ombudsman's remit includes investigating complaints about treatment and about disciplinary decisions (though not about convictions, sentence lengths, or release dates). His powers extend only to the making of recommendations, including the making of ex gratia payments (but not compensation) to prisoners. His independence is somewhat compromised by the fact that he is heavily reliant upon information provided by prison staff and this may make it difficult for a prisoner to establish that their grievance is well founded. They are likely to be successful only if they can show that a rule has been broken or their entitlements have been denied. Like the Chief Inspector of Prisons, the holders of the office of Ombudsman have been robust in their responses to prisoners' complaints and have worked hard to improve accessibility to prisoners. The increasing number of complaints to the Ombudsman suggests that prisoners regard this office as an important resource.

There remain many improvements that might increase legitimacy further still, not least opening up prisons to external scrutiny. The Boards of Visitors, ostensibly charged with the task of monitoring and oversight,

---

[99] Reading at random from the Chief Inspectors' Reports one cannot help but be struck by the generally negative tone struck. See <http://www.homeoffice.gov.uk/justice/prisons/inspprisons/inspectionreports/f.html>.

[100] <http://www.hmprisonservice.gov.uk>.

[101] Morgan, R., 'Imprisonment: a Brief History, the Contemporary Scene, and Likely Prospects' in Maguire, Morgan, and Reiner (eds), *The Oxford Handbook of Criminology* (3rd edn, Oxford: Oxford University Press, 2002) 1142.

[102] <http://www.homeoffice.gov.uk/ppoweb/>.

[103] These include making a complaint to the prison governor, chaplain, medical officer, Board of Visitors, or the Area Manager of the Prison Service.

appear to have had little effective power in this role. It remains to be seen whether their replacement by new **Independent Monitoring Boards** will satisfy the purpose of ensuring autonomous scrutiny and oversight.[104] Providing adequate resources to ensure that all grievances are heard within a reasonable time frame would reduce delay and thus injustice in the individual case. Many of the grievances brought by prisoners are suffered not only individually but also collectively. Since their resolution might better be secured by policy change than individual redress, it has been argued that new procedures should be introduced to deal with collective grievances. These might also furnish a forum for mediation or collective negotiation where disputes are unlikely to be resolved by more formal processes.

In the absence of a code of prisoners' rights or a fully independent grievance body with full powers of enforcement, prisoners have sought legal protection under the Prison Rules and under general principles of common law in the ordinary courts. What remains lacking is a fully developed conception of the purposes of imprisonment, of the status of prisoners, and of their rights. In the absence of a clear legal framework, prisoners' rights have developed on an ad hoc basis. They are limited also by the fact that the courts have been very cautious in their forays into the field of prison administration.

PRISON PRIVATIZATION

The move to privatization is one of the most controversial aspects of present-day prison policy. Privatization can mean many things. It may refer to no more than the contracting out of supplies, cleaning, or catering services. Nevertheless, given the importance of the environment of a closed institution to its inmates, one should not underestimate the impact of this low-level privatization. Privatization may refer to the contracting out of the construction of prison buildings and provision of facilities, which are then run by the state. And it is most commonly used to refer to the wholesale transfer of responsibility to private contractors for the provision and daily running of penal institutions. Each of these different forms and degrees of privatization carry different implications to which we need to be alert in the discussion that follows.

Unlikely as it seems, one radical response to the problem of ensuring

---

[104] Introduced in 2003 following the recommendation of Lloyd, P., *Review of the Boards of Visitors* (London: Home Office, 2001).

legitimacy in prisons has been to advocate privatization. Although, of course, privatization has other quite different drivers too, it is argued that private prisons provide an opportunity to raise standards and increase accountability.[105] Privatization is said to add market mechanisms of accountability to those of the political process; to introduce objective performance measures by which to judge service delivery; and permit the government to act as independent monitor of service provision rather than having to monitor itself. By separating the purchase of prison services from provision, it is theoretically possible for the state to act as a rational consumer seeking out the best provider of services. Privatization also has the potential to improve the policing of prisons because the state is no longer in the position of having to defend its own failings but can freely challenge the private provider for any failure of contract or legal breach. Further, by fostering a market in provision, privatization is said to encourage rival competitors to act as watchdogs upon each other. The introduction of contracts is lauded as a means of specifying detailed service standards and of holding contractors to these standards through the threat of financial penalties for non-performance. Because contracts are time limited, they are said to serve also as a means of maintaining standards by repeating the requirement to tender at the end of each contract period.

Evidence as to whether it is, in practice, the case that private prisons provide for better conditions is complicated by the fact that only certain types of prison have so far been privatized, inhibiting meaningful comparison. To the extent that there is evidence of better performance, it is said that this improvement is enjoyed not only by the private sector but in the public sector as well both because private prisons serve as an example and because competition requires that public sector prisons improve their standards in order to win new contracts. Given the considerable cost of providing decent prisons and the unpopularity of spending from the public purse on prison improvement, it is argued that private finance arrangements permit the capital costs of new prison building to be smoothed over by long-term mortgage arrangements under which private contractors finance prison buildings which the government then leases back. Further cost savings are said to reside in the greater efficiencies of the market. Finally, and perhaps most importantly, to the charge that prisons are a non-delegable function of the state, advocates of

---

[105] Logan, C., *Private Prisons: Pros and Cons* (Oxford: Oxford University Press, 1990).

privatization draw a distinction between allocation and delivery.[106] If the state retains control of the allocation, it is argued, then provided satisfactory means can be found to regulate delivery, the objection to privatization evaporates.[107] One of the more sophisticated advocates of privatization, Logan, thus insists that 'the motivation of those who apply a punishment is not relevant either to the justice or the effectiveness of punishment'.[108]

Against these arguments, opponents of privatization argue that imprisonment is not merely a state function, it is a core responsibility of the state. For the state to delegate this coercive power is to abrogate responsibility. Sentences are executed in the name of the state and it is improper for the state to delegate this to a private agency. The claim that it is possible to draw a line between allocation and delivery of punishment rests upon an artificial distinction. Those working in private prisons are involved in disciplinary proceedings against prisoners that may result in sanctions such as removal to punishment cells. They are also responsible for awarding privileges and permitting prisoners petty licence, and have the power to tolerate minor offences against the regime or enforce sanctions against them. In all these decisions, prison staff can be said to determine not only the delivery but also the amount of punishment suffered. Complex difficulties arise in the case of prisoner grievance. The question of who should be held liable and to what extent the state should be permitted to evade liability by arguing that delivery has been delegated only raises more concerns about the legality of privatization.

Given that the move toward privatization has been driven in part by the need to house the growing prison population, further concerns arise about the relationship between private provision and prison growth. Parkinson's Law suggests a tendency toward expansion if places are made available. Witness the case of the announcement by the Corrections Corporation of America, one of the major providers of private prisons, that it would build three prisons in California as an entirely speculative venture. An unnamed executive of CCA was quoted as saying: 'If you can build in the right place, the prisoners will come'.[109] The very arguments used by

---

[106] Ibid.

[107] For a very cautious set of arguments about the possibility of regulating delivery see Moyle, P., 'Separating the Allocation of Punishment from its Administration' (2001) 41 *British Journal of Criminology* 77–100.

[108] Quoted in Shichor, D., 'Private Prisons in Perspective: Some Conceptual Issues' (1998) 37 *Howard Journal* 82–100 at 87.

[109] Considine, J., *Restorative Justice: Healing the Effects of Crime* (Lyttelton, NZ: Ploughshares Publications, 1995) 67.

proponents of privatization in favour of private financing are thus exposed as permitting unrestrained prison expansion away from the public eye and the constraints of the Treasury. Leaseback arrangements are further criticized as a means of mortgaging the future that offends against the constitutional principle of not tying the hands of future governments, as well as irrationally preferring present to future fiscal benefits. The profit motive not only permits prison expansion but is said to be unsuited to administering prisons since it may drive private providers to ensure a continuing supply of prison inmates; discourage early release of prisoners when supply is short; and lead private providers to lobby government to increase usage of the prison in order to defend their vested commercial interests.[110] The introduction of harsher sentencing regimes is masked by the fact that the intervention of the private sector normalizes imprisonment, making it seem more akin to other areas of administrative and commercial life. Christie argues that it transforms imprisonment into a profitable industry or 'crime-control complex'.[111] In so doing, it is said to erode the 'dismaying' nature of state punishment.[112] To the extent that prisoners are driven around in vans displaying a commercial logo and are guarded by staff who do not wear the insignia of the Crown, it is argued that the communicative power of the prison as a place of *state* punishment is eroded.

Concerns have also been raised about the prospect of private providers reducing prisons to benign warehouses that contain prisoners humanely but have little aspiration beyond this minimum. Any suggestion that early attempts at privatization have resulted in prisons that set higher standards and are well thought of by prisoners is dismissed as a honeymoon period whilst private providers establish their credibility or the result of careful selection by prison authorities of non-problematic prisons as suitable targets of privatization. To the extent that it can be shown that private prisons are better than their state counterparts (though this comparison is very difficult to make), the danger arises that privatization creates a two-tier system leaving poorly funded state prisons to deal with the most recalcitrant inmates in what might become 'sink establishments' unable to escape from their second-class status because the private sector has been allowed to cream off the best staff and least troublesome

---

[110] Shichor, D., 'Private Prisons in Perspective: Some Conceptual Issues' (1998) 37 *Howard Journal* 82–100 at 85–6.

[111] Christie, N., *Crime Control as Industry* (London: Routledge, 1994).

[112] Harding, R. W., *Private Prisons and Public Accountability* (Buckingham: Open University Press, 1997).

inmates. The threat that failing prisons must raise their standards or face privatization may be a lever to improvement but it is no guarantee of it.

In addition to these larger arguments, the characteristics of commercial organizations threaten the accountability of prisons. Commercial organizations are driven by profit, they are accountable primarily to their shareholders, and to the extent that they are in competition with other providers they defend secrecy on the grounds of commercial interest. Where those administering prisons are called upon to balance the interests of their shareholders against those of the regime, problematic conflicts of interest arise. The extent to which these problems of accountability can be mitigated by the requirement that every private prison be overseen by a Controller (who is a governor-grade Prison Service employee) is hotly contested. It is also argued that the necessary interpolation of the Controller between private prison and the Prison Service adds a layer of bureaucracy at odds with the economic imperatives of privatization.

Finally, opponents of privatization maintain that it is inherently objectionable to permit anyone to profit from the pains of punishment. Sparks describes objections such as this as 'intuitionist. They begin and end with the feeling that "it is wrong to profit from punishment" ' and he suggests that they are 'a slight basis for a critical perspective'.[113] It might be countered that this objection is neither a matter of mere intuition nor slight. Although it is said that there is no inherent incompatibility between the making of profit and the pursuit of justice, it could equally be argued that the objection to making profit out of pain constitutes a developed ethical position that undermines all the pragmatic arguments raised in defence of privatization.

The theoretical arguments for and against privatization have been partly overtaken by state commitment to contracting out and market testing. Private prisons now hold about 5,000 prisoners, around 7 per cent of the prison population.[114] Given that the shift to privatization has now advanced so far as to be practically irreversible, it might be more productive to focus on the problems of regulation and accountability. Even within the remaining public-sector prisons, it might be argued that the dominance of managerialism, with its emphasis on efficiency and effectiveness, already occludes issues of justice. To the extent that all the Prison Service

[113] Sparks, R., 'Prisons, Punishment, and Penality' in McLaughlin and Muncie (eds), *Controlling Crime* (2nd edn, London: Sage, 2001) 242.

[114] Prison Reform Trust, *Briefing from Prison Reform Trust October 2003* (London: Prison Reform Trust, 2003).

is concerned with is efficient service delivery then it is morally neutral who delivers. The damage is already done.

CONCLUSION

So many roles have been mooted for the prison in the course of this chapter, as a place of treatment, custody, coercion, and punishment amongst others, that we should not be surprised to find that sentencers remain wedded to its use; that they have tended to increase sentence length; and that, at the margins, they prefer custodial sentences over those in the community.[115] The Home Office predicts that the prison population at the end of the first decade of the twenty-first century will exceed one hundred thousand.[116] In order to slow this predicted increase, one favoured means of attempting to reduce reliance upon imprisonment is the interpolation of new measures that, standing between prison and community sentences, might divert some of the burgeoning prison population into the community. Detention and training orders for young offenders (under which half the sentence is served in custody, half in the community) and the home detention curfew scheme are examples of such measures.[117] The latter scheme was introduced in 1999 in order to allow the early release of eligible prisoners on an electronically monitored curfew. The introduction of intermittent or 'weekend' custody;[118] of 'Custody Plus',[119] and 'Custody Minus'[120] are further attempts to reduce reliance upon the prison for less serious offenders. Although these measures are intended to tackle the problem of short-term prison sentences, there is a danger that they will tend toward further expansion in use of the prison.

[115] Hough, M., Jacobson, J., and Millie, A., *The Decision to Imprison: Sentencing and the Prison Population* (London: Prison Reform Trust, 2003).

[116] Home Office predictions quoted in Prison Reform Trust, *Briefing from Prison Reform Trust October 2003* (London: Prison Reform Trust, 2003).

[117] Mortimer, E., *Electronic Monitoring of Released Prisoners: an Evaluation of the Home Detention Curfew Scheme* (London: Home Office, 2001). In order to ease prison overcrowding an emergency extension of the programme was ordered in 2003.

[118] The Criminal Justice Act 2003 s.183 allows custody to be served at weekends or on weekdays and the offender to be on licence in between in order to permit employment or care responsibilities to continue in cases where the court decides the offence is so serious as to require a period of imprisonment.

[119] The Criminal Justice Act 2003 s. 181 replaces custodial sentences of less than 12 months with the apportionment of the penalty by the court between custody and a period on licence during which requirements from the options available under the new generic Community Order may be attached.

[120] Criminal Justice Act 2003 s. 189. This is, in essence, a sentence of Custody Plus suspended for a period from six months to two years during which the court sets requirements from the options available under the new generic Community Order.

There is little to prevent intermittent custody being imposed upon those who would not formerly have received a custodial sentence. And in respect of Custody Plus and Custody Minus, the conditions imposed during the sentence served in the community increase the danger of breach, which in turn raises the risk of return to prison. Moreover, since these orders only apply to sentences of less than 12 months, they leave open the possibility of evasion by courts setting marginally longer sentences. Another major problem is that the bulk of those in prison at any one time are serving long sentences, for which these alternatives are not likely to be thought appropriate. Weaning popular and judicial opinion away from the prison might be a more effective, if more ambitious, solution.

The dangers of expansion are only exacerbated by the fact of privatization. As Feeley has shown, 'the most distinctive feature of the involvement of private contractors in the administration of criminal justice is that they have expanded not contracted the government's capacity to effect social control'.[121] It is to this complex relationship between state and private provision that we turn in the final chapter.

---

[121] Feeley, M., 'Entrepreneurs of punishment: the legacy of privatization' (2002) 4 *Punishment and Society* 321–44 at 322–3.

8

From Criminal Justice to the Security Society?

Anderton said 'You're acquainted with the theory of precrime of course. I presume we can take that for granted.'

'I have the information publicly available,' Witwer replied. 'With the aid of your precog mutants, you've boldly and successfully abolished the postcrime punitive system of jails and fines. As we all realize, punishment was never much of a deterrent, and could scarcely have afforded comfort to a victim already dead.' . . .

Anderton said: 'You've probably grasped the basic legalistic drawback to precrime methodology. We're taking in individuals who have broken no law.'

'But they surely will,' Witwer affirmed with conviction.

'Happily they don't—because we get them first, before they can commit an act of violence. So the commission of the crime itself is absolute metaphysics. We claim they're culpable. They, on the other hand, eternally claim they're innocent. And, in a sense, they are innocent.' . . .

'In our society we have no major crimes,' Anderton went on, 'but we do have a detention camp full of would-be criminals.'[1]

INTRODUCTION

Much of this book has been concerned with the ways in which the criminal justice system responds to crime; what Philip Dick, in the excerpt above, calls *postcrime*. This chapter[2] will be concerned with sweeping changes some of which, at least, are captured by his notion of *precrime*. The changes we will explore do not involve *precog mutants* wired up to prophesy crimes before they occur but they are only a little less radical.

[1] Dick, P. K., *Minority Report* (London: Gollancz, 2002) 2–3.

[2] Some of the ideas developed in this chapter first appeared in previous articles: Zedner, L., 'The Pursuit of Security' in Hope and Sparks (eds), *Crime, Risk and Insecurity: Law and Order in Everyday Life and Political Discourse* (London: Routledge, 2000); Zedner, L., 'Dangers of Dystopias in Penal Theory' (2002) 22 *Oxford Journal of Legal Studies* 341–66; Zedner, L., 'The concept of security: an agenda for comparative analysis' (2003) 23 *Legal Studies* 153–76; Zedner, L., 'Too much security?' (2003) 31 *International Journal of the Sociology of Law* 155–84.

Any general shift in the common understanding of crime directly affects society's policies toward it. We have examined several different ways of thinking about crime, all of which shared a conception of crime as a departure from the norm. We have observed how this conception of crime invites, even requires, the state to respond—whether to censure and sanction, to deter, incapacitate, reform, or otherwise make good. And the criminal processes, the trial, sentence, and institutions of punishment that we have examined are, for the most part, logical consequences of these basic assumptions.

These existing criminologies are being challenged, even overtaken, by a radically different conception of crime not as an aberration but as a normal social fact. According to this conception, attempts to cure or punish appear less logical than do moves to manage crime and minimize its costs. The consequence is profound changes in the governance of crime, changes that include the rise of statistical risk assessment, prudential strategies, and social and situational crime prevention. Whilst these developments have roots within existing criminal justice practice, the crucial difference is that they are occurring increasingly on the margins of and outside the public sphere. Crime control is contracted out to private providers wielding state franchises, delegated to individuals and communities, or completely over taken by the growing private security industry. In many jurisdictions private security is outstripping public policing. Punishment is being transformed by popular demands for protection and the presumption that safety is a public good is being usurped by the private commodity of security. These changes call into question the modernist assumption that the state should have primary responsibility for crime control. For the moment, private security has joined, not replaced, public policing, and punitivism remains an important corollary to demands for public protection. The future dominance of public criminal justice over private crime control is less clear.

CHANGES IN THE CONSTRUCTION OF CRIME

In the post-welfare state, crime is increasingly conceived not as pathology or abnormality, nor even as deviance or aberration. Rather it is accepted as 'a routine activity' or 'opportunity',[3] a 'fact of everyday life,'[4] or 'normal

---

[3] Clarke, R., 'Situational Crime Prevention' in Tonry and Morris (eds), *Crime and Justice: An Annual Review of Research* (Chicago: University of Chicago Press, 1995) 91–150 at 91.
[4] Felson, M., *Crime and Everyday Life* (3rd edn, London: Sage, 2002) ch. 11.

social commonplace aspect of modern society'.[5] This re-conception of crime as ordinary and everyday recognizes that the overwhelming majority of crimes are minor property offences, such as petty theft and motor vehicle theft, or minor public order offences, such as public drunkenness and disorderly conduct. Only a small proportion of recorded crimes are offences of violence, and sexual offences make up less than 1 per cent. Even the most serious crimes are less dramatic than media representation and public perception would suggest. One leading exponent of the idea of crime as a normal social fact, Marcus Felson, wryly observes: 'the path toward murder is not much different from that of an ordinary fight, except that, unfortunately, someone happened to die. Most murder is the tragic result of a stupid little quarrel. Murder has two central features: a lethal weapon too near and a hospital too far.'[6]

This re-conception of crime owes much to the influence of rational choice theory, derived from economics and increasingly influential in neighbouring social sciences. The impact of rational choice theory has been described as 'nothing short of the invasion of economic man . . . the ultimate imperialist assault of economics on sociology—the subordination of *homo sociologicus* to *homo economicus*'.[7] Economic analysis of crime has gained currency partly because it provides an intellectually respectable explanation for the failure of the deviancy model and partly because it mirrors prevailing libertarian models of individual freedom and personal choice. It is, therefore, entirely consistent with the dominant political paradigm of neo-liberalism. Several immediate consequences stand out.

First, crime is no longer presented as a deviation from the norm but rather as **continuous with normal social interaction** and motivated by the same urge to utility maximization. Those who commit crimes are said to be much like the rest of us: self-interested and inclined to pursue that interest unless the costs of so doing outweigh the benefits. In general, criminals are portrayed not so much as pathological or poorly socialized but rather as rational actors taking advantage of opportunities.[8] The rational offender is not so much immoral as amoral. As Garland has observed, 'this criminal figure—sometimes described as "situational

---

[5] Garland, D., *The Culture of Control: Crime and Social Order in Contemporary Society* (Oxford: Oxford University Press, 2001) 128.

[6] Felson, M., *Crime and Everyday Life* (3rd edn, London: Sage, 2002) 2.

[7] Baert, P., *Social Theory in the Twentieth Century* (Cambridge: Polity Press, 1998) 154.

[8] Felson, M., and Clarke, R. V., *Opportunity Makes the Thief: Practical Theory for Crime Prevention*, Police Research Papers No. 98 (London: Home Office, 1999).

man"—lacks a strong moral compass or any effective internal controls, aside from a capacity for rational calculation and a healthy will to pleasure'.[9] Many criminologists see this as the most fundamental of the conceptual shifts dictated by economic analysis of crime.[10] It should be noted, however, that this shift is resisted by the persistent countervailing view of offenders as 'wicked' and even 'monstrous', for which we will offer some explanations below.[11]

Secondly, it follows that most crimes can be conceived less as threats to our moral order or culpable acts in need of punishment than as **calculable costs**. Understood this way, crime has little to do with the threat it poses to shared values and or the responsibility of the offender, and everything to do with the physical, psychological, and material losses it imposes. This re-conception of crime has been most plausible in respect of property offences. Attempts to reconstruct violent and sexual offences in terms of the costs they impose, rather than as subjects of moral outrage, have proved more problematic. These remain more naturally located within the logic of moral censure with the result that palpable tensions arise in the attempt to re-conceptualize all crimes as hazards to be minimized and harms to be calculated or insured against.

Thirdly, orientation around the costs of crime entails a shift from retrospective concern with crimes past to **prospective concern with future offences**.[12] This reorientation toward future crimes greatly expands the scope of offending under view from that already known to that which is as yet only estimable.[13] In part this reorientation arises from the increasing sophistication of statistical techniques that makes such estimation possible. As Feeley and Simon observe: 'Instead of training in sociology or social work, increasingly the new criminologists are trained in operations research and systems analysis. The new approach is not a

---

[9] Garland, D., *The Culture of Control: Crime and Social Order in Contemporary Society* (Oxford: Oxford University Press, 2001) 129.

[10] Although few economists would accept criminologists' caricatured account of modern rational choice theory, with its sophisticated regard for information costs, time discounting, and other elements of bounded rationality: Jolls, C., Sunstein, C. R., and Thaler, R., 'A Behavioral Approach to Law and Economics' (1998) 50 *Stanford Law Review* 1471–550.

[11] Simon, J., 'Managing the Monstrous. Sex Offenders and the New Penology' (1998) 4 *Psychology, Public Policy and Law* 1–16; Young, J., *The Exclusive Society: Social Exclusion, Crime and Difference in Late Modernity* (London: Sage, 1999) ch. 4, 'Essentializing the Other: Demonization and the Creation of Monstrosity'.

[12] Feeley, M., and Simon, J., 'Actuarial Justice: The Emerging New Criminal Law' in D. Nelken (ed.), *The Futures of Criminology* (London: Sage, 1994) 173.

[13] Shearing, C., 'Punishment and the Changing Face of Governance' (2001) 3 *Punishment and Society* 203–20.

criminology at all, but an applied branch of systems theory.'[14] Despite advances in computational techniques and actuarial models, risk assessment is necessarily an inexact science that can never predict with certainty and can never remove individuals from the vagaries of their social context.[15] It is all the more striking that, despite the imprecision of its predictive power, risk assessment is now presented as a central tool in the management of crime.[16]

Fourthly, economic analysis de-dramatizes crime and presents it as an ordinary activity carried out by ordinary individuals exposed to everyday criminogenic situations. Rises in crime are explained less according to changes in demography, social structure, or socialization processes, and instead by reference to **the multiplication of opportunity**. The growth of small, light, and valuable consumer goods (the mobile phone is a paradigmatic example here) becomes more important in explaining rising property crime than any claim of moral or social breakdown. Mass car ownership creates the possibility of preying upon distant neighbourhoods, allows for fast getaways, and provides an unguarded object for theft, vandalism, and joyriding. The ready availability of alcohol, the expansion of the leisure industry, and, in particular, the night-time economy of clubs and bars creates occasions for drunkenness, disorder, and interpersonal violence.[17] In short, wealth, wide availability of consumer goods, and increased leisure activity create new temptations and new opportunities for crime. This analysis rejects older understandings of crime as the product of social deprivation, inequality, and inadequate social control as both vague and excusatory. Instead, economic analysis of crime relies upon several basic assumptions, namely: that the risks of crime can be calculated; that the costs of prevention are lower than the costs of crime; and that it is more effective to target the opportunity than the offender. Together these central assumptions have important implications for criminal justice to which we will now turn.

---

[14] Feeley, M., and Simon, J., 'The New Penology: Notes on the Emerging Strategy of Corrections and its Implications' (1992) 30 *Criminology* 449–74 at 466.

[15] Crawford, A., *Crime Prevention and Community Safety: Politics, Policies, and Practices* (London: Longman, 1998) 256; Ericson, R., and Haggerty, K., *Policing the Risk Society* (Oxford: Oxford University Press, 1997) 92.

[16] See, for example, Home Office, *Risk Framework Document* (2002): <http://www.homeoffice.gov.uk/new_indexs/riskframe.htm>.

[17] Hobbs, D. *et al.*, *Bouncers: Violence and Governance in the Night Time Economy* (Oxford: Oxford University Press, 2003).

CHANGES IN THE ORIENTATION OF
CRIMINAL JUSTICE

The values, processes, and institutions of criminal justice do not stand unaffected by these changes in thinking about crime. The existing criminal process of investigation, trial, and punishment makes sense only where crime is regarded as the moral responsibility of the offender. Where crime is reconceived as the morally neutral product of rational choice or occasioned by opportunity, the logic of criminal justice begins to look less certain. As Sparks observes, 'The state cannot any longer simply perform punishment as a matter of sovereign right. It must also thereby promise something. And increasingly what it promises is protection.'[18]

As we have seen in the preceding chapters, the criminal justice process is centred on the individual offender and the wrong that they are suspected of committing. Crudely put, policing focuses upon the identification of individual suspects; investigation upon known crimes; trials upon establishing the innocence or guilt of the defendant; sentencing upon censuring their action and determining a penalty apposite to the offence. Although the classical orientation of criminal justice is backward looking, many aspects of the criminal process are prospectively orientated. Policing, though chiefly reactive, has always been in part preventive and deterrent, and innovations like CCTV augment these aspects. Desert-based sentencing is retrospective in orientation, but consequentialist theories of sentencing look to the future, justifying punitive action by claiming to secure larger social goods such as rehabilitation, deterrence, and reparation. Aside from their punitive function, community sentences and imprisonment have been used to fulfil future-oriented goals like incapacitation. Likewise remand and parole decisions are based in part upon risk assessment and calculations as to the probability of offending on release. In short the seeds of another world-view were always contained within criminal justice.

The increasingly prospective orientation of crime control draws upon technologies familiar to the criminal justice repertoire but uses them in different and more extensive ways. Conceiving crime as rational choice requires above all that opportunities for offending be foreseen and

---

[18] Sparks, R., 'Perspectives on Risk and Penal Politics' in Hope and Sparks (eds), *Crime, Risk and Insecurity: Law and Order in Everyday Life and Political Discourse* (London: Routledge, 2000) 136.

forestalled. Statistical calculation of probability and proactive measures to reduce opportunity through situational crime prevention, target-hardening, risk assessment, and monitoring and surveillance become central tools replacing traditional patterns of policing and punishment. The imposition of curfews, the use of electronic monitoring, technological innovations in surveillance, and provisions for recording offenders' names on risk registers are prime examples here.

Where crime is regarded as the product of rational choice, punishment continues to have some limited capacity as a pricing mechanism. But given the remote likelihood of detection, still less conviction, it appears to have little purchase upon the calculations of the would-be offender.[19] Faced with the immediate, sure, and palpable reward of the stolen object versus the remote and improbable prospect of suffering a penalty, however harsh, the rational (but, it is presumed, amoral) offender will steal. If the criminal justice process is an ineffective means of maximizing the opportunity costs of crime, it cannot but be marginal to the larger task of prevention.

Unsurprisingly, the shift toward prevention, surveillance, and security has been the subject of considerable criminological attention. Several commentators consider the changes in the orientation, goals, technologies, and practices of crime control to be so radical as to constitute the end of the criminal justice state.[20] For example, Bayley and Shearing claim that 'Modern democratic countries . . . have reached a watershed in the evolution of their systems of crime control and law enforcement. Future generations will look back on our era as a time when one system of policing ended and another took its place.'[21] Others, like Jones and Newburn, doubt the universal applicability of this transformation. Although they acknowledge that significant shifts have occurred in public policing and that there has been a substantial expansion of private-sector policing, they argue that criminologists have tended 'to overstate the novelty and

[19] von Hirsch, A. *et al.*, *Criminal Deterrence and Sentence Severity: An Analysis of Recent Research* (Oxford: Hart Publishing, 1999).

[20] Bayley, D., and Shearing, C., 'The Future of Policing' (1996) 30 *Law and Society Review* 585–606; Shearing, C., 'Punishment and the Changing Face of Governance' (2001) 3 *Punishment and Society* 203–20; Loader, I., and Sparks, R., 'Contemporary Landscapes of Crime, Order, and Control: Governance, Risk, and Globalization' in Maguire, Morgan, and Reiner (eds), *The Oxford Handbook of Criminology* (3rd edn, Oxford: Oxford University Press, 2002).

[21] Bayley, D., and Shearing, C., 'The Future of Policing' (1996) 30 *Law and Society Review* 585–606 at 585.

the "epochal" nature of current trends[22] and overlook continuities with the past in the race to identify new 'master patterns'.

The question of what forms these changes are taking is more contested still. Bayley and Shearing describe them as a system restructured around preventive governance.[23] Ericson and Haggerty see policing as shifting from 'traditional modes of crime control and order maintenance towards provision of security through surveillance technologies designed to identify, predict, and manage risks'.[24] Policing the risk society, they argue, operates within a negative logic that focuses on fear: 'Collective fear and foreboding underpin the value system of an unsafe society, perpetuate insecurity, and feed incessant demands for more knowledge of risk. Fear ends up proving itself, as new risk communication and management systems proliferate.'[25] O'Malley identifies the rise of a new 'prudentialism', geared to preventing loss and insuring against risk.[26] Feeley and Simon suggest that the 'Old Penology' 'rooted in a concern for individuals, and preoccupied with such concepts as guilt, responsibility and obligation, as well as diagnosis, intervention and treatment of the individual offender' is being abandoned.[27] In its place, and in striking contrast, they argue, a 'New Penology' is emerging: 'it is actuarial. It is concerned with techniques for identifying, classifying and managing groups assorted by levels of dangerous.' The qualities of the individual, their failings, or amenability to reform or reintegration slip from view. Instead the focus is on targeting suspect populations and making actuarial assessments of their likelihood of offending in particular circumstances or when exposed to certain categories of opportunity. It does so in order to influence the decision-making processes of those deemed likely to offend by identifying, exposing, and deterring them. Profiling is designed to generate reflexivity about risk: as high-risk subjects become aware of their profile, the hope is that they will alter their behaviour accordingly. The tactics of

---

[22] Jones, T., and Newburn, T., 'The Transformation of Policing? Understanding Current Trends in Policing Systems' (2002) 42 *British Journal of Criminology* 129–46 at 130.

[23] Bayley, D., and Shearing, C., 'The Future of Policing' (1996) 30 *Law and Society Review* 585–606 at 585.

[24] Ericson, R., and Haggerty, K., *Policing the Risk Society* (Oxford: Oxford University Press, 1997) xi.

[25] Ibid. 6.

[26] O'Malley, P., 'Risk, Power, and Crime Prevention' (1992) 21 *Economy and Society* 252–75.

[27] Feeley, M., and Simon, J., 'The New Penology: Notes on the Emerging Strategy of Corrections and its Implications' (1992) 30 *Criminology* 449–74; Feeley, M., and Simon, J., 'Actuarial Justice: The Emerging New Criminal Law' in D. Nelken (ed), *The Futures of Criminology* (London: Sage, 1994) 173.

reactive risk are extended also to the general public who are engaged as self-calculating monitors of risk and inveighed upon to minimize their self-exposure and limit opportunities for harm.

In practice there is considerable overlap between the old and new penologies. The old assumptions continue to infect the new scientific calculations of probability and the new risk-managers do not abandon their preconceptions. Indeed, by enumerating the characteristics of suspect populations, the new penology lays bare the bases of categorical suspicion and makes starkly evident the stereotypes and prejudices that inform them. But it also has the power to reconfigure the objects of anxiety as statistical profiling generates categories of likely suspects upon whom police attention focuses. That groups of youngsters, badly dressed persons, or the otherwise 'suspect' individuals are routinely excluded from mass-private property is well documented.[28] Likewise, the effect of mass CCTV in public, quasi-public, and private spaces in Britain has been to identify and target suspicious or undesirable persons known either from past observation or because they fit predetermined offender profiles.[29] Should those so identified come to the camera operator's notice, their presence will likely trigger observation and possible subsequent intervention by public police officers or private security guards. Actuarial calculation thus becomes its own self-fulfilling prophecy as those so targeted are more likely to be drawn into the criminal justice net.

The new penology or actuarial justice has a complex relationship with the economic analysis of crime that spawned it: 'Economic analysis and actuarial justice share several important features. Both emphasize utilitarian purposes of punishment over moral considerations. They both prefer quantitative analysis over qualitative analysis. They both focus on the performance of the criminal process as a *system*.'[30] But there are important differences also. Crucially, whereas economic analysis presumes that all individuals are rational actors liable to respond to pricing signals sent out, for example, through deterrent punishments, actuarial justice targets entire categories of high-risk people. It does so both with the intention of

[28] Wakefield, A., 'Situational Crime Prevention in Mass Private Property' 125–45; and von Hirsch, A., and Shearing, C., 'Exclusion from Public Space' 77–96, both in von Hirsch, Garland, and Wakefield (eds), *Ethical and Social Perspectives on Situational Crime Prevention* (Oxford: Hart Publishing, 2000).

[29] Goold, B. J., 'Public Area Surveillance and Police Work: the Impact of CCTV on Police Behaviour and Autonomy' (2003) 1 *Surveillance & Society* 191–203.

[30] Feeley, M., and Simon, J., 'Actuarial Justice: The Emerging New Criminal Law' in Nelken (ed.), *The Futures of Criminology* (London: Sage, 1994) 188. Though we would point out that Utilitarianism is, of course, a form of moral reasoning.

influencing their decision making and in order to classify and incapacitate them. But to the extent that it is about classifying rather than altering potential offenders, Feeley and Simon see actuarial justice as a departure from the logic of economic analysis.

It is possible, however, to see actuarial justice as broadly consistent with economic analysis. A fundamental assumption thereof is that individuals act rationally according to the perceived costs and benefits of their decisions. For that portion of the population commonly identified as 'the underclass', two major inhibitions to their susceptibility to disincentives exist. First, the fine-tuning of penal disincentives presumes that it is possible to set the costs so high as to inhibit deviant behaviour. To the extent that members of the underclass appear immune to these disincentive structures, it is not that they fail to act rationally. It is rather that they have, so to speak, nothing to lose.[31] Secondly, to the extent that they live on the margins of consumer society, they are outside the range of normal economic signals and it is questionable, therefore, whether they are susceptible to manipulation by punitive pricing mechanisms. It is for this reason that techniques of profiling, preventive detention, and incapacitation come into play where punishment and deterrence do not and cannot work. The further implication of this analysis is that, since recalcitrant or intractable populations cannot be changed through conventional methods of penal and rehabilitative intervention, they must be managed, contained, or excluded. Actuarial justice may have as its primary goals the prevention of crime and the minimization of risk, but the draconian curtailment of individual liberty and the mass expulsion into penal warehouses[32] so licensed can scarcely be deemed morally neutral or unproblematic.

It follows that the reorientation of criminal justice around risk reflects some but by no means all the changes in conceptions of crime considered above. Most significantly, whereas the presentation of crime as a routine and everyday event promised a cooler, less moralistic attitude toward crime, recent developments in criminal justice policy have succeeded in incorporating the future orientation of this analysis without moving one iota away from the idea that offenders are distinct, dangerous, and to be demonized. Political and media obsession with sex offenders, mentally disordered offenders, and those with less clearly defined personality

---

[31] Taylor, I., *Crime in Context: A Critical Criminology of Market Societies* (Cambridge: Polity Press, 1999) 15 ff.

[32] Simon, J., 'From the Big House to the Warehouse: Rethinking State Government and Prisons' (1999) 3 *Punishment and Society* 213–34.

disorders similarly reflect the persistence of dangerousness as a defining category. Provisions within the Sexual Offenders Act 2003 for new civil preventative orders,[33] for risk of sexual harm orders,[34] and for foreign travel orders[35] all impose stringent conditions on those with a record of sexual offending. The fact these conditions are imposed upon those who should be presumed innocent, until proven guilty of a new offence, would appear to have been forgotten. In part, at least, this willingness to demonize arises from the logic of actuarial justice. The categories of offenders currently targeted are precisely those so out of range of normal economic signals that they are 'natural' targets of classification, containment, and exclusion.

It has been observed that these changes dash 'the hope that the development of new, depersonalized techniques of crime control aimed at prevention and unconcerned with the moral well-being of offenders would reduce dependency on criminal justice . . . and that the moral distance between offenders and other community members would diminish'.[36] But it can be argued that these depersonalized techniques of crime control were only ever targeted at that large swathe of criminal activity and criminal actors susceptible to manipulation through the imposition of high opportunity costs. The continuing, even augmented, tendency to demonize those resistant to economic signals was, as we have shown, entirely predictable. Hence provisions for the 'imprisonment for public protection for serious offences' (an indeterminate and reviewable sentence for dangerous offenders under the Criminal Justice Act 2003),[37] sit alongside concerted efforts to reduce reliance upon imprisonment for lesser offenders in a bifurcated approach that is now all too familiar a feature of criminal justice policy.

If criminal justice is not yet the quaint anachronism that the proponents of the 'engineered society' had hoped it would become, the question remains, can criminal justice stand unscathed by the challenges it

---

[33] Sex Offender Orders (Crime and Disorder Act 1998 s. 2) and Restraining Orders (Sex Offenders Act 1997 s.5) have been combined into a new Sexual Offences Prevention Order (Sexual Offences Act 2003 s. 104).

[34] The Sexual Offences Act 2003 s. 123 is specifically designed to protect children from sexual harm.

[35] The Sexual Offences Act 2003 s. 114 can be used to prevent an offender with a conviction for a sexual offence against a child from travelling to countries where he is at risk of abusing children.

[36] Hudson, B., 'Punishment, Rights and Difference: Defending Justice in the Risk Society' in Stenson and Sullivan (eds), *Crime, Risk and Justice: The Politics of Crime Control in Liberal Democracies* (Cullompton, Devon: Willan Publishing, 2001) 157.

[37] Criminal Justice Act 2003 s. 225.

now faces? Is it, as Garland argues, that the 'normality of high crime rates' forces the sovereign state to recognize its limits and drives the state to two simultaneous but mutually incompatible responses?[38] Obliged to accept its impotence to control crime, the criminal justice state resorts to a series of 'adaptive responses'[39] which include the withdrawal of the police from the community and the rationing of justice; contracting out or privatizing of police, court escorts, and prisons; 'defining deviance down';[40] redefining success in terms of service delivery rather than outcome; attending to the consequences of crime (victimization, fear of crime) rather than its causes; and relocating responsibility for the control of crime to others (the private sector, the community, and individual citizens). Simultaneously, the state is driven into an expressive or 'hysterical' response to its predicament that manifests itself in recourse to punitive rhetoric and draconian penalties.[41] The state appears torn between admission of failure in its self-appointed role as sole provider of security; denial of its predicament; and simultaneously, expressive reassertion of its power to control crime through punitive law and order policies. Garland's characterization attempts to make sense of the fact that the criminal justice state appears to be withdrawing its claim to be sole provider of security by dispersing responsibility through civil society, whilst simultaneously pursuing a policy of mass incarceration at odds with this withdrawal.

Other penal theorists have suggested alternate readings of the reactions of the criminal justice state to the normality of high crime rates.[42] O'Malley sees these developments as 'volatile and contradictory', driven more by changing political paradigms of government than by any reaching of

[38] Garland, D., 'The Limits of the Sovereign State: Strategies of Crime Control' (1996) 36 *British Journal of Criminology* 445–71.

[39] Garland, D., *The Culture of Control: Crime and Social Order in Contemporary Society* (Oxford: Oxford University Press, 2001) 113.

[40] The strategic implementation of tactics and filters designed to decriminalize low-level, low-visibility crimes through non-investigation, police cautioning, and diversion from prosecution.

[41] Garland, D., op. cit. 131–5.

[42] See Braithwaite, J., 'The New Regulatory State and the Transformation of Criminology', and Rose, N., 'Government and Control', both in Garland, and Sparks (eds), *Criminology and Social Theory* (Oxford: Oxford University Press, 2000); Sparks, R., 'Perspectives on Risk and Penal Politics' in Hope and Sparks (eds), *Crime, Risk and Insecurity: Law and Order in Everyday Life and Political Discourse* (London: Routledge, 2000) 129–45; O'Malley, P., 'Volatile and Contradictory Punishment' (1999) 3 *Theoretical Criminology* 175–96; and Zedner, L., 'Dangers of Dystopias in Penal Theory' (2002) 22 *Oxford Journal of Legal Studies* 341–66.

the limits of the sovereign state.[43] Sullivan, on the other hand, has argued that the criminal justice state has by no means reached its limit but rather the appearance of instability in fact reflects the 'two faces' of neo-liberalism and conservatism which leads to the 'ironic conclusion that the sovereignty of [the state] . . . has seldom been on more solid ground'.[44] Certainly this latter interpretation would seem to be borne out by the fact that policing and the criminal process attract considerable political attention and a corresponding portion of the state budget, and the prison population stands at unprecedented levels. To all appearances, the criminal justice state has never been in more robust and gross good health.

As we have already intimated, yet another reading is possible. Instead of interpreting the rhetorical assertion that prison works and the identification of 'paedophiles' and 'super-predators' as emotive responses by a state and citizens angered by problems they cannot control, we have argued that containment of those deemed immune to the incentive structures of rational choice theory is entirely consistent with economic analysis of crime. The prison works not as an expressive alternative to effective crime control but precisely to contain or exclude those outside the market. And the demonizing of dangerous, sexual, and persistent offenders may be less the 'politicized discourse of the collective unconscious',[45] than a predictable outcome of the recognition that such groups are not rational actors manipulable by incentive structures and that they represent, therefore, a particular threat to the state. It is thus possible to see recent developments in criminal justice as less contradictory, polarized, or volatile and more closely causally related than some penal theorists have allowed.

Several causal relationships between the two modes of managerialism and punitivism can be identified. First, it is possible that the pursuit of technicist risk-management strategies so fail to satisfy basic punitive instincts that they inadvertently stimulate demands for symbolic displays of vengeance. Understood this way, the simultaneous re-emergence of popular punitivism alongside the arcane actuarial language of risk-orientated managerialism is not contradictory but directly related.

[43] O'Malley, P., 'Volatile and Contradictory Punishment' (1999) 3 *Theoretical Criminology* 175–96.
[44] Sullivan, R. R., 'The Schizophrenic Self: Neo-Liberal Criminal Justice' in Stenson and Sullivan (eds), *Crime, Risk and Justice: The Politics of Crime Control in Liberal Democracies* (Cullompton, Devon: Willan Publishing, 2001) 29–47 at 45.
[45] Garland, D., *The Culture of Control: Crime and Social Order in Contemporary Society* (Oxford: Oxford University Press, 2001) 135.

Secondly, it is possible that the larger 'disembedding' processes, in part brought about by technological change, managerialist techniques, and prudential strategies, have created a widespread sense of insecurity that feeds popular punitivism.[46] Thirdly, it may be that actuarialism allows the passionate vengeful reactions unleashed by popular punitivism to be reduced to questions of internal efficiency or utility maximization. Complex moral problems become issues of a technical consequentialist rationality. And public sentiment, expressed through punitively orientated legislation, can be neutralized by the bureaucracy of the system.[47]

A final, and arguably most promising, reading is that it is simply a mistake to regard contemporary penality as displaying two contradictory faces. Actuarial techniques of risk assessment and incapacitation derive historically from the handling of dangerous offenders and have been generalized to other groups in such a way as to expand the very definition of dangerousness. Most importantly, both risk assessment and incapacitation are founded upon the same notions of individual responsibility and grounded in rational choice theory.[48] This being so, managerialist techniques of risk assessment and increasing punitiveness, although they appear to be contrary developments, share greater commonality than at first appears. Further, although the growth of incarceration is presented as the product of popular punitivism, it is arguable that what is occurring is 'not so much an intensification of "punitiveness" *tout court* as an increasing preoccupation with confinement as such . . . its conditions and the perfection of its security'.[49] Taken together, these various ways of thinking about the apparently contradictory faces of contemporary penality suggest more commonality and coherence than at first appears.

FROM POSTCRIME TO PRECRIME?

How far do the changes so far discussed presage the rise of Philip Dick's 'precrime' society?[50] Do they signify a shift from the retrospective orientation of 'postcrime' criminal justice to prospective concern with

[46] Bauman, Z., *Globalization: The Human Consequences* (Cambridge: Polity Press, 1998) 116.

[47] van Swaaningen, R., *Critical Criminology: Visions from Europe* (London: Sage, 1997) 183.

[48] O'Malley, P., 'Risk, Power, and Crime Prevention' (1992) 21 *Economy and Society* 252–75.

[49] Sparks, R., 'Perspectives on Risk and Penal Politics' in Hope and Sparks (eds), *Crime, Risk and Insecurity: Law and Order in Everyday Life and Political Discourse* (London: Routledge, 2000) 136.

[50] Dick, P. K., *Minority Report* (London: Gollancz, 2002) 2–3.

risks as yet unrealized? Such a shift in temporal perspective would also entail a move in substantive focus away from the workings of the criminal process, trial, and punishment, and toward the physical environments and opportunity structures in which crime is committed. The criminal justice process becomes but one tool in an array of preventative activities undertaken by the community, local authorities, and private enterprise. State policing remains important but, in significant respects, it too moves outside the norms and conventional roles of the criminal justice process. Community policing is less about responding to crime, still less drawing offenders into the criminal justice process, than about seeking to prevent crime and foster communal self-help. The police encourage the proliferation of CCTV surveillance systems less to solve past crimes than to identify and monitor suspect populations.[51] The significant expansion of local authority involvement in community safety programmes, the running of community patrols, and the development of local crime reduction strategies are likewise orientated around prospective crime prevention rather than the largely reactive criminal process.[52] When we talk about developments outside the criminal justice process therefore, we are not necessarily talking about developments beyond the state.

The growth of situational crime prevention[53] is a prime example of the way in which the work of criminal justice agents has moved outside the criminal process. Prevention is sought not only through the conventional means of deterrence, punishment, or reform but also through reduction of opportunity, finely calculated disincentives, imposition of controls, and modification of routines. Prevention is served by practices directly geared to reducing temptation and maximizing disinhibitors. Target hardening shifts focus from the putative offender to the predicted site of risk. Routine activity theory, lifestyle analysis, and environmental criminology[54]

---

[51] Goold, B. J., 'Public Area Surveillance and Police Work: the Impact of CCTV on Police Behaviour and Autonomy' (2003) 1 *Surveillance & Society* 191–203. Goold, B. J., *CCTV and Policing: Public Area Surveillance and Police Practices in Britain* (Oxford: Oxford University Press, 2004).

[52] As required under the Crime and Disorder Act 1998. See Crawford, A., *Crime Prevention and Community Safety: Politics, Policies, and Practices* (London: Longman, 1998). Though it is arguable that the assumption of responsibility for community safety by local authorities through projects like 'City Challenge', 'Safer Cities', and regional 'partnerships' was as much about securing social welfare goals through generously funded crime prevention policies as about crime control.

[53] Clarke, R., 'Situational Crime Prevention' in Tonry and Morris (eds), *Crime and Justice: An Annual Review of Research* (Chicago: University of Chicago, 1995) 225–56.

[54] Bottoms, A. E., and Wiles, P., 'Environmental Criminology' in Maguire, Morgan, and Reiner (eds), *The Oxford Handbook of Criminology* (3rd edn, Oxford: Oxford University Press, 2002).

drive new technologies of control and prevention that extend well beyond the scope of conventional criminal justice to include environmental design, street architecture, and the planning of urban space. Examples include closing city centre streets to encourage pedestrian traffic which provides 'natural surveillance', improving street lighting, toughening glass in pub and shop windows, and installing gates and barriers to create gated communities. In pursuit of situational crime prevention, the urban planners become agents of criminal justice and criminal justice agents become urban planners.

Whereas criminal justice and punishment are, in theory at least, the obligation and preserve of the state, preventing crime is not, and has never been, solely a state responsibility. Although many commentators present the role of private entrepreneurs as a new phenomenon, Feeley rightly observes that 'many now taken-for-granted institutions in the criminal process were originally promoted by contractors'.[55] Until well into the nineteenth century hierarchical social relations and communal self-policing were the primary sources of social order.[56] The regulation of social life, including crime, was the responsibility of civil society under the limited gaze of the nightwatchman state. Accordingly, the current devolution of state provision for security to private bodies can be read as the reversal of a historical process whereby state responsibility for internal security itself grew out of private practices. This 200-year-old trajectory has been stalled by a partial move back to communal self-help and private industry.

This is not to downplay the fact that significant developments are occurring beyond the state. These include the growth of neighbourhood watch groups, of citizens' patrols, and of community safety initiatives. Attempts to reconnect police forces with their local communities reflect the spirit of the 'new localism' and are endorsed by all the main political parties as a means of encouraging communities to share responsibility for their own safety. Another significant development is the expanding role for insurance. In a development identified as 'post-Keynesian Prudentialism' risks are increasingly made the subject of private insurance instead

---

[55] Feeley, M., 'Entrepreneurs of punishment: the legacy of privatization' (2002) 4 *Punishment and Society* 321–44 at 324.

[56] Hay, D., 'Crime in eighteenth- and nineteenth-century England' in Tonry and Morris (eds), *Crime and Justice: An Annual Review of Research* (Chicago: University of Chicago Press, 1980) vol. 2: 45–84 at 48.

of being managed collectively by social institutions.[57] Insurance companies can be seen as prime movers in the expansion of the security industry.[58] They provide incentives for investment in security measures through reductions in insurance premiums; they require corporate and private clients to purchase security equipment and services; and they provide advice, propose service providers and police take-up, and monitor quality of installations.[59] The burgeoning of the private security industry thus derives from the pressure on individuals and communities to protect themselves; from the demands of the insurance industry; and from the enormous profits to be made from this lucrative area of commercial endeavour.[60]

Whether or not the changes so far observed signify merely a more modest conception of the power of the criminal justice state; constitute a more complex reconfiguration of state governance of crime; or portend the death of the criminal justice state is a matter of intense academic debate.[61] The first, most moderate, position is that changes in the governance of crime signify a more modest conception of state power moving away from primary responsibility for crime control and toward a more attenuated conception of the state's role. Given that in many countries private security agents now outnumber state police, criminal justice would seem to be losing ground.[62] Community organizations, charities,

---

[57] Stenson, K., 'Communal Security as Government—The British Experience' in Hammersicht (ed), *Jahrbuch für Rechts- und Kriminalsoziologie* (Baden-Baden: Nomos, 1996) 109.

[58] Ericson, R., Barry, D., and Doyle, A., 'The Moral Hazards of Neo-Liberalism: Lessons from the Private Insurance Industry' (2000) 29 *Economy and Society* 532–58; Ericson, R., Doyle, A., and Barry, D., *Insurance as Governance* (Toronto: University of Toronto Press, 2003).

[59] For example, subscribers to private alarm centres in the Netherlands grew by 1100 per cent in the 15 years to 1998: van Dijk, F., and de Waard, J., 'The Private Security Industry in the Netherlands' in Pakes and McKenzie (eds), *Law, Power and Justice in the Netherlands* (Westport: Greenwood, 2001).

[60] Johnston, L., and Shearing, C., *Governing Security: Explorations in Policing and Justice* (London: Routledge, 2003) ch. 5.

[61] Taylor, I., *Crime in Context: A Critical Criminology of Market Societies* (Cambridge: Polity Press, 1999); Young, J., *The Exclusive Society: Social Exclusion, Crime and Difference in Late Modernity* (London: Sage, 1999); Hope, T., and Sparks, R. (eds), *Crime, Risk and Insecurity: Law and Order in Everyday Life and Political Discourse* (London: Routledge, 2000); Stenson, K., and Sullivan, R. R. (eds), *Crime, Risk and Justice: The Politics of Crime Control in Liberal Democracies* (Cullompton, Devon: Willan Publishing, 2001); Garland, D., *The Culture of Control: Crime and Social Order in Contemporary Society* (Oxford: Oxford University Press, 2001); Shearing, C., 'Punishment and the Changing Face of Governance' (2001) 3 *Punishment and Society* 203–20.

[62] Jones, T., and Newburn, T., *Private Security and Public Policing* (Oxford: Oxford University Press, 1998) ch. 2.

and other non-governmental organizations increasingly take responsibility for crime prevention and even community penalties. The rapid rise and spread of restorative justice initiatives privatize dispute resolution by handing formerly state responsibilities over to victims, families, and communities. Simultaneous moves to render parents responsible for their offspring's delinquency, for example, under Parenting Orders, can be seen as a means to legitimate state withdrawal.[63] It is debatable whether this withdrawal is best understood as a tacit acknowledgement that the state has failed to control crime; a means of maximizing self-regulation in reaction to the perceived 'dependency culture' of penal welfarism; or, more cynically, as a means of cost cutting and shrinking state capacities.

The relative openness of the criminal justice state to the diffusion of its functions to other institutions, groups, and individuals is perhaps surprising. It is curious that this most coercive manifestation of state power should open itself to informal intervention; permit policing by those other than state criminal justice professionals; and admit realignment of its punitive functions. One interpretation is that criminal justice has always been but the most extreme and coercive point of a continuum of social ordering practices. The post-war welfarist model that presumed state responsibility for crime control and that ordained increases in state policing as crime worsened was both stronger theoretically than it ever was in practice and, in any case, short-lived.

A second position is that the changes here observed signify a significant transformation or reconfiguration of criminal justice and, in particular, of the distribution of responsibility for crime control. A central question here is whether these changes marginalize criminal justice or expand the remit of what Braithwaite calls the 'new regulatory state'.[64] It is equally possible that they do not so much evidence the retreat of the criminal justice state as extend its remit, and do not so much replace state police as add to their number. Private security guards double the number of police on the beat and ultimately rely upon state policing and punishment to enforce their functions and interests. It is likely, therefore, that they will trawl more suspects into the criminal justice net. Private

---

[63] Under the Crime and Disorder Act 1998 parents are made responsible for the payment of their offspring's fines or compensation orders, can be bound over to ensure their good behaviour, and be made subject to Parenting Orders intended to inculcate good parenting practices. Zedner, L., 'Sentencing Young Offenders' in Ashworth and Wasik (eds), *Fundamentals of Sentencing Theory* (Oxford: Clarendon Press, 1998) 165–86 at 177.

[64] Braithwaite, J., 'The New Regulatory State and the Transformation of Criminology' in Garland and Sparks (eds), *Criminology and Social Theory* (Oxford: Oxford University Press, 2000).

security firms operating in commercial, transit, and shopping areas are commonly overseen by the local police and rely upon police back-up to detain, investigate, and prosecute suspects. Security guards are themselves the subjects of police video surveillance. And videotapes generated by private CCTV cameras are turned over to the police investigating crimes.

The growth of regulatory legislation, provision for licensing, inspection, and the auditing of its activities have all accompanied the rise of private security.[65] These new regulatory provisions, far from diminishing the criminal justice state, generate new tiers of activity that effectively extend its ambit.[66] Likewise restorative justice initiatives expand control over the lives of delinquents, consume more time and resources than formal cautions or even court appearances, and are not constrained by any requirement of proportionality. Similarly, promotion of parental responsibility could be said to extend rather than limit state control mechanisms. The assignment of responsibility for their offspring imposes a duty upon parents that, if not satisfactorily fulfilled, renders them directly answerable to the court.[67] As a result, parents are not only being involved as the informal police of their own families, but also being held to account by the state. Policing is as much of, as by, the parents. And the state, whilst appearing to withdraw, simultaneously extends its ambit of control.[68]

It is striking that the growth of private and semi-private provision for crime control does not mirror that obtaining in other spheres.[69] Whereas the growth in private provision for education, health, and pensions has effected a decrease in reliance upon state provision by those opting out, in respect of crime these developments are 'an adjunct to, not an alternative to, state provision' and as such represent a 'rolling out' not a 'rolling back' of the state.[70] Although privatization is promoted as a means of reducing

---

[65] In Britain the Private Security Industry Act 2001 is the primary legislative instrument of control. For an overview of regulatory provision in other European countries, see de Waard, J., 'The Private Security Industry from an International Perspective' (1999) 7 *European Journal on Criminal Policy and Research* 108–12.

[66] Rose, N., and Miller, P., 'Political Power Beyond the State: Problematics of Government' (1992) 43 *British Journal of Sociology* 173–205.

[67] Crime and Disorder Act 1998 ss. 8 and 9.

[68] Zedner, L., 'Sentencing Young Offenders' in Ashworth and Wasik (eds), *Fundamentals of Sentencing Theory* (Oxford: Clarendon Press, 1998) 179.

[69] O'Malley, P., 'Risk, Power, and Crime Prevention' (1992) 21 *Economy and Society* 252–75.

[70] Hudson, B., 'Punishment, Rights and Difference: Defending Justice in the Risk Society' in Stenson and Sullivan (eds), *Crime, Risk and Justice: The Politics of Crime Control in Liberal Democracies* (Cullompton, Devon: Willan Publishing, 2001) 156.

government activity, one of the curious features of private entrepreneur-ship in this area is that it has tended to expand state involvement and expenditure on crime control.[71] To the extent that there is any public-sector retrenchment, it is in the employment of social workers and other welfare agents. It is for this reason that Braithwaite concludes 'While the welfare state is wound back, the punitive state is not.'[72]

Running in parallel to these changes has been the development of voluntary or communal ventures operating on the margins of the state. These vary from grassroots initiatives, through charitable endeavours in crime control, local crime prevention programmes, to non-governmental organizations (NGOs) working in close association with state agencies. Rarely are they wholly autonomous either in origin or in operation. Instead, the language of 'partnership', 'inter-agency cooperation', and 'multi-agency approach' captures the close linkages and intimate inter-actions between state, charitable, and private bodies. Neighbourhood watch groups function as adjuncts to the police, surveying their streets, reporting suspicious behaviour, and providing evidence in support of police investigations. Generally, new community safety programmes arise at the instigation of the police or local authority rather than through grassroots initiatives. To the extent that citizens involve themselves in neighbourhood watch schemes or citizens' patrols, they do so because they have been encouraged by central government campaigns or local community police officers. These campaigns invite public participation in activities once reserved to the police and seek to impose upon the public a sense of responsibility for their own protection. What have been described as 'responsibilization' strategies are commonly understood as means of deflecting former criminal justice state obligations upon private citizens.[73]

Rather than seeing these trends as transferring responsibility from the state, we can read them instead as evidence that non-state bodies are being integrated into the realm of the criminal justice state. Understood this way partnerships do not hand over state crime control functions so much as subject individuals, community groups, and NGOs to state

[71] Feeley, M., 'Entrepreneurs of punishment: the legacy of privatization' (2002) 4 *Punishment and Society* 321–44 at 322–3.

[72] Braithwaite, J., 'The New Regulatory State and the Transformation of Criminology' in Garland and Sparks (eds), *Criminology and Social Theory* (Oxford: Oxford University Press, 2000) 53.

[73] Garland, D., 'The Limits of the Sovereign State: Strategies of Crime Control' (1996) 36 *British Journal of Criminology* 445–71 at 451–2.

accountability, not least through the mechanism of funding. State control is thus extended over what were once essentially private and voluntary crime control endeavours. These shifts have perhaps best been captured by the notion of corporatism. This entails interpenetration of public and private provision; eroding lines of demarcation between state and private agencies; and the incorporation of local community groups, businesses, and entrepreneurs.[74] Together, individual, communal, and private security provision is blurring the boundary between criminal justice and private policing.

The third, more radical position is that the changes here described will eventually spell the end of the criminal justice state as individual, communal, and, above all, private initiatives come to supplant state policing and punishment as the primary motors of crime control. Whilst it would appear premature to toll the death knell of criminal justice, the scale of change raises questions about its future. Privatization of security is now a billion-pound business that has led to private provision outstripping public in many Western countries.[75] Substantial spheres of private and semi-private life are now largely subject to private rather than state control. Shearing and Stenning argue that central to the growth of private security is the widespread emergence of 'mass private property'.[76] The proliferation of the privately owned public spaces that are shopping malls, gated housing communities fortified and sometimes patrolled against external threat, the growth of large-scale private recreational, industrial, and commercial complexes, and of privately owned college and university campuses shift more and more public life into the private domain. The result is that 'people are now more likely to be living, working, shopping, and spending leisure time in places which are protected by private security rather than the public police'.[77] The activities of private security firms limit access to what was once public space and create privatized streets, housing estates, shopping malls, and leisure parks open only to those able

[74] Crawford, A., 'The Partnership Approach to Community Crime Prevention: Corporatism at the Local Level?' (1994) *Social and Legal Studies* 497–518. .

[75] Though the distribution of private security is very uneven. This raises intriguing questions about why some countries are more resistant to privatization of state functions than others and with what consequences. See Hall, P. A., and Soskice D. (eds), *Varieties of Capitalism: The Institutional Foundations of Comparative Advantage* (Oxford: Oxford University Press, 2001).

[76] Shearing, C., and Stenning, P., 'Modern Private Security: Its Growth and Implications' in Tonry and Morris (eds), *Crime and Justice: An Annual Review of Research* (Chicago: University of Chicago Press, 1981) 193–245.

[77] Jones, T., and Newburn, T., *Private Security and Public Policing* (Oxford: Oxford University Press, 1998) 105.

to buy their right to be there. Those gaining admission to this mass private property or 'club goods' are then subject to an array of situational, social, and other controls that seek to reduce aberrant or offensive behaviour. This said, the 'new feudalism' identified by Shearing and Stenning as the natural consequence of the proliferation of private space in North America is less developed in Britain and only just emerging in continental Europe.[78]

Private provision for security is justified on the grounds that private-sector involvement improves economic efficiency, increases quality of service, subjects the state to the pressures of market competition, and permits consumers to exercise their choice to buy protection where and in what measure they please. Pro-market analysts argue that encouraging those with resources to buy protection frees up state resources which then can be directed toward those most in need and least able to enter the market. Against these claims it can be seen that the burgeoning market in private security creates inequalities and imposes costs that are unacceptable in a democratic liberal society.[79] Inevitably, where private enterprise effectively replaces the state as chief provider of security, its distribution is regulated more by market forces than political will. Indeed to the extent that the pursuit of security is the subject of commercial venture, it is arguable that to posit it as a direct analogue to criminal justice or potential usurper of criminal justice functions is mistaken. One of the more striking aspects of private security provision is that its techniques have become curiously disassociated from crime itself. Indeed crime is essential to the health of the security market: without it shares would surely tumble. Instead, the pursuit of security has become an end in itself, the success or failure of which is gauged by quite other criteria than crime rates. What the private security industry sells is less risk reduction than the promise of protection and, above all, freedom from anxiety and insecurity for those who buy its products. Satisfying consumers and shareholders is more important than solving the crime problem. To ask whether we are moving from criminal justice state to security society may be, therefore, to pose a false dichotomy.

---

[78] Zedner, L., 'The concept of security: an agenda for comparative analysis' (2003) 23 *Legal Studies* 153–76, Jones, T., and Newburn, T., 'The Transformation of Policing? Understanding Current Trends in Policing Systems' (2002) 42 *British Journal of Criminology* 129–46.

[79] Loader, I., 'Consumer Culture and the Commodification of Policing and Security' (1999) 33 *Sociology* 373–92; Hope, T., 'Inequality and the clubbing of private security' in Hope and Sparks (eds), *Crime, Risk and Insecurity* (London: Routledge, 2000).

CONCLUSION

It is as unrealistic to regard crime as the exclusive province of the criminal justice system as it is to regard the criminal justice system as the sole source of crime control. The formal apparatus of criminal process, trial, and punishment has no more than a partial role in controlling crime. The fact that just a few per cent of known crimes result in caution or conviction does not surprise the student of criminal justice.[80] But it should cause them to reflect upon the place of criminal justice in the larger control of crime.

The criminal justice process, trial, sentence, and punishment described in this book share certain distinctive features. Formally they are the preserve of the state; they are invoked only by a suspected violation of the criminal law; and they are constrained by legal principles and legal rules. Granted these are ideal rather than invariable features of criminal justice but they set norms against which departures can be observed and, where appropriate, sanctioned. Punishment as pain inflicted by the state self-evidently requires special justification. It has rightly attracted the scholarly attention of moral philosophers and legal and penal theorists concerned to give an account of why, how, and in what measure the state may exercise its punitive powers to inflict pain upon its citizens. Security as an apparent public good, by contrast, risks being seen as needing no special justification. Because its methods of dealing with crime generally appear to be less intrusive than traditional punitive methods, it appears self-evidently preferable. But pursuing security is not without costs. It lacks any clear normative or principled framework; suffers from few and variable legal constraints; and in its extreme manifestations such as vigilantism, protection rackets, or the Mafia, it stands outside the law entirely. Although it overtly pursues risk reduction, the commercial enterprise of security is predicated upon the persistence of crime. The expansion of the security industry has enlarged not diminished the penal state. And though security is posited as a universal good, its pursuit tends to exclude those deemed as risks, erodes civil liberties, and corrodes trust, the very cement of civil society.[81] Identifying the costs of pursuing security is the

---

[80] Known, that is, to the British Crime Survey. Home Office, *Information on the Criminal Justice System in England and Wales: Digest 4* (London: Home Office, 1999) 29.

[81] Walklate, S., 'Trust and the problem of community in the inner city' in Hope and Sparks (eds), *Crime, Risk and Insecurity* (London: Routledge, 2000). For further elaboration of these charges see Zedner, L., 'Too much security?' (2003) 31 *International Journal of the Sociology of Law* 155–84; Hudson, B., *Justice in the Risk Society: Challenging and Re-affirming Justice in Late Modernity* (London: Sage, 2003).

first step to developing a normative framework according to which this expanding industry might be regulated. The recognition that crime is a permanent and endemic feature of modern society has forced some hard rethinking about the role and the capacity of the criminal justice state. Recognizing the limits to this capacity is not, however, tantamount to an open invitation to the market to provide what the state apparently cannot.

As yet, the emerging security society has not supplanted the criminal justice state. Security does not exclude nor render obsolete policing and prosecution. It adds to the burdens of punishment rather than replacing them, and the criminal justice system must continually mop up the casualties of the market society. But it is effecting profound changes in our understanding of crime and our responses to it. A book with this title written a decade hence will no doubt need to contend with a very different beast than the many-headed Hydra encountered here.

Select Bibliography

General

Cavadino, M., and Dignan, J., *The Penal System: An Introduction* (3rd edn, London: Sage, 2002).

Lacey, N. (ed), *A Reader on Criminal Justice* (Oxford: Oxford University Press, 1994).

McConville, M., and Wilson, G. (eds), *The Handbook of the Criminal Justice Process* (Oxford: Oxford University Press, 2002).

Maguire, M., Morgan, R., and Reiner, R. (eds), *The Oxford Handbook of Criminology* (3rd edn, Oxford: Oxford University Press, 2002).

Tonry, M. (ed), *Handbook of Crime and Punishment* (New York: Oxford University Press, 1998).

Chapter 1 Criminal Justice

Bowling, B., and Phillips, C., *Racism, Crime and Justice* (London: Longman, 2002).

Cohen, S., and Scull, A. (eds), *Social Control and the State: Historical and Comparative Essays* (Oxford: Basil Blackwell, 1983).

Crawford, A., and Goodey, J. (eds), *Integrating a Victim Perspective within Criminal Justice* (Aldershot: Ashgate, 2000).

Downes, D., *Contrasts in Tolerance: Post-war Penal Policy in the Netherlands and England and Wales* (Oxford: Clarendon Press, 1993).

Hudson, B., *Understanding Justice: An Introduction to Ideas, Perspectives and Controversies in Modern Penal Theory* (2nd edn, Buckingham: Open University Press, 2003).

King, M., *The Framework of Criminal Justice* (London: Croom Helm, 1981).

Nelken, D. (ed), *Contrasting Criminal Justice* (Aldershot: Ashgate Dartmouth, 2000).

Tyler, T., *Why People Obey the Law* (New Haven: Yale University Press, 1990).

Walklate, S., *Gender, Crime and Criminal Justice* (Cullompton, Devon: Willan Publishing, 2001).

Zedner, L., and Ashworth, A. (eds), *The Criminological Foundations of Penal Policy* (Oxford: Oxford University Press, 2003).

Chapter 2 Crime

Downes, D., and Rock, P., *Understanding Deviance: A Guide to the Sociology of Crime and Rule Breaking* (3rd edn, Oxford: Oxford University Press, 2003).

Felson, M., *Crime and Everyday Life* (3rd edn, London: Sage, 2002).

Norrie, A., *Crime, Reason and History: A Critical Introduction to Criminal Law* (London: Weidenfeld & Nicolson, 2001).

Simon, J., *Governing Through Crime: Criminal Law and the Reshaping of American Government, 1965–2000* (New York: Oxford University Press, forthcoming).

Sparks, R., *Television and the Drama of Crime: Moral Tales and the Place of Crime in Public Life* (Buckingham: Open University Press, 1992).

Taylor, I., *Crime in Context: A Critical Criminology of Market Societies* (Cambridge: Polity Press, 1999).

van Swaaningen, R., *Critical Criminology: Visions from Europe* (London: Sage, 1997).

Wilson, J. Q., *Thinking about Crime* (New York: Vintage, 1985).

Chapter 3 Punishment

Braithwaite, J., and Pettit, P., *Not Just Deserts: A Republican Theory of Justice* (Oxford: Oxford University Press, 1990).

Duff, R. A., *Punishment, Communication, and Community* (Oxford: Oxford University Press, 2001).

Duff, R. A., and Garland, D. (eds), *A Reader on Punishment* (Oxford: Oxford University Press, 1994).

Garland, D., *Punishment and Modern Society: A Study in Social Theory* (Oxford: Oxford University Press, 1990).

Hart, H. L. A., *Punishment and Responsibility* (Oxford: Oxford University Press, 1968).

Lacey, N., *State Punishment: Political Principles and Community Values* (London: Routledge, 1988).

Matravers, M. (ed), *Punishment and Political Theory* (Oxford: Hart Publishing, 1999).

von Hirsch, A., *Censure and Sanctions* (Oxford: Oxford University Press, 1993).

von Hirsch, A., Roberts, J., and Bottoms, A. E. (eds) *Restorative Justice and Criminal Justice: Competing or Reconcilable Paradigms?* (Oxford: Hart Publishing, 2003).

Chapter 4 Criminal Process

Ashworth, A., *The Criminal Process: An Evaluative Study* (2nd edn, Oxford: Oxford University Press, 1998).

Choongh, S., *Policing as Social Discipline* (Oxford: Clarendon Press, 1997).

Dixon, D., *Law in Policing: Legal Regulation and Police Practices* (Oxford: Clarendon Press, 1997).

Ericson, R., and Haggerty, K., *Policing the Risk Society* (Oxford: Oxford University Press, 1997).

Hawkins, K., *Law as Last Resort: Prosecution Decision-Making in a Regulatory Agency* (Oxford: Oxford University Press, 2002).

Loader, I., and Mulcahy, A., *Policing and the Condition of England* (Oxford: Oxford University Press, 2003).

McBarnet, B., *Conviction* (London: Macmillan, 1981).

Morgan, R., and Newburn, T., *The Future of Policing* (Oxford: Oxford University Press, 1997).

Packer, H., *The Limits of the Criminal Sanction* (Stanford, Cal.: Stanford University Press, 1968).

Reiner, R., *The Politics of the Police* (3rd edn, Oxford: Oxford University Press, 2000).

Sanders, A., and Young, R., *Criminal Justice* (2nd edn, London: Butterworths, 2000).

Chapter 5 Court

Ashworth, A., *Sentencing and Criminal Justice* (3rd edn, London: Butterworths, 2000).

Ashworth, A., and Wasik, M. (eds), *Fundamentals of Sentencing Theory* (Oxford: Clarendon Press, 1998).

Hood, R., *Race and Sentencing* (Oxford: Oxford University Press, 1992).

Rock, P., *The Social World of an English Crown Court: Witness and Professionals in the Crown Court Centre at Wood Green* (Oxford: Clarendon Press, 1993).

Rex, S., and Tonry, M. (eds), *Reform and Punishment: The Future of Sentencing* (Cullompton, Devon: Willan Publishing, 2002).

Shapiro, M., *Courts—A Comparative and Political Analysis* (Chicago: University of Chicago Press, 1981).

Tonry, M., and Frase, R. (eds), *Sentencing and Sanctions in Western Countries* (New York: Oxford University Press, 2001).

von Hirsch, A., and Ashworth, A. (eds), *Principled Sentencing: Readings on Theory and Policy* (2nd edn, Oxford: Hart Publishing, 1998).

Young, R., and Hoyle, C. (eds), *New Visions of Crime Victims* (Oxford: Hart Publishing, 2002).

Chapter 6 Financial and Community Penalties

Bottoms, A. E., Gelsthorpe, L., and Rex, S. (eds), *Community Penalties: Change and Challenges* (Cullompton, Devon: Willan Publishing, 2003).

Braithwaite, J., *Crime, Shame and Reintegration* (Cambridge: Cambridge University Press, 1989).

Brownlie, I., *Community Punishment: A Critical Introduction* (London: Longman, 1998).

Cohen, S., *Visions of Social Control* (Cambridge: Polity Press, 1985).

Crawford, A., *The Local Governance of Crime: Appeals to Community and Partnership* (Oxford: Clarendon Press, 1997).

Crawford, A., and Newburn, T., *Youth Offending and Restorative Justice: Implementing Reform in Youth Justice* (Cullompton, Devon: Willan Publishing, 2003).

McGuire, J., (ed), *What Works: Reducing Reoffending* (Chichester: Wiley, 1995).

Chapter 7 Prisons

Christie, N., *Crime Control as Industry* (London: Routledge, 1994).

Foucault, M., *Discipline and Punish: The Birth of the Prison* (Harmondsworth, Middlesex: Peregrine, 1979).

Garland, D. (ed), *Mass Imprisonment: Social Causes and Consequence* (London: Sage, 2001).

Harding, R. W., *Private Prisons and Public Accountability* (Buckingham: Open University Press, 1997).

James, A., Bottomley, A. K., and Liebling, A., *Privatising Prisons: Rhetoric and Reality* (London: Sage, 1997).

Mathiesen, T., *Prison on Trial: A Critical Assessment* (London: Sage, 1990).

Morris, N., and Rothman, D. (eds), *The Oxford History of the Prison: The Practice of Punishment in Western Europe* (Oxford: Oxford University Press, 1995).

Sparks, R., Bottoms, A. E., and Hay, W., *Prisons and the Problem of Order* (Oxford: Oxford University Press, 1996).

Chapter 8 From Criminal Justice to the Security Society?

Crawford, A., *Crime Prevention and Community Safety: Politics, Policies, and Practices* (London: Longman, 1998).

Garland, D., *The Culture of Control: Crime and Social Order in Contemporary Society* (Oxford: Oxford University Press, 2001).

Hope, T., and Sparks, R. (eds), *Crime, Risk, and Insecurity: Law and Order in Everyday Life and Political Discourse* (London: Routledge, 2000).

Hudson, B., *Justice in the Risk Society: Challenging and Re-affirming Justice in Late Modernity* (London: Sage, 2003).

Hughes, G., and Edwards, A. (eds), *Crime Control and Community: The New Politics of Public Safety* (Cullompton, Devon: Willan Publishing, 2002).

Johnston, L., and Shearing, C., *Governing Security: Explorations in Policing and Justice* (London: Routledge, 2003).

Jones, T., and Newburn, T., *Private Security and Public Policing* (Oxford: Oxford University Press, 1998).

Stenson, K., and Sullivan, R. R. (eds), *Crime, Risk and Justice: The Politics of Crime Control in Liberal Democracies* (Cullompton, Devon: Willan Publishing, 2001).

von Hirsch, A., Garland, D., and Wakefield, A. (eds), *Ethical and Social Perspectives on Situational Crime Prevention* (Oxford: Hart Publishing, 2000).

Young, J., *The Exclusive Society: Social Exclusion, Crime and Difference in Late Modernity* (London: Sage, 1999).

Index